Missouri

THE HEART OF THE NATION

Missouri

THE HEART OF THE NATION

Third Edition

William E. Parrish
Charles T. Jones, Jr.
Lawrence O. Christensen

Harlan Davidson, Inc.
Wheeling, Illinois 60090-6000

Visit us on the World Wide Web at www.harlandavidson.com.

Library of Congress Cataloging-in-Publication Data

Parrish, William Earl, 1931–
    Missouri, the heart of the nation / William E. Parrish, Charles T. Jones, Jr.,
Lawrence O. Christensen.—3rd ed.
        p. cm.
Includes bibliographical references and index.
    0-88295-997-2 (alk. paper) — 0-88295-996-4 (hardcover)
    1. Missouri—History. I. Jones, Charles T. II. Christensen, Lawrence O.
III. Title

    F466.P27 2004
    977.8—dc21

                                              2003013266

Manufactured in the United States of America
06 05 04 03 1 2 3 4 5 VP

Contents

Introduction
to the Third Edition

The history of Missouri is rich and varied. The state stands at the crossroads of America in "the Heart of the Nation." It has played a pivotal role in much of the nation's history, most particularly in the development of the American West. The writers have been concerned to present the story of Missouri and its people in a clear and concise manner. It is a panorama of the interaction of political, economic, and social activity. From earliest times to the present, the history of the state has been a story of people and their attempts to relate to their environment and changing circumstances. The writers hope that they have captured herein the full impact of those people and the forces that have shaped Missouri into the state it is today.

What we have tried to provide here is an overview arranged generally in chronological sequence but with topical development. It is impossible to go into numerous details in a book of this sort. For those who wish to pursue various aspects of Missouri history further, the writers have provided Suggestions for Reading at the end of each chapter. These have been revised in this edition to include the wealth of works that have appeared in the past decade. Missouri's past is indeed a rich gold mine for historians, and it is good to see the digging that is currently occurring. The most thorough account of the state's development remains David D. March, *The History of Missouri*, 4 vols., Chicago, Lewis Publishing Co., 1967, even though it is somewhat dated. It should be supplemented by the *Sesquicentennial History of Missouri* series in 5 volumes, Columbia, University of Missouri Press, 1971–1997 (revised editions of Vols. I–III, 1999–2001), of which William E. Parrish is General Editor. These cover the state's history from its beginnings to 1953 and contain extensive bibliographies beyond what we can furnish here. A sixth volume bringing the story to the present is in preparation. These volumes are cited in the Suggestions for Readings as appropriate. Milton D. Raffery, *Historical Atlas of Missouri*, Norman, University of Oklahoma Press, 1982, offers illustrative maps of considerable use. Another important work dealing with a particular group is Lorenzo J. Greene, Gary R. Kremer, and Antonio F. Holland, *Missouri's Black Heritage,* rev. ed., Columbia, University of Missouri Press, 1993. For those interested in their local history, a good general source is Marian M. Ohman, *A History of Missouri's Counties, County Seats and Court House Squares,* Columbia, University of Missouri Press, 1983. The best general history of St. Louis is James Neal Primm, *Lion of the Valley: St. Louis, Missouri, 1764–1980,* 3d ed., St. Louis, Missouri Historical Society Press, 1998. For Kansas City, see A. Theodore Brown & Lyle W. Dorsett, *K.C.: A History of Kansas City,* Missouri, Boulder, CO, Pruett Publishing, 1978. Histories of other communities are cited at different places in the Suggestions for Readings as appropriate.

A most important supplement, which has appeared in the past decade, is the *Dictionary of Missouri Biography,* edited by Lawrence O. Christensen, William E. Foley, Gary R. Kremer, and Kenneth H. Winn, Columbia, University of Missouri Press, 1999. Here one will find brief biographies of most significant Missourians in all walks of life, written by a variety of scholars. Other important biographical sources are *Show Me Missouri Women: Selected Biographies,* edited by Mary K. Dains and Sue Sadler, 2 vols., Kirksville, Thomas Jefferson University Press, 1989, 1993; Jerena East Giffin, *First Ladies of Missouri: Their Homes and their Families,* 2d ed., Jefferson City, Giffin Enterprises, 1996; Jean Carnahan, *If Walls Could Talk: The Story of Missouri's First Families,* Jefferson City, MMPI, L.L.C., 1998; and Carla Waal and Barbara Oliver Korner, eds., *Hardship and Hope: Missouri Women Writing About Their Lives, 1820–1920,* Columbia, University of Missouri Press, 1997.

Missouri is fortunate to have two excellent historical libraries in the State Historical Society of Missouri at Columbia and the Missouri Historical Society at St. Louis. The former is coordinated with the Western Historical Manuscripts Division of the University of Missouri, which now has extensive centers on all four of the University's campuses. These facilities contain all types of materials dealing with the state's past. The back issues of the societies' respective publications, the *Missouri Historical Review* and *Gateway Heritage,* formerly *The Bulletin,* are a treasure trove of lore on all aspects of the state's history. In addition Missouri has many local historical societies, some with museums, libraries, and/or publications. And many local libraries have special corners with materials of their region's past. Students would do well to acquaint themselves with these where they are available in their local community. The heritage of Missouri is rich not only at the state level but at the grassroots of its towns and counties, and students can find many fascinating things to study right at their front door if they but look for them.

We wish to thank the staffs of the State Historical Society of Missouri, the Missouri Department of Transportation, and the Missouri State Archives for their help in the selection of the pictures and maps that are used herein. We also wish to express our appreciation to the following for their assistance in the initial enterprise: Thomas W. Carneal, the late Carl H. Chapman, William E. Foley, James W. Goodrich, Alan R. Havig, Gary R. Kremer, B. B. Lightfoot, David D. March, Patrick E. McLear, Franklin D. Mitchell, the late George P. Rawick, Robert W. Richmond, and J. Christopher Schnell. Professor Parrish would like to thank the University of Missouri Press for permission to use materials from some of his previous books and the Johns Hopkins University Press for permission to use excerpts from his chapter "Reconstruction Politics in Missouri, 1865–1870," in Richard O. Curry, ed., *Radical, Racism, and Party Realignment: The Border States During Reconstruction*, 1969. Permission to use the quotation in Chapter 12 from Lawrence Goodwyn, *The Populist Movement*, has been granted by the Oxford University Press. Since the publication of the first edition, our esteemed mentor, Lewis E. Atherton, has passed away. His heritage of devotion to state and local history and to the preservation of Missouri history is hereby gratefully acknowledged.

Finally, a special word of thanks to our wives, HelenSue Parrish, Barbara Jones, and Maxine Christensen, for their assistance in many ways and for their patient endurance throughout this and other enterprises.

William E. Parrish
Charles T. Jones, Jr.
Lawrence O. Christensen

ONE

The Original Missourians

W hen Mark Twain's unforgettable character, Tom Sawyer, scolded Huckleberry Finn for thinking that Illinois was green and Indiana pink because they appeared that way on the map, Huck demanded, "What's a map for? Ain't it to learn you facts?" Although the illiterate Huck could not read a map, he knew its purpose. The Missouri map can teach us many important geographic facts that will increase our understanding of its history.

Missouri and Mid-America

Between the Appalachian Mountains in the east and the Rocky Mountains in the west is mid-America, a land with a variety of physiographic regions drained by a great inland water system formed by the Ohio, Mississippi, and Missouri rivers and their 250 tributaries. These "western waters" give mid-America its geographic unity and help furnish the key to its history. Situated in the west north central part of mid-America, Missouri lies somewhat east and a little north of the geographical center of the United States. Between 36° and 40° 35' north latitude and 89° and 95° 42' west longitude, Missouri's total area of 69,686 square miles makes it nineteenth in size among the states. It is one of only two states bordered by eight other states: Illinois, Kentucky, and Tennessee on the east; Arkansas on the south; Oklahoma, Kansas, and Nebraska on the west; and Iowa on the north. Looked at in terms of population, the 1980 federal census showed that the nation's population center shifted westward from Illinois to Missouri, while the 2000 federal census showed a 9.3 percent gain in Missouri's population over the previous decade to 5.5 million.

The Mississippi River

The Mississippi River forms all but twenty miles of the eastern boundary of the state. Named "Missi-Sipi" (big river) by the Algonquin Indians, the river flows 2,350 miles through the heart of the United States from its source in northern Minnesota to the Gulf of Mexico. The upper Mississippi travels through a great valley with high ground and bluffs on both banks. The bluffs between Louisiana and Clarksville in northeast Missouri are among the highest along the river. When it reaches Cape Girardeau, the river widens, emerging from the wooded bluffs and limestone cliffs to shape the Mississippi flood plains that stretch to the Gulf.

Awed by its size, the Indians called it "The Father of Waters." The French fur traders and priests followed its courses in search of wealth and converts. Early French forts, trading posts, and settlements appeared on higher ground overlooking the river on both the Illinois and Missouri sides. Its changing currents, sand bars, ice, flooding in low-lying areas, submerged debris, and driftwood have made the river dangerous to both travelers and inhabitants. A young French soldier on his way upriver to his outpost reported in 1750 that he nearly drowned when trees like "flying buttresses" crashed into his boat and dumped him and his companions into the turbulent waters.

From 1763 to 1783, the Mississippi divided Great Britain and Spain in North America. After the American Revolution it became the western boundary of the new United States, separating it from Spanish territory. Questions over its navigation and the use of the Port of New Orleans for American products led to controversy between the United States and Spain and later France, eventually resulting in the Louisiana Purchase of 1803. Before the Civil War, enslaved blacks saw "upriver" as the way to freedom, while to be "sold downriver" meant bondage and the loss of hope. During the Civil War (1861–65), Union forces fought to control the river and to divide the Southern states. In time this strategy was decisive in the collapse of the Confederacy. Many artists, authors, folklorists, ragtime composers, and jazz musicians, influenced by their river experiences, have greatly enriched the cultural history of the American people. Mark Twain, who grew up on its banks at Hannibal, piloted a Mississippi River steamboat and used it as a setting for three of his best-known books. He described it as "the crookedest river in the world, since in one part of its journey it used up one thousand three miles to cover the same ground that the crow would fly over in six hundred and sixty five."

The Missouri River

The state's most distinctive geographical feature is the Missouri River. From its headwaters high in the northern Rockies of western Montana to its confluence with the Mississippi, it flows 2,714 miles, making it the longest river in the United States. Joined by northern and southern tributaries as it moves across Montana and North Dakota, it increases in volume and current. Running through rocky areas, which serve as a natural filter, the water remains clear, but once it washes into the plains country of the Dakotas it begins to assume a muddy color. Following a course predetermined by large polar ice masses during the Ice Age, it continues in a southerly direction until it joins the Kansas River at Kansas City. There it bends and meanders 577 miles across the state to join the Mississippi seventeen miles above St. Louis.

Major tributaries in the state are the Little Platte, Grand, and Chariton rivers to the north and the Lamine, Osage, and Gasconade to the south. Although relatively short, these tributaries provide considerably more water than the plains tributaries causing the river to widen and pick up current speed. Because the Missouri fluctuates in its current more than the Mississippi, it has frequently changed its channel and washed away shorelines, farms, and even towns. In 1804 the American explorers Meriwether Lewis and William Clark, on their way to the Pacific Ocean, noted in their journals that the Missouri's current was very "rapid" and that its "violence" moved sandbars and caved in banks. One of their most difficult tasks was navigating their crafts upriver against the charging current.

The brownish coloration of the water is due to the great amount of silt and solid matter carried by the river. It is estimated that the river dumps 500 million tons of solid matter into the Mississippi annually. When Father Jacques Marquette and Louis Jolliet saw the Missouri for the first time in 1673, they wrote that it was "all muddy and could not get clear." Francis Parkman, an American historian, wrote in his great travel book, *The Oregon Trail*, that "the river was constantly changing its course . . . continually shifting . . . [the] water is so charged with mud and sand that, in spring, it is perfectly opaque, and in a few minutes deposits a sediment an inch thick in the bottom of a tumbler." Missourians call the river "Big Muddy," and to this day they say unceremoniously that it is "too thick to drink and too thin to plow."

In 1944 the United States Congress authorized the Missouri River Basin Project, involving Missouri and nine other states, for the purposes of taming "the wide Missouri," halting stream pollution, building recreational areas, providing for hydroelectric power and irrigation. Present-day ecological concerns dictate that more be done to conserve the wildlife once so abundant along its shores. It is hoped that an aroused public opinion will insist on somehow saving one of the state's greatest natural resources.

The Lay of the Land

During the Ice Age thousands of years ago, great mountains of ice ground into Missouri and then receded, leaving behind a land composed of four physiographic regions. North of the Missouri River is the Glacial Plains. Here the glaciers left behind rolling hills, gentle valleys, some rock formations of limestone and sandstone, and prairie land similar to that of Iowa and Illinois. In addition to the glaciers, powerful winds carried a sediment (loess), and deposited it across the land, adding to the uniform texture and fertility of the soil. Some of the state's most productive land is in this region.

South and southeast of the river is the Ozark Plateau or "highlands," which extend from Illinois into southern Missouri, Arkansas, Kansas, and Oklahoma. Located a few hundred miles southeast of the center of the United States, the Ozarks is a land of rocky hills, deep valleys, cliffs, tablelands, springs, and forests. The elevation ranges from 1,200 to 1,700 feet above sea level. Taum Sauk Mountain in Iron County, rising 1,772 feet above sea level, is the highest point in the state. The Ozark soil is not as fertile as that of the Glacial Plains because of chert (a compact siliceous rock), but a diversity of plant and tree life abounds.

The name Ozarks is from "aux arcs," a French abbreviation of "to the Arkansas Post"—an outpost established on the Arkansas River when the French first arrived in the Mississippi Valley. Wild rivers, such as the Meramec, Black, White, Big Niangua, and Current run through the region, creating scenes of rugged beauty. The headwaters of some of these rivers are freshwater springs, from many of which flow over a million gallons a day. Big Springs in Carter County has a daily measured flow of 840 million gallons. Saline springs and salt licks are numerous in the region. The man-made Lake of the Ozarks has become a national tourist attraction. Many Missourians believe the region's wild rivers, wilderness areas, springs, and scenic landscapes are among the state's most precious resources. ·

In the western part of the state are the Osage Plains, a triangular area extending from a point in Pettis County southwesterly and sloping into the Great Plains. The plains environment is conducive to the growing of grasses and hay. The raising of livestock has become one of the major industries in this region.

The southeastern lowlands, popularly known as the bootheel, is similar to the Mississippi Delta. Bounded on the east by the Mississippi River and on the west by the St. Francis River, it juts thirty-five miles into the northeast tip of Arkansas. Although unglaciated, flat, and poorly drained, the soil is rich and productive, with cotton and soybeans being the major crops. Between 230 and 350 feet above sea level, the lowest point in the state is where the St. Francis River meets the southern state line of the heel. Seismologists believe that the geologic unrest of these lowlands (which caused the New Madrid earthquake of 1811–1812) still exists. One man even predicted the exact date of a major earthquake to occur in 1990—a prediction that terrified many Missourians who live in the area of the New Madrid fault. Fortunately no quake occurred.

Summers in Missouri are generally hot and sultry, especially along the Mississippi River with July, the hottest month, averaging 77° Fahrenheit (25° Celsius). Winters can be long and rigorous with January, the coldest month, averaging 30° Fahrenheit (-1° Celsius). Annual average temperatures are 50° Fahrenheit (10° Celsius) in the northwest and 60° Fahrenheit (15° Celsius) in the southeast. The annual rainfall averages 30–35 inches in the north, 40–45 inches in southern portions, and 48 inches in the southern lowlands. An annual average of 21 inches of snow falls in the north, with 16 inches in the southern lowlands. Sudden drops and rises in temperatures occur in the interior when cold Arctic air meets head on with the warm air from the Gulf.

Lead, iron, and zinc attracted early pioneers to the new land. The Irish Wilderness, so-called because of Irish immigrants who came to Oregon County in 1850, is one of the richest stores of zinc in the world. Other minerals found in the state are coal, copper, barite, uranium, and cobalt. Sand and gravel are extracted from streams and rivers; limestone is used in the making of cement; clay is mined and used in the making of firebrick; what little oil there is tends to be heavy and is used primarily in the blacktopping of roads.

Missouri remains a land with a great variety of flora and fauna. Botanists have discovered and classified 2,400 different species of ferns and flowering plants in the state. It has been estimated that at the time of settlement two-thirds of Missouri was covered with forests. Even today in some Ozark counties between 60 and 80 percent of the land is in timber. Some of the trees found in the state are different species of oak, linden, hickory, sweet gum, walnut, catalpa, cottonwood, hornbeam, ash, sugar maple, papaw, southern buckhorn, pine, red bud, and dogwood (the state tree). A few birds native to the state are the cardinal, mourning dove, bobwhite quail, bullfinch, red-wing blackbird, crow, hawk, blue jay, woodpecker, brown thrush, robin, wren, passenger pigeon, and bluebird (the state bird). Although large game like bison, elk, and antelope have disappeared, the red fox, otter, deer, wild turkey, squirrel, rabbit, skunk, raccoon, opossum, coyote, and a few black bears in the Ozarks of southwestern Missouri still exist and, in some cases, are increasing in population as a result of conservation practices.

Early Inhabitants of Missouri

Perhaps as long as 40,000 years ago a small band of hunters crossed a then existing land bridge over the Bering Strait from Asia to North America. Their descendants, in search of big game now extinct, began to drift south into the interior of the continent. These ancestors of the North American Indians left behind evidence of their existence and means of survival. In the vicinity of Clovis and Folsom, New Mexico, archaeologists have uncovered artifacts that show human habitation there as early as 10,000 B.C. Recently in Mastadon State Park south of St. Louis, archaeologists discovered a flintlike spear point similar to one found at Clovis. They believe that "Clovis man" may have been in the lower Missouri and central Mississippi valleys before appearing in New Mexico. Although subject to debate, this may mean that early humans followed a north to southeast migration route into the V-shaped area formed by the Missouri and Mississippi rivers. Furthermore, based on archaeological finds throughout this region, some archaeologists believe that these early wanderers spread their culture from this area east to the headwaters of the Ohio River, south along the Mississippi, and west to the prairies and plains.

The Early Hunter Period (12,000 to 8,000 B.C.)

Prehistoric people in the region that became Missouri passed through various stages of development. The first was the Early Hunter Period. They inhabited a physical environment that was supportive of human life. Camping near fresh water, these people hunted wild game for food, using the bones for tools and skins for clothing. From stone they fashioned spear points, knives, scrapers, and choppers. Dependent on animals for their food supply, these early hunters traveled great distances, continually following the herds. During the Early Hunter Period people were nomads, never remaining in one place for long.

The Archaic Period (8,000 to 500 B.C.)

The Archaic Period brought significant changes in these early people's lifestyle. Staying in one site for longer periods of time, they sought out caves and overhanging rocks as natural shelters. Although hunting continued to provide their main food source, their lifestyle became less nomadic and more sedentary. They foraged for wild roots, berries, nuts, and fruits. They made new weapons for the hunt, as well as new tools for the preparation of the food they gathered. In the Early Hunter Period, tools for grinding seeds were rare, but in the Archaic Period they became quite common. These early inhabitants refined some of their weapons and tools, making them more useful. The bone needle, for example, enabled them to make animal skins fit tighter. As the size of the individual groups grew, semblances of social organization appeared. Archaeological evidence shows the emergence of ceremonies and rites associated with the mysteries of nature and death.

Archaeological sites that reflect the transition of these early dwellers in the Archaic Period from hunters to hunter-gatherers can be found throughout Missouri. Graham Cave, located in Montgomery County, has provided bits of information that show how these early people foraged as well as hunted, thereby increasing and diversifying their food supply, adapted more effectively to their environment and climate, increased in population, and engaged in ceremonies and rites. The Dalton sites in the lowland areas of southeastern Missouri, the Jakie Shelter in Barry County, a village area and burial site near Troy in Lincoln County, and sites around Sedalia have supplied more evidence to tell us about the life of the foragers in the Archaic Period.

The Woodland Period (c. 1,000 B.C.–A.D. 900)

The chief development of the Woodland Period was the invention of pottery, a simple craft of firing clay pots and jars that made it possible for people to store the food they gathered. This meant that they could spend more time in one place and in activities other than hunting. If they could not find natural shelters, they constructed crude dwellings using the materials close at hand. It is believed that these early Woodland Indians began to branch out into new areas encountering and trading with other groups.

Midway through the Woodland Period the Hopewell culture began to spread into Missouri. So named because archaeologists excavated important artifacts of these people on the Hopewell farm in Ohio, this ancient Indian culture greatly influenced the lifestyles of the people with whom it came in contact. Besides hunting and gathering, the Hopewell Indians grew crops (corn). They molded their pottery in different forms and sizes, covering it with interesting designs and patterns. They built large earthworks and mounds, which served as the focal point for the village. Often animal-shaped, these large mounds were used for celebrations and burial rites. Hopewell people made tools and weapons from different kinds of materials such as mica, shells, and copper, which suggests extensive trade with other Indian cultures.

Appearing quite suddenly in Missouri, the Hopewell Indians settled near the mouth of the Lamine River and along the Missouri River to the Kansas River. Their culture is evidenced in the weapons, tools, mounds, and fragments of pottery on village sites they left behind. In Van Meter State Park in Saline County, an earthwork called "The Old Fort" serves to remind us that centuries before the arrival of Europeans in Missouri a still somewhat vigorous Indian culture existed in the central part of the state.

Toward the end of the Woodland Period small but isolated Indian villages began to develop regional groupings in different geographical areas of Missouri. Larger towns grew up. Adapting to environmental conditions and building on the remnants of the Hopewell culture, these Indian groups established technological and cultural characteristics that distinguished them from Indians living in other regions.

The Mississippi Period (A.D. 900 To 1500)

As the Woodland Period merged into the Mississippi Period, a large Indian town grew up in the Cahokia–St. Louis area, its culture spreading up and down the Mississippi River and into the hinterland of Missouri. Archaeological evidence shows its impact in southeastern Missouri, as far west as Kansas City, and even to the very western edge of Oklahoma. The rise of this new culture and its influence on other groups marked a new chapter in the history of Missouri Indians.

The enterprising townspeople migrated up and down the Mississippi River. Their culture, described as riverine, reflected the importance of the Mississippi River to their way of life. They hunted its water-dwelling animals, collected its mussels, fished in its waters, and

Hopewell Indian Mound, Van Meter State Park, Saline County. *Courtesy State Historical Society of Missouri*

Diagram of Hopewell Indian Mound, Van Meter State Park, Saline County. *Courtesy State Historical Society of Missouri*

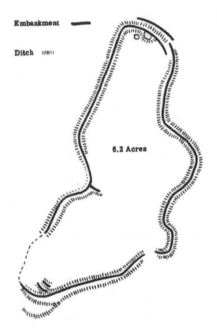

Embankment

Ditch

6.2 Acres

traveled it to trade with other Indians. The remains from their gardens, however, indicate that they were skillful gardeners and probably grew as much food as they hunted. Their pottery, highly decorated and shaped into a variety of forms, was used as a major trade item. In making tools, weapons, and art objects, these Indians used different materials, such as flint, stone, bone, antlers, copper, clay, cloth, and wood. They were early miners, extracting flint and chalcedony from areas along the Meramec River. Using large dugout canoes, they traded extensively and interacted with various other Indian groups.

The townspeople's dwellings were square or rectangular wood frame covered with thatched roofs. Each major town contained a large flat-topped temple mound where the inhabitants practiced their religious ceremonies. Because of the number of mounds in and around the St. Louis area, the town sometime in the past was nicknamed the "Mound City." Examples of the group's religious symbolism can be found carved on rocks (petroglyphs) in Washington State Park, Washington County. There one can see carvings of snakes, birds, an arrow, fish, and weeping eyes. At Cahokia on the east bank of the Mississippi, the Old Village shows the great development of the later Indian civilization in mid-America. When the first European explorers penetrated the Mississippi Valley early in the sixteenth century, they encountered descendants of the Mississippi townspeople.

The Oneota Culture (c. A.D. 1350 to 1500)

During the decline of the townspeople of the Mississippi Period, another widespread Indian culture manifested itself throughout the central hinterland of Missouri. It was the cultural base from which the historic tribes, the Missouri and the Osage, developed and was prominent by the time the Europeans appeared in mid-America. The term used to designate this culture is Oneota.

The general characteristics of the Oneota were not unlike those of the townspeople of the Mississippi Period. Trash sites excavated by archaeologists show piles of animal bones that attest to their hunting skills. It is believed they searched great distances for large game. As gardeners, they grew corn, squash, and beans. The wild fruit, berries, and nuts that they gathered added variety to their diet. Excelling in the shaping of bone tools, they made handles from antlers and needles and beads from the bones of smaller animals. Ornaments, spoons, and jewelry were fashioned from shells, some of which they acquired from other Indians as far away as the Gulf of Mexico. They dug large pits where they cached food and valuable items and which they later filled with trash. Their religious symbolism was very much like that of the townspeople, which suggests a continuity of religious practices and beliefs between cultures. Their stone technology was typified by knives, arrowheads, and drills. They made catlinite pipes and smoked tobacco.

The influence of the Oneota culture extended beyond Missouri into southern Minnesota, Iowa, Nebraska, and Illinois. Near the mouth of the Grand River in Saline County the Utz archaeological site has furnished considerable information about this culture and its impact on the later Indian tribes.

The Transitional Tribes: The Quapaw Indians
(c. A.D. 1500 to 1800)

Between the decline of the townspeople of the Mississippi Period and the coming of the Spanish explorer Hernando de Soto in 1541, the Quapaw Indians settled at the mouth of the Arkansas River. Indian tradition recorded that at some distant time a tribe searching for new homes separated at the mouth of the Ohio River—one group ("the upstream people") included the Omaha, Kansas, Ponca, and Osage Indians. They migrated up the Missouri River, some settling on the banks of the Osage River and its tributaries, the others moving farther west. The second group, the Quapaw ("the downstream people"), moved southwest and established strong villages at the mouth of the Arkansas River. Like other Indians, they made tools and weapons from stone and bone, hunted the Ozark Plateau north into Missouri, and engaged in agriculture. They built large mounds on which they placed their chief buildings. From these, archaeologists have taken some of the finest specimens of pottery made by the Indians. Early accounts of this tribe describe them as being tall and well shaped.

Hernando de Soto may have visited their villages when he arrived at the Mississippi Valley. Some years later the French established a post at the mouth of the Arkansas River, traded with the Quapaw, and, according to Captain Amos Stoddard, intermarried with them to preserve peace and to secure their trade. Stoddard maintained that by 1812 most of the inhabitants of their villages were of "mixed blood."

The Historic Tribes:
The Missouri Indians (c. A.D. 1500 to 1800)

Although the origin of the Missouri tribe is obscure, traditions indicate that they were part of a larger group of southeastern Indians who migrated to the Great Lakes region and there divided into two segments. One, the Winnebago, remained in that area while the other pushed farther west, dividing again into the Ioway, Oto, and Missouri tribes. In 1673 the French explorers Father Jacques Marquette

and Louis Jolliet located the Missouri Indians on their map as living near the mouth of the Grand River. The French Canadian Étienne de Bourgmond, who arrived in 1714, traded with both the Missouri and the Osage Indians in the general vicinity of Van Meter State Park in Saline County. From this time on, the story of the Missouri Indians is one of decline. Victimized by their enemies, the Sauk Indians, and by smallpox, this once large and powerful tribe slowly disintegrated until the remnants moved west to combine with the Oto tribe in Kansas.

Little Stabbing Chief of the Sauk Tribe. *Courtesy State Historical Society of Missouri*

The Missouri tribe's way of life was similar to other Indians, before Europeans invaded their lands. In the winter they tracked the bison, elk, deer, and wild turkey, while in other seasons they gathered berries, nuts, and wild fruit. In their gardens they grew corn, beans, and squash. Lewis and Clark wrote that the Missouris wore breachcloths, blankets, and buffalo robes and adorned themselves with bracelets of bone, copper, beads, and brass. They made pottery, stone tools, bone needles from the shoulder blades of buffalo, and flint scrapers. Their dwellings appear to have been similar to wigwams, a framework of poles covered with reed mats. Since they did not use the horse until after the coming of the Europeans, the Missouris traveled by foot. Dogs pulled their travois, warned the village of intruders, and often ended up in a kettle of stew. Little is known of the Missouri's social organization other than that the tribe, headed by a chief, was divided into clans that were named after birds and animals.

The Missouris traded extensively with Europeans during the first half of the eighteenth century and did not resist the intrusion of either the French or the Spanish into their territory. By the time the Americans entered the area in increasing numbers at the end of the century, the tribe had joined the Otoes, leaving only their name to the river and state where they had once been numerous.

The Historic Tribes: The Osage Indians
(c. A.D. 1600 to 1830)

The most important tribe in the early history of Missouri was the Wazhazhe ("the upstream people"), a word that the French abbreviated to Osage. Father Marquette located them on his map in the region of present-day Vernon County. They were composed of two principal groups, the Grand and the Little Osage, who had their villages close together and were on friendly terms. They hunted across the Ozark highlands south of the Missouri River to the Arkansas and into the western plains.

The Osage represented a blending of Indian cultures, possessing traits that could be described as Plains and Woodland. John Bradbury, a botanist on his way up the Missouri River in 1811, commented in his journal that they were "tall, robust, broad shouldered people resembling giants." It was not uncommon for adult males to reach six feet in height. Osage warriors had been known to run sixty miles in one day and to possess the physical strength to put an arrow through a grown buffalo. They painted and decorated their shaved heads. The Osage male wore a breechcloth, leggings, and a general blanket coverall that he draped over his shoulder. When he addressed someone, he lowered the blanket and tied it around his waist. Early visitors to the Osage villages were also impressed by the comeliness of their young women, who wore buckskin dresses. Both men and women wore moccasins.

The spring hunt began in March and lasted until May, when the Osage returned to plant their crops of corn, beans, and pumpkins. They also hunted in the summer, returning to their villages in late August or early September to harvest their crops and to gather walnuts, hazelnuts, pecans, grapes, papaws, roots, and acorns. They continued the hunt in the fall, but remained close to their villages during the cold months of January and February.

In Osage society, the men hunted and engaged in warfare, while the women gathered firewood, cured the meat, cooked the meals, and reared the children. There was considerable social organization, with the tribe divided into clans or families, each of which had a chief. The head chief was chosen by members of a particular clan or family. Bradbury described the Osage lodges as "circular in form, constructed by placing mats of coarse rushes over forks and poles." The women wove the mats from wild rushes and "leaves of flags or typha palustris."

Charles Claude Dutisne, the first French explorer to cross the Ozark highlands early in the eighteenth century, found a country filled with bison. He also met the Osage, whom he described as a tribe that hunted on horseback. Both the bison and the horse were important to the Osage way of life. From the bison they

Osage warriors, drawn by George Catlin. *Courtesy State Historical Society of Missouri*

Osage woman with child. *Courtesy State Historical Society of Missouri*

got meat, hides, and bones for tools and ornaments. The horse was used primarily for hunting as the Osage went to war on foot. The Osage secured their horses by trading, stealing, and capturing them wild on the plains. To bring in a stolen horse was an honor for the Osage brave equal to the taking of an enemy scalp, although neither habit was cultivated until after the coming of whites in the early eighteenth century.

In their religion the Osage worshiped Wah'Kon-Tah, the Mystery Force of sun, wind, and lightning, accepting their victories and their defeats as divine will. The most important rituals had to do with preparing for war and mourning the dead. The "Mourning Dance" was held upon the death of a chief or a great warrior. A chief mourner went into the forest to grieve for thirty days. When he came back to the village, he led the other mourners in a dance to Wah'Kon-Tah. During the dance six braves mounted their ponies and rode off in search of an enemy scalp. On their return they presented to the medicine man the scalp impaled on a spear or a pole. This symbolized the passing of the deceased into the "happy hunting ground." A feast followed, and when it was over the widow returned to her lodge, washed herself, and resumed her chores.

In the first decade of the nineteenth century, approximately 6,300 Osage Indians lived in present-day Bates and Vernon counties. Captain Zebulon M. Pike, an American explorer, visited them in 1806. Struck by the beauty of the Osage River and the "prairie crowned with rich and luxuriant grass," Pike predicted that the Osage lands would soon be occupied by American farmers and herders. Less than two years later, in 1808, the Osage gave up their rights to Missouri east of a line drawn from the village of Sibley in Clay County due south. By treaty in 1825, the United States took what was left of Osage land in Missouri and removed the remnants of the tribe to Kansas and eventually to the Indian Territory (Oklahoma).

Besides the Missouri and the Osage, there were other tribes in Missouri for brief periods of time during the late eighteenth and early nineteenth centuries. Most of them had once held sway over various parts of the eastern United States. These transient tribes made little impact during their short time in Missouri and had only a slight influence on its history. Once forces to be reckoned with by white settlers advancing across the eastern half of the United States, they had become weak and helpless by the time they were forced west of the Mississippi River. These remnants of a people whose former glory had become only a memory were quickly pushed aside by the surge of white settlement into Missouri.

From earliest times Missouri's land and rivers, its abundance of wild animals and variety of plant life attracted and sustained the life of the prehistoric peoples and their descendants, the Indians. For thousands of years Missouri's early inhabitants developed cultures in harmony with nature and its demands. The story of their development is only partially known, but each new archaeological discovery adds a further dimension to it. By the time the European explorers and, later, white settlers came to Missouri, distinctive Indian tribes lived and hunted along the rivers, across the Ozark Plateau, and into the prairies and the plains. But within a relatively short time these tribes declined, weakened, and eventually retreated in the face of forces they neither understood nor were able to control.

Suggestions for Reading

A good survey of Missouri's geography and natural resources is James Collier, *Geographic Areas of Missouri*, Parkville, Missouri Council for Social Studies, 1959. For the classic surveys of the land and its influence on the early inhabitants of Missouri, see Carl H. Chapman, *The Archeology of Missouri*, Vol. I, Columbia, University of Missouri Press, 1975, and Carl H. and Eleanor F. Chapman, *Indians and Archeology of Missouri*, Rev. ed., Columbia, University of Missouri Press, 1983. More recent works on Missouri's prehistoric period can be found in Michael J. O'Brien and W. Raymond Wood, *The Prehistory of Missouri*, Columbia, University of Missouri Press, 1998, and Michael J. O'Brien, *Paradigms of the Past: The Story of Missouri Archeology*, Columbia, University of Missouri Press, 1995. For concise and informative articles on the state's great rivers, see Robert W. Durrenberger, "Missouri River" and "Mississippi River" in Howard R. Lamar, ed., *The*

New Encyclopedia of the American West, rev. ed., New Haven, Yale University Press, 1998. For a more comprehensive study of the Missouri, see C. Young, "That Damned Missouri," *National Geographic,* September 1971, and for the Mississippi, Nora Davis and Joseph Holmes, *The Father of Waters: A Mississippi River Chronicle,* San Francisco, Sierra Club/Yolla Bolly Books, 1982. An authoritative work on Missouri wildlife is Charles W. Schwartz and Elizabeth R. Schwartz, *The Wild Mammals of Missouri,* rev. ed., Columbia, University of Missouri Press, 1983. For the history of Missouri's major Native American tribe, turn to John Joseph Mathews, *The Osage: Children of the Middle Waters,* Norman, University of Oklahoma Press, 1961; Willard H. Rollings, *The Osage: An Ethnohistorical Study of Hegemony on the Prairie Plains,* Columbia, University of Missouri Press, 1988; and Terry P. Wilson, *The Osage,* Broomall, PA, Chelsea House Publishers, 1988. Their eventual removal from Missouri is covered in J. Frederick Fausz, "Becoming a 'Nation of Quakers': The Removal of the Osage Indians from Missouri," *Gateway Heritage* (Summer 2000).

The French and the Spanish

Toward the end of the fifteenth century, the nations of western Europe began the age of discovery, exploration, and colonization of the "Great Frontier." An eminent historian defined the Great Frontier as "all the lands discovered by Christopher Columbus and his associates." Missouri, standing in the heart of the vast Mississippi Valley region of North America, was a part of that Great Frontier. When the first European explorer entered the Mississippi Valley and encountered the mighty river, he opened the first chapter of the recorded history of Missouri.

Hernando De Soto

In 1539 Hernando de Soto, a wealthy Spanish noble who had been with Francisco Pizarro in the conquest of Peru, landed on the west coast of Florida with 600 men, 213 horses, large herds of swine, packs of dogs, and a quantity of provisions. Strongly motivated to expand Spain's dominion over the New World, to convert the Indians to Christianity and, more importantly, to amass great fortunes of gold and silver, de Soto set forth on a journey that would take him west to the Mississippi. Indian captives told him of rich lands, cities, and people who wore golden helmets when they went into battle farther to the west. De Soto's band crossed into Arkansas on barges just south of present-day Memphis in 1541. On the west bank he learned from the Indians that not far from their encampment were salt and a yellowish metal. He dispatched two of his men to accompany the Indians in search of these materials. They may have reached the Saline River near Ste. Genevieve before they returned with specimens of salt and copper. If so, de Soto's men were the first Europeans to come in contact with the land and the Indians of Missouri.

During the winter of 1541–42, the Spaniards camped at the junction of the Arkansas and Canadian rivers. In the spring they retraced their steps to the Mississippi. After four years of hardship, De Soto "took to his pallet" with fever and died. Fearing the Indians would learn of his death and attack them, the survivors took his body, wrapped it in a shroud filled with sand, and during the night buried it in the river. By 1543 the desperate survivors finally reached the Gulf of Mexico and made their way back to Spain.

Nearly 150 years after De Soto, Europeans would again navigate the great river and intrude upon the lands and inhabitants of the Mississippi Valley. This time they would come under the French flag and in the simple dress of a Catholic priest and a fur trader.

Marquette And Jolliet

By 1665 the ambition of France to expand its religious, political, and economic interests in North America led to the naming of Jean Talon as administrator of Canada. The enterprising Talon encouraged missionaries and traders to push farther into the interior of New France and to seek out new Indian tribes to convert and to trade tools, cloth, and guns for furs. Among these were Father Jacques Marquette and Louis Jolliet, whom Talon sent to explore the "Colbert River" (French name for Mississippi). In these two men were embodied the French objectives in the New World, a zeal for souls and a desire for profit.

Father Marquette descending the Mississippi River, 1673, as painted by Oscar E. Berninghaus. *August A. Busch, Jr. Courtesy State Historical Society of Missouri*

On May 15, 1673, the two explorers departed St. Ignace on Green Bay, where Father Marquette had labored among the Indians since 1670, and traveled by way of Green Bay, the Fox River, and the Wisconsin River toward the Mississippi. On June 17 they reached the Mississippi and began its descent in their birch bark canoes, carefully noting in their journals the lay of the land, the Indian tribes they encountered, and the nature of the rushing river. At the confluence of the Mississippi and Missouri rivers they were at first frightened by the loud noise and turbulence of the water. They could not believe "a mass of large trees, entire, with branches, real floating islands," belching from "Pekitanoui" (Indian name for Missouri River). "Its agitation" was "so great that the water was all muddy and could not get clear." They canoed as far as the mouth of the Arkansas River, where they realized that the Mississippi did not flow into the Pacific Ocean but rather into the Gulf of Mexico. Disappointed that they had not discovered the all-water route to the Pacific, they nevertheless were excited about the possibilities of a connection from the Great Lakes to the Gulf of Mexico. They returned to Quebec in 1674 by way of the Illinois River.

Father Marquette and Jolliet brought back considerable information that in time would be used by others coming into the Mississippi Valley. When Father Marquette resumed his work at St. Ignace, he sketched a map based on his notes in which he called the Missouri River, "Pekitanoui," placed ten Indian tribes living in the general area where the "broad stream" enters the Mississippi, and identified one Indian village near there as "Ou-Missouri," referring to the tribe of that name. In time the word Missouri was used to designate the river. Marquette's map, now preserved in the archives of St. Mary's College in Montreal, has been termed by modern cartographers "the Mother Map of Missouri."

Marquette and Jolliet did not open the Mississippi Valley to great numbers, but their journey provided useful information about it and sharpened the ambition of the French to establish themselves there. Their exploits also encouraged the evangelizing activities of the Catholic Church and influenced the great French empire builder Robert de La Salle.

Robert de La Salle

Following the expedition of Father Marquette and Jolliet, La Salle conceived the plan to strengthen France's control of the Mississippi

Valley by establishing a series of forts and trading posts at various points along the river. Backed by the powerful French governor of Canada, Count de Frontenac, La Salle set forth in January 1682 to explore the river and to claim land, natural resources, and inhabitants for his king.

La Salle's expedition, consisting of twenty-three French and twenty-eight Indians, ten of whom served as cooks, moved across the Great Lakes to the upper reaches of the Mississippi. Accompanying the explorer was Father Zenobe Membré, a strong-willed Franciscan priest who represented the interest of Catholic Christianity on the frontier. La Salle's chief lieutenant, Henry Tonty, an Italian known as "Iron Hand" because of a metal hand replacing one he had lost, kept a detailed journal that contained much information and valuable insights about what he called the "lands of the Mississippi." Especially descriptive in his accounts about Indian life, he once noted that the fat faces of the Indians, presumably Chickasaws, resembled "large soupplates." Tonty recorded that extensive forests lined the river banks, wild game and fur-bearing animals abounded, and fresh water was plentiful. He even predicted that if silkworm eggs were introduced to thrive on the mulberry trees in the area, the Indians would become silk makers. Tonty's account would add immeasurably to the growing information about the Mississippi Valley.

Camping one night near the confluence of the Missouri and Mississippi rivers, La Salle interrogated a young Pawnee Indian boy, "age sixteen or seventeen," who had escaped from the Missouris. From the boy La Salle learned that the Missouri River flowed from west to east, was navigable, and extended far west of the Mississippi. The Pawnee boy erred when he told La Salle that the Missouri River was only a tributary of the Platte River far to the west.

The expedition navigated the Mississippi River all the way to the Gulf of Mexico. There La Salle, on April 9, 1682, claimed the valley, stretching from the Appalachian Mountains on the east to the Rocky Mountains on the west and from Canada on the north to the Gulf of Mexico on the south, for France and named it Louisiana in honor of the French King Louis XIV. On his way back to Quebec, La Salle built Fort St. Louis on the Illinois River. La Salle sailed for France to secure additional funds and workers to erect a post at the mouth of the Mississippi River to protect Louisiana from the encroachments of Spain and England.

In the spring of 1686, Tonty, who had been left behind, went down the Mississippi River to rejoin La Salle, whom he believed had returned from France. Tonty did not know that La Salle had left France in 1684 but had failed to find the mouth of the Mississippi River. Landing in Texas, La Salle attempted to return to Louisiana but his mutinous crew murdered him. In the meantime, Tonty established a small settlement of ten people on the Arkansas River to reinforce La Salle on his anticipated return. La Salle's tragic death temporarily set back France's development of Louisiana, but his exploits clearly added to the knowledge of the region, its inhabitants, its potential for trade and profit, and its opportunity for the missionary endeavors of the Catholic Church. In 1698 a French-Canadian, Le Moine d'Iberville, sailed from France and found the mouth of the river that La Salle had missed.

The Work of the French Missionaries

Although the French did not pour into Louisiana after La Salle, the two principal agents of French activity in frontier America, the priests and the fur traders, appeared in search of water routes to the Pacific, furs, trade with the Indians, and opportunities to spread the Roman Catholic faith. Called "Black Robes" by the Indians, the priests followed the river courses and narrow Indian trails into country never before seen by Europeans. Like Father Pierre Charlevoix, who explored the Mississippi River in 1721 and wrote that its confluence with the Missouri was the grandest in the world, the Catholic priests probed the wilderness of the Mississippi Valley. They established semipermanent missions to work with the Indians. In 1700 Father Gabriel Marest established St. Francis Xavier (a mission for the Kaskaskia Indians) at the mouth of the River des Peres on the west bank of the Mississippi, considered the first white settlement in Missouri. The village disappeared in 1703 as the Kaskaskia Indians sought refuge from the unhealthy conditions of the site and the proximity of unfriendly Indians. On the east bank of the river the Catholic priests planted the seeds of Cahokia (1699) and Kaskaskia (1703), which in time became leading settlements in the Illinois country of Louisiana.

In addition to their evangelizing work, the priests gave pastoral care to the French pioneers, administered the sacraments, gave religious instruction, and often at their own expense built churches and rectories. Later, the presence of the Catholic Church and its priests gave a measure of stability to the tiny French settlements along the banks of the Mississippi River.

These priests served not only the Catholic Church but also the state on the Louisiana frontier. French officials used their observations in determining the sites of military outposts. Cartographers in Paris made maps of Louisiana based on the data sent by them. In conferring with the Indians or serving as "listening posts" for potential danger to French activity, they assumed a diplomatic role. Even their reports and letters often advertised the frontier and excited would-be entrepreneurs and adventurers to come and seek their fortunes in Louisiana.

Despite their lack of funds or protection, the missionaries faced the dangers of the Louisiana frontier without fear or trembling. Many lost their lives suddenly and violently, while others became enfeebled by harsh frontier conditions. The Archbishop of Paris once asked a poor priest among the Illinois Indians if there might be wealth in that place to fill the Church treasury and to undergird the missionary work. Writing to his superior the priest said, "The only riches to be won are sufferings." The influence of the Catholic Church and its missionary priests in the early history of Louisiana can still be seen in the Mississippi Valley and in Missouri towns and cities near the two great rivers.

Fort Orleans

Along with the missionary priests, the French fur traders paddled up unknown rivers and into unexplored areas of Louisiana. Exchanging beads, trinkets, vermilion, tools, blankets, and brandy for furs, the "coureurs de bois" (traders and trappers) and "voyageurs" (boatmen) established trade with the Indians, explored the wilderness, and named rivers and places. Their endeavors fit well into the theory of mercantilism, whereby the colony was to provide the natural resources that would make the "Mother Country" economically self-sufficient and independent.

French traders and hunters, as early as 1687, ascended the Missouri River as far as the mouth of the Osage. During 1714 Étienne de Bourgmond explored the Missouri River as far north as the Platte River, logged his journey, and lived with the Indians. Nine years later Bourgmond returned to establish Fort D'Orleans on the north bank of the Missouri near the Grand River in present-day Carroll County. The French intended to strengthen their relationship with the Indians, to increase the Indian trade, and to defend the area from the intrusion of the Spanish. By the spring of 1724 it had become a busy center where Indians from as far away as present-day Kansas came to trade furs and listen to the preaching of Father Jean Baptiste Mercier. Fort Orleans remained a French outpost in the wilderness until 1729, when it had to be abandoned because of excessive costs. During its brief existence, however, Bourgmond managed to persuade a group of Indian chiefs to go with him to France where they created a mild sensation in the royal court and among the French intellectuals.

Charles Claude Dutisne explored the Missouri as far as the Osage and Gasconade rivers in 1718, but hostile Indians forced him to retreat to Kaskaskia. In 1729 the dogged Dutisne followed Indian and bison trails across the Ozark highlands of southwest Missouri where he planted the French flag and made official contact with the Osage Indians. This was the first recorded trip across the land surface of Missouri.

The Discovery of Lead

Early French explorers knew of the existence of iron and lead deposits in Louisiana but yearned for gold and silver. When the French mineralogist Le Sueur reported in 1700 that there was lead in the Illinois country, d'Iberville petitioned the French king for permission to work the mines there. Unlike gold and silver, lead did not entice the French king, and d'Iberville was denied his request. French interest in the economic potential quickened, however, as reports of gold and silver in the region reached the authorities. In 1712 Antoine Crozat, a French banker, sought and received a fifteen-year trade monopoly in the region with the encouragement of Governor Antoine de la Motte Cadillac. The governor personally set out to search for silver in February 1715. At Mine La Motte (Madison County), about thirty-five miles southwest of Ste. Genevieve, Cadillac dug for silver and found lead. Pressed by financial problems, Crozat surrendered his patent in 1717.

Not long after that French investors organized the Company of the Indies to exploit the wealth of frontier Louisiana. Philippe Renault, a Parisian banker and director general of the company's mining operations, came to Louisiana in 1720 and supervised new efforts southwest of the Meramec River and at Mine La Motte. Renault brought with him a work force of fifty miners and some black slaves. They extracted, melted, and molded the lead. Hauled to the river in wagons pulled by oxen, the lead was then loaded on a

Old Ste. Genevieve as depicted in the murals at the state capitol. *Walker-Missouri Commerce, courtesy State Historical Society of Missouri*

barge and shipped upriver to Fort Chartres in Illinois, the company headquarters. There it was weighed and reloaded on barges bound for New Orleans. The lead-mining industry expanded in southeast Missouri, but Renault's failure to find silver finally bankrupted the company. In spite of his debts and troubles with the Fox Indians, Renault continued his mining operations until 1744, when he returned to France.

Although the lead yielded little profit, it did attract miners, farmers, traders, and missionaries to the general vicinity of the mines. Early in the 1730s a few Creole families at Kaskaskia crossed the river and settled on its west bank at a site later named Ste. Genevieve. This tiny village became the first permanent white settlement in Missouri. Although the official date of its founding is set at 1735, there were undoubtedly French settlers there earlier. The original settlement some three miles below the present town proved susceptible to flooding and was later moved to a safer site. The area provided the French settlers with the basics of a stable settlement: fresh water, wild game, salt, furs, fertile soil, lead, and the river highway to New Orleans. The village's growth, although not spectacular, was steady. Evidence of its French heritage still abounds in the modern town of Ste. Genevieve.

The Founding of St. Louis

France ceded Louisiana west of the Mississippi to Spain through the Treaty of Fontainebleau (1762) in return for its assistance in the

Seven Years War against England. Spain had entered the war late and was promptly and decisively defeated by England, which claimed Florida from it as a prize. The Peace of Paris (1763) brought the war to an end. France gave up to England all Canada and Louisiana, east of the Mississippi. Although Spain was anxious to establish control of its share of Louisiana as a buffer state between its empire in Mexico and the expanding English colonies east of the Mississippi River, the first Spanish governor did not arrive until 1766. In the interlude between the Treaty of Fontainebleau and Spain's actual takeover, the French established St. Louis, the second permanent settlement on the west bank of the Mississippi.

News traveled at a snail's pace in the eighteenth century, especially to faraway places like Louisiana. Early in 1763 the French governor, unaware that worldwide developments had stripped France of Louisiana, granted to the firm of Maxent, Laclede & Company the exclusive right to trade with the Indians in present-day Missouri for a period of eight years. Gilbert Antoine Maxent, a wealthy New Orleans merchant, furnished the money while his partner, Pierre Laclede Liquest, was to select a site on the west bank of the Mississippi and build a trading post that would take full advantage of the Missouri fur trade.

After gathering his supplies and equipment, Laclede, Madame Therese Chouteau, and their thirteen-year-old son, Auguste Chouteau, whom Laclede had adopted, departed New Orleans in the summer of 1763 on their way to upper Louisiana. Laclede had hoped to lay over at Ste. Genevieve, store their goods, and wait for fairer weather, but he discovered that Ste. Genevieve lacked adequate facilities. The French commandant of Illinois, DeVilliers, invited Laclede to come to Fort Chartres. Reaching there on November 3, 1763, the party stored their goods, and Laclede and the young Chouteau crossed the Mississippi early in December to scout a location for the post. When Laclede spotted a place on a bluff some thirty feet above the water's edge, he knew instinctively he had found what he had been seeking. It had a commanding view of the river, good soil, and was surrounded by rich timberland. In February 1764, Laclede left to the young Chouteau the responsible job of supervising the building of the post. With Laclede's directions, Chouteau saw to the construction of a number of log houses and a stone building to serve as the company's headquarters. Laclede named the post St. Louis in honor of King Louis IX, the patron saint of the reigning King Louis XV. By

Pierre Laclede Liguist, the founder of St. Louis.
Courtesy State Historical Society of Missouri

April 1764, the unexpected news of the transfer of Louisiana to Spain and England influenced a number of French families on the Illinois side of the river to migrate to St. Louis to escape the English. At first St. Louis experienced little population growth, but became the seat of government for the Spanish regime. Developing early a quaint Old World charm and lifestyle, St. Louis was to thrive as a fur trading center and the gateway to the hinterland of Missouri.

The "Joie De Vivre"

Although wilderness conditions imposed many hardships on the French pioneers in Louisiana, they held to their Old World ways and traditions, which have been termed *joie de vivre* (the joy of life). The American explorers Meriwether Lewis and William Clark saw the French people as being happy, hospitable, and full of vivacity, but at the same time often neglecting their occupations. In 1751, a young military officer on his way to an assignment in Illinois commented in a series of delightful letters on French life in Louisiana. "There is," he wrote, "a great deal of hunting, fishing, and other pleasures of life . . . the land is filled with wild game and birds." His initial homesickness was all but cured when he tasted for the first time a consommé made from buffalo tongue and knew that the French natives had not lost their cooking skills. They filled their leisure hours with card playing, horse racing, family affairs, and games. Sunday was a day of worship. Special days were called celebrations. La Guignoile (New Year's Eve) saw the people dressed in outlandish costumes, going from house to house, dancing and singing for a liquid reward. The King's Ball, held annually between Twelfth Night and Shrove Tuesday, included dancing, singing, and feasting.

French dwellings, similar to the ones constructed in Normandy and Quebec with a few alterations, were well adapted to the hot muggy summers and the blistering cold winters of Upper Louisiana. Most houses were constructed with logs erected vertically, rather than horizontally, like American log cabins. High-pitched roofs, plenty of plaster in the log cracks, and coats of whitewash provided what are now recognized as sound insulating techniques. The "galerie," a porch on three or four sides, provided an early form of air-conditioning, protecting the house from the sun and rain and opening it to the breeze. Later glass was used in casement windows that swung on hinges in the more elegant homes. Interior furnishings most likely included bedsteads, cupboards, chairs, tables, and a chest for clothing. The kitchen was often separate from the house. Some houses in the villages doubled as shops. The storekeeper kept his wares in a chest and the storeroom was a part of the house. For patrons who needed a nap, merchants often kept a bench handy for this purpose.

Unlike the independent American farmers, the French practiced a blend of individual and collective farming. "Le grand champ" (the common field) near the village of Ste. Genevieve comprised several thousand acres, with each family owning at least one long, narrow strip of land stretching from the river westward. This arrangement was similar to that of French-Canadian fields along the St. Lawrence river today. To provide pasture and woodlot, a second tract of land, the "commons," was reserved near each village. A common storage place was also a part of French agricultural practices. Once planted, the growing crops were left pretty much on their own until harvesttime. The main crops were corn, spring wheat, oats, barley, pumpkins, watermelons, muskmelons, peaches, and apples. Livestock included hogs, cattle, and horses. The French made a delicious brandy from peaches, and cider from apples. From sweet grapes they made a red wine. If we are to believe Lewis and Clark, the French were not great farmers, but as gardeners they excelled.

The dominant church in Louisiana was, of course, the Roman Catholic. The priests performed the pastoral role and brought, as well, a strain of French civilization to the lonely outposts in the wilderness. Generally as the size of a village increased, so did the size and ornateness of the church building. Roman Catholicism had some impact on native religions in Missouri as evidenced by the crucifixes left behind by the Indians, although a corresponding influ-

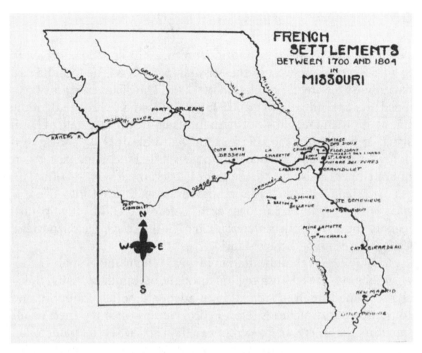

French settlements between 1700 and 1804 in Missouri. *Courtesy State Historical Society of Missouri*

ence of native religion on Catholicism seems minimal. The Catholic priests conducted themselves and their duties as they had been taught while their congregations worshiped and prayed as had their ancestors. Both the Catholic religion and community gave a sense of security and continuity to people facing daily the insecurity and isolation of the frontier.

Major forms of transportation on land were horseback and wagons pulled by oxen. Small two-wheeled carts called *charettes* and more elegant two-wheeled carts called *calaches* were used extensively. On water the keelboat, bateau, canoe, and pirogue were employed. The waterways were the highways in frontier Louisiana.

The end of the French control of Louisiana in 1763 did not end the influence of French ways, language, lifestyle, traditions, or Catholicism. The *joie de vivre* would cast long shadows over the developments of Spanish Louisiana. In time a more restless and rambunctious breed, the American pioneer, would lessen the shadows of *joie de vivre*, but never completely dispel them.

The Spanish Regime

When the new Spanish governor, Don Antonio de Ulloa, arrived in Spain's new colony west of the Mississippi in 1766, he found a vast territory with a small population of 1,000. The Spanish regime organized the area into Lower and Upper Louisiana, with the dividing line at approximately the northern limits of the present state of Louisiana. Appointed by the king and subject to his directives, the governor resided in New Orleans. In turn he selected the lieutenant-governor of Upper Louisiana, whose seat of government was St. Louis. Upper Louisiana, which included Missouri, was divided into five districts with a commandant over each. Before the end of the Spanish regime, the five districts were St. Charles, St. Louis, Ste. Genevieve, Cape Girardeau, and New Madrid.

Characterized as authoritarian in government and Roman Catholic in religion, the Spanish regime throughout four decades in Louisiana remained small in size, without adequate military support, and constantly short of funds. Don Pedro Piernas once reported to his superiors that there never were more than six or seven Spaniards in Ste. Genevieve, one of the permanent settlements in Upper Louisiana. Although Spanish was the official language, most of the inhabitants spoke French. Relying on the French who had been in Louisiana for three quarters of a century, the Spanish regime followed their advice and counsel in dealing with the Indians, competing against the British fur traders, and locating sites for forts and settlements. Some French even served in the government. On July 17, 1765, Louis St. Ange De Bellerive, the French commander at Fort Chartres moved his troops to St. Louis where he remained as the civil and military head until he was finally replaced by the Spanish lieutenant governor Don Pedro Piernas in 1770.

The Population of Upper Louisiana

The population of Upper Louisiana, mainly French with a few Spaniards, Anglo Americans, black slaves, and Indians, came from French Canada, the lower Mississippi Valley, and across the river in Illinois. Direct immigration of colonists from Spain and France was minimal. African slaves had been imported to Upper Louisiana to work in the lead mines, to clear the land, and to serve as domestic servants. Although a few Indians camped near the settlements, except for fur traders the larger tribes who lived in the hinterland of Upper Louisiana had little to do with the settlers. French and Spanish law prohibited Indian slavery, though a few Indians were enslaved. Most of the French and Spanish fur traders were too shrewd to consider Indians as candidates for chains when they could be used as partners in the fur trading industry. And then, the vast wilderness provided the means of escape for the few Indians who might be subjugated by the whites. After 1800, Indian slavery ceased to exist. From the time of Spain's occupancy of Upper Louisiana until the end of the century, the population increased slowly, reaching nearly 10,000.

Expansion Around St. Louis

The Spanish regime built Fort San Carlos to strengthen St. Louis's defenses. Many of the French inhabitants resented helping to defray the cost of the fort named in honor of Charles II, the Spanish king. Carondelet, near the mouth of the River des Peres, was founded the same year. Nicknamed *vide poche* (empty pocket) either because St. Louisans who gambled at the racetrack there often lost or because of the poverty of Carondelet, the little village reflected its French background.

Louis Blanchette, a French fur trader, started a trading post on the Missouri River about twenty-one miles from its confluence with the Mississippi. First called by the French *Les Petites Côtes*, in time it became St. Charles. When Lewis and Clark ascended the Missouri on their way to the Pacific in 1804, St. Charles had grown to a village of 450. Later it was a jumping-off place for pioneers moving into the interior of Missouri.

The American Revolution

The American Revolution erupted in 1775, and its effects were felt in Spanish Louisiana. The Indian tribes, torn between their loyalty to the Spanish and British fur traders, disrupted the fur trade, the economy, and the commerce on the Mississippi River. The French inhabitants, who had no love for their old enemy Great Britain, sympathized with the American cause. This sympathy was strengthened as a result of the French Alliance in 1777. After this France gave direct aid in the form of soldiers, a navy, and loans to the American rebels.

During the Revolution, Great Britain attempted to secure the country west of the Appalachian Mountains all the way to the Mississippi River. Their efforts were stymied by General George Rogers

Clark who, with the help of French inhabitants in the area, overran Cahokia, Kaskaskia, and Vincennes in the Illinois country by July 1778. Lieutenant-governor Henry Hamilton, Britain's principal agent in the West, sensing that the loss of these important settlements threatened Britain's hold on this territory, moved against the Americans late in 1778. Nicknamed "Hair-buyer" because of his alleged practice of paying Indians for American scalps, Hamilton recaptured Vincennes in December 1778. Clark, however, rallied his forces and with the financial assistance of some St. Louisans attacked Vincennes several months later and drove out the British.

The Spanish regime leaned toward the Americans in the hope that an American victory would force the British to return Florida to Spain. Lieutenant-Governor Fernando de Leyba moved to bolster the defenses at St. Louis when he learned that on July 8, 1779, Spain had declared war on Great Britain. On May 26, 1780, Spanish troops, with the aid of French inhabitants of St. Louis and reinforcements from Ste. Genevieve, repulsed a combined force of British soldiers and Indians in their attempt to take St. Louis and gain control of the Mississippi River. After this serious setback the British threat to the Mississippi Valley ended.

Postrevolutionary Expansion

In the Treaty of Paris of 1783, ending the American Revolution, Great Britain gave the United States its claim to the land between the Appalachian Mountains and the Mississippi River. The spirited advance of Americans into that area gave Spain more concern. Caught between the desire to people Louisiana with American colonizers and the fear of American expansion east of the river, Spain closed the Mississippi River to American commerce and trade. Infuriated by this act, the American pioneers threatened disunion if the government did not act aggressively to force Spain to open the river since the free and open navigation of the river and the use of New Orleans as a port were essential to their interests. After fruitless negotiations during the Confederation period (1781–87), this issue was finally resolved by the Pinckney Treaty (1795) between Spain and the United States. This treaty gave Americans free navigation privileges on the Mississippi and the right to store goods at New Orleans in transshipment.

In the years immediately following the American Revolution, official Spanish policy held little promise for Americans on the other side of the river, who looked hungrily toward Upper Louisiana and its unlimited frontier resources. In 1787, however, the Spanish minister to the United States offered Colonel George Morgan a large Spanish land grant on the west bank of the Mississippi River south of Ste. Genevieve if he would settle the area with American colonists. Morgan thought enough of the proposition that he visited Upper Louisiana, selected a site for a settlement where some French were already living, and named it New Madrid. Governor Miro at New Orleans, in accord with official policy, nullified the arrangement and Morgan returned home. Some of Morgan's followers did remain, however, and added to what became an important settlement on the Mississippi.

Before the outbreak of the American Revolution, Louis Lorimier, a French Canadian Indian trader, established a trading post in the Ohio country among the Shawnee and Delaware Indians. During the Revolution, his trading post became the center of British intrigue and military activity in the West until George Rogers Clark overran it. Lorimier barely escaped with his life. In 1787 he arrived in Upper Louisiana to escape his creditors and to recoup his financial losses. He settled near St. Mary's, a little southeast of Ste. Genevieve, where he worked with the Spanish commandant in the Indian fur trade. Lorimier recruited some of his former Shawnee and Delaware allies, who were being pressured by the Americans, to come to Louisiana. Early in 1793 the Spanish authorities gave Lorimier permission to settle himself and his Indian bands in the general vicinity of Cape Girardeau. In time Lorimier became a leading trader, an extensive landowner, the commandant of Cape Girardeau, and an important citizen of Upper Louisiana. A handsome man with long black hair that he braided into a riding whip, Lorimier could neither read nor write, but he spoke several foreign languages. After the American occupation of Louisiana, Lorimier laid out Cape Girardeau from his own land grants. The United States government did not confirm his land grants, however, until after his death in 1812.

As late as 1792, Lieutenant-Governor Trudeau received orders to prohibit Americans from entering Upper Louisiana. By 1795 the belief was growing that allowing Americans to settle in Upper Louisiana and become Spanish citizens and good Catholics would strengthen the colony, increase prosperity, and weaken the expanding American territories in the West. This moved Spain to relax its prohibitions against American settlers. Two Americans drawn to Up-

Daniel Boone. *Courtesy State Historical Society of Missouri*

per Louisiana by what they believed to be excellent opportunities for land and economic gain were Moses Austin and Daniel Boone. A native of New England, Austin had joined a mercantile company that had expanded its operations to lead mining. Sent to western Virginia to supervise the company's mining operation, he learned from a traveler that there were rich lead producing areas across the Mississippi in Upper Louisiana. Leaving Virginia in the late fall of 1796, Austin rode horseback across the country, losing his way in a violent snowstorm in Illinois before reaching his destination in St. Louis. Cordially received, Austin was permitted to journey to the lead-producing areas near Potosi. Impressed by the lead which he described as "better quality than any I have ever seen either from the Mines in England or America," Austin returned to Virginia, packed his family and goods, and came back to Upper Louisiana. Austin became wealthy, developed new lead-mining techniques, opened a store, and invested in a St. Louis bank. After the United States acquired Louisiana, Austin became one of Missouri's most prominent citizens. Wiped out by the panic of 1819, Austin conceived the idea of starting an American colony in Texas. He died before he could complete his venture, but his son, Stephen F. Austin, took up his father's work and led Americans into yet another frontier.

Lieutenant-Governor Trudeau offered Daniel Boone 1,000 arpents of land in 1798 to settle in Upper Louisiana, and the Kentuckian joined his sons on the Femme Osage Creek not too distant from St. Louis the following year. The Spanish regime appointed him a syndic, which means judge or magistrate, of the Femme Osage district. The stump of the giant oak under which Boone held court still stands today at his son's home near Defiance, Missouri. For two decades Boone farmed, hunted, explored the Missouri River, and manufactured salt with his sons. An important trail leading from St. Louis to the salt licks in Howard County bore the name Boonslick Trail.

Austin and Boone represented the type of Americans who were being attracted in increasing numbers to Upper Louisiana by the late 1790s. Restless, land hungry, versatile, optimistic, and motivated by economic opportunity, the American farmers, artisans, fur traders, adventurers, and merchants crossed the Mississippi River to swell the populations of St. Louis, Florissant, St. Charles, Cape Girardeau, Ste. Genevieve, New Madrid, and adjacent areas.

The Louisiana Purchase

In decline as a major European power by the end of the eighteenth century, Spain faced a crumbling empire, a need for funds to bolster a sagging economy, and a Louisiana becoming more of a burden than a benefit. France, on the other hand, under the leadership of Napoleon, was seeking to rebuild its empire in the Caribbean and in the Gulf of Mexico, beginning with Santo Domingo and Louisiana. Determined to keep Louisiana out of the hands of Great Britain, France offered Spain the European principality of Tuscany for Louisiana in the secret treaty of San Ildefonso of 1800. Until such time as Napoleon could order his affairs in Europe and Santo Domingo, Spain retained possession of Louisiana.

Rumors of the secret arrangement filtered across the Atlantic slowly. American reaction to the transfer of Louisiana was one of shock and then anger. Westerners feared that French power would be able to close the Mississippi and the port of New Orleans again and back it up with French military might. When the Spanish intendant at New Orleans mistakenly denied the United States storage rights there, many Americans wanted to take the river by force and settle the issue once and for all. The Spanish governor apologized for the error and disavowed the act, but the damage had been done. "If this is done in the green tree," one American queried, "what shall be done in the dry?" If Spain closes the port of New Orleans by mistake, what will the French do on purpose?

By 1802 President Thomas Jefferson had a crisis on his hands. Not wanting a war for the young nation, but facing a dangerous situation, he wrote Robert Livingston, American minister in France, to seek negotiations with the French over the question of the river. He also instructed Livingston to offer to buy New Orleans and West Florida, which would give the United States control of the mouth of the Mississippi. If this failed, Jefferson threatened that the United States might have to "marry itself to the British fleet" to secure its interests on the Mississippi River. To reinforce American demands, the President dispatched James Monroe to France to assist Livingston. Before Monroe arrived in the spring of 1803, however, Napoleon declared, "The season of deliberation is now over." He had decided to dispose of all of Louisiana to the United States.

Why did Napoleon make such a sudden move? Sent to Santo Domingo to put down a revolution and to secure the Caribbean island, a crack French army under the command of General Leclerc had been decimated by the native forces of Toussaint L'Ouverture and a more deadly enemy, yellow fever. Two-thirds of the French Army, including General Leclerc and fifteen members of his staff, died of the disease. The army never reached North America, and the disaster at Santo Domingo seemingly convinced Napoleon that Louisiana would be too costly to defend. He needed money to renew war against Great Britain. By selling Louisiana to the United States, he would also keep it out of the hands of Great Britain, prevent an Anglo-American alliance, and enable Americans to become in future years a major rival to the British.

Monroe and Livingston quickly worked out the treaty for the Louisiana Purchase, which was signed April 30, 1803. In exchange for an area of land that covered 827,987 square miles, the United States would pay France $11,250,000 and assume $3,750,000 worth of American claims against France. All French and Spanish vessels and merchandise would be admitted into all ports of Louisiana with commercial privileges not extended to other nations. The United States would incorporate Louisiana into the Union as soon as possible and the people there would enjoy the same rights and privileges as other citizens of the United States.

Most Americans approved the Louisiana Purchase, and President Jefferson soothed the disgruntled opposition in his message to Congress on October 17, 1803, when he promised that Louisiana would aid our treasury, secure an outlet for the produce of western states, and provide an opportunity to spread "the blessings of freedom and equal laws."

On December 20, 1803, the French tricolor, which had floated only briefly over Louisiana, was lowered at New Orleans and the American flag raised. Governor William C. Claiborne proclaimed that the government of the French Republic in Louisiana had ceased, "and that of the United States of America is established over the same." Before the government house in St. Louis a similar ceremony took place on March 9, 1804, when Captain Amos Stoddard, representing both the United States and France, accepted the transfer of Upper Louisiana from Lieutenant-Governor Carlos Delassus.

In his journal of 1796–97 Moses Austin wrote of Upper Louisiana, "It is Not possible a Country which has with in its self everything to make its settlers Rich and Happy can remain unoticed [sic] by the American people." The next chapter in the history of the area would see the fulfillment of that prophecy.

Suggestions for Reading

The best overview of preterritorial Missouri can be found in William E. Foley, *The Genesis of Missouri: From Wilderness Outpost to Statehood*, Columbia, University of Missouri Press, 1989. An updated bibliography is included in Foley, *A History of Missouri, Vol. I, 1673 to 1820*, rev. ed., Columbia, University of Missouri Press, 1999. Additional information on early European explorers of the Mississippi Valley and Missouri is in John B. Brebner, *Explorers of North America, 1492–1806*, New York, Doubleday, 1955. French exploration and colonization efforts in the Mississippi Valley are covered in Charles Balesi, *The Time of the French in the Heart of North America, 1673–1818*, Chicago, Alliance Francaise, 1992; Carl J. Ekberg, *French Roots in the Illinois Country: The Mississippi Frontier in Colonial Times*, Urbana, University of Illinois Press, 1998; and John F. McDermott, ed., *Frenchmen and French Ways in the Mississippi Valley*, Urbana, University of Illinois Press, 1969. Frank Norall, *Bourgmont: Explorer of the Missouri, 1698–1725*, Lincoln, University of Nebraska Press, 1988, traces the career of the man who first penetrated the Missouri valley beyond St. Louis. For the influence of the Spanish in preterritorial Missouri, see the documentary collection in Lawrence Kinnard, *Spain in the Mississippi Valley, 1765–1794* in the Annual Report of the American Historical Association, 1945, vols. II–IV, Washington, 1946, and John F. McDermott, ed., *The Spanish in the Mississippi Valley*, Urbana, University of Illinois Press, 1972. An interesting source of an early traveler to Upper Louisiana during the Spanish regime is George P. Garrison, ed., "Moses Austin's Journey . . . to The Province of Louisiana West of the Mississippi, 1796–97," *American Historical Review,* April 1900. Significant studies on the founding of St. Louis are John F. McDermott, "Myths and Realities Concerning the Founding of St. Louis," in McDermott, ed, *The French in the Mississippi Valley,* Urbana, University of Illinois Press, 1965, and William E. Foley and C. David Rice, *The First Chouteaus: River Barons of Early St. Louis,* Urbana, University of Illinois Press, 1983. Missouri's oldest settlement is beautifully described in Carl J. Ekberg, *Colonial Ste. Genevieve: An Adventure on the Mississippi Frontier,* Gerald, MO, Patrice Press, 1985. For an account of the epic Louisiana Purchase, see Alexander DeConde, *This Affair of Louisiana,* New York, Scribners, 1976.

THREE

The Coming of the Americans and the Statehood Crisis

T he citizens of Upper Louisiana were undoubtedly curious as to what they could expect under their new
rulers, the Americans. Captain Amos Stoddard, who had been appointed acting commandant for the region, noted that "a cordial ac-
quiescence seems to prevail among all ranks of people." Hoping to
avoid needless antagonism, the War Department had instructed
Stoddard to deal fairly with the people and to assure them that their
religious and property rights would be upheld. Until such time as
Congress established a permanent government for the area, Stoddard
would exercise both military and civil functions as the appointee of
the President.

In October 1804, Congress attached the area to the Territory of
Indiana, with its capital at Vincennes. This did not set well with the
local citizens, who objected to being governed from such a distance.
They were also concerned with the effects this might have on slavery,
which was illegal in Indiana. As a result, the following year Congress
created the Territory of Louisiana, which consisted of the region beyond the Mississippi River above the 33rd parallel. When the area
south of that line became the state of Louisiana in 1812, the name of
the northern part was changed to the Territory of Missouri.

Following the pattern that had been laid down by the Northwest
Ordinance of 1787, Missouri became a first-class territory in 1805.
This allowed for the appointment by the President of a governor, a
secretary, and three judges to rule the area. There was no legislature,
and the people had no direct voice in governmental affairs. The
territory's first governor was General James Wilkinson, a highly controversial figure who had a checkered career of intrigue dating back
to the American Revolution. At the time of his appointment he
had been holding secret conversations with Aaron Burr, presumably

about encouraging revolution in the West. Earlier in Kentucky he had been a secret agent for the Spanish with a mission to persuade that area to withdraw from the Union and join itself to Louisiana.

The arrival of Governor Wilkinson in July 1805 brought the emergence of political factionalism to the Missouri frontier. The American takeover had made the established French leadership in St. Louis and elsewhere edgy about policy with regard to land claims, slavery, and Indian affairs. They exerted a strong influence over the self-seeking Wilkinson, who quarreled with the territorial judges, refusing to meet with them to establish laws. An anti-Wilkinson group soon emerged consisting largely of recently arrived Americans, many of them lawyers, who wished to play a major role in land speculation and territorial politics.

Wilkinson stayed until August 1806 when it became obvious that his usefulness had ended because of continuing political turmoil. The governorship remained vacant until President Jefferson appointed Meriwether Lewis to the post in March 1807. Lewis did not arrive in St. Louis until a year after his appointment. In the meantime affairs were handled by Acting Governor Frederick Bates, whose real position was territorial secretary, and William Clark, who had been named superintendent of Indian affairs. Bates brought order out of the political chaos left by Wilkinson. He met with the judges and enacted a series of general laws to take care of a whole variety of problems.

Fort Osage and Fort Madison

One of the problems still festering when Governor Lewis arrived was the matter of establishing better relations with the Indian tribes of the area. Clark had dealt with some of these a year earlier, but then he had taken a lengthy trip east to visit relatives and get married. Now, with both men on the scene, they moved rapidly to deal with the Indians. The Osage, who had long been the area's dominant tribe, with their base in southwestern Missouri, had enjoyed the protection of the American government as they had that of the Spanish earlier. But they and other tribes farther west had grown increasingly restless as white settlers began to move into their lands and the American government seemed to show little concern. They wanted the government to build a trading post in their area to better service their needs, and Lewis and Clark agreed. In August 1808, Clark negotiated a new treaty with the Osage whereby they gave up some 200 square miles of land between the Missouri and Arkansas rivers. In return the government agreed to maintain a permanent trading post with a blacksmith shop and mill for the Indians' use and to give the tribe an annual grant of $1,500. Fort Osage, established for this purpose on a high bluff overlooking the Missouri River in Jackson County, would remain a vital outpost on the Missouri frontier until 1822, except for a brief period during the War of 1812 when it was abandoned.

During the winter of 1808–09, Lewis and Clark made a similar attempt to establish a fort on the upper Mississippi near the mouth of the Des Moines River, in part to strengthen territorial defenses against the hostile Shawnees in that area. This tribe was being stirred up by one of its chiefs, Tecumseh, in an effort to head off white movement into its lands throughout the upper Mississippi Valley. Presumably the British in Canada stood behind Tecumseh; and as British-American relations worsened generally, it caused concern in St. Louis that they might push the Indians into an attack on that settlement. Fort Madison took shape slowly while Governor Lewis also ordered block houses built in the St. Charles district as a final line of defense should an attack come from the north.

The War of 1812

In 1811 Governor William Henry Harrison of Indiana Territory sought to put an end to the Indian menace by attacking Tecumseh's village of Tippicanoe. He found the Indians bearing British arms. When the War of 1812 broke out the following year, the frontier was ablaze with Indian raids. By this time small settlements dotted the Missouri landscape along both rivers, and the Indians struck at several of these. With only 250 regular American troops available for duty west of the Mississippi, the settlers were forced to provide their own defense. Most communities erected wooden stockades around themselves, with sturdy log forts projecting above them at each corner. This slowed the Indian attacks, with only one village being hit thereafter. That was Côte sans Desseins in Callaway County, which was attacked in 1815. The Indians set the stockade there on fire but then fled in terror when the flames reached the community powder magazine, which erupted with a tremendous explosion.

When complaints to Washington failed to bring adequate reinforcements, the territorial officials organized local rangers called "the Minute Men of the Frontier." Each volunteer had to provide his own

Fort Osage (Jackson County) as depicted by George F. Green. *Courtesy of the artist*

horse, rifle, and provisions. Led by Captain Nathan Boone, this outfit maintained a constant patrol along the Missouri River and generally kept the Indians under control.

The war officially ended with the signing of the Treaty of Ghent on Christmas Eve, 1814, but it was several months before word of this reached Missouri. When the terms were disclosed, they aroused considerable concern along the frontier. Article IX drew particular objections. It provided for an immediate end to hostilities against the Indians providing they resumed peaceful ways. In return the tribes were to have the full restoration of their prewar rights and privileges. With reports of occasional attacks on outlying posts still current, many settlers shared the opinion of Christian Wilt of St. Louis that "we shall not have peace with the Indians until we drub them soundly into it."

The Indians themselves were caught off guard by Britain's sudden withdrawal from the war, which left them isolated and vulnerable. While some continued the struggle, nineteen tribes agreed to meet with American peace commissioners in July 1815 at Portage des Sioux just north of the mouth of the Missouri River. Led by William Clark, the Americans distributed $20,000 in presents among the Indians to aid in the signing of peace treaties. The following year ten more tribes sent representatives to St. Louis for a similar purpose.

Although many Americans resented "buying off" the Indians, these treaties effectively ended the frontier menace. As more settlers poured into the territory in the years following the war, the various

Indian tribes gradually relinquished their claims to Missouri soil. Clark, who had become governor in 1814, took the lead in arranging Indian treaties. Over the years the tribes had come to trust him, and he consequently knew how to persuade them to exchange their Missouri lands for those farther west in present-day Kansas and Oklahoma.

Territorial Growth

Although the war years tended to slow growth slightly, the American territorial period was one of strong population gains for Missouri. At the time of the American takeover in 1804, the population stood at 10,000—most of it centered in the area between St. Louis and New Madrid. Within the next six years that number had doubled to 20,000, which then trebled in the following decade to stand at 67,000 in 1820. Most of the new settlers came from Tennessee, Kentucky, North Carolina, and Virginia. They were attracted by the prospect of plentiful land at fairly reasonable prices. As southerners they bypassed the territories north of the Ohio River because the Northwest Ordinance forbade slavery there.

In the years following the War of 1812, these new settlers moved increasingly into the Boonslick region of central Missouri. This area had been so named because the sons of Daniel Boone had made the

A pioneer Missouri cabin, 1820. *Courtesy State Historical Society of Missouri*

PIONEER LIFE IN MISSOURI IN 1820.

first extensive exploration of it following their discovery of salt springs in Howard County in 1807. The region abounded in fertile land and good natural resources. River transportation flourished, and towns sprang up across the landscape to furnish supplies for those who were taking up farms nearby. One of the most prominent settlements was Franklin, which was established on the north bank of the Missouri in 1817 and quickly became the county seat of Howard County which then covered all of northwest Missouri. Within three years Franklin had 1,000 citizens and numerous businesses, a federal land office, and a newspaper serving the expanding region. Rival towns grew up in Chariton (1818) and Boonville (1819). By 1820 the Boonslick region had grown to 20,000—nearly a third of Missouri's total population. One of the territorial legislature's regular functions during this period was to divide and redivide the land into counties, whose number had grown to fifteen by 1820.

The Land Problem

The influx of settlers intensified a serious problem that had been festering since the United States acquired Louisiana in 1804—the question of land titles. This problem stemmed from three major sources. The first of these was the so-called Spanish land grants. The last of the Spanish governors, Carlos Delassus, like his predecessors, had often ignored formal procedures in making land transfers. It was also suspected that in the period between the transfer of the territory to France in 1800 and the American takeover in 1804, Delassus had made extensive land grants to friends and relatives, primarily for speculative purposes. Aggravating the matter further was the failure of many bona fide settlers under the Spanish regime to "perfect" their titles, which required the signed approval of officials at New Orleans. Because of the fear of fraud and overlapping claims, Congress refused to honor any title changes that had occurred between 1800 and 1804. This caused a tremendous uproar. As a result, in 1805 Congress established a board of land commissioners for Upper Louisiana to examine each claim and determine its validity. Over the next seven years the board looked at some 3,300 claims and continuously found itself a storm center of political controversy, for many of the territory's leading citizens, who had extensive holdings, were involved.

In its final report in January 1812, the board confirmed 1,340 claims—most of them small. But subsequent legislation enabled territorial officials, notably Frederick Bates as the Recorder of Land Titles, to continue the process of review. He approved many additional claims over the next four years while rejecting an almost equal number. Given the pressure of decision making, his was not an enviable job. Indeed the controversy over the Spanish land claims continued long after statehood, with the final claim being settled in the 1880s.

The second source for land problems was a natural disaster of gigantic proportions that occurred in December 1811. This was the New Madrid earthquake, so named because that small town appeared to be at the center of the disturbance. One of the most devastating tremors ever to shake the North American continent, the New Madrid earthquake was felt to some degree as far away as New York and Pennsylvania. Periodic aftershocks continued through March 1812. At the heart of the quake in the New Madrid area, some buildings shifted from their foundations and cracked while wooden dwellings were demolished. Giant crevices split the earth, and landslides were common along the riverbanks and streams. Travelers caught on the Mississippi that December night claimed that the motion of the earth actually caused the river to flow backward. Uprooted trees and other impediments clogged the river for months thereafter making travel difficult.

In spite of the quake's intensity, property damage and casualties were relatively light in the sparsely settled region. But in the wake of the earthquake many packed their remaining possessions and moved to what they considered safer areas. Unlike today, when disaster teams are quickly on the spot offering all kinds of aid, pleas for assistance then went generally unheeded because of the government's absorption with the pending outbreak of war. Finally in 1815, however, Congress passed legislation permitting any person to exchange his damaged land, up to 640 acres, for the same amount of the public domain elsewhere. Unfortunately this law benefited speculators more than actual settlers. Many of the latter had long since left the region, and speculators came into the area in droves in the spring of 1815 to buy up claims—in some cases before the landowners had even heard of the new law. Among those engaging in this activity was Governor Clark, who found the temptation for a few quick dollars a bit too great. So much suspected fraud occurred over the next five years that in 1820 the United States attorney general ruled that the New Madrid claims could not be transferred by their original owner except through an estate.

But many of those with New Madrid land claims had already sought compensation in the rapidly developing Boonslick country. As this area filled up following the War of 1812, many settlers found themselves "squatting" on government land that had not yet been surveyed and offered for sale. Congress had tried to protect these settlers by extending to Missouri the right of preemption in 1814. Such a right presumed that squatters would have the first opportunity to buy the land on which they had settled when it was put up for sale by the government. But Secretary of the Treasury William H. Crawford ruled that this did not apply to the lands in Howard County. This touched off a furor as New Madrid claimants swarmed over the area seeking good lands, many of which were already occupied. Crawford quickly reversed himself and, in March 1819, Missouri's congressional delegate, John Scott, pushed through a law formally extending the right of preemption to Howard County.

All of this was aggravated by the third source of land difficulties: the slowness with which the government surveyed the public domain and made it available for sale. Part of this delay came from the

The New Madrid earthquake, December 1811. *Courtesy State Historical Society of Missouri*

necessity of clearing Indian land titles. The first public land sales in Missouri did not occur until June 1818, by which time squatters had not only moved rather freely onto government land but Indian lands as well. The federal law provided that tracts be sold in no smaller quantities than 160 acres by the bid system, with a minimum price of two dollars per acre. Depending on the quality of the land and the improvements that might have been put on it by some squatter, the price went up sharply from there. Credit was fairly easy to obtain, and speculation was rampant. The better lands in the St. Louis area brought from four to twelve dollars an acre while one tract near Franklin, which had been highly improved, sold for better than twenty-six dollars.

Frontier Lawlessness

As was true with any frontier, Missouri early acquired a reputation for lawlessness. Portraying Missourians as uncouth savages, one eastern newspaper recounted numerous duels between prominent and not-so-prominent citizens. It warned that the area was overrun with "individuals quick to fight with dirks and pistols or to engage in personal encounters in which the eyes of opponents were gouged from their sockets and ears and noses bitten off." This prompted one would-be immigrant from Pittsburgh, Pennsylvania, to write the editor of the *Missouri Gazette* in St. Louis asking if it was true that the people there carried knives and guns so as to continually endanger a person's life. No doubt the raw frontier area that was Missouri attracted its share of the lawless element, but certainly no more so than any other similar community. For all its controversies, Missouri remained attractive to immigration. The *St. Louis Enquirer* noted in the fall of 1819: "The emigration to Missouri is astonishing. Probably from thirty to fifty wagons daily cross the Mississippi at the different ferries, and bring an average of from four to five hundred souls a day."

The Frontier Church

Those who came wanted to develop in Missouri the cultural advantages that they had known elsewhere. Among these were churches and schools. The Catholic Church had been the dominant religious institution throughout the French-Spanish colonial period because it received state support. Following 1804 it went into rapid decline as congregations were thrown on their own to support their priests, many of whom left because of the sudden scarcity of funds with which to pay them. The church drifted leaderless until the arrival in 1818 of Bishop William L. DuBourg. An energetic man with vision, he quickly revitalized a dormant church and began construction of what is now known in St. Louis as the "Old Cathedral." He secured a number of European priests to assist him in the parishes and persuaded the Congregation of the Priests of the Mission of St. Vincent de Paul to open a badly needed seminary to train new ministers. DuBourg also pushed the establishment of Catholic schools throughout his diocese. Perhaps his greatest achievement in this regard was to persuade the Order of the Sacred Heart to send Mother Philippine Duchesne and four other nuns to establish a school for girls at St. Charles. It was later moved to Florissant. Mother Duchesne soon earned a reputation for working with the poor and became a much beloved figure among the Catholics in the area.

With the coming of the Americans in greater numbers after 1804, Protestantism followed, with the Baptists, Methodists, and Presbyterians taking the lead. The Twappity Baptist Church near Cape

Girardeau became the first of its denomination in the new territory in 1805, but others soon organized. Congregations met in homes or, during good weather, out of doors. Ministers were not always numerous so lay leadership played a major role in some of these early churches. The Baptists did not require a formal education for their ministers, as some other denominations did, which meant that would-be preachers could readily emerge from the congregation. Means of support were scarce, and most ministers supported themselves with a regu-

The circuit rider. *Courtesy State Historical Society of Missouri*

lar occupation while they preached on Sundays. In 1817 a group of eastern Baptists sent John Mason Peck and James Welch to the frontier to reach blacks as well as whites. They founded an African Baptist Chapel in St. Louis, which later evolved into the First African Baptist Church.

The Methodists, who kept a tighter control over their clergy than did the Baptists, sent out preachers known as "circuit riders." The first of these to come to Missouri was John Travis, who arrived in 1806. These dedicated ministers rode for miles through all kinds of weather and environmental conditions to reach the faithful scattered across the frontier. Although paid by their conferences rather than the congregations they established, these ministers received meager salaries that had to be stretched far. The circuit riders frequently stayed in the homes of friendly settlers, who were eager for whatever news the minister might have to offer; but often they slept under the stars. They followed a set pattern, hence the "circuit," holding services and Bible classes wherever they could find a sufficient crowd. Where there was enough interest they organized a church. The first known Methodist congregation was the McKendree Church established in 1806 near Jackson. By 1810 the Methodists had five circuits in Missouri with over 500 members.

The Presbyterians arrived a decade later than the Baptists and the Methodists. Samuel J. Mills and Daniel Smith came west in 1814 under the sponsorship of the Philadelphia Bible and Missionary Society and spoke in St. Louis, but they left behind no permanent organization. That remained for Salmon Giddings and Timothy Flint, who arrived two years later through the efforts of the Connecticut Missionary Society. Giddings organized Missouri's first Presbyterian congregation, the Concord Church in Washington County, ten miles south of Potosi, in 1816 and a year later helped establish another group in St. Louis that became that community's first Protestant church.

Early Schools

The establishment of schools tended to follow in the wake of churches. These were "subscription schools," in which a teacher announced that he would hold classes for a set term with each student paying a fee to attend. Many of the early missionaries did this as a means of making a living, given the meagerness of congregational support. Most towns of any size had some kind of school by 1820. The quality of a school depended on the background of the teacher. The greater stress was on education for boys than for girls in a male-dominated society, but at least eleven "female academies" are known to have operated in Missouri during the two decades before statehood. For the boys emphasis was usually placed on languages and mathematics with some elementary science, while girls were taught the basics of reading and writing with a large smattering of those skills thought to be useful around the home. Most schools were segregated by sex, but coeducational institutions existed in St. Louis, Potosi, Jackson, and Franklin during the territorial period.

Territorial Newspapers

Cultural opportunities were not limited to church and school, although they were scarce when one got beyond St. Louis. Newspapers were eagerly sought after as sources of information. Heavily political in nature, they did not hesitate to take sides on the various issues of the day. The territory's first newspaper was the *Missouri Gazette,* which began publication in St. Louis on July 12, 1808. Its publisher, Joseph Charless, had been encouraged by Governor Lewis to come from Kentucky to try his journalistic fortunes; and he proved quite successful. Charless had news in both English and French to appeal to as broad a reader base as possible. A subscription cost three dollars cash or four dollars "in country produce." Various rivals appeared from time to time, but all proved shortlived until the establishment of the *St. Louis Enquirer* in 1818, which had Thomas Hart Benton as its editor. During the next two years Benton used that paper as a political stepping-stone to a seat in the United States Senate, where he would remain for the next thirty years. The first newspaper in the interior was the *Missouri Intelligencer and Boon's Lick Advertiser* established at Franklin in 1819 by Benjamin Holliday. It must be kept in mind that many Missourians during this period could not read because of limited educational opportunities. Books were scarce. For many the Bible would be their only book, if they could afford that. Libraries were the luxury of the wealthy, although a small group at Franklin organized a semiprivate library there in 1819. In St. Louis, Charless invited citizens to use his newspaper office. By 1818 a "Reading Room & Punch House" had opened near the *Gazette.*

The territorial counties of Missouri. *Courtesy State Historical Society of Missouri*

Changes in Territorial Government

As Missouri increased in population it also began to mature politically. It became a second class territory on the eve of the War of 1812, which meant that the people for the first time could elect the lower house of their territorial legislature and choose a nonvoting delegate to sit in the national House of Representatives. The President still appointed the territorial governor, judges, various other officials, and the upper house of the legislature. In the latter, however, he was limited to selecting nine persons from a slate of eighteen nominated by the lower house. At the local level, government was managed by county officials appointed by the governor. These had no legislative power, but they could assess and collect taxes. They also supervised the construction of roads and other public works, licensed businesses, and administered local justice. To vote in a Missouri election or hold public office, one had to prove citizenship by furnishing a tax receipt from a territorial or county official. In 1816 Missouri advanced to third-class status, which meant that the people could elect both houses of the legislature. This was the final step before statehood.

The Movement For Statehood

Petitions to accomplish statehood began circulating around the territory in 1817 and were presented to Congress early the following year by John Scott, Missouri's territorial delegate. When that body took no action, the territorial legislature passed a formal memorial requesting admission in the hope that this would have a greater impact. Among other things it contended that Missouri's population stood a "little short of one hundred thousand souls." Later historians have estimated the real figure at closer to 50,000, but then westerners had always been known for their tendency toward exaggeration.

The proposal went routinely to committee in the House of Representatives, and that group recommended an enabling bill in February 1819. Debate had hardly begun when James Tallmadge, Jr., a one-term congressman from New York City, dropped a bombshell into the proceedings by proposing the gradual extinction of slavery in Missouri Territory. Under his amendment no more slaves would be allowed to enter the territory. All children of slave parents already there, who might be born after its admission as a state, would be freed although they might be kept in servitude until the age of twenty-five. Tallmadge was apparently motivated by several factors: a humanitarianism that formed a part of the whole social reform movement then getting underway nationally; the presence of several voting wards in his district where blacks made a critical difference; and the emerging struggle between the commercial and industrial East and the agrarian South for control of certain national policies such as the tariff.

John Scott opposed the Tallmadge amendment on the grounds that the Louisiana Purchase treaty had guaranteed that Missouri's citizens could keep all their property, which included slaves. Since Congress had not put any restrictions on other territories seeking statehood, it had no right to do so with Missouri. In spite of his arguments, the House passed the bill with the Tallmadge amendment attached. The Senate refused to go along. With compromise impossible, Congress adjourned, leaving Missouri's future still in doubt. The two houses did agree to the separate organization of Arkansas Territory without any restrictions on slavery, however, although similar efforts had been made to limit slavery there. This indicated that perhaps it was Missouri's northern latitude and not its trans-Mississippi location that gave many representatives cause for concern.

The news of the congressional impasse touched off a wave of protest throughout Missouri. Most of the territory's inhabitants considered themselves westerners not southerners even though many had come from southern states, bringing with them their slaves and their attitudes toward race. While many might look upon slavery as "an evil," they considered it a necessary one from both an economic and a social point of view. Furthermore, it had been introduced with the coming of the French and had been a long established institution. By 1820 there were 10,222 slaves in Missouri, constituting nearly one-sixth of the total population. Consequently the white Missourians' southern and French antecedents mixed with their western inclinations to make them resent what they considered "yankee meddling" in their affairs.

Many feared that the controversy might dry up further immigration from the South, while a successful Tallmadge amendment, though not leading to immediate emancipation, would certainly bring a future inundation of northerners and restrictionists. A strong campaign against the amendment got underway immediately, spearheaded by the territory's newspapers. The *Gazette* thundered: "Bear in mind, fellow-citizens, that the question now before us is not whether slavery shall be permitted or prohibited in the future State of Missouri, but whether we will meanly abandon our rights and suffer any earthly power to dictate the terms of our constitution."

Few persons raised their voices in Missouri against this outcry. One who did so somewhat effectively called himself "A Farmer of St. Charles Country." He wrote six letters to the *Gazette* in the early summer of 1819. In one of these he spoke to the argument that Tallmadge wanted to destroy the rights of property. As the "Farmer" saw it, the amendment did not interfere with present property in any way but only with its future offsprings. It reminded him, he said, "of the tavern keeper, who, when a traveler obtained from him a dinner of eggs, charged him with the price of all the hens and chickens which *might have been* produced from those eggs to the end of time."

Meanwhile the antislavery forces were holding meetings throughout the North that fall to secure support for the Tallmadge amendment. While some moral arguments were brought forward, most frequently these gatherings stressed the political implications in the spread of slave territory as the Union stood balanced between eleven free and eleven slave states. Southern meetings denounced northern attempts to restrict slavery where it already existed while pointing up the same critical balance. With the southern states falling behind the North in total population, that region was already losing ground in the House of Representatives, which was chosen on the basis of population. Its strongest hope was to maintain an even balance of free and slave states to keep its position of equality in the Senate and thereby protect its interests.

The Missouri Compromise

With the convening of Congress in December 1819, the major scene of action shifted back to Washington while the Missouri press continued its agitation. Although Tallmadge no longer sat in the House, having made a try for a New York State Senate seat and lost, his friend John W. Taylor reintroduced his amendment, which the House ultimately attached to its Missouri bill. This once again proved unacceptable to the Senate, where the proslavery element had picked up two new Alabama senators and several additional allies from the northern states. The situation had become further complicated in the meantime by the agreement of Massachusetts to allow its district of Maine to petition for separate statehood. The South now had an opportunity to pair Missouri off, and it proceeded to make the most of it. Under the leadership of House Speaker Henry Clay of Kentucky and Senator Jesse B. Thomas of Illinois, the famous Missouri Compromise was enacted. By its terms Maine would become a free state while Missouri would be allowed to draw up a constitution with slavery. Slavery would be prohibited in the remainder of the Louisiana Purchase north of 36 30′, the southern boundary of Missouri.

During the debates on the issue, the Senate galleries were crowded with interested spectators including many of Washington's blacks. The latter obviously knew that the debates concerned slavery or freedom and might ultimately affect their condition. Hence, to quote one observer, "As one side or other of the question preponderates, they rejoice or are depressed." There is no record of how the blacks of Missouri felt, but one can readily imagine their thoughts to the extent that they may have been informed.

The Constitutional Convention

With the compromise accepted, the last cannon shot in celebration had scarcely ceased its roar before hats were being thrown into the political ring. Balloting for members of a constitutional convention took place early in May. To qualify to vote one had to be free, white, male, twenty-one years of age, and a resident of the territory for three months prior to the election or be "qualified to vote for representatives to the General Assembly." The forty-one delegate seats were apportioned among the various counties on the basis of population. Given the absence of organized political parties, the contest turned largely into a battle of personalities in most counties. In terms of debatable issues, only three occupied much attention: whether there should be a property restriction on voting, whether voting should be by ballot or orally, and whether the future immigration of slaves into the state should be restricted. Of these, the last stirred the most controversy.

Those favoring some restriction on slavery were not numerous, but they were vocal. Most of them were concentrated in Cape Girardeau, Jefferson, and St. Louis counties, although restrictionists also filed for seats in Lincoln and Washington counties. Generally their opposition to the peculiar institution rested on moral and economic grounds. Although some might be abolitionists or emancipationists at heart, none openly advocated interference with existing slave property. Rather they looked toward some "reasonable time" in the future when Missouri might prohibit the further introduction of slaves, with the hope of emancipating those in bondage at some additional vague time beyond that. When the votes were cast, however, not a single restrictionist secured election. Indeed the proslavery supporters outclassed their rivals by at least seven to one. Southern immigration over the past three years, when added to the heated congressional controversy, simply proved too strong a barrier for even a mild form of slavery restriction to overcome. In addition, slavery represented too large an investment to be tampered with.

The Missouri Constitutional Convention met at the Mansion House Hotel in St. Louis on June 12, 1820, and completed its work in only thirty-eight days, apparently with a minimum of controversy. Of the forty-one delegates, two were native to the Upper Louisiana region while thirty-nine had immigrated from elsewhere, mostly from the South. Most of the recognized political leaders in the territory participated although no one person dominated the proceedings. Many of them would later play prominent roles in the state's political development, including David Barton, who presided over the convention and later served as one of the first two United States senators; Edward Bates, brother of Frederick, who would later serve in Congress and lead the Missouri Whig party before ending his career as President Lincoln's Attorney-General; John Scott, territorial delegate, who would become Missouri's first representative; and Alexander McNair, who would shortly be elected Missouri's first governor. The delegates were mainly those of financial means, with businessmen and lawyers predominating. Better than 60 percent had some college education. In political ideology they appeared to be a generally homogeneous group.

Missouri's First Constitution

The constitution that this group drafted followed generally traditional lines, drawing most heavily on the constitutions of Alabama, Illinois, and Kentucky. It provided for the usual three branches of government with a bicameral legislature. Senate members were to serve four-year terms, House members two years, with each county being guaranteed one representative. The governor and lieutenant governor were to be elected for four-year terms—something a bit unusual at the time as most states still chose their executives for one or two years. The remaining officials in the executive branch—the secretary of state, the auditor, the attorney general—would be appointed by the governor with the consent of the Senate and serve for four years. A state treasurer was to be elected by the General Assembly every two years. The judiciary was to consist of a supreme court, a chancery court (abolished in 1822), and a series of circuit courts. The General Assembly could establish additional lower courts as it thought necessary. The matter of how judges should be appointed raised one of the few serious divisions in the convention. The majority, led by Edward Bates, wanted an independent judiciary and pushed through their proposal that judges be appointed by the governor with the consent of the Senate to serve "during good behavior," which meant for life. A minority, led by future Governor Alexander McNair, called for the election of judges for set terms. This issue carried over into popular debate following the convention, with public opinion seemingly supporting the McNair position. No changes were immediately forthcoming, however.

As to the issues mentioned earlier that aroused general debate during the campaign for delegates, the convention provided for universal white manhood suffrage at the age of twenty-one (there would be no property qualifications for voting), for the written ballot, and for a strongly entrenched system of slavery. The general outline of the constitution's slavery provisions will be discussed in Chapter 6. It is enough to mention here that the constitution provided that there could be no general statewide abolition of slavery without full compensation to each owner.

In most other matters the constitution conformed to the general pattern of the day. A few items of more than passing interest need to be mentioned, however. With regard to a permanent capital the constitution called for the establishment of a commission to choose a site that had to be on the Missouri River and not more than forty miles from the mouth of the Osage River. This would guarantee a central location. Perhaps because of the American reaction to the French Catholic heritage of the territory, with its close church-state relationship, the constitution forbade any minister to serve in public office other than that of justice of the peace. Fearful that the state might attract an influx of free blacks and mulattoes, who might cause unrest among the slave population, the constitution required the first legislature to pass a law forbidding their immigration into Missouri.

Unlike today's procedures, which require a popular referendum on constitutional changes, Missouri's first basic document provided that amendments had to be proposed by a two-thirds vote of each house in one legislative session and then ratified by the same majority at the first session of the next legislature. This allowed the people a voice in such matters only in that proposed amendments might be major issues in legislative elections.

The convention formally adopted the constitution on July 19, 1820, with celebrations throughout the territory. The document was not submitted to the people for ratification—a procedure that seemed to bother few at the time. In addition to its basic handiwork, the convention passed an ordinance agreeing to the exemption from taxes for set periods of public lands sold after January 1, 1821, and those that had been given for military service in the War of 1812. In return Congress agreed to give one section of land in each township to help establish public schools and to set aside four sections for a state capital and thirty-six sections to help underwrite a state university. Five percent of the new proceeds from the sale of public lands in the new state was to go to help promote internal improvements such as roads and canals. Finally, the state was given ownership of all salt springs, not to exceed twelve, with six sections of adjacent land to keep anyone from getting a monopoly on this vital frontier resource. By means of this agreement the federal government sought to use land, its most valuable commodity, to assist new states in establishing their basic institutions.

The 1820 State Elections

Elections under the new constitution were scheduled for August 28, which left little time for an extensive campaign. Although political parties as such did not exist in Missouri, two factions quickly emerged to contest for office. The most prominent of these was dubbed the "little junto" by Joseph Charless of the *Missouri Gazette*. It consisted of those who had long dominated territorial politics—the old French element and their American allies who had a strong mutual interest in land and the fur trade. Although not highly organized as we think of political parties today, this group tended to support William Clark, who had served as territorial governor for the past six years, for the governorship. Generally challenging the "little junto" was a Charless-led group who opposed the recognition of the Spanish land grants. They wanted to see the old power bloc broken up, with greater opportunity for more recent arrivals. Their gubernatorial candidate was Alexander McNair, a native Pennsylvanian who had administered the federal land office at St. Louis since 1818. McNair had used that post to work against the interests of the "little junto" while favoring the newly arrived immigrant who was seeking a place on the frontier.

McNair conducted an active campaign across the new state while Clark remained absent in Virginia, looking after his ill wife. The vote count revealed that McNair had won a surprisingly easy victory. To many in the out-state area, this represented a revolt by rural Missouri against the "St. Louis Clique," as some termed it. William H. Ashley of Potosi, who was successfully engaged in the manufacture of gunpowder and would later gain prominence in the fur trade, was elected lieutenant governor over Nathaniel Cook, who came from southeast Missouri but was tied to the St. Louis Clique. Of the latter group only John Scott of Ste. Genevieve survived the election, gaining Missouri's lone seat in Congress where he had already been serving as territorial delegate.

Selection of a State Capital

The first General Assembly convened on September 18, 1820, at the Missouri Hotel in St. Louis, and the next day witnessed the inauguration of Governor McNair. Early in the session it decided upon St. Charles as the temporary capital until a permanent site could be located in accordance with the constitutional provision. The legislature appointed a five-member commission for this purpose. That group selected four sections of public land on the site of present-day Jefferson City but then recommended that the capital be placed at Côte sans Dessein in Callaway County, which was the largest existing town within the area designated by the constitution. Apparent fear of speculation and unclear land titles clouded that recommendation in the minds of many legislators although there is not a complete record of the debate in the General Assembly. Whatever the case, that body instructed its commissioners, early in 1822, to lay out a town on the selected public lands, which it named the City of Jefferson in honor of the President who had acquired the Louisiana Purchase. The capital was moved there permanently in 1826.

Missouri's First Senators

On October 2, 1820, the General Assembly met in joint session to select two United States senators—a function that the legislature would continue to have under the federal constitution until 1914. With a majority vote required, the two houses chose David Barton and Thomas Hart Benton on the first ballot. Both men were from Tennessee. Barton had arrived in the territory shortly before the War of 1812 and had

Alexander McNair, Missouri's first governor. *Courtesy State Historical Society of Missouri*

served subsequently as attorney general and circuit judge before turning to the private practice of law. He had recently presided over the
constitutional convention and was possibly the most popular political figure in the new state. He had avoided aligning himself with either faction in the recent election and hence could claim support
from both. Benton had come to Missouri after the War of 1812 and
had quickly carved out a prominent and controversial role in territorial affairs as a lawyer and as editor of the St. Louis *Enquirer*. He was
generally aligned with the "little junto," but had gained considerable
popularity out-state because of his strong editorials against restriction. In the decade ahead Benton and Barton would reveal differing
philosophies on most issues, and around them would form the Missouri equivalent of the two new political parties—Democrat and National Republican, later Whig—which were to emerge nationally.

The Second Missouri Compromise

Barton and Benton left for Washington with John Scott in late November to take their seats as representatives of the Union's twenty-
fourth state. But while Missourians had been busy launching their
state government, pressures had been building in northern antislavery circles to make one last effort to block the territory's admission.
Seizing upon that clause in the new Missouri constitution that would
bar the immigration of free blacks and mulattoes into the state,
Missouri's opponents argued that it conflicted with the provision of
the federal Constitution that "The Citizens of each State shall be entitled to all Privileges and Immunities of Citizens in the several
States." Although Congress had never definitively settled the question of national citizenship for blacks, several states did recognize
them as full citizens. Hence the antislavery advocates felt that they
stood on strong constitutional ground and might rally thereto some
who had gone for compromise in the previous session.

When Congress convened in December, Scott, Barton, and
Benton were admitted to seats in their respective houses with all the
privileges of membership except voting. The House technically recognized Scott as territorial delegate, to which label he refused to answer roll call while insisting on full membership as the *state* of
Missouri's representative. The Senate quickly agreed to Missouri's
new constitution with what Professor Glover Moore has called the

"Pontius Pilate proviso." This simply asserted that the admission of Missouri did not imply sanction for anything in its constitution that might contradict the federal constitutional provision already mentioned. The following day, the House, after lengthy debate, rejected the Missouri charter outright by a vote of ninety-three to seventy-nine, placing the area in a sort of limbo, with its territorial government having ceased to function and its state government not yet recognized.

Scott, Barton, and Benton bombarded their constituents with letters, which received wide publication, denouncing the northern representatives as unfairly holding up the final admission of an already existent state. Into the breach stepped Henry Clay of Kentucky, who used his great skill behind the scenes to put together the "Second Missouri Compromise." It provided that Missouri be admitted by presidential proclamation once its legislature had agreed through "a solemn public act" that no law should ever be passed under the questionable clause in its constitution. Congress set the fourth Monday of November 1821 as a deadline for compliance.

Word of Clay's achievement reached Missouri by late March through Kentucky newspapers brought up the Mississippi. Missourians saw their latest triumph not as a victory for statehood—they already had that in their own eyes—but as a vindication of their determined stand against their "yankee foes," the eastern restrictionists. The *St. Louis Enquirer* summed up their feelings in its editorial on March 24: "The fate of Missouri is at last decided. She has been admitted to her just rank in the confederacy, a member of the Union which every true American ardently hopes may be perpetuated. . . . The schemes of unprincipled and ambitious men have been disappointed, the ocean which has been agitated by the tempest will soon become calm."

Governor McNair called a special session of the General Assembly for June 4 to deal with the matter. Meeting at the temporary capital of St. Charles, the legislators argued at great length over phrasing before passing the necessary promise. Their resolution was worded in such a finger-crossing, sarcastic manner, however, that the antislavery press was stirred once again to fever pitch. For President Monroe this did not matter. He wanted to be rid of an exceedingly irksome problem. Consequently when he received the official copy of the legislature's resolution he issued a final proclamation on August 10,

1821, formally admitting Missouri into full partnership in the Union.

Within four years a new General Assembly would violate the spirit of this initial resolution by requiring that any free black or mulatto coming from another state must bring a certificate of citizenship. Two decades later still another legislature would completely repudiate the promise of 1821 by banning free black or mulatto immigration altogether. Yet this lay in the future, which President Monroe could not control.

Suggestions for Reading

The best overall study of Missouri's territorial period is William E. Foley, *The Genesis of Missouri: From Wilderness Outpost to Statehood*, Columbia, University of Missouri Press, 1989. Three of the territorial governors have had biographies written about them: James Ripley Jacob, *Tarnished Warrior, Major-General James Wilkinson*, New York: Macmillan, 1938; Richard H. Dillon, *Meriwether Lewis: A Biography*, New York: Coward-McCann, 1965; and Jerome O. Steffen, *William Clark: Jeffersonian Man on the Frontier*, Norman, University of Oklahoma Press, 1977. Other biographies of important territorial figures are John Mack Farragher, *Daniel Boone: The Life and Legend of an American Pioneer*, New York, Henry Holt & Company, 1993; R. Douglas Hurt, *Nathan Boone and the American Frontier*, Columbia, University of Missouri Press, 1998; William E. Foley & C. David Rice, *The First Chouteaus: River Barons of Early St. Louis*, Urbana, University of Illinois Press, 1983; David Kaser, *Joseph Charless: Printer in the Western Country*, Philadelphia, University of Pennsylvania Press, 1963; and Dick Steward, *Frontier Swashbuckler: The Life and Legend of John Smith T*, Columbia, University of Missouri Press, 2000.

James L. Penick, Jr., *The New Madrid Earthquakes*, rev. ed., Columbia, University of Missouri Press, 1981, covers that topic well. Stuart Banner, *Legal Systems in Conflict: Property and Sovereignty in Missouri, 1750–1860*, Norman, University of Oklahoma Press, 2000, details the struggle to replace the old French and Spanish legal order with the American legal system. The efforts to develop and populate the area beyond St. Louis can be found in R. Douglas Hurt, "Seeking Fortune in the Promised Land: Settling the Boon's Lick Country, 1808–1825," *Gateway Heritage*, Summer 1992. Efforts to fortify the frontier are dealt with in Kate L. Gregg, "The History of Fort Osage," *Missouri*

Historical Review, July 1940; and Donald Jackson, "Old Fort Madison, 1808–1813," *The Palimpsest,* January 1966. The War of 1812 is covered in Kate L. Gregg, "The War of 1812 and the Missouri Frontier," *Missouri Historical Review,* October 1938, January 1939, and April 1939. Good studies on territorial churches are William Barnaby Faherty, "The Personality and Influence of Louis William Valentine DuBourg: Bishop of Louisiana and the Floridas (1776–1833)," in John F. McDermott, ed., *Frenchmen and French Ways in the Mississippi Valley,* Urbana, University of Illinois Press, 1969; and Lucy Simmons, "The Rise and Growth of Protestant Bodies in the Missouri Territory," *Missouri Historical Review,* October 1928. On the matter of schools, see Monia C. Morris, "Educational Opportunities in Early Missouri," *Missouri Historical Review,* April 1939 and July 1939. Marian M. Ohman, "Missouri County Organization, 1812–1876," *Missouri Historical Review,* April 1982, is a good treatment of that topic. A general overview of the new state is to be found in Lewis E. Atherton, "Missouri's Society and Economy," *Missouri Historical Review,* July 1971. Floyd C. Shoemaker, *Missouri's Struggle for Statehood, 1804–1821,* Jefferson City, Hugh Stephens Printing Co., 1916, is the standard work on that subject and especially good for Missourians' reactions to the problem, while the crisis at the national level is well covered by Glover Moore, *The Missouri Controversy, 1819–1821,* Lexington, University of Kentucky Press, 1953.

Missouri and the Opening of the American West

In the first decade of the nineteenth century, Missouri stood between a line of Anglo American population advancing westward and what we today call the American West. West of the great bend of the Missouri River (95th meridian) lay a vast area of land still largely unknown and unchartered. Part of this land fell within the Louisiana Purchase, but a greater portion still belonged to Spain's overseas empire. Composed of a variety of physiographic regions, the American West begins with the Great Plains, extending north to the Canadian border, south to the Rio Grande, and continues west across the Rocky Mountains to the Pacific Ocean. The Great Plains stretch treeless and dry to the very foot of the Rocky Mountains. For years Americans viewed it as the Great American Desert, a land fit for "savages" and "misfits" and unworthy of the enterprise of American settlers. Down its western side, the Rocky Mountains spread from Canada into northern New Mexico. Pioneers on their way to the "promised land" of Oregon or the "get rich quick" gold fields of California found the "backbone of the continent" a towering obstacle to overcome. Beyond the mountains are river plateaus, mesas, basins, deserts, more mountains, canyons, forests, and grasslands. Not too distant from the Sierra Nevada in California looms the Pacific Ocean. The American West offered challenge, adventure, and opportunity to those who would explore and conquer it.

The Lewis and Clark Expedition

Little was known of this land before 1800 except its vastness. Long before he made the Louisiana Purchase, Thomas Jefferson had expressed considerable interest in learning more about this great expanse. When he became President, Jefferson persuaded Congress to appropriate $2,500 to explore the area from the Mississippi River to the far northwest. American explorers would follow the Missouri River to its headwaters, portage across the continental divide to the Columbia River, and then canoe down the Columbia to the Pacific Ocean. They would find the "road to India," an all-water route with short portages that would link the United States with trade opportunities in the Far East. As American emissaries, they would make peace with the Indian inhabitants and prepare the way for future trade relations. By keeping a sharp eye they would locate sites for American trading posts and forts. Their presence in Oregon would strengthen American claims if a dispute arose between nations over its ownership. Above all, they would be scientists, collectors of specimens, and recorders of geographic, geological, botanical, zoological, and meteorological facts. They would be, in fact, a "Corps of Discovery."

Jefferson selected Meriwether Lewis, a fellow Virginian and his private secretary, to head the expedition. Having served the United States Army on the frontier, Lewis possessed the necessary qualities to lead a group into the wilderness. He knew frontier techniques, the Indian character and customs, how to survive in the wilderness, and how to discipline fairly those under his command. Though well educated, he went immediately after his appointment to Philadelphia to work with scientists, familiarizing himself with the technical vocabulary of the natural sciences.

Lewis thought it necessary to have a co-commander of the expedition in case he was incapacitated or killed. He recommended William Clark, brother of the Revolutionary hero, George Rogers Clark. Although outranked by Lewis, Clark shared equally in the command of the expedition. He excelled as a frontiersman, hunter, and judge of people. Of the two, Clark probably was more effective in dealing with the Indians. Both men brought to their mission their own distinctive talents and abilities.

Lewis organized the expedition. He collected the Indian trade goods and supplies and designed a fifty-five-foot keelboat with a sail, twenty-two oars, and small cannons mounted fore and aft. Two pirogues, flat-bottomed boats rowed with oars, completed the tiny flotilla. Clark recruited the members of the expedition, selecting each one on the basis of physical condition, ability to handle a rifle, and a sense of humor. The expedition consisted of fourteen regular soldiers, nine Kentucky frontiersmen, two French and a French interpreter, and Clark's slave, York. Additionally a corporal, six soldiers, and nine voyageurs would accompany them as far as the Mandan Indian villages in present-day North Dakota, and then return to the United States with specimens and scientific data.

The two leaders conferred with fur traders in St. Louis to gain some general knowledge of what to expect in the country into which they were heading. On May 14, 1804, the expedition set sail "under a gentle breeze" up the Missouri River for the adventure that awaited them.

The powerful current of the river enabled them to average only ten miles a day. Both officers kept a journal and noted Indians in the forests along the banks and the variety of flora and fauna. As they navigated the great bend of the Missouri River and headed north, the only fatality occurred when Sergeant Charles Floyd died of "bilious colic" (probably appendicitis).

The expedition reached the Dakota country before winter set in. There they lived among the Mandans and prepared for the next leg of the journey. While waiting for the long winter to break, they enlisted the services of Toussaint Charbonneau and his Shoshoni Indian wife, Sacagawea, as interpreters and guides. Though Charbonneau was of some assistance to the expedition, his Shoshoni wife, Sacagawea, became a valuable addition. Contrary to popular belief, the Indian woman did not lead the explorers across the continent, but she was instrumental in saving them when they were caught in an early snowstorm at the foot of the Rockies. Seeing the Indian mother and

Lewis and Clark Expedition, as painted by Oscar E. Berninghaus. *August A. Busch, Jr., courtesy State Historical Society of Missouri*

her child traveling with the party may also have convinced potentially hostile Indians that the expedition posed no threat to their mountain domain.

With the spring thaw Lewis and Clark resumed their journey across the Rocky Mountains. Late in May 1805, they sighted the Rocky Mountains and Lewis recorded in his journal that "the Rocky Mountains covered with snow" gave him "a secret pleasure in finding myself so near the head of . . . the boundless Missouri." He also thought of the problems those great peaks would present when they started to cross them. For a solid month they tried to find their way through the mountains. They reached the Three Forks of the Missouri late in July and by mid-August crossed the continental divide, where mountain streams begin to flow in a westerly direction. Lost, hungry, and in desperate need of horses to continue on to the Pacific, they were discovered by a band of Shoshoni Indians led by Sacagawea's own brother. Through her, Lewis and Clark were able to communicate with the Indians and purchase the needed horses to carry them on to their destination. Many days later they found the Columbia River. After facing a food shortage and shooting the dangerous rapids of the Columbia, they reached the Pacific Ocean on November 15, 1805. Awed by the immense waves of the ocean, they camped on the "highest spot" they could find. That winter of 1805– 1806 the expedition built a fort, which they named after the Clatsop Indians. Unlike the previous winter with the hospitable Mandans, the party endured cold rainy weather, poor hunting, pilfering Indians, and fleas. As soon as the weather permitted, they started back to the United States.

Forging their way through the mountains by summer, they divided their command, with Lewis exploring the Marias River valley and Clark going to the Yellowstone River. Lewis skirmished with a band of Gros Ventre Indians and beat a retreat to join Clark at the Yellowstone. On the way back Lewis suffered a gunshot wound in the leg when one of his own band mistook him for a bear. When they finally reached the Missouri River, they rode the swift current toward St. Louis. On the way they met traders and trappers already ascending the river on their way to the fur-trading grounds on the upper Missouri. Arriving in St. Louis on September 23, 1806, they found the village turned out to give them a warm welcome. Jefferson, believing the expedition had perished, proclaimed, "Never did a similar event excite more joy through the United States. The humblest of its citizens . . . look forward with impatience for the information it would furnish."

The Lewis and Clark expedition had a profound effect upon Missouri and the nation. It helped to open the American West by exploring thousands of miles of new lands, blazing trails, mapping the Missouri River to its headwaters, and giving names to rivers, streams, lakes, and mountains that still stand today. It encouraged the fur trade by recommending sites for forts and trading posts and advertising the trans-Mississippi West. Lewis and Clark returned with extensive information about the area's Indian inhabitants. They made peace with some but gained the enmity of others. Their journals were filled with scientific information. They showed that one could reach the Pacific Ocean overland, although the way they traveled was not necessarily the best nor the easiest route to go. As noted in Chapter 3, both Lewis and Clark later served as territorial governors of Missouri, and Clark played a major role in working out treaties with the various Indian tribes in the area.

Zebulon M. Pike

While Lewis and Clark probed the northern Rockies in 1805, another government explorer, Zebulon M. Pike, searched for the source of the Mississippi River. Although unsuccessful, Pike returned to St. Louis with enough information for cartographers to make a more accurate map of the upper Mississippi Valley. Although not as experienced as Lewis and Clark, Pike secured the confidence of American leaders and they selected him to explore the southwestern part of the Louisiana Purchase. In 1806, he departed St. Louis with some Osage and Pawnee Indians to escort them back to their villages. After delivering the Indians, he struck out for southeastern Colorado where he discovered the mountain that bears his name and suffered through the winter for which he and his band were poorly prepared and trained. Although given strict orders to stay out of Spanish territory, Pike, for reasons not altogether clear, strayed across the border and was captured by Spanish soldiers. Convinced they had American spies, the Spaniards detained Pike and his band, confiscating their papers. Their captors finally escorted them across northeastern Mexico and southern Texas to the Louisiana border where they were released. Pike lost most of his notes, but did smuggle out a few by rolling them into small balls and ramming them into gun barrels. On their way across Spanish territory, Pike made mental notes of the lay of the land and its potential for American settlement.

Actually Pike's report, which he composed mostly from memory in 1810, became public before those of Lewis and Clark. His glowing descriptions of Indian land in Missouri, of fur-bearing animals in the southern Rockies, of Santa Fe's need for trade, and of the Spanish southwest excited land-hungry farmers, fur trappers, traders, and American expansionists alike. However, Pike believed that the Great Plains of Kansas and southeastern Colorado were fit only for "Indian savages." "The American Desert" he said would deter the westward movement and force settlers to remain east of the bend of the Missouri River to build American civilization. The image of the great American desert persisted for several decades until traders and pioneers along the Santa Fe and Oregon trails became aware of the agricultural and livestock-raising potential of the Great Plains.

Major Stephen H. Long

Following the War of 1812, interest in and immigration to the trans-Mississippi West increased. Secretary of War John C. Calhoun proposed the establishment of a government fort at the confluence of the Yellowstone and Missouri rivers for purposes of checking the Indians and protecting American fur traders from the British. He selected Major Stephen H. Long to make a scientific study of the area. Long enlisted several scientists to accompany him on his mission, including Edwin James, a botanist and geologist, who published in 1823 a full account of their investigation of "the face of the country, water courses, and productions."

Leaving St. Louis in June 1819, Long's expedition proceeded up the Missouri River by steamboat as far as Council Bluffs. The next spring they explored the Rocky Mountains, named a mountain peak after their leader, and climbed Pike's Peak, which Pike had thought unconquerable. They also discovered the confluence of the Canadian and Arkansas rivers. Returning to Missouri in 1820, Long and his specialists added their observations to the growing body of knowledge about the American West and its flora and fauna. Long, like Pike, believed the desert-like plains country would never support white settlements.

Fur trading post. *Courtesy State Historical Society of Missouri*

Traders and Trappers

In the history of the American frontier, the fur traders and trappers
have usually been among the first Europeans to explore and to exploit a new area. In Missouri the French fur traders searched the great
rivers and their tributaries for furs and traded with the Indians. Many
of the earliest settlements in Missouri during the French period trace
their beginnings to the fur trade. St. Louis started as a trading post in
1764 while seventy-five years later, at the opposite end of the state,
Joseph Robidoux, a fur trader, saw St. Joseph grow into a town from
the site of the trading post he had established in 1826. The fur-trading industry remained a major economic activity in Missouri for a
hundred years. The beaver was the fur most in demand. In Europe
and in America the fashionable top hat was made from beaver skin.
As long as the top hat was in style, the demand for beaver was high,
but by the 1840s men's fashion in headpieces changed and the demand for beaver fell accordingly. The trappers endured hardships,
faced danger from hostile Indians and angry animals, and lived
lonely lives in their endless quest for the beaver skin. Fur trappers

and traders were not builders of white civilization, but they paved the way for those who were.

One of the important early figures in the Missouri fur trade was Pierre Chouteau, whose half-brother had helped establish St. Louis. While sprinkling his conversation with Latin phrases, he boasted that he was educated in the school of the Osage Indians. From 1794 to 1802 Chouteau, with his brother Auguste, monopolized the Osage trade, but when the monopoly was given to Manuel Lisa, Chouteau persuaded the Osage to move into the vicinity of the "Three Forks of the Arkansas" where he had trading privileges. Because of his rapport with the Osage, President Jefferson appointed him an Indian agent to that tribe. After being one of the dominant figures in the Missouri fur trade for many years, Chouteau helped organize the Missouri Fur Company in 1809 to expand his operation to the upper Missouri River and the Rocky Mountains. When the company went bankrupt in 1813, Chouteau reduced his activity and went into semiretirement at his home on the outskirts of St. Louis. Chouteau was an example of many traders and merchants who helped establish the position of St. Louis as a leading trade center on the Mississippi River.

Another important fur trader and merchant was Manuel Lisa who had arrived in St. Louis in 1790 at the age of eighteen. Impressed by the reports of Lewis and Clark, Lisa organized a trading venture with forty-two traders in 1807 and set out for the upper Missouri River. Reaching the mouth of the Big Horn River, Lisa built Fort Manuel and spent the winter in the Rocky Mountains gathering furs and trading with the Indians. On his return to St. Louis, he formed the Missouri Fur Company to exploit the fur trade in the Rocky Mountains. Among the investors in his company were William Clark, Pierre Chouteau, and Major Andrew Henry. From the outset, the company faced overwhelming difficulties. Intense competition from other groups, angry Indians, a variety of bad luck, the War of 1812, and savage winters drove the company into bankruptcy by 1813. Not until after the War of 1812 did the interest in the Rocky Mountain fur trade revive. Lisa then reorganized and was active in trading near present day Omaha until his death in 1820.

In the 1820s two Missourians, Major Andrew Henry, an experienced trader who had been with Lisa, and Lieutenant Governor William Henry Ashley, a wealthy St. Louis businessman, organized a new company to trade and to trap furs in the Rocky Mountains. In 1822 they advertised in a St. Louis newspaper for a hundred "enterprising young men" to join the trading venture. Due to some severe losses and setbacks because of hostility from Indians, Ashley decided to shift his operation from the northern to the central Rockies. In November 1824, he set out to see for himself if trade could be established in this new area. On his journey, Ashley came up with an idea that was to revolutionize the fur-trading industry. Instead of building trading posts and forts among the Indians which seemed to aggravate them, he conceived the plan whereby the traders and trappers would explore and trap individually or in small groups and then would exchange their furs for supplies and Indian trade goods transported by a St. Louis caravan. The "rendezvous system" became a permanent part of the fur-trading industry until its decline in the 1840s. It offered greater flexibility at less expense than the old system.

The importance of the fur-trading industry to the early economy and settlement of frontier Missouri can hardly be overstressed. As discussed in Chapter 2, the fur traders followed closely the French explorers into the wilderness, making contact with the Indians, charting their own courses into the back country, and encouraging the tiny settlements that slowly cropped up along the banks of the Mississippi and Missouri rivers. During the Spanish regime, the most popular furs were, according to Auguste Chouteau, the beaver and the shaved deer skin, whose average annual sale on the St. Louis market between 1789 and 1804 totaled $204,750. Since specie (gold, silver) was scarce on the frontier, furs were used as a medium of exchange. Amos Stoddard in 1804 reported that a pound of shaved deer skins was worth 40¢; a 100-pound bundle of beaver furs, $189, lynx, $500, otter, $450, marten, $300; a buffalo robe, $6, and a bear skin, $3.

During the territorial and early statehood period, the fur trade continued to be a leading industry with its expansion to the upper reaches of the Missouri River and into the Rocky Mountains. Ashley recorded that from 1822 to 1826 the proceeds of the Rocky Mountain Fur Company totaled $250,000. However, by the late 1830s and early 1840s, the trade declined noticeably as European and American fashion no longer dictated that the well-dressed male must wear a beaver top hat, as the wild animal supply dwindled after years of excessive trapping, and as competition from other industries, such as the textile, intensified. Caught squarely between declining profits and the inadequate supply of raw furs, the fur trade soon fell from a major to a minor economic activity in Missouri. However, it should be pointed out that St. Louis still remains a center for the "raw fur" market in the country.

Many traders and trappers who lived in the mountains had little contact with white civilization. Although they lived a hard and dangerous existence, they became symbolic of the "free spirits" who exchanged the trappings of civilization for an unpretentious and exciting life in the mountains. Some lived alone, others lived with the Indians. They hunted, trapped, and came to the "rendezvous" in the spring. Among the more famous of the mountain men were Jedediah Strong Smith, James Beckwourth, Jim Bridger, and Kit Carson.

A New Yorker by birth, Jedediah Smith moved to St. Louis in 1816. Joining Ashley's expedition in 1822, Smith and two partners later purchased his business and operated the Rocky Mountain Fur Company until the late 1820s, when they in turn sold out to two others. From 1826 to 1830 Smith explored extensively the American West from the Great Salt Lake, across the Mohave Desert into California and into the Oregon country. These journeys into unknown areas were the first by white Americans. Because of them, Smith ranks among the great explorers in American history. After returning from the Rocky Mountains in 1831, he entered the Santa Fe trade. At a water hole near the Cimarron River in the summer of 1831, a Comanche hunting party attacked him and his company and Smith was killed. Unlike the stereotypical wild and illiterate mountain man, Smith was gentle by nature, schooled in the ways of the mountains, and a dedicated Christian who carried his Bible with him at all times.

Like Jedediah Smith, Jim Beckwourth was also a member of Ashley's famous 1822 expedition. A St. Louisan, Beckwourth was a mulatto who may have gone with Ashley to escape social ostracism by St. Louis society. His exploits grew into legends as he lived with the Indians and became a chief of the Crow Nation. After Beckwourth finally returned to Missouri, he told his life's story to an eastern writer who lionized the old mountain man and overly sentimentalized his love affair with Pine Leaf, the daughter of a Crow chief. The book is valuable for its picture of the everyday life of the mountain man, but must be read with the understanding that Beckwourth was known not only for his bravery but for his boastfulness as well.

Another important member of the 1822 expedition was Jim Bridger, who migrated from Virginia to St. Louis in 1812. For twenty years he stayed in the mountains, roaming the area between Canada and southern Colorado, and from the Missouri River to Idaho and

Utah. When the fur trade declined, he established a way station on the Oregon Trail in Wyoming for the overland pioneers. After ten years at Fort Bridger, he retired to a farm not far from present-day Kansas City, but was enlisted by the United States government to serve as a scout and explorer. One of his assignments was to measure the distance of the Bozeman Trail from Fort Kearney, Nebraska, to Virginia City. In 1868 he again returned to his farm, where he lived until his death in 1881. Although he began as a fur trader, his later career was described as being "with eyes and the ears" of overland travelers, government workers, and army personnel in the American West.

Perhaps the best known of the frontiersmen associated with Missouri and the opening of the American West was Christopher "Kit" Carson. Kit came from Kentucky to Missouri in 1811 and settled in the Boonslick area. He got his start in the Santa Fe trade in 1826 as a "cavvy boy" (one who tended the saddle horses). From the Santa Fe trade he got into trapping and trading, hunting buffalo to supply Bent's Fort and, eventually, scouting for the United States Army. Carson married an Arapaho woman who bore him a daughter before she died in 1842. Although he himself was illiterate, Carson took his child to St. Louis, enrolled her in a school, and then returned to the mountains. His fame grew when he joined John Charles Frémont's western expeditions as a scout in the 1840s. It was Frémont who wore the badge of "The Pathfinder," but it was Kit Carson who deserved it. In 1857 he dictated his life's story to Lieutenant Colonel DeWitt C. Peters who, Carson said, "laid it on a leetle [sic] thick . . ." in the book that was later published. When the Civil War broke out, Carson returned to the army and fought against the Indians in the Southwest.

Trailblazers like Smith, Beckwourth, Bridger, and Carson probably did more to open the trans-Mississippi West than any single group. They were the ones who went where no white people had been before, found the passes through the mountains, advertised the West, helped reduce Indian resistance, contributed to the economic wealth of Missouri and the nation, and became characters in an important chapter in the history of the American West.

The Santa Fe Trail

Located in the Spanish province of northern New Mexico, Santa Fe was one of the oldest towns in North America. Founded in 1609, the town was supplied with Spanish trade goods across a fifteen hundred-mile trail from the seaport of Vera Cruz. Since Spain had outlawed trade with the United States, American traders who attempted to get through to Santa Fe were turned back at the border by Spanish authorities. In 1821 Mexico achieved its independence from Spain and reversed the trade policy by lifting the ban on trade with the United States. William Becknell, a Missouri trader, was one of the first to learn of this and to take advantage of it.

In the fall of 1821 Becknell, with twenty men and a pack train loaded down with trade goods was in the southern Rockies to barter for furs. He and his band happened to meet Mexican soldiers who told them that their new nation welcomed trade with the United States. Becknell hastened to Santa Fe where his party quickly disposed of their goods, and the travel-weary traders found more than their share of fun and fandangos. After his successful return to Missouri, Becknell organized another trading venture that left Franklin in June 1822 for Santa Fe eight hundred miles away. He moved across Kansas to the Arkansas River, turned south to blaze a desert crossing to the Cimarron River, which he followed into New Mexico. Other traders followed, and by 1824 commerce on the trail was well established. The trade continued without interruption until 1843, when it was temporarily shut down by Mexican authorities because of a brewing diplomatic crisis with the United States over Texas.

Independence, a hundred miles closer to Santa Fe, became the starting point by 1830. The journey was hard and dangerous. Josiah Gregg, an eastern physician who came west for health reasons and stayed to engage in the Santa Fe trade, left a classic account of what it was like to travel on the trail in his book *Commerce of the Prairies*. Convoys with as many as a hundred wagons each, drawn by eight horses or mules, rolled in four columns across the level plains country. At Council Grove, a hundred miles west of Independence, the train halted to elect a captain and to organize for the rest of the trip. At night they made camp by placing the wagons in a square and interlocking the wheels to form a barricade against Indian attack and a corral for livestock. To take one's turn standing guard at night was a duty no one dared shirk. Composed of every "grade and class of society, one could see among the convoy's members "the fustian frock of the city bred . . . merchant the leather hunting shirt of the backwoodsman . . . the blue jean coat of the farmer . . . and the flannel-sleeve vest of the wagoneer." Well armed with "scatter guns," rifles, pistols, and knives, they kept alert to roaming bands of Kiowas and

Comanches. There was safety in numbers, and loners and stragglers gambled their lives on the Santa Fe Trail. From 1820 to 1830 the United States Army escorted the traders because of Indian resistance. According to Gregg, the Santa Fe Trail was no place for the "softer sex," "the listless loafer," "the amateur tourist," or "the genteel idler."

It was on the Santa Fe Trail that Americans learned the techniques of traveling great distances overland. The pioneers on their way to Oregon or California adopted some of the same organizational structures and rules followed by the Santa Fe traders. Mexican silver stimulated the Missouri economy and helped make possible the strong stand of Senator Thomas Hart Benton for a "hard money economy." Gregg estimated that total profits of more than $3 million were realized from the Santa Fe trade during the twenty years of the trail's existence. The Mexican burro entered Missouri, by way of the trail, mated with Belgian draft horses in the German settlements, and produced the true Missouri mule. In time Missouri became a leading mule breeding and exporting state. The Santa Fe Trail focused attention on trade with the Indians in the Southwest. Men and some women traveled the trail and returned to Missouri convinced that the Southwest was another land of opportunity. The Santa Fe trade was another example of white settlers coming into an area seeking economic gain and ending up possessing the territory. Word of the ex-

Independence, 1839, the starting point for the long trek West. *Courtesy State Historical Society of Missouri*

ploits of the Santa Fe trader, soldier, adventurer, and fur trader certainly helped to encourage American expansion in the 1840s.

Independence

The Santa Fe Trail made Independence. When Lewis and Clark passed by the town's future site, they described it as a land "full of wild apples, deer and bears." It became the jumping-off place for those traveling to the American West. Steamboats brought trade goods from St. Louis and deposited them at two river ports, the Upper (Wayne City) and Lower (Blue Mills) landings. Trading companies made the town the base of their operations. In time it attracted famous people, including Washington Irving and many of the characters associated with the western movement. One such person was the historian Francis Parkman, who like Josiah Gregg came west to regain his health and wrote a book about his experiences. In *The Oregon Trail*, Parkman caught the spirited atmosphere of this frontier town in the 1840s when he observed:

> The town was crowded. A multitude of shops had sprung up to furnish the emigrants and Santa Fe traders with necessaries for their journey; and there was an incessant hammering and banging from a dozen blacksmiths' sheds, where the heavy wagons were being repaired, and the horses and oxen shod. The streets were thronged with men, horses and mules. While I was in town, a train of emigrant wagons from Illinois passed through, to join the camp on the prairie, and stopped in the principal street. A multitude of healthy children's faces were peeping out from under the covers of the wagons. Here and there a buxom damsel was seated on horseback, holding over her sunburned face an old umbrella or a parasol. . . . The men, very sober looking countrymen, stood about their oxen . . .

Independence was not only the beginning of the Santa Fe Trail but also became the rendezvous for the emigrants heading west to Oregon in the 1840s.

Manifest Destiny

The decade of the 1840s saw white settlers whipped into a frenzy over expansion into the West. Expansionists in Congress and on the street corners declared unabashedly that God had destined the United States to spread to the Pacific Ocean. It was Manifest Destiny that the Republic of Texas be annexed, that Americans settle in California, and that the Oregon country by every right under God and known to humankind belonged to the United States. The Mexicans in the Southwest, the British in Oregon, and the Indians throughout the West were to be swept aside in the rush of Americans toward the Pacific. Regardless of the difficult political, social, ethical, and diplomatic questions that such an attitude raised, James K. Polk and the Democratic party in 1844 campaigned on the platform of American expansion and defeated Henry Clay, the Whig candidate, who failed to match his opponents' promises of Manifest Destiny.

Texas

Originally from Connecticut, Moses Austin migrated from Virginia to Missouri before the Louisiana Purchase. He settled in the vicinity of Potosi, mined lead, farmed, skirmished with Indians, raised a family, and invested in a bank in St. Louis. When the panic of 1819 wrecked him financially, Austin, now an old man, looked for ways to recoup his losses. At one time a citizen of Spanish Louisiana, he believed he could use his Spanish citizenship to secure a land grant in Texas for the purpose of establishing an American colony. He set out on the long journey to Texas, finally reaching Mexico City, where he received permission to proceed with his colonizing scheme. On the return to Missouri, he became ill from exposure and exhaustion and died. His son, Stephen F. Austin, picked up the project and successfully carried through his father's dream.

Many Missourians were part of that first colony. Others migrated to Texas later and fought in the Texas Revolution of 1836. By the 1840s, they were numbered among those who urged the annexation of Texas by the United States, as discussed in Chapter 5.

"Oregon Fever"

The Oregon country was claimed by Great Britain, the United States, Spain, and Russia. In 1818 the British and the Americans signed a treaty agreeing to joint occupation of the area. During the following decade, Spain and Russia withdrew their claims. About the time Moses Austin was riding back from Mexico to Missouri in 1821, Dr. John Floyd, a Virginia congressman, was urging his colleagues to pass a bill for the complete acquisition of the Oregon country by the United States. Senator Thomas Hart Benton said Floyd's proposal was "the first blow struck" for the takeover of Oregon. The bill failed to pass, but occupation of Oregon had bulled its way into the public's awareness.

During the 1820s and 1830s, propagandists for American expansion kept alive interest in Oregon. A number of expeditions went to Oregon and planted the seeds of American settlements. Both Catholic and Protestant missionaries labored there, bringing the gospel to the Indians and good news about Oregon to missionary boards and supporting congregations back home. One such example was the missionary endeavors of the tireless Father Jean-Pierre de Smet, a Jesuit priest who came to America in 1821. De Smet's first charge brought him to St. Louis in 1823 to serve in a new novitiate that became the Catholic University of St. Louis. After fifteen years of service in the St. Louis vicinity, he became a missionary to the Indians, working first among the Potowatomi. In 1840 he was sent to the northwest to survey the possibilities of establishing Catholic missions among the Indians. Convinced that the Catholic Church had a mission to the Indians, de Smet traveled over 180,000 miles in America and Europe, raising funds and support for the establishment of missions among Indians of the Far Northwest. Called "Blackrobe" by the Indians, Father de Smet was representative of both Catholic and Protestant missionaries who not only converted Indians to Christianity but also advertised in Oregon and paved the way for the coming of the American pioneers.

Senator Lewis F. Linn of Missouri was one of the strongest proponents of American occupation of Oregon. Appointed to the Senate in 1833, the former physician and booster of Missouri's interests worked well with Senator Benton. Linn supported measures that he believed would build up Missouri and the western United States. He supported internal improvements, a liberal land policy, and the occupation of Oregon. In 1838, "Missouri's model senator" proposed a bill for the occupation of Oregon, its organization as a territory, and land grants of 640 acres to every settler. The bill passed the Senate but not the House of Representatives. Linn died in 1843, before the Oregon issue was resolved, but his vigorous efforts for its acquisition and settlement helped to stamp Oregon as a land of opportunity. His successor, David R. Atchison, took up the Oregon cause in the Senate and was one of those who pushed it through to a successful conclusion.

By the 1840s "Oregon Fever" raged in almost every part of the Union. The depressed economic conditions in the Mississippi Valley caused by the panic of 1837, the reported high prices for agricultural products in Oregon, and the spirit of Manifest Destiny led many Missourians to migrate to Oregon.

One man who was struck by Oregon fever was Peter H. Burnett of Platte County who in 1843 went from village to village lecturing, spreading the word about Oregon, and recruiting men, women, and children to go with him to the far northwest. That year young Edward Lennox went with his father to hear Burnett and later recalled how the enthusiastic stump speaker had extolled the greatness of Oregon. According to Lennox, Burnett, with a twinkle in his eye, said,

> . . . and they do say, gentlemen, they do say that out in Oregon the pigs are running about under the great acorn trees, round and fat, and already cooked, with knives and forks sticking in them so that you can cut off a slice whenever you are hungry.

Before the day ended, Edward's father signed his name to go with Burnett to the land where pigs were "round and fat and already cooked."

The Oregon Trail

Although small parties pioneered the Oregon Trail in 1840 and 1841, it was not until 1843 that large numbers of emigrants traveled the route to the extent that one traveler actually complained that "the road from morning till night, is crowded like Pearl Street [sic] or Broadway." The trail began at Independence, moved up the Missouri to the Platte River, the North Platte, Sweetwater to South Pass, then by the valley of the Bear to Snake River, and along the route of the Snake and Columbia to the Pacific coast. Far from a four-lane highway, it was, nevertheless an excellent trail. Food, water, and forage were nearby and it was relatively safe from Indians. The South Pass was a good way to get through the Rocky Mountains.

Gathering at Independence, St. Joseph, and other Missouri River frontier towns, the overland pioneers equipped themselves and commenced their long journey in the early spring to avoid the winter on the trail. Relying on lessons learned from the Santa Fe traders and from the personal experiences of those who first took the trail to Oregon, they elected strong leaders, made strict rules, traveled light, used oxen instead of draft horses to pull the Conestoga wagons, and wore thick shoes. In time they even created a "roadside telegraph," nailing messages to trees and posts for those who followed as to the availability of grass and water and to potential dangers. Cattle raised in Missouri and Illinois and accustomed to prairie grasses trailed the emigrant train in what was called "the cow column."

Indian attacks on wagon trains have been exaggerated, but Indians and white renegades disguised as Indians did commit many acts of depredation and thievery. Travel on the Oregon Trail was long and hard, but as time went by, it did become easier as the government, mountain men, friendly Indians, and people like Jim Bridger were often on hand to give aid and direction. The health of the individual traveler and sheer good luck were, however, two important factors that made for a successful journey.

Travel on the Oregon Trail in the 1840s and 1850s may well have had a strong nationalizing and democratizing effect on the emigrants. One traveler, David DeWolf, who traveled with people from Missouri, Mississippi, Tennessee, Illinois, and Ohio wrote in his diary that "we are a mixed up multitude but we all get along fine. Some of them get in a spur now and then but soon get over it. This trip binds us together like a band of brothers." Many of these brothers and sisters on the Oregon Trall were instrumental in pressing for the final acquisition of Oregon in 1846. The Oregon Trail opened the provinces of the American West, and for years was one of the main arteries between the Pacific Ocean and the Mississippi Valley over which flowed the travel and trade of an expanding nation.

On June 15, 1846, the United States signed the Oregon Treaty with Great Britain that ended nearly a half century of controversy over the Oregon country. Although the treaty was not to the complete satisfaction of the American expansionists, nevertheless, it provided for a boundary along the forty-ninth parallel between the two nations. With the acquisition of Oregon, President Polk and the Democratic party had fulfilled another campaign promise and now turned their attention to the Mexican War which had already begun.

Gateway To The West

In the westward movement, Missouri was first a frontier, a new land, a "going to" place for fur traders, backwoods dwellers, cattle raisers, merchants, and explorers. By the early 1800s it became a territory, and then by 1821 a state. From Missouri there came many people who explored and settled the trans-Mississippi West that made the United States a continental nation. No other phrase so accurately denotes the place of Missouri in the history of the American West as the one written on the great arch that rises above the Mississippi River at St. Louis—"the gateway to the West."

Suggestions for Reading

Two scholarly treatments of the entire history of the westward movement are Ray Allen Billington, *Westward Expansion*, New York, Macmillan, 1967, and Frederick Merk, *History of the Westward Movement*, New York, Knopf, 1978. Another valuable and comprehensive work on the history of the American West is William H. Goetzmann, *Exploration and Empire*, New York, Knopf, 1966. Important works on the Lewis and Clark Expedition include Stephen E. Ambrose, *Undaunted Courage: Meriwether Lewis, Thomas Jefferson and the Opening of the West*, New York, Simon & Schuster, 1996; Paul R. Cutright, *Lewis & Clark: Pioneering Naturalists*, Urbana, University of Illinois Press, 1989; James P. Ronda, *Lewis and Clark Among the Indians*, Lincoln, University of Nebraska Press, 1984; and the companion volume to the television documentary by Dayton Duncan and Ken Burns, *Lewis and Clark: The Journey of the Corps of Discovery: An Illustrated History*, New York, 1997. *We Proceeded On*, the quarterly magazine of the Lewis and Clark Trail Heritage Foundation Inc., P.O. Box 3434, Great Falls, MT, 59403, publishes articles and book reviews related to the expedition, as well as reports of the activity of the Foundation. The best biography of Clark is Jerome O. Steffen, *William Clark: Jeffersonian Man on the Frontier*, Norman, University of Oklahoma Press, 1977.

The classic work on the fur trade is Hiram M. Chittenden, *The American Fur Trade of the Far West*, 2 vols., New York, Barnes & Noble, 1935. Biographies of significant figures in the fur trade include Richard Clokey, *William H. Ashley: Enterprise and Politics in the Trans Mississippi West*, Norman, University of Oklahoma, 1980; Cecil J. Alter, *Jim Bridger*, Norman, University of Oklahoma Press, 1962; William R. Nester, *From Mountain Man to Millionaire: The "Bold and Dashing Life" of Robert Campbell*, Columbia, University of Missouri Press,

1999; Richard E. Oglesby, *Manuel Lisa and the Opening of the Missouri Fur Trade*, Norman, University of Oklahoma Press, 1963; Charles T. Jones, Jr., *George Champlin Sibley: The Prairie Puritan (1782–1863)*, Independence, Jackson County Historical Society, 1970; and Dale L. Morgan, *Jedidiah Smith and the Opening of the West*, Indianapolis, Bobbs Merrill, 1953. There are also short biographies of many participants in the fur trade in LeRoy Hafen, ed., *The Mountain Men and the Fur Trade of the Far West*, 10 vols., Glendale, CA, Arthur R. Clark Publishing Co., 1965–1972.

The classic account of the Santa Fe Trail and trade is in Josiah Gregg, *Commerce of the Prairies*, ed. Max L. Moorhead, Norman, University of Oklahoma Press, 1990. For a more than adequate treatment of the history of the Santa Fe Trail, see Stephen G. Hyslop, *Bound for Santa Fe: The Road to New Mexico and the American Conquest, 1806–1848*, Norman, University of Oklahoma Press, 2002. It should be supplemented by William E. Brown, *The Santa Fe Trail*, St. Louis, The Patrice Press, 1988, and Mark L. Gardner, *Wagons for the Santa Fe Trade: Wheeled Vehicles and Their Makers, 1822–1880*, Albuquerque, University of New Mexico Press, 2000. Another interesting study is William Patrick O'Brien, "Hiram Young: Pioneering Black Wagonmaker for the Santa Fe Trade," *Gateway Heritage*, Summer 1993. The man who established the Santa Fe Trail is well covered in Larry Beachum, *William Becknell: Father of the Santa Fe Trail*, El Paso, Texas Western Press, 1982. For a firsthand account of the experiences of a young army wife traveling the Santa Fe Trail in the 1840s, see *Down the Santa Fe Trail and into Mexico: The Diary of Susan Shelby Magoffin, 1846–1847*, ed. Stella M. Drum, 3d ed., New Haven, Yale University Press, 1979.

An exhaustive study of travel across the American West is John D. Unruh, Jr., *The Plains Across: The Overland Emigrants and the Trans-Mississippi West, 1840–1860*, Urbana, University of Illinois Press, 1979. A literary and historical masterpiece of the excitement and romance of the westward movement is Francis Parkman, *The Oregon Trail*, New York, New American Library, 1955.

FIVE

The Age of Benton

The United States had become virtually a one-party nation at the time of Missouri's admission as a state. The Federalist party had fallen into disgrace during the War of 1812 and failed thereafter to provide effective opposition to the Democrat-Republicans. Consequently President Monroe was reelected in 1820 with all of the nation's electoral votes except one. Missouri politics reflected a similar situation. All voters bore the Democrat-Republican label. Yet that party quickly became factionalized around certain personalities and issues. The lines between factions tended to remain somewhat fluid during the 1820s as each voter and politician sought to find the niche in which he felt most comfortable. By the end of the decade, however, two distinct parties had emerged at the national level—the Democrats and the National Republicans, who later became the Whigs. Most Missourians thereafter found their place in one or the other of these groups.

The Emergence of Political Differences

Differences began to emerge in Missouri's First General Assembly over two interrelated issues: the question of what kind of public relief should be offered the people as a result of the panic (or depression) of 1819; and the matter of certain controversial parts of the new constitution, especially those relating to the courts, salaries, and appointive powers. The panic of 1819 had ended the boom times that followed the War of 1812. It began in the East, but its full effect was not felt in Missouri until the winter of 1820–21. It had been brought on by extended land speculation backed by a too liberal credit policy. Numerous banks had issued loans based on unsound currency for which they did not have adequate backing of gold or silver. When the collapse came, it triggered many bank and business failures. Prices fell drastically, and credit dried up almost overnight.

In Missouri the depression affected every class of people. The flood tide of immigrants slowed to a trickle. Those who had bought surplus land, frequently on credit with the hope of reselling it at a profit to the newcomers, now found themselves holding greatly depreciated property with no buyers. Many farmers had a difficult time marketing their crops, while others had to sell their produce at prices far less than their costs of production. Merchants found that persons could not afford to buy their goods. Once the panic hit, it had a steamrolling effect. Poor management caused both of Missouri's banks, established during the territorial period, to fail and left the new state without adequate credit just when it was badly needed. In this crisis, people on all sides turned to the new state government for help.

The legislature, following a pattern of numerous other states, responded with two major relief measures, neither of them overly radical. First, it passed a series of stay laws under which debtors were given ample opportunity to recover property that might be foreclosed. Second, it established a state loan office that could lend up to $1,000 against either land or personal property. In the case of the loan office, its loan certificates could be used to pay taxes or any other state debts; and private creditors were urged to accept them in payment. Missourians divided sharply over the necessity for these measures. Those who owned and worked the land tended to favor them while merchants, lawyers, and others to whom they might owe money opposed them. In reality, the new laws proved complicated and gave little actual relief. The Missouri courts quickly declared them unconstitutional. Still, the controversy indicated a sharp difference of opinion about the government's responsibility for the well-being of its citizens during difficult times.

Missourians divided along similar lines over attempts to amend the state's new constitution. They argued about salaries set for judges and the governor and whether the appointive power over judges and executive officers should be in the hands of the governor, as the constitution provided, or those of the legislature. The First General Assembly passed ten amendments giving the legislature power to set a flexible salary schedule, abolishing the chancery court with its powers being given to regular courts, vacating all judicial offices, and transferring appointive powers to the legislature. The major argument in support of increasing legislative powers was that the General Assembly was closer to the people. Those opposing the amendments feared that this might be a move to get a new set of judges who would uphold the recent relief legislation.

Under the terms of the constitution the amendments had to be passed by a two-thirds vote of two successive legislatures. This meant that the questions raised became issues in the election of a new legislature in 1822. That contest saw an almost complete turnover in the General Assembly, but the tide was toward conservatism. The older leaders, realizing that they could not take elections for granted, exerted their full energies toward getting candidates acceptable to their point of view. By the time of the election, the initial burst of discontent had subsided, aided in part by the quick action of the courts in striking down the relief acts. Consequently the new legislature passed only the three amendments abolishing the chancery court, repealing minimum salaries, and vacating judicial offices. Because they did not pass the amendments transferring the appointive power from the governor to the legislature, the trend toward presumably more popular government was postponed until another day. Governor McNair simply reappointed the existing judges, who carried on as before.

The two issues of the relief legislation and the constitutional amendments clearly indicated that division of opinion existed in Missouri. In the absence of organized political parties and strong leadership, those who advocated more popular government had to await new events to help focus attention on the need for change. As the 1820s progressed, a series of national and state elections helped provide the necessary focus and leadership that had been lacking. The result was the emergence by the end of the decade of the Jacksonian movement with Senator Thomas Hart Benton as one of its strongest leaders.

Thomas Hart Benton

Benton, who had been elected to the Senate in 1820 with but a single vote to spare, had come to realize early that he had to broaden his base of support to retain his office. He had ties to the special interests of the so-called St. Louis Clique, but he also had established a statewide appeal with his strong editorials in the *Enquirer* on the restriction issue during the statehood crisis.

A strong egotist and opportunist, Benton proved a forceful leader in the rough and-tumble politics of frontier Missouri. He played one group against another while emerging as the champion of the common people. He particularly spoke for western interests against the encroachments of a remote central government in Washington. In so doing, Benton established himself as the dominant force in Missouri politics for the next thirty years.

Realizing his dependence of the moment upon the St. Louis Clique, Benton pushed legislation in the Senate to meet their needs. In so doing, however, he emphasized that his measures would also help the average citizen. For example, he secured a liberal policy with regard to final settlement of the Spanish land grants and noted that it would help the small farmer with his claims as well as the large landholder. He worked to abolish the old factory system, represented in Missouri by Fort Osage, whereby the government set up special outposts for Indian trade in competition with the private trader. He unsuccessfully introduced legislation to provide for private management of government-owned Missouri lead mines. In all of this, he appeared as the champion of private enterprise.

The 1820s saw most states provide for the popular election of presidential electors, where previously they had been chosen by the state legislatures. Benton went one step further in 1824 by proposing a constitutional amendment abolishing the electoral college alto-

gether on the grounds that it was undemocratic. Congress refused to approve his proposal, but Benton had begun to move toward a leadership role in the blossoming democratic movement that would find its national symbol in Andrew Jackson.

A second measure introduced by Benton at the close of the 1824 congressional session was also designed to help him broaden his base. This became known as his "graduation policy" because it proposed to graduate downward

Senator Thomas Hart Benton. *Courtesy State Historical Society of Missouri*

THOMAS H. BENTON SPEAKING AT HIS DESK.

the price of public land each year that it remained unsold after first being offered. The idea was to make less desirable land available at a cheaper price to someone willing to take a chance on working it. Congress had no opportunity to act on it at this session nor would it do so later, but the idea had a popular appeal.

The Election of 1824

The election of 1824 began the breakdown of the Democrat-Republican party at the national level and hastened the reemergence of a two-party system. With President Monroe completing his second term, numerous candidates vied for the public's favor to replace him. This would be the first presidential election in which substantial numbers of electors would be chosen by popular voting so that it began to take on some of the excitement of a modern campaign. The field narrowed down to four finalists by the fall of 1824: Secretary of State John Quincy Adams, Secretary of the Treasury William H. Crawford, Speaker of the House Henry Clay, and General Andrew Jackson. Of the four, Clay and Jackson had the greatest appeal to Missourians. Both were westerners—Clay from Kentucky and Jackson from Tennessee—and were well known, at least by reputation, to many Missourians who came from those states.

Clay had a strong edge over Jackson within the state, primarily because of his role in helping secure statehood. His platform, which he called the "American System," also brought him wide support as it advocated a strong balanced economy through a national bank, protective tariffs, and federal aid for internal improvements such as canals and roads. Senator Benton, who was related to Clay by marriage, campaigned actively for him. The Kentuckian also had the support of Barton and Scott. This undoubtedly helped him secure the state's electoral vote. The final Missouri balloting showed Clay with 2,042 votes; Jackson, 1,168; Adams, 186; and Crawford, 37. Unfortunately for Clay, things did not go that well for him nationally as he finished fourth behind Jackson, Adams, and Crawford in that order. The vote was so split, however, that none of the four received a majority in the electoral college, as required by the constitution. Consequently the decision was thrown to the House of Representatives where each state would have but one vote with a majority needed to select a president.

By placing fourth, Clay was eliminated from further consideration, but as Speaker, he quickly became the powerbroker in the

House election. After some deliberation Clay threw his support to Adams against his fellow westerner, Andrew Jackson. It was done, Clay said, because he believed the secretary of state to be the more experienced candidate. John Scott, Missouri's lone representative who had just been reelected, found himself on the horns of a dilemma as he would be solely responsible for casting the state's vote in the House election. Jackson had run strongly behind Clay in Missouri, but the latter's endorsement of Adams had to carry weight. Scott asked the legislature for instructions on how to vote, but its members could not agree. Senators Barton and Benton split on the issue with the former favoring Adams while Benton, sensing the wave of the future, came out for Jackson. In the end, Scott cast Missouri's vote for Adams, who was elected President by a bare majority. In doing so, he helped set the stage for the emergence of two fairly clearcut political factions within the state. On the one hand, there was the Adams-Clay group, headed by Scott and Senator Barton, which increasingly favored a strong national program at the possible expense of the states. On the other, there was the Jackson group, headed by Senator Benton, which came to advocate a broader democracy with a strong western flavor.

For the moment, it would appear that the faction headed by Barton and Scott had control in Missouri. They had chosen the winning side in the national election as Adams moved into the White House with all the patronage that the presidency could bestow. In spite of Benton's active opposition, Barton was handily reelected to the Senate by the new legislature in November 1824. And the conservative candidate, Frederick Bates, had recently been elected governor with the strong support of the St. Louis business interests.

The Jacksonians Gain Ground

All of this would quickly change, however, as a result of circumstances in both Washington and Missouri. Shortly after his election by the House, Adams announced his cabinet and revealed that Henry Clay would become his secretary of state. The Jacksonians, who had taken his election rather calmly up to this point, now cried "corrupt bargain." They were certain that Clay had sold his influence in the House for a political post that could put him in a stronger position to move toward the presidency. Consequently they developed an effective opposition in Congress, led in part by Senator Benton, and began planning for the election of 1828.

An opportunity for the display of partisanship came in Missouri when Governor Bates died of pleurisy in August 1825, only eight months after taking office. Under the Missouri constitution a special election had to be held to fill the vacancy because more than eighteen months remained on the unexpired term. In the interim, Abraham J. Williams, the president pro tem of the Senate, became acting governor. The election was held in December 1825 with four announced candidates. All indicated their independence of any faction, but Benton and Barton endorsed different candidates and campaigned actively on their behalf. Benton's choice was John Miller of Franklin, who had been registrar of the federal land office there since 1817, while Barton and Scott supported Judge David Todd of St. Louis. Miller won handily and secured reelection in 1828 without opposition. At least one newspaper proclaimed his victory as a triumph for the Jacksonians, and there are indications that Miller used the state patronage to help build the Missouri Democratic party over the next six years.

When Scott sought another term in the House of Representatives in 1826, he came under strong criticism for having supported Adams. He tried to justify it on the grounds that Adams had the election already locked up so that he assured Missouri of being on the

George Caleb Bingham's painting *The County Election* from an engraving by John Sartain. *Courtesy State Historical Society of Missouri*

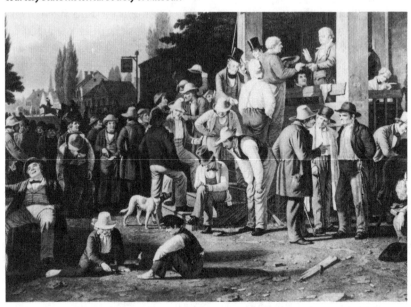

winning side. He also argued the importance of commercial connections with the northeast that Adams represented, but to no avail. He was challenged by Edward Bates, brother of the late governor, who ran as an independent candidate with a mild endorsement of Henry Clay's American System. Primarily, however, the ambitious Bates sought to take advantage of Scott's dilemma over the 1824 election. He received Jacksonian support for lack of another candidate and won handily. The Jacksonians soon discovered what some had already suspected—that they had simply replaced one Adams supporter with another as Bates came quickly into opposition to Benton on most issues. Benton meanwhile won reelection to the Senate handily.

The Election of 1828

It was a forgone conclusion that the presidential race in 1828 would be a rematch between Jackson and Adams. The former's partisans in Missouri organized early. They held an unofficial convention at Jefferson City in January 1828, which endorsed Jackson and his vice presidential running mate, John C. Calhoun, chose presidential electors, and established a state committee to conduct the campaign. The Adams supporters countered with their own meeting in March, but they could not begin to match the enthusiasm of the Jacksonians. As spring gave way to summer, the latter held rally after rally around the state. While the Adams supporters stressed their "respectability," the Jacksonians emphasized the importance of the average citizen.

The only cloud on the Jacksonian horizon was the announcement of two candidates for Congress to challenge Edward Bates. One was Mayor William Carr Lane of St. Louis; the other, Spencer Pettis of Cole County, had strong out-state support from a group of emerging politicians centered in Howard County who would soon become known as the Central Clique. Fearful that a split in the Jacksonian vote would give the election to Bates, Benton stepped in as umpire with both Lane and Pettis agreeing to abide by his decision. He chose the latter as the official candidate, thereby moving toward an alliance with the Central Clique through which they would dominate Missouri politics for the next twenty years. In the state election that August, Pettis easily defeated Bates; and John Miller received another term as governor unopposed. The new legislature would have a strong Jacksonian majority.

This was but a prelude to the national election in November in which Jackson swept everything before him on his march to the White House. The general carried every county in Missouri as he tallied 8,372 votes to only 3,407 for Adams. The Age of Jackson had arrived, and Thomas Hart Benton was its chief architect in Missouri. During the next eight years Benton would also establish himself as the floor leader of the Jackson forces in the Senate and become an important figure in the inner circles of the national Democratic party.

The Tactics of the Opposition

The party machinery that had put together the winning campaign in Missouri was quickly dismantled, however, for no one then saw the need for organization except at election time. Political alliances remained loose knit and fluid. The Jacksonians generally assumed the Democratic label, while their opponents, who rallied around Henry Clay and his American System, merely called themselves anti-Jackson or the Opposition. By the end of the 1830s, the latter would emerge as the Whig party. Their chances of winning statewide elections in Missouri were negligible as they had few avowed candidates beyond the legislative level. Many office seekers in sympathy with them took the Jackson label to give themselves greater assurance of election, and Opposition leaders soon learned to support these wolves in sheep's clothing as their best means of thwarting the Jacksonians.

Such was the case in 1830 when David Barton reached the end of his second Senate term. Plagued by ill health and alcoholism, Barton had no chance of reelection. Benton wrote his allies in central Missouri suggesting that the honor go to Governor Miller. But several candidates jumped into the contest under the Jackson label. Edward Bates quietly lined up Opposition legislators behind Alexander Buckner of Cape Girardeau County, a former state senator, who was chosen with their help on the first ballot while the Jacksonians split their votes among a variety of others, with Governor Miller coming in second. Buckner subsequently supported rechartering of the Bank of the United States and maintenance of the existing protective tariff, both of which were Clay measures. Benton discovered that Barton had been replaced by another Adams-Clay candidate albeit one with a Democratic label.

A parallel situation occurred when Spencer Pettis, who had been reelected to Congress in 1831, was killed in a duel, necessitating a special election to fill the vacancy. William H. Ashley, the prominent fur trader and former lieutenant governor, quickly announced his candidacy on a platform favoring the reelection of Jackson but otherwise supporting the American System. Bates gave him the Opposition's endorsement, and Senator Buckner announced his support. Aware of Ashley's great popularity, the Jacksonians sought to head him off by arranging a convention that nominated Robert W. Wells, who followed Benton's lead on such matters as the Bank, the tariff, and internal improvements. Although rejected by the convention, Ashley refused to withdraw from the race. He split enough Jacksonian votes away from Wells so that, with the help of the Opposition endorsement, he won the election by less than 100 votes.

The Election of 1832

Having been stung twice, the Jacksonians sought to make a greater effort at weeding out those who joined them in name only as they approached the election of 1832. With the President running for reelection and Benton up for a third term in the Senate, it was important to sweep into office those sympathetic with Jacksonian principles. The most critical issue in that election was the rechartering of the Second Bank of the United States. Henry Clay, who had been nominated by the National Republicans to oppose Jackson for the presidency in 1832, had pushed a recharter bill through Congress that spring only to have the President veto it in stinging language.

Henry Clay saw the Bank as a cornerstone of the American System because it could make credit readily available where needed and hopefully regulate a flexible paper currency. His followers were called "soft money" men. In Missouri they tended to come from the merchant class, especially in St. Louis, those involved in mining, and the large farmer-slave owner class along the Mississippi and Missouri rivers. These groups needed fluid capital for the management of their respective enterprises.

But Jackson and Benton believed that the Bank represented special privilege at the expense of the average citizen. They disliked the way it managed the currency, expanding it at one time and contracting it at another. They believed that it exercised inadequate control

A pioneer Missouri village. *Courtesy State Historical Society of Missouri*

over local banks that issued paper currency in a reckless fashion without sufficient coinage to back it. Such paper fluctuated sharply in value, and the small debtor suffered in the process. Benton believed that paper money should be limited to bills of twenty dollars denomination or higher, with gold and silver coins for anything below that. This earned him the nickname "Old Bullion," and his supporters were known as "hard money" men. They were made up of the small farmers and store owners in the outlying areas and the growing working class in St. Louis and the larger towns.

The election of 1832 was a strong triumph for the Jacksonians in Missouri and elsewhere. Jackson swept the state with 70 percent of the vote and won reelection handily. Daniel Dunklin, Potosi lawyer and innkeeper, easily took the governorship on the Jacksonian ticket; and the new General Assembly sent Benton back to the Senate for a third term by an overwhelming vote. The following year Senator Buckner died in a cholera epidemic that struck Missouri. Governor Dunklin appointed Dr. Lewis F. Linn of Ste. Genevieve, an ardent Jacksonian, to replace him; and the General Assembly elected Linn to fill the unexpired term at its next session. Now Benton had a colleague with compatible views, and the two worked closely together in the Senate.

The Platte Purchase

The Dunklin administration proved relatively uneventful, although there were several unsuccessful efforts to adopt constitutional changes similar to those of the early 1820s. Dunklin resigned the governorship in the fall of 1836 to accept an appointment from President Jackson as surveyor general for Missouri, Illinois, and Arkansas. Lieutenant Governor Lilburn W. Boggs of Jackson County, who had already won election to a full term as governor on the Democratic ticket in August, filled out the remaining days of Dunklin's term.

Boggs was the first governor from the rapidly growing western part of the state. His administration proved to be a very active one. In June 1836, in large part because of the efforts of Senators Benton and Linn, Congress agreed to expand Missouri's original western boundary, which had been drawn through the point where the Kansas River empties into the Missouri near present-day Kansas City. The region to the north, between this line and the Missouri River, was fertile land upon which white settlers began casting covetous eyes almost as soon as they came into northwest Missouri. But various Indian tribes held title to it, and they also recognized its value. Agitation to extinguish the Indian titles got underway seriously with a petition from the Missouri legislature in 1831 calling for the region's annexation. In response William Clark and other government agents began negotiations with the various tribes, who accepted what seemed inevitable and quickly came to terms. By November 1836, treaties had been signed granting the tribes lands in Kansas in exchange for their rights to the Platte country. And on March 28, 1837, President Martin Van Buren formally proclaimed the region to be a part of Missouri. From it six counties were formed: Platte, Buchanan, Andrew, Holt, Nodaway, and Atchison.

The Bank of Missouri

Following the election of 1832, President Jackson had successfully terminated the Bank of the United States, whose charter expired in 1836. This eliminated the St. Louis branch of the B.U.S. as well and led to demands for a state-chartered bank to replace it as a means of providing adequate credit for Missouri's economic development. The major concern of Senator Benton and the Jacksonians in any such move was that the bank be soundly financed and adequately controlled in relation to its currency policy. Wildcat banking, so-called because of the minimum amount of control or restraint over it, had begun to flourish in many other areas with the demise of the Bank of the United States, resulting in a flood of worthless paper currency.

Benton had no desire to see that process repeated in Missouri. Governor Boggs recommended to the legislature in November 1836 that it charter a state bank with limited ability to issue paper currency based strictly on an adequate specie (gold and silver) backing. The General Assembly responded favorably. It created a bank capitalized at $5 million in which the state owned one-half of the stock, and the legislature appointed the president and half of the directors. Notes could not be issued in denominations of less than ten dollars, and other rigid restrictions sought to guarantee the bank's soundness. The success of the bank's conservative management was reflected in part by its ability to survive the panic of 1837, a severe national financial crisis, that wiped out many other lending institutions.

Indeed, for a variety of reasons, Missouri, unlike other states to the East, weathered the depression that followed the panic of 1837 fairly well. It had enjoyed a steady growth in population and trade throughout the decade. The traffic over the Santa Fe Trail generated

Early day in banking Missouri. *Courtesy State Historical Society of Missouri*

hundreds of thousands of dollars of specie. Government activity in the West required large sums of federal monies, and many of these funds found their way into the Bank of Missouri inasmuch as Jefferson Barracks at St. Louis served as the center for most of the government's western operations. As the migration west over the Oregon Trail began in the 1840s, those towns in central and western Missouri outfitting the caravans also experienced a boom time.

The Advance of Education

The first steps toward the establishment of a comprehensive public school system were taken during the Boggs administration. Building on a study done during the Dunklin administration, the General Assembly passed the Geyer Act in 1839 which provided, on paper at least, for a structure ranging from elementary school through a state university. In the initial stages, however, the state provided no monies to assist school districts other than funds that it received from various federal programs such as the sale of public lands. Because these funds went only to districts that had already made some local efforts of their own, nothing was done to assist other areas in getting schools started. St. Louis organized the first high school in 1852, with St. Joseph following suit on the eve of the Civil War. The legislature established the state university at Columbia in 1839 but gave it no direct appropriations from state funds until after the Civil War.

In 1853 the General Assembly adopted the Kelly Act, which provided the first state monies to support public schools. This required that 25 percent of the state's general revenues be divided among the counties on a proportional basis for this purpose. With this boost the amount of money for public education increased tenfold during the 1850s to approximately $262,000. During the same decade the legislature also established a state school for the deaf at Fulton and one for the blind at St. Louis.

Despite the enactment of the Geyer and Kelly Acts, education in Missouri continued to be primarily a private concern, with the subscription schools dominating the elementary level and private academies and colleges, most of them church related, providing opportunities beyond that. The General Assembly granted some ninety charters to various private schools in the three decades prior to the Civil War, and it has been estimated that an additional 100 probably existed without a charter.

First capitol erected in Jefferson City, 1826. Presented to Cole County Historical Society by Marcel Boulicoult , March 15, 1955. *Courtesy State Historical Society of Missouri*

A New State Capitol

One of Governor Boggs's major concerns was the inadequacy of the existing state capitol. A two story brick structure of rectangular design, it had originally served as both capitol and governor's mansion, with the intention that it would become the latter entirely as soon as a permanent government building could be erected. The reverse happened, however, as a separate mansion was built during the Dunklin administration. Following Boggs's recommendation, the legislature authorized $75,000 for the construction of a new capitol. But the project had hardly begun before the original structure caught fire and burned on the night of November 15, 1837, destroying all of the state papers. Only the absence of a high wind prevented the fire from spreading to the new mansion nearby. A new capitol now rose slowly on the hillside overlooking the Missouri River. Its cost far outstripped the original estimate, eventually reaching $250,000. This brought on a legislative investigation, but no evidence of fraud was discovered. The new capitol was an imposing classical structure surmounted by a large dome, which was becoming the popular style of the day for public buildings. It remained the seat of government until it, in turn, was destroyed by fire in 1911.

The Mormon War

While the Boggs administration was marked by progress in several areas, it was also a period of confrontation and violence. One of the saddest episodes in Missouri history was the Mormon War of 1838. It grew out of a smoldering conflict of some seven years' duration between the religious group known as the Church of Jesus Christ of Latter Day Saints and those to whom they referred as their "Gentile" neighbors along the western Missouri frontier. The Saints, or Mormons as they were popularly known, were disciples of Joseph Smith, who had organized the church in western New York in 1830. Having established himself as a prophet through a series of divine visions, Smith determined that Jackson County should be the location of what he called the "New Zion." He led a small band of followers there in the winter of 1830–31 and then returned East to encourage further immigration.

From the outset the Mormons proved an aggressive, dynamic body. By 1833 they numbered some 1,200, perhaps a third of the total population of Jackson County. The Saints sent missionaries into present-day Kansas to work with the Indians. They also tended to be strongly antislavery, and there were rumors that a considerable number of free black converts might soon join them. Well organized and clannish, the Mormons believed strongly in the rightness of their views. Their newspaper, *The Evening and the Morning Star*, reflected their attitudes and convinced non-Mormons in the area that the Saints intended to make Jackson County their exclusive domain.

Violence broke out on July 20, 1833, when a mob destroyed the Mormon printing office and dumped its press unceremoniously into the Missouri River. The mob also attacked nearby Mormon shops and homes and tarred and feathered two prominent leaders. Threats to do them further harm forced the Saints to agree to abandon the county in stages, with the stipulation that all would be gone by April 1834.

The Mormons petitioned Governor Dunklin for protection. He replied sympathetically but suggested that the Saints try to resolve their problems through the courts. This they did, but with little success. When it became apparent that the Mormons would not keep their promise to leave, mob violence resumed at the end of October 1833. The governor called out the militia but mistakenly put them under the command of Colonel Thomas Pitcher, a staunch anti-Mormon, who disarmed the Saints and then broke his promise to confiscate the weapons of the mob. The Mormons, who now had no choice but to flee, found refuge across the Missouri River in Clay County. A court of inquiry, ordered by Governor Dunklin, got nowhere because of continued hostility in Jackson County. Attempts to settle Mormon claims for lost property came to naught when the two sides failed to reach agreement during their periodic negotiations. Just how much property was involved and what finally became of it has never been clear.

Over the next three years the Mormons did fairly well in Clay and surrounding counties, but their increasing numbers eventually caused concern among their new neighbors. To help alleviate this, one of their attorneys, Alexander W. Doniphan, who had been elected to the legislature from Clay County, worked out an informal agreement setting aside the newly created county of Caldwell as Mormon territory. Most of the Saints migrated there in 1837 and 1838, laying out the town of Far West as their "capital" and county seat. Joseph Smith arrived there in March 1838 after financial difficulties, brought on by the panic of 1837, forced him to flee Kirtland, Ohio, his previous headquarters. The new county soon had a population of 5,000, most of whom were Mormons. They held all the county offices and organized their own militia.

Before long, Caldwell County became too small to contain all of the Saints who were migrating to western Missouri, and they began

The attack on the Mormons at Haun's Mill (Caldwell County), October 1838. *Courtesy State Historical Society of Missouri*

to spill into neighboring Carroll, Clinton, Daviess, and Livingston counties. Because they tended to vote and act as a unit, the Mormons frequently had the power to decide the outcome of elections in counties where the opposing political factions were evenly matched. Violence erupted on August 6, 1838, at Gallatin in Daviess County when Mormons attempted to participate in a local election. As tension mounted that fall, both the Saints and their neighbors armed themselves. Each group undertook intermittent raids against the other. What ensued is known as the Mormon War. Governor Boggs called out the militia at the end of August, but they proved ineffective. Boggs was from Jackson County and had been associated with the anti-Mormon leadership there in 1833. He now concluded that the Saints were the source of all of the difficulties in western Missouri and issued what came to be known as his "Extermination Order." On October 26, he directed General John B. Clark of the militia as follows: "The Mormons must be treated as enemies, and must be exterminated or driven from the State if necessary for the public peace—their outrages are beyond all description."

The Saints planned a final stand at Far West; but when militia units under General Samuel Lucas, an old enemy, surrounded the town, Smith realized that it would be hopeless to resist. He surrendered with other leaders and agreed to stand trial for treason. The Mormons gave up all their arms and saw their property confiscated to pay for damages that they had allegedly caused. A mass migration of some 15,000 Mormons followed as Brigham Young, one of Smith's lieutenants who had been absent on a missionary journey during the fighting, led them to a new settlement adjacent to the Mississippi River in western Illinois. Joseph Smith and the other leaders who had been arrested were given a preliminary hearing at Gallatin in April 1839. Their lawyers arranged for their trial to be transferred to Boone County, where it could be held in a less hostile atmosphere. While they were being transferred from one jail to another, a judicious bribe provided the means for their escape; they rode quickly to join their fellow Saints in Illinois.

The Honey War

The winter of 1839–40 saw a confrontation of another sort in northeast Missouri along the Iowa border. The boundary between the two areas had come into dispute as a result of different surveys authorized by the Missouri legislature and by Congress. Both Missouri and

Iowa claimed jurisdiction over a strip approximately nine to eleven miles wide. An attempt by Sheriff Uriah Gregory of Clark County, Missouri, to collect taxes in the region brought first hostility and then his arrest by his counterpart in Van Buren County, Iowa. When Governor Boggs called up local militia to reinforce Missouri's jurisdiction, Governor Robert Lucas of the Iowa Territory suggested that Congress draw the boundary. Boggs rejected that idea whereupon Lucas called up his own militia, and a fight seemed eminent. Fortunately cooler heads prevailed among the militia commanders on both sides, who negotiated a truce. With Boggs remaining adamant against a congressional settlement, the matter was finally resolved ten years later by the United States Supreme Court, which divided the disputed region equally between the two. In the meantime the whole incident had come to be known as the "Honey War" because a Missourian found cutting down several bee trees in the area was fined $1.50 by an Iowa territorial court. John L. Campbell satirized the whole affair in a poem called "The Honey War" published in the Palmyra *Missouri Whig and General Advertiser*, and it became a popular song of the 1840s sung to the tune of "Yankee Doodle."

The Seminole War

Missourians also fought beyond the state's boundaries during the Boggs administration. In 1835 the Seminole Indians in Florida began actively resisting United States efforts to relocate them farther west. Two years later Senator Benton received a request from President Van Buren for Missouri troops to join with others in stemming the Seminole War. Some 600 men volunteered from central Missouri under the command of Colonel Richard Gentry of Columbia. Only about half of them saw actual combat. Those who did suffered heavy casualties, including the loss of Colonel Gentry, while participating in a battle at Lake Okeechobee on Christmas Day, 1837. General Zachary Taylor, who commanded the overall American force, later charged the Missouri troops with cowardly behavior. His allegation aroused a storm of protest throughout the state. A legislative committee investigating the matter interviewed many participants in the battle. Its reports completely exonerated Gentry's troops, pointing out the loss of 138 Missourians in the battle, and called on President Van Buren to investigate the charges, but nothing further came of the matter. Gentry had been a close personal friend of Benton—even to the naming of one of his sons after the senator—and Old Bullion now saw to it that his widow was appointed postmistress at Columbia with a federal pension in addition.

Strains Within the Democratic Party

During the early 1840s the Democratic power base that Benton had built so carefully over the previous two decades started to show signs of strain. Many Democrats, especially in St. Louis, began to support the Whig stand for a relaxation of currency restrictions because they feared a negative effect on business growth. These "Softs" urged a more liberal policy by the Bank of Missouri in issuing paper currency and accepting the notes of out-of-state banks. These notes floated rather freely in St. Louis mercantile circles as did the commercial paper of a number of companies chartered for other purposes. The "Hards," who stood firmly behind Benton's conservative banking policies, opposed such tactics. In 1843 they pushed through the legislature bills making it illegal for any corporation, public or private, to receive or circulate any paper currency of less than ten dollars value or the notes of any bank which did not pay in specie. The new laws further outlawed the exercise of banking functions by private corporations. These measures had the full support of Governor Thomas Reynolds, who had succeeded Boggs in 1841. The new governor tended to be very anticorporation and refused to recommend any relief measures when the effects of the depression following the Panic of 1837 finally began to be felt in Missouri in 1842.

Other issues tended to divide Soft and Hard Democrats as well. As the population grew, there was an increasing demand for legislative reapportionment and for the election of congressmen from individual districts rather than from the state at large. The reapportionment issue became critical because the constitution limited the number of House seats to 100 and guaranteed each county one representative. The General Assembly increased the number of counties to seventy-seven in 1841 and then created an additional nineteen in 1845 which left little room for the more populous counties, such as St. Louis, to have the extra representation to which they were logically entitled.

With its increase in population, Missouri gained three additional congressional seats (making a total of five) after the 1840 census. Congress passed legislation in 1842 requiring each state to establish separate congressional districts; but the Missouri legislature under the influence of the Central Clique refused. Under the at-large system, wherein all voters statewide cast ballots for each congressional seat, the Clique controlled the Democratic nominations and hence those who were sent to Washington. This was a power they did not care to relinquish.

Interestingly enough, on both of these issues Benton found himself on the horns of a dilemma for each tended to give more power to the people, something he had long advocated as a Jacksonian, while threatening to destroy his rural power base. Under the circumstances he tried to dodge both issues. And in the midst of all this debate yet another concern from an earlier era continued to crop up periodically: the popular election of appointed state officials, including judges. The battle lines were slowly being drawn between the people and the politicians.

Two unfortunate deaths also affected the Democratic party during this period. Senator Linn died unexpectedly in October 1843, leaving Governor Reynolds the task of appointing a temporary successor. He chose David R. Atchison of Platte County. A popular circuit judge, Atchison had steered clear of factional struggles. His appointment gave recognition to the growing northwestern corner of the state. Shortly after this, in February 1844, Reynolds committed suicide at the mansion, leaving a note that indicated he could no longer take the stress of party divisions. Lieutenant Governor Meredith M. Marmaduke of Howard County, a member of the Central Clique, succeeded him.

The Election of 1844

Against this background Missourians faced the election of 1844. The Softs made a strong effort to control the state Democratic convention early in April. The best they could do, however, was to force a compromise candidate for governor. Realizing that Governor Marmaduke would be too divisive, the Hards put forward instead former Congressman John C. Edwards of Cole County, a staunch Benton supporter but a moderate on the currency issue. Miller also favored congressional districting and a constitutional convention to deal with legislative reapportionment. The state convention avoided taking a stand on any of the controversial issues plaguing the party; rather it called on all Democrats to support the ticket and the election of legislators pledged to return Benton and Atchison to the Senate. The Softs refused to support Edwards, however. One of their number, Charles H. Allen from northwest Missouri, announced his candidacy in opposition to Edwards and secured Whig endorsement. Edwards still won by 5,000 votes, but it was the closest margin of any Democratic candidate in the 1840s.

The Constitutional Convention of 1845

The agitation over reapportionment and other issues led to the calling of a constitutional convention in November 1845 to draft a new basic law for Missouri. The constitution that it proposed was a mixed bag reflecting the deep-seated political divisions within the state. On legislative reapportionment it continued the policy of each county having one representative but allowed the more populous ones additional seats under a ratio system with no restriction on the total. It greatly limited the legislature's powers to charter banks and corporations or incur debts, reflecting the group's strong rural bias. Circuit judges were to be elected although the governor would continue to appoint state supreme court judges, but both were limited to set terms: six years for the former, and twelve years for the latter. In line with broadening democratic concepts, the General Assembly was to establish and finance free public schools through the use of state monies. All future constitutional amendments were to be approved by popular referendum. The convention submitted its own handiwork to the people in August 1846, only to have it narrowly turned down. Too many diverse groups opposed the various changes.

The entire procedure was not without benefit, however, as the legislature undertook some corrective measures through the amending process over the next few years. It had already passed legislation establishing congressional districts in 1845. Four years later it approved a provision for reapportionment similar to that proposed in the defeated constitution. Then in 1851 it provided for the popular election of all judges from the supreme court down and set their terms at six years while making the offices of secretary of state, attorney general, auditor, treasurer, and registrar of lands elective for four-year terms. Two years later it undertook the financing of public schools with state monies.

Benton and Texas

While Missouri made strides toward greater democracy through these changes, events were occurring outside the state that would have a profound effect on its political future. The legislature returned both Atchison and Benton to the Senate in November 1844, but Old Bullion had the closest contest of his career since his first election in 1820. He had alienated himself from many of his constituents on a national issue thrust into the 1844 election: the annexation of Texas. The Texas question had been simmering since that area gained its independence from Mexico eight years earlier. President John Tyler had worked hard to secure a treaty that provided for annexation on the eve of the election. Benton disliked the Tyler treaty because it had been drawn up by his old enemy, Secretary of State John C. Calhoun, whom he accused of using Texas to advance the cause of slavery and thereby disrupt the Union. Old Bullion also feared war with Mexico if annexation was carried out. Most Missourians, on the other hand, wanted Texas regardless of the consequences. Among these were Senator Atchison, an ardent expansionist, and several members of the Central Clique.

The Democratic party endorsed annexation at its national convention that year and nominated as its candidate for the presidency James K. Polk of Tennessee, a strong advocate of such a policy. In the election that followed, Polk defeated Henry Clay, the Whig candidate, who had been lukewarm on the issue. Benton opposed without success an attempt by outgoing President Tyler to annex Texas by joint resolution of Congress that winter. By the summer of 1845 the Lone Star Republic had become a part of the United States.

The Mexican War

Mexico severed diplomatic relations with the United States in protest and when efforts at negotiation failed the following winter, war broke out between the two countries along the Rio Grande in May 1846. Governor Edwards soon called for volunteers to join an expedition being organized by General Stephen W. Kearny to capture Santa Fe. There was a strong response, and Kearny's army of 1,600 that set out over the Santa Fe Trail included some 400 Missourians. Colonel Alexander W. Doniphan of Liberty commanded the First Missouri Volunteers. Santa Fe was taken without a fight, and Kearny left Doniphan in charge there while he went on to California. In September an additional 1,200 Missourians arrived under Colonel Sterling Price.

Doniphan now undertook expeditions against the warring Navajos and persuaded them to sign a peace treaty in early December.

Taking 500 men, he then moved into the neighboring province of Chihuahua where he scored two significant victories over larger Mexican forces and occupied El Paso and the capital, Chihuahua City. Covered with glory, Doniphan and his troops returned to St. Louis in July 1847 after being discharged in New Orleans. They received tumultuous welcomes there and in other cities across Missouri.

Among those who greeted them with lengthy speeches were Senators Atchison and Benton. The latter had supported the war reluctantly at first, believing that insufficient efforts had been made to work out differences peacefully. Later Benton suggested himself as a combination military leader-diplomat to head an expedition to take Mexico City and arrange a peace settlement. President Polk favored this idea, but it fell through when Congress refused to create the position of Lieutenant General which Benton insisted upon having for himself. in the end Major General Winfield Scott received the military leadership of the expedition while the diplomatic responsibility was entrusted to Nicholas Trist, a clerk in the State Department. Scott's army captured Mexico City in September 1847, but it took Trist until February 1848 to negotiate a peace treaty with Mexican authorities. The Treaty of Guadalupe Hidalgo confirmed the annexation of Texas and transferred to the United States the territory between there and the Pacific Ocean. Out of this conflict would arise a new issue—in reality the old one supposedly laid to rest by the Missouri Compromise, namely, whether slavery should be extended into new territories. It would create additional friction, as we shall see in Chapter Seven, and lead to Benton's removal from the Senate, an open fracturing of the old Jacksonian coalition, and continuous political turmoil in the 1850s.

Suggestions for Reading

The best general study on Missouri during the Jacksonian period is Perry McCandless, *A History of Missouri, Vol. II, 1820 to 1860*, rev. ed., Columbia, University of Missouri Press, 2000. The principal biography of Thomas Hart Benton is William N. Chambers, *Old Bullion Benton: Senator from the New West*, Boston, Little Brown, 1972. His later rival for political power is covered in William E. Parrish, *David Rice Atchison of Missouri: Border Politician*, Columbia, University of Missouri Press, 1961. Benton's relation to state politics has been well analyzed in Robert E. Shalhope, "Thomas Hart Benton and Missouri State Politics: A Re-Examination," *The Bulletin*, April 1969. For a study of the political opposition, one should read John V. Mering, *The Whig Party in Missouri*, Columbia, University of Missouri Press, 1967. Its leader is the subject of Marvin R. Cain, *Lincoln's Attorney General: Edward Bates of Missouri*, Columbia, University of Missouri Press, 1965. For a discussion of the state's role in banking and other economic policies, see James Neal Primm, *Economic Policy in the Development of a Western State, Missouri 1820–1860*, Cambridge, Harvard University Press, 1954. An interesting study of an important aspect of Missouri life during this era is Dick Steward, *Duels and the Roots of Violence in Missouri*, Columbia, University of Missouri Press, 2000. Stephen C. LeSueur, *The 1838 Mormon War in Missouri*, Columbia, University of Missouri Press, 1987, is an excellent study of that conflict. The best general history of the Mormons is Leonard J. Arrington and Davis Bitton, *The Mormon Experience—A History of the Latter-Day Saints*, New York, Vintage Books, 1980. Missourians' participation in the Mexican War is best related in Joseph C. Dawson III, *Doniphan's Epic March: The 1st Missouri Volunteers in the Mexican War*, Lawrence, University of Kansas Press, 1999. A good biography of its leader if Roger D. Launius, *Alexander William Doniphan: Portrait of a Missouri Moderate*, Columbia, University of Missouri Press, 1997.

Slavery in Missouri

As mentioned in an earlier chapter, the first black slaves were introduced into Missouri from Santo Domingo by the French in 1720 to work the lead mines. By the time of the statehood crisis, slavery had become an ingrained part of Missouri's economic and social life. It is impossible to defend the institution from the perspective of late twentieth century America, but most Missourians of 130 years ago simply accepted it with little question as an integral aspect of their lives. Given the French and Spanish background, which included slave labor and the migration of the bulk of Missouri's early American population from the southern states where slavery had already been long established as an economic and social "necessity," this is not too surprising.

Legal Basis for Slavery

Although some Indian slavery had existed under the French and the Spanish, the few vestiges that remained had pretty well died out during the territorial period. The state supreme court officially declared Indian slavery illegal in 1834. Hence to Missourians, *slave* and *black* became interchangeable terms. All blacks were presumed to be slaves unless they could prove otherwise. Missouri law defined a black as anyone whose grandfather or grandmother had been African; but to most whites, any black ancestry was sufficient to make any biracial person a suspected slave.

In accepting the fact of slavery, the Missouri Constitution of 1820 assumed that slaves were the personal property of their owners. It provided that no slave could be emancipated or set free without the express agreement of the owner and only with appropriate compensation for the loss. Slave owners might manumit or free a slave voluntarily, but in so doing they had to guarantee that the individual was mentally stable and would not become a public charge. Slave owners, if freeing a slave during their own lifetime, must furnish that individual with formal proof signed either by two witnesses or certified by a justice of the peace. Some slaveholders freed slaves out of kindness or because of certain special acts that the slaves may have performed for them. The large number of biracial persons among those manumitted would suggest that these might be the slave owner's children by an African woman. Others allowed slaves to accumulate money in a variety of ways, which might then be used to buy their freedom. Some, especially in the 1850s, freed their slaves because the institution now conflicted with their political views. Most, if they were going to do anything of the sort, arranged to free their slaves through their wills.

Occasionally a slave might be freed by act of the legislature if there were special circumstances. Much more frequently a slave who believed that he or she was being held illegally would resort to the courts to secure freedom. These cases might involve violations of wills or the kidnapping of free blacks. Most common were suits involving slaves who had been taken into territory made free under the Northwest Ordinance of 1787 and the Missouri Compromise and then returned to Missouri. The courts were fairly liberal in their interpretation of these cases, and a number of slaves had been freed before the famous Dred Scott decision of 1857 changed all that. (See Chapter 7.) All told, however, only a few hundred Missouri slaves, constituting less than one-tenth of one percent of the total, were manumitted in the pre–Civil War era.

Laws Affecting Slaves

One of the first laws passed by the General Assembly in 1821 was a general slave code to regulate the system. Based primarily on that of Virginia, this established the concept of slaves as personal property and gave owners the right to sell or trade them as they wished. A slave, on the other hand, could not hold property nor buy or sell anything without the owner's consent. A particular concern was liquor. Anyone found guilty of having sold any alcohol to a slave without the owner's consent might be held liable for damages if that slave became drunk or died because of it. Slaves had no right to sue in court, unless it was to seek their freedom under the circumstances mentioned above, nor could they testify in court against a white in any

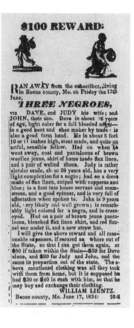

$100 REWARD:

RAN AWAY from the subscriber, living
in Boone county, Mo. on Friday the 13th
June,

THREE NEGROES,

viz DAVE, and JUDY his wife; and
JOHN, their son. Dave is about 32 years
of age, light color for a full blooded negro—
is a good boot and shoe maker by trade : is
also a good farm hand. He is about 5 feet
10 or 11 inches high, stout made, and quite an
artful, sensible fellow. Had on when he
went away, coat and pantaloons of brown
woollen jeans, shirt of home made flax linen,
and a pair of welted shoes. Judy is rather
slender made, about 26 years old, has a very
light complexion for a negro; had on a dress
made of flax linen, striped with copperas and
blue; is a first rate house servant and seam-
stress, and a good spinner, and is very full of
affectation when spoken to. John is 9 years
old, very likely and well grown; is remark-
ably light colored for a negro, and is cross-
eyed. Had on a pair of brown jeans pantaloons, bleached flax linen shirt, and red flan-
nel one under it, and a new straw hat.
    I will give the above reward and all reas-
onable expenses, if secured in any part of
the State, so that I can get them again, or
$50 if taken within the State—$30 for Dave
alone, and $20 for Judy and John, and the
same in proportion out of the state. The a-
bove mentioned clothing was all they took
with them from home, but it is supposed he
had $30 or $40 in cash with him, so that he
may buy and exchange their clothing.
                    WILLIAM LIENTZ.
    Boone county, Mo. June 17, 1834:   52-8

circumstance. In some cases a slave might be allowed to tell his or her story to a white who would then take the witness stand on the slave's behalf.

Slaves were forbidden to hold any kind of meeting without their owner's permission, and even then the rule required that a white person be present. Under no circumstances could they bear arms, and any suspicion of rebellion or insurrection brought severe penalties. Slaves were subject to the state's criminal codes, with three penalties imposed in most instances: death for murder, intended murder, or insurrection; mutilation for other severe crimes; and whipping for most misdemeanors.

Beyond the crimes covered in the regular criminal code, the worst offenses committed by slaves were disobedience or disrespect for the slave owner or an attempt to escape. In most cases of this sort, the whip administered a punishment of at least thirty lashes. Persistent troublemakers found themselves "sold South," as the saying went, to work on the large labor gangs of the lower Mississippi Valley. Most slaves feared this more than physical punishment. Such slave reminiscences and other records as we have indicate that whippings were a common occurrence in the lives of Missouri slaves. The owner's word was law, and there was no appeal for those slaves who provoked anger. A slave's movements were quite restricted. Any slave found off the owner's farm without a pass authorizing an errand could be assumed to be running away and punished accordingly. County courts sometimes organized patrols to hunt down slaves where trouble was suspected, and these units had virtually unlimited powers of search and arrest. Beyond all these measures, town and county governments would frequently pass laws thought necessary for slave control.

Although slaves were considered property and severely restricted in their movements and privileges, they were not completely helpless. The Constitution of 1820 required the General Assembly to "oblige the owners of slaves to treat them with humanity, and to abstain from all injuries to them extending to life or limb." Slaves did have the right to trial by jury should they be suspected of crime although, as already mentioned, slaves could not testify against a white person even in their own defense. While owners had virtually complete control over their slaves under ordinary circumstances, the law specifically forbade a white to mistreat a black who belonged to someone else, and cases occasionally arose of whites being tried in such instances. Slave owners varied; some were cruel, others highly protective. Many were both, depending upon the circumstances. As property, slaves lived a life of constant toil and uncertainty. At the slightest whim the owner could administer the lash or decide to sell the slave to the farmer next door or to a slave trader who could carry the slave hundreds of miles away.

Geographical Distribution of Slavery

Slavery in Missouri generally followed the river systems from the southeast corner up the entire line of the Mississippi and swinging west along the Missouri into the state's northwest corner. By far the strongest concentration of slaves was to be found in that group of central Missouri counties from Callaway west to Clay. The slave population of the state rose steadily in the forty years before the Civil War, from 10,222 in 1820 to 114,931 by 1860. But its growth did not keep pace with white population increase. While slaves made up 15 percent of the population in 1820, by 1860 the ratio had dropped to 9.7 percent. This made Missouri the second smallest slaveholding state next to Delaware. Over this same time span the biggest noticeable change was in St. Louis, where the black population increased considerably but was dwarfed by the tidal flood of whites. Slavery had its strongest gains in the counties from Callaway west to the Kansas border which were undergoing a similar surge of white population while retaining a basically agricultural economy.

There were at least a few slaves in every county. By 1860 Lafayette had the greatest number, with 6,374, while Howard had the highest concentration, with 36.4 percent of its population slave. Other large slaveholding counties were Boone, Callaway, New Madrid, Saline, and St. Louis. Slaves were sparsest in the Ozarks region. For example, Carter, Oregon, Stone, Ozark, and Shannon counties each had less than twenty-five slaves. This area was settled later by immigrants from the Appalachian hill country of North Carolina, Tennessee, and

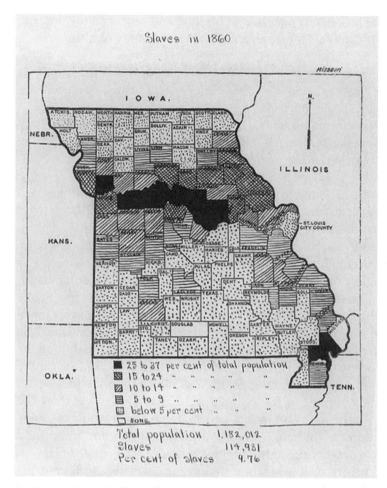

Distribution of slaves in Missouri, 1860. *Courtesy State Historical Society of Missouri*

Kentucky. Neither the land they left nor their new home lent themselves to the production of crops that required slave labor.

Average Slaveholdings and Type of Work

Missouri did not have the large slaveholding plantations worked by
hundreds of slaves that one might find farther south. Jabez Smith of
Jackson County is generally considered to have been Missouri's largest slave owner, with 244 slaves in 1850. But he was far from being
typical. More frequently the "large" slaveholder in the central Missouri region owned between ten and fifty slaves. Here hemp was the

114 **Missouri: The Heart of the Nation**

principal product. It was used in bagging and rope, and the demand was considerable. One observer in Lafayette County recalled,

> I can remember how twenty or thirty negroes would work in line cutting hemp with sickles. it was then left to rot till January. Then it was broken and the pith removed by means of a heavy crusher which the slaves swung up and down. He often received the lash if not breaking his one hundred pounds. I have seen a long line of wagons loaded with hemp extending from the river nearly to the court house.

Slaves were expected to break 100 pounds a day at a minimum. For anything in excess of that they would usually receive a penny a pound or some free time. This was called the "task system."

Missouri's second most important agricultural product was tobacco. Although some cotton was grown in south Missouri, it was done mainly on small farms, and slaves were seldom used in its cultivation. On those farms with large numbers of slaves, the owner might choose one of them to serve as the "driver" with the responsibility of directing the work of the others. In some cases where the owner had an older son, he might be given the job of handling the slave work schedule. The hiring of an "overseer," so familiar on the large plantations in the Deep South, was not common in Missouri.

Seventy percent of the state's slaveholders owned less than five slaves each. In many instances a person might own a family of slaves: father, mother, children. It was not uncommon that the father could work on a neighboring farm. In these cases the slaves performed general field work or house labor, depending upon the need, and frequently the master and his family would work side by side with them in the fields to scratch out a living from the Missouri dirt. Even in the larger slaveholding counties, most owners possessed only a few. In Boone County the 1860 census revealed 885 slaveholders with an average of 5.7 slaves among them while in neighboring Callaway 636 owners had an average of 4.67 slaves. In the latter, 173 held one slave each while another 102 had only two. As one commentator of the time remarked: "Every decent Missouri family has at least one, and usually from two to four, as house servants."

"Hiring Out"

Many owners "hired out" their slaves when they had more than they could use for one reason or another. This was a common practice in

St. Louis and the larger towns, but it also occurred in the countryside. Especially where a slave possessed a particular skill such as carpentry or stone masonry, he could be much in demand. Newspapers carried frequent announcements of slaves for hire, listing their skills if they had one. In addition to being hired for general or skilled labor in town, slaves were sometimes used to supplement riverboat crews if there was a shortage of free labor. Hired slaves were also used in mining, especially in the earlier periods of French and Spanish rule. At a later date, the Maramec Iron Works in Phelps County and similar outfits would often hire excess slaves from area farmers for semi-skilled and unskilled tasks.

While some owners may have looked on their slaves as a good investment in this regard, there is no evidence of deliberate planning along these lines. In many instances slaves for hire might be tied up in an estate settlement, with the widow or children of the deceased owner wishing to have cash income while waiting for the final disposition of the estate. Most slaves would be hired out under a specific contract that spelled out the term, the payment, and the abilities of the hirer for their maintenance. In a few cases the slave might be hired out for a short term to a neighboring farmer or someone in a nearby town. In such instances he might continue to reside with his owner at night or on weekends, especially if he had a wife or family. But usually hiring meant going to live elsewhere, with the hirer guaranteeing adequate lodging and good treatment. Most contracts would be for a year at a time. The fees themselves varied, depending upon the slave's value. Those with specific skills came higher. Harrison A. Trexler, who wrote the standard history of Missouri slavery, estimated that rentals averaged 14 percent of the slave's monetary worth.

Although the law specifically forbade the practice, some owners, especially in St. Louis and some of the larger towns, allowed slaves to make their own contracts. In these cases the slave could usually keep a certain percentage of the hiring fee. Many slaves saved the money they gained thereby to buy their own freedom and/or that of their families. Under various codes, owners who allowed their slaves this privilege might find themselves subject to fines of $20 to $100, but the law was difficult to enforce and so frequently ignored. The general fear seemed to be that such arrangements gave slaves too much freedom in terms of movement. An 1824 St. Louis editorial, for instance, complained: "Slaves hiring their own time of their masters . . . take upon themselves at once the airs of freemen and often resort to illicit modes to meet their monthly payments." Ten years later a St. Louis mass meeting was called to deal with the continuing problem and a committee was appointed to put a halt to the practice. There is little evidence that the group met with much success.

Slave Prices

One of the continuing arguments among historians and economists is whether or not slavery was an economically profitable system. Regardless of how one evaluates the question, it would appear that most Missourians, like their fellows elsewhere, thought that it was. As will be discussed later in this chapter and in Chapter 7, efforts to rid the state of slavery met with determined and successful resistance until the Civil War. The slave trade remained active and vigorous, and prices for slaves rose steadily. These varied from one area to another and depended upon the age and sex of the slave. In general, slave prices tripled between 1830 and 1860. In 1830 a male slave in good health and in his twenties or thirties would usually bring between $450 and $500; by the end of the period his price would average $1,300. A woman generally averaged about a fourth less. Children and older slaves brought considerably less because of their reduced labor value. The newspapers carried frequent notices of slave auctions or estate sales. In the lives of most Missourians who lived along the rivers, such sales were a common occurrence.

The Records of Slavery

What was it like to be a slave in Missouri before the Civil War? Much of our picture of slavery has come from records left by whites—farm accounts, probate proceedings, newspapers, diaries, letters, etc. Not many African slaves recorded their feelings. Few slaves could read or write—indeed it was illegal to teach them to do so after 1847—and consequently left no diaries or letters. A few wrote memoirs after the war, and we can catch a glimpse of slavery through their reflections. Ninety-six former Missouri slaves were interviewed in the 1930s as part of the Federal Writers' Project, a New Deal program to help unemployed writers. These black interviewees were advanced in years at the time. Most of them had been young children or in their early teens at the time of the Civil War, but their memories of slavery generally and of certain vivid incidents in particular come through

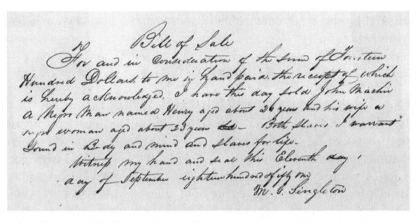

A slave bill of sale, 1851. *Western Historical Manuscripts, University of Missouri Columbia*

clearly. It is from such meager black sources that historians are beginning to piece together how blacks felt under slavery.

Slave Work Patterns

Rural slaves usually worked from sunup to sundown. William Wells Brown, a Missouri slave who escaped and wrote his memoirs, recalled that they were awakened at four o'clock in the morning by the ringing of a large bell. They had half an hour to eat their breakfast and get to the field, with a horn sounding at four thirty to indicate that the workday had begun. Anyone who showed up late was given ten lashes. This was an extreme situation, but regardless the workday was long and hard. House slaves usually got a little extra sleep, but their chores also began early with the preparation of breakfast and then carried through a variety of activities all day and often into the evening. Slaves in town had a varied schedule depending upon what was required of them. But in an age when everyone—white and black—worked long hours, few questioned the length of the workday. The law required that slaves be given Sunday as a free day, and many in Missouri received Saturday afternoons off as well. These were usually times for hunting or fishing or catching up with odd chores around the cabins. Many slaves recalled dancing and singing as major outlets in those moments they had for recreation. Horseshoes and other makeshift games also provided occasional entertainment. Brown recalled the occasion when his master "got religion," and suddenly some of the freedoms enjoyed on Sunday became restricted by the requirement that all of his slaves attend church services with him.

Religious Activities

Many slaves were highly religious. Where allowed to do so, they would attend their master's church, usually sitting in the balcony or at the back or side in a segregated section. In some cases, where permitted, they would gather in some centrally located field with perhaps one or two of their numbers doing informal preaching. In other cases they would be allowed to hold their own services in white churches on Sunday afternoons, but in all such instances some white person from the local community would be present to oversee the proceedings. In their own services, singing predominated, and here they would pour out their hearts with the spirituals whose music frequently was a carry-over from African rhythms but whose words came from the soul of their current experience.

Occasionally slaves might be allowed to attend "camp meetings," or religious revivals, which could stretch over several days in the off-season. They looked forward to these with eager anticipation because of the time off from work as well as for religious satisfaction. One former slave recalled such a meeting in Cooper County where the Africans constructed a "brush arbor" on one of the farms. This consisted of a series of forked poles that held a frame over which brush was placed to serve as a roof against excessive sun or rain. Slaves walked five or six miles to attend. Singing and praying predominated over preaching, and those attending were caught up in an emotional experience that helped to sustain them through their difficulties for another year.

Living Conditions

Regardless of the size of the work force, the slave quarters stood in back of the owner's house. These were frequently nothing more than one- or two-room shanties built of the cheapest lumber available, sometimes with dirt floors, sometimes elevated on puncheons that allowed for some storage underneath the floor. Eliza Overton recalled that her family's cabin in Ste. Genevieve County had "a corded bed, trundle bed to slip under the big bed to save room, home made split bottom chairs, tin-plates, wooden boxes and a fire-place."

Where no fireplace existed, the slaves had to rely on outdoor hearths for food preparation. The food supply usually consisted of what could be raised on the farm itself: hog jowls or bacon, turnip greens, potatoes, cabbage, beans. Occasionally this diet might be supplemented by molasses and coffee. There would also be homemade bread and fish caught from a nearby stream. Quantity varied from one place to another and sometimes with the season.

On holidays many owners would give extra rations, including whiskey sometimes, to help create a festive air. Several former slaves recalled Christmas as a particularly special time. Malinda Discus mentioned that if any of the slave children on her farm could get out the words "Christmas gift" that day to any of the master's family before they spoke to them it would mean a treat, usually some clothes or stick candy. August Smith, whose Pennsylvania Dutch owner was undoubtedly an exception, recalled that his master not only gave his slaves Christmas off but the entire month of January during which they were free "to go and come as much as we pleased." He remembered other special occasions on their Osage County farm such as

Missouri slave cabin. *Courtesy State Historical Society of Missouri*

"quiltin's, dancin', makin' rails, for days at a time." William Black, who grew up in Ralls County, recalled a time when the slaves thought their master had left the farm and they proceeded to have a party. Either the master got suspicious or came home early. Suddenly Black's sister looked up to see him at the edge of the crowd dressed up to look like a slave and observing their dancing. Once discovered he apparently joined in the festivities, for Black indicated that nothing came of the incident because the owner "had too good a time hisself."

Slave clothing was simple and usually homespun. Mark Discus remembered that during the summer down in Dade County they wore a "shift," which was a long, one-piece cotton garment somewhat like a nightshirt. In the winter they wore the castoff clothes of the owner's family. Marie Simpson recalled that on the Crawford County farm where she lived they raised their own sheep and spun the wool into yarn which they dyed with indigo secured from the drugstore in Steelville. All of the women sewed and made their own clothes from whatever scraps or materials they had available to them. Most slaves remember going barefoot in summer and usually well into cold weather. Their feet would crack and bleed and give them the most pain of any part of their body. In really cold weather they might have split-leather shoes with no lining, which did little to protect their feet.

Master-Slave Relationships

The personal relationships between master and slave varied from one situation to another. Many owners treated their slaves as fairly as conditions would allow. On small farms worked by one or two slave families a "patriarchal" atmosphere frequently prevailed with the owner and his family taking a strong personal interest in all aspects of their slaves' lives and activities and with this feeling being reciprocated with a deep loyalty on the part of the blacks. But even in such situations blacks knew there was a certain line beyond which they dared not step. They were still slaves and subject to any whim that might strike their owner or to any punishment he might care to hand out if they aroused his displeasure. Work on these farms was hard. It always seemed that there was more to do than there was labor available to do it. Many owners who had maintained good relationships with their slaves for years were amazed at how quickly these same blacks deserted them when the opportunity for freedom came. There were some blacks, on the other hand, who remained loyal to their owners long after emancipation.

Missouri had more than its share of cruel masters who did not hesitate to use the whip at the slightest infraction. one slave recalled being whipped for breaking an ax handle, several others for being what they called "too proud in spirit," which simply meant any display of independence. August Smith remembered a particularly mean owner on a neighboring farm who used the whip frequently and brutally. He kept his slaves hungry to such an extent that a seventy-year-old grandmother in desperation stole a chicken from his yard one night. When he caught her cooking it in her cabin, he forced her, in his anger, to get a spoon and drink the boiling water sip by sip until it was gone. She died that same night.

Slave Trading

One of the cruelest aspects of slavery was the ever-present threat of sale and possible separation from one's family. Such incidents were as prevalent in Missouri as they were in other places where slavery held sway. Slave traders made their rounds frequently, traveling the rivers to certain points and then covering the interior by stage or buggy. They would go among the various towns and farms buying any surplus that might be available. Local newspapers carried the announcement that traders were in the neighborhood. Those slaves gathered in the interior of the state would usually be taken to the St. Louis market, and, if not salable there, would be sent down the Mississippi River.

To be caught in the slave trader's web was a degrading situation for the blacks personally.

A country slave auction. *Courtesy State Historical Society of Missouri*

When en route along roads or on board a boat, slaves were treated like cattle, with the males usually kept in chains. The pens in which they were held pending sale were barren and cold although the slaves were usually well fed to keep them in good shape for sale. Most slave traders sought to present their wares in the best light possible. William Wells Brown, who at one time had been hired out to assist a trader, recalled being ordered "to have the old men's whiskers shaved off, and the gray hairs plucked out where they were not too numerous, in which case he had a preparation of blacking to color it, and with a blacking-brush we would put it on." Mark Discus remembered being auctioned from a big stump at a young age. He recalled that they greased the bodies of the older slaves to make them glisten. Buyers would stick pins in their muscles to test them and examine their teeth carefully. Being sold was not a pleasant experience.

Most slave sales in out-state Missouri, however, were local matters and in many cases involved the settlement of estates. Owners frequently died without wills and so in debt that their property, including slaves, had to be sold to clear the estate. Often the widow simply could not maintain the household or farm after her husband's death. One such case involved the slaves of Hiram Sloan of Cape Girardeau, who died in 1855. He had had a good relationship with his slaves—

some twenty-four in all—but the widow could not keep them. The night before the sale they crowded into her home to ask what was to become of them and whether any attempt would be made to keep families together. Mrs. Sloan assured them that the auctioneer had been told to avoid separations if at all possible. The next morning she personally walked the courthouse corridors, where the sale took place, visiting with friends who had come to buy and expressing her hope that they would purchase with an eye to keeping families together. As it

William Wells Brown, Missouri slave who escaped to become a prominent author and lecturer in the antislavery movement. *Courtesy State Historical Society of Missouri* turned out, her wish and that of the slaves was granted in every case. But not all slaves sold were so fortunate, and the separation of husband from wife and mother from child was not uncommon. The heartbreak and pain in such cases may well be imagined, for in many instances they would never see each other again.

The Free Blacks

In addition to its 114,931 slaves in 1860, Missouri had 3,572 free blacks. Of these approximately 60 percent lived in St. Louis city and county. Most of the rest were scattered in other urban locations around the state. Hannibal, for instance, had 44 out of the 78 living in Marion County, with another 12 in Palmyra. Cole County had a small group, most of whom lived in Jefferson City. Boone County had 53, with most of these in Columbia. Missouri's free blacks tended to live in urban areas because of the greater economic opportunities there.

White Missourians did not look favorably upon free blacks as already noted in the controversy over the Second Missouri Compromise. They saw them as potential troublemakers who set a bad example for their slaves and were an ever-present reminder to the slaves of the possibilities of freedom. Free blacks were constantly suspected of being willing to aid and abet escaping slaves. Beyond this there was a strong racist strain among Missouri's whites—typical of most of the country in the nineteenth century—who pictured any sizable proportion of free blacks as an economic and social threat.

Because of these attitudes, state and local governmental authorities placed all kinds of restrictions on the free black population. Under an 1835 law, free blacks who could not prove citizenship from one of the other states (something hard to do) had to obtain a license from their local county court to reside in Missouri. This required posting a sizable bond and giving assurance that the person was of good behavior and employable. The license could be immediately revoked if the black was caught in a felony or keeping a gambling establishment. Any black who was picked up without a license might be sent back into slavery as a runaway by a justice of the peace. An 1843 law went even further by limiting free blacks in Missouri to those who were natives or citizens of other states or who had lived in Missouri since 1840. Others should stay out. Four years later the legislature took the final step in violating the Second Missouri Compromise by prohibiting the further immigration of any free blacks into the state. At the same time it outlawed any form of education for this group, with heavy fines and possible imprisonment for those caught teaching them.

Free blacks found their civil rights greatly restricted. They could own property, including slaves, and enter into contracts. They could sue and be sued, but they could not testify against whites in court nor did they enjoy the right of habeas corpus as did other free persons. They could not hold public meetings unless a white person was present. Nor could they have any kind of weapon or ammunition without a special license from a justice of the peace. Finally, they did not have the right to vote or hold public office.

For all these restrictions, free blacks did manage to carve out a place for themselves in Missouri society. Although not numerous, they made a definite contribution to the economic life of St. Louis and other river towns. They pursued a variety of occupations. Some of them had jobs on the river as stewards, engineers, or firefighters. Many in St. Louis worked as servants until displaced by Irish and German immigrants in the 1850s. There were thirty-three free black barbers in the city, and several owned elegant "tonsorial parlors" with an exclusive white clientele. The 1850 census listed eleven seamstresses, including Elizabeth Keckley, who later found service with Mrs. Abraham Lincoln in Washington and left her confidential memoirs of that experience.

There were several prominent free black ministers in St. Louis. Two in particular wielded considerable influence. John Berry Meachum had arrived there in 1815 and with the help of a white missionary, John Mason Peck, organized the First African Baptist Church. At the time of his death in 1854, the church had a membership of more than 500, free and slave, with a Sunday school attendance averaging between 150 and 300. Meachum was much more than a minister to his congregation. He served as the real leader of the city's black community, working constantly to improve their economic and educational opportunities. When the legislature passed its antiblack education law in 1847, he purchased a steamboat and turned it into a "Freedom School." Operating in the middle of the Mississippi River, he contended that his school was under federal rather than state jurisdiction. Meachum was also active in purchasing slaves, freeing them, and helping them find jobs whereby they could repay him to help buy someone else. The black minister's spiritual successor was J. Richard Anderson, who got his early training in the Peck-Meachum Sunday school and later helped organize the Second African Baptist Church. He carried forward his mentor's work into the war years, dying in 1863. At his funeral more than 175 vehicles made their way to the cemetery carrying those who would honor him.

A number of free blacks managed to acquire considerable property. Meachum for instance had purchased two brick homes and an Illinois farm by the late 1830s. A directory of the "colored aristocracy" of St. Louis was published in 1858 by Cyprian Clamorgan, presumably a prominent barber and descendant of one of St. Louis's old-line free black families. It identified other prosperous free blacks, including Mrs. Sarah Hazlett, who owned property worth $70,000 and sent her two daughters to boarding school in Philadelphia; Samuel Mordecai, a former riverboat steward and gambler who "is good for one hundred thousand dollars when 'flush'"; and William Johnson, Sr., a barber and real estate speculator whose wealth Clamorgan places at over $100,000 while the 1860 census estimates it more modestly at $21,000. Many of the leading free blacks could trace their roots back to French territorial days with their ancestors being the products of a mixed marriage or liaison. Their property holdings came down to them through inheritance. Whatever their circumstances, Clamorgan leaves a clear picture of a well-structured black society in St. Louis. Similar examples, but on a smaller scale, could be cited in other Missouri towns with a free black community. One of the most prominent out-state blacks was Hiram Young of Independence, who made a small fortune with his wagon factory and blacksmithing business from those settlers heading west to Oregon and California.

The free blacks were concerned for both the spiritual and educational welfare of their community. St. Louis had five African churches—three Baptist and two Methodist—with a combined membership of nearly 1,500 including numerous slaves. Hannibal had an all-black Second Baptist Church, but there is no indication of any other such congregations in out-state Missouri. The attendance of slaves at their owners' churches has already been noted. Most congregations had a mixed membership, with the church records noting equal participation in the various ordinances.

Although legally prohibited after 1847, black schools did exist in St. Louis and occasionally elsewhere. Blacks used their Sunday schools for broader educational purposes. The Catholic Church, which had numerous African members, promoted special classes taught by nuns from time to time, depending upon how strongly the law was enforced. Meachum's Freedom School has already been noted. There were others in various underground locations, most of them charging a monthly tuition of one dollar. Out-state black schools are known to have existed at various times in Jefferson City and Glasgow, where they were taught by Quakers, and at Hannibal in the Second Baptist Church.

Most whites feared and distrusted free blacks as evidenced by the attempts at restricting their numbers in Missouri. One nongovernmental effort to reduce the black population was the organization in 1825 of a group that became the Missouri Colonization Society. Part of a nationwide movement, this was an attempt by prominent St. Louis whites to raise funds with which to send free blacks to Africa. It worked closely with local churches, especially the Methodists, around the state to carry out its program; but it had little overall success. Probably not more than 100 Missouri blacks were assisted by its efforts in the thirty-five years prior to the Civil War—a record which generally paralleled that of the national organization. The group made its greatest headway in the 1850s, and the legislature even appropriated $3,000 to its work in 1856 at a time (as we shall see in the next chapter) when there was increasing concern to restrict free blacks even more drastically.

Antislavery Activity

Throughout its history there were many who tended to associate the colonization society with abolitionism even though its leaders were quick to assure the public that they were only interested in helping blacks already freed. The extent of antislavery sentiment in Missouri prior to 1850 is difficult to assess. It was noted in Chapter 3 that there had been some opposition to slavery on moral and economic grounds at the time of the 1820 constitutional convention. Most of the arguments then centered on the question of restricting further slave immigration into the state. Those favoring such a move hoped to phase out slavery gradually by reducing the numbers of slaves through attrition and eventually emancipating those who remained. "Restrictionists" were few in number. Many belonged to religious sects such as the Friends of Humanity, and none of them secured election to the 1820 convention.

During the next three decades few Missourians openly questioned slavery. If they did talk about ending it, they spoke usually in long-range terms. Even nonslaveholders tended to defend the system because of their hopes that they might someday acquire bondspeople or simply as necessary to preserve an "enlightened" social order. Some emancipationist sentiment reappeared in the mid-1830s with the increased immigration of northern settlers. Elijah P. Lovejoy, a native of Maine who had studied at Princeton Theological Seminary in New Jersey, represented that influence. He arrived in St. Louis in November 1833 and began publishing the *St. Louis Observer* as a Presbyterian newspaper. A man of strong opinion, Lovejoy filled the columns of his journal with attacks on Catholics and antislavery sentiment, which quickly aroused the anger of many in the community. Matters came to a head in May 1836, when Lovejoy denounced the lynching by burning of a mulatto sailor Francis McIntosh, who had been charged with stabbing a police officer. When a local judge, who happened to be a Catholic, came to the defense of the mob, Lovejoy condemned him for failing to defend McIntosh's civil rights. The minister-editor had already decided to seek a more friendly climate in Illinois, but before he could make the move a mob attacked his newspaper office and threw his printing press into the Mississippi River. Lovejoy moved to Alton, Illinois, and resumed his efforts only to meet continued resistance. He died there at the hands of a mob in November 1837 still clinging staunchly to his beliefs.

Emotions were running high during this same period in Marion County. The Presbyterians had recently established a new college near Palmyra, and some of its leadership apparently had antislavery leanings. In the spring of 1836, the Rev. David Nelson, the school's president, read in open assembly a letter from John Muldrow, one of the trustees. Muldrow offered to establish a $10,000 fund from which to reimburse slave owners if the government would authorize an emancipation program. He challenged others to add to it. Muldrow and a proslavery citizen came to blows with the latter being seriously hurt. The college trustee stood trial and was acquitted; the minister-president fled the state. Simultaneously, angry citizens drove two others from the county when it was discovered that they had been receiving literature from the American Colonization Society.

Five years later in 1841, Marion County again became the scene of considerable agitation when a trio of abolitionists crossed the Mississippi River from Quincy, Illinois, where they had been studying at an antislavery college. The three had made plans for a rendezvous with several slaves whom they planned to lead to freedom. The blacks they proposed to help had informed their masters out of fear, with the result that the abolitionist trio found sheriff's deputies waiting for them. A sensational trial followed during which the slaves, who could not openly testify in court under Missouri law, told their story to their masters, who in turn relayed it from the witness box. The three abolitionists were sentenced to twelve years in the state penitentiary where one of them, George Thompson, who became known as the "prison bard," wrote the story of their misadventures. It circulated widely in the North as an antislavery tract. In March 1843, a proslavery vigilante group crossed the river in the opposite direction and burned the college which had nurtured the trio. Escaping in the darkness, the arsonists were never brought to trial. The whole episode finally closed in 1846 when Governor John C. Edwards pardoned all three of the men originally involved. They had served five years of their twelve-year sentence.

This incident caused widespread repercussions throughout Marion and other counties along the border. Many townships organized vigilante groups to stop strangers and question them about their activities. If they could not give a good account for themselves, they would be forcibly escorted to the state line with a warning of fifty lashes if they tried to return. Any blacks found away from home were also suspect as runaways unless they could produce a pass from their owner. When a constitutional convention met in 1845, a lone delegate introduced an antislavery petition under the obligation, so he said, that a constituent had given it to him. The convention rejected it sixty-four to zero and included in its final document a provision requiring all newly freed slaves to leave Missouri. The voters rejected the constitution, but this whole action was symptomatic of the times.

The Mexican War which broke out the following year, with its potential for adding vast territories to the United States, gave new life to the antislavery cause nationally through the birth of the Free Soil movement. This ushered in a decade and a half of turbulence which ended in civil war. This controversy had a direct and forceful impact on Missouri as will be seen in the next chapter.

Suggestions for Reading

The standard although dated work on Missouri slavery is Harrison A. Trexler, *Slavery in Missouri, 1804–1865,* Baltimore, Johns Hopkins Press, 1914. Important recent studies are R. Douglas Hurt, *Agriculture and Slavery in Missouri's Little Dixie,* Columbia, University of Missouri Press, 1992, and George R. Lee, *Slavery North of St. Louis,* Canton, Lewis County Historical Society, 2000. These should be supplemented with the following articles in the *Missouri Historical Review:* George R. Lee, "Slavery and Emancipation in Lewis County, Missouri," April 1971; Philip V. Scarpino, "Slavery in Callaway County, Missouri, 1845–1855," October 1976 and April 1977; James William McGettigan, Jr., "Boone County Slaves: Sales, Estate Divisions and Families, 1820–1865," January 1978 and April 1978; Dennis Nag-lich, "The Slave System and the Civil War in Rural Prairieville," April 1993; and Barbara L. Green, "Slave Labor at the Meramec Iron Works, 1828–1850," January 1979. Two articles in *The Bulletin* are also helpful: Lyle W. Dorsett, "Slaveholding in Jackson County, Missouri," October 1963, and Lloyd A. Hunter, "Slavery in St. Louis, 1804–1860," July 1974, as is Robert Moore, Jr. "A Ray of Hope Extinguished: St. Louis Slave Suits for Freedom," *Gateway Heritage,* Winter 1994. A poignant account of one slave's experience is Melton A. McLaurin, *Celia, A Slave,* Athens, University of Georgia Press, 1991. The slaves' own stories are told in George P. Rawick, *The American Slave: A Composite Autobiography,* Supplement, Series I, 12 vols., West-port, CT, Greenwood Press, 1977. The Missouri stories are in Vol. II.

Missouri's free blacks are discussed in Donnie D. Bellamy, "Free Blacks in Antebellum Missouri, 1820–1860," *Missouri Historical Review,* January 1973; and Judy Day and M. James Kedro, "Free Blacks in St. Louis: Antebellum Condition, Emancipation, and the Postwar Era," *The Bulletin,* January 1974. One should also consult Cyprian Clamorgan, *The Colored Aristocracy of St. Louis,* ed. Julie Winch, Columbia, University of Missouri Press, 1999.

Benjamin G. Merkel, *The Anti-Slavery Controversy in Missouri, 1819–1865,* St. Louis, Washington University, 1942, remains the standard treatment of that subject. One of the movement's leading figures is dealt with in Merton L. Dillon, *Elijah P. Lovejoy, Abolitionist Editor,* Urbana, University of Illinois Press, 1961. Opposition to its efforts is detailed in Bonnie E. Laughlin, "'Endangering the Peace of

Society': Abolitionist Agitation and Mob Reaction in St. Louis and Alton, 1836–1838," *Missouri Historical Review,* October 2000. An interesting aspect of the movement is discussed in Donnie D. Bellamy, "The Persistence of Colonization in Missouri," *Missouri Historical Review,* October 1977.

Political Turmoil
and the Kansas War

A lthough the questions of currency, reapportionment, and Texas annexation had shown that Senator Thomas Hart Benton's firm hold on the loyalties of Missouri Democrats might be weakening in the 1840s, the party went into the 1848 election campaign united. They chose Austin A. King of Ray County, a soft-money man who had stayed generally aloof from intraparty quarrels, as their compromise candidate for governor while balancing the remainder of their ticket with representatives of the various factions. Their convention adopted strong resolutions of support for Benton. King easily defeated the Whig candidate, James S. Rollins of Boone County, in the August state elections with a margin of 15,000 out of 83,000 votes cast.

The Jackson Resolutions

Rumblings of discontent began to be heard concerning Benton, however, in the interim before the national elections in November. While Senator David Rice Atchison and other party regulars campaigned enthusiastically for Lewis Cass of Michigan, the Democratic nominee for President, Old Bullion remained in Washington where he officially endorsed the party ticket but did nothing to help it. Missouri's senior senator found himself on the horns of a dilemma in the 1848 election. His close friend, former President Martin Van Buren, had led a split from the regular Democrats to organize the Free Soil party behind his own candidacy. This group took its name from its opposition to the extension of slavery into the newly acquired territories in the West. Cass and the regular Democrats, on the other hand, favored the doctrine of popular sovereignty by which the people in the territories would decide the issue of slavery for themselves.

Many in Missouri believed that Benton could have talked Van Buren out of this dangerous schism. The senator did not believe that the Free Soil movement had any chance of success, although he agreed with many of its goals. To him it simply was not feasible that the western territories could sustain slavery economically because of their climate and topography. Consequently it jeopardized the Union to agitate the question, and he wanted to avoid it. Yet he refused a chance to visit Van Buren personally and try to influence him. Benton was hurt further when his ally, Frank Blair, established a Free Soil newspaper in St. Louis and worked actively for Van Buren. When the Free Soil defection threw the national election to the Whigs, many in Missouri and elsewhere could not refrain from condemning the senator for his inactivity.

When the General Assembly convened in December 1848, the Democratic majority decided to lay the issue on the line with Benton. Led by Claiborne F. Jackson of Saline County, long a leader in the Central Clique, they overwhelmingly passed resolutions asserting that Congress did not have the authority to limit slavery in the territories and upholding popular sovereignty. The Jackson Resolutions also denounced antislavery agitation by the northern states which, they claimed, threatened the peace established by the Missouri Compromise. While sanctioning the extension of a compromise line through the new territories, if that would keep the peace, the resolutions concluded by vowing that Missouri should act jointly with the rest of the South if "northern fanaticism" continued. To make certain that Benton understood their message, the Democratic leadership included an instruction that the state's senators act in conformity with their resolutions.

Frank Blair immediately charged that a plot had been laid by Senator John C. Calhoun of South Carolina, a longtime Benton enemy, to get rid of the Missouri senator. According to this scenario, Claiborne Jackson and his fellow legislators were but pawns in Calhoun's game. In reality, the Central Clique was moving toward the belief that Benton had ruled Missouri Democratic politics too long; they saw him as being too Washington oriented and hence out of touch with his constituents' concerns. The Jackson Resolutions were meant to be a warning, but Old Bullion took them differently. He wrote a supporter from Washington: "I shall be out among them as soon as Congress adjourns & drive them out to open war."

The "Southern Address"

While the Missouri legislature was passing the Jackson Resolutions, Senator Calhoun was attempting to unify southern senators and members of the House in Washington against a resolution passed by the House of Representatives to outlaw the slave trade in the District of Columbia. After numerous meetings, a small group of them hammered out a statement called the "Southern Address." It traced the history of northern antislavery offenses culminating in the Free Soil movement, which it saw as an attempt to deny the South's "just claim" to its share of the new territories. The address left it to the southern states to decide what should be done to counteract this northern aggression. Senator Benton refused from the outset to have anything to do with this document, and in the end only 48 of 121 southern congressmen signed it. But prominent among the authors and signers was Senator Atchison of Missouri, who had been coming increasingly under Calhoun's sway. When Benton threw down the gauntlet to the Missouri Democratic leadership a few months later, it was Atchison who took it up.

Benton's Appeal

While Benton had always agreed previously with the idea that the legislature, which elected the state's senators, could instruct them on issues before the Congress, he refused to accept the Jackson Resolutions. He returned to St. Louis in the spring of 1849 for the first time in two years. On May 9 he issued an appeal through the press to "The People of Missouri," asking them to overrule the action of the General Assembly by their votes in the next election. Benton then launched a speaking tour across the state in which he spelled out the reasons for his action. He accused Calhoun of working with Missouri's dissident Democrats to try to unseat him and argued that the Jackson Resolutions were divisive of the Union because they sought "to array one-half of it against the other." Benton defended the right of Congress to legislate regarding slavery in the territories. He then took the fatal step of personally embracing Free Soilism by declaring his opposition to the extension of slavery and announcing that if it did not already exist in Missouri he would oppose its introduction there. To the state's Democratic leadership this was heresy of the worst kind. Benton recognized this and proclaimed "between them and me, henceforth and forever, *a high wall and deep ditch!* and no communication, no compromise, no caucus with them." Rank-and-file Missourians would do better to equate their economic interests with those of northern workers, he asserted, than to line up with southern traitors.

Atchison, Jackson, and other state Democratic leaders now criss-crossed the state to answer Benton's charges and ride him out of the party. They pictured him as selling out to Free Soilism and thereby going contrary to the best interests of Missouri's citizens. Although the election for a new legislature was still a year distant, the summer of 1849 bore all the appearances of a campaign year as rallies were held on both sides of the issue in nearly every county. Old Bullion returned to Washington in November full of confidence, but Atchison assured a friend that his colleague "has as good a chance to be made Pope, as to be elected Senator."

That winter Congress struggled with numerous issues including the petition of California for admission to the Union as a free state and the establishment of some kind of territorial government for New Mexico and Utah. After ten months the Congress agreed to the Compromise of 1850, which brought California into the Union on its own terms and organized New Mexico and Utah as territories with the provision that popular sovereignty would determine the issue of slavery there. In nearly every vote Benton and Atchison found themselves on opposite sides. And while the debates went on in Congress, they continued in Missouri as well.

Benton's Downfall

After being a very weak minority for the past decade and a half, the Whig party suddenly became a force to be reckoned with as the balance wheel between the two Democratic factions. It was helped by a new Whig administration in Washington that could dispense local patronage. The August 1850 election returns revealed significant Whig gains as the rival Democratic groups frequently ran separate candidates. The Whigs carried three of Missouri's five congressional seats and gained a plurality in the new General Assembly over what came to be known as the pro-Benton and the anti-Benton Democrats. When the legislature met in January 1851, it struggled for twelve days and

forty ballots before compromising on Henry S. Geyer, a proslavery Whig from St. Louis, as Benton's replacement. Throughout the balloting the followers of Old Bullion remained faithful to their leader, but in the end the anti-Benton men swung to Geyer in return for a Whig pledge to support their candidates for all other offices that the General Assembly had to bestow. Thomas Hart Benton's senatorial career of thirty years had come to an end.

The Election of 1852

Realizing the danger of continued division after the election debacle of 1850, the Democrats managed to patch up their differences two years later and unite behind Sterling Price of Chariton County as their candidate for governor. A hero of the Mexican War, he handily defeated the Whig candidate, James Winston of Springfield. The Democrats also restored unity at the national level as the Free Soilers rejoined the regulars to elect Franklin Pierce of New Hampshire as President. One small cloud appeared on the Missouri horizon, however, as Thomas Hart Benton made a comeback of sorts by winning election to the national House of Representatives from Missouri's first district. He promptly indicated that he would be a candidate for the Senate when Atchison's term expired in 1855.

The latter meanwhile had moved increasingly to the foreground of southern leadership in the Senate. He had been chosen almost continuously since 1849 as president pro tem of that body and wielded considerable power behind the scenes in committee assignments and the flow of Senate business. He belonged to a close-knit group of southern senators who boarded together and, because of their seniority, controlled several of the key committees. The

Atchison group was definitely one to be reckoned with in a new Democratic administration.

The Kansas-Nebraska Act

During the 1852 campaign a new issue had begun to stir along the western border of Missouri that would have far-reaching consequences for the future of both state and national politics. Interest had been increasing in the organization of the area beyond Missouri known generally as Nebraska Territory. This region had been consigned to various Indian tribes in the 1820s and 1830s and thus closed to white settlement. But with the rapid development of California following the Gold Rush of 1849, discussion had begun of the need for a transcontinental railroad. Benton early advocated construction along "the Great Central Route" across Nebraska which would link St. Louis and San Francisco. Congressman Willard P. Hall of St. Joseph had introduced legislation to organize the region and open it to settlement in December 1851, but the bill had failed to get out of committee.

The following summer pressure began to grow in northwest Missouri in the form of public meetings as many people there saw speculative opportunities awaiting them if the territory was developed. The Wyandot Indian tribe, which occupied eastern Nebraska, also saw advantages and sent Abelard Guthrie, a white who had married into the tribe, as a lobbyist to Washington that winter. He tried to enlist Atchison's support but found the senator cool to the idea because of the Missouri Compromise restrictions on slavery there. Nevertheless, Congressman Hall reintroduced his bill, which this time passed the House by a wide margin. It came up in the Senate on the closing day of the session, and Atchison left the president's chair to speak to it. He admitted his opposition because of the restrictions while acknowledging that there was little chance of changing them. He also expressed concern that Indian land titles be properly taken care of so that the tribes would not be despoiled by white speculators. But Atchison realized the growing agitation for action; and while he deplored the idea that Missourians could not take their slaves with them if they went into the territory, he indicated that he would support the movement for organization at the next session.

Atchison undoubtedly knew that Benton was already gearing up his campaign to replace him. Indeed, the very next day, Old Bullion released a statement to the press announcing his candidacy for the Senate and indicating that the construction of a railroad by the Great Central Route and the consequent necessity for organizing Nebraska would be his key issues. In opposing these, Atchison, according to Benton, would place a major roadblock in the path of Missouri's future economic development.

Although the election to choose a new legislature was still a year and a half away, the two men crisscrossed the state that summer of 1853 seeking support. Atchison reiterated his new stand in support of the organization of Nebraska and further indicated that he would try to find some way by which slaveholders could go into the territory on an equal footing with other citizens. It was not clear what he had in mind; but time revealed that he was coming around to a position already suggested by some other southerners, namely, that the Compromise of 1850 with its principle of popular sovereignty had supplanted the Missouri Compromise in relation to all existing territories.

When Congress convened in December 1853, new versions of the Nebraska bill were quickly introduced in both houses. it was generally agreed, however, that the Senate would take the lead through its Committee on Territories chaired by Stephen A. Douglas of Illinois, who had been a champion of the proposal for nearly a decade. Over the next six months, before its final passage as the Kansas-Nebraska Act in May 1854, Atchison played a major role in reshaping the bill to fit southern demands. Although he initially supported Douglas's plan to allow the Compromise of 1850 to supplant that of 1820, he changed his mind in midstream because of a fear that such an indirect move might not withstand a court test should the Free Soilers bring one. In the end Atchison insisted on the outright repeal of the Missouri Compromise as the only sure means of allowing slaveholders to enter the territory. Douglas acquiesced because of Atchison's control of key southern votes needed for the bill's passage. The two of them, with some others, secured President Pierce's official support, which improved the measure's chances. The Iowa congressional delegation now insisted that the territory be divided into two parts, hence Kansas-Nebraska, because of its fear that Missourians would dominate a single territory. The bill passed the Senate 37 to 14 in March, and, after lengthy debate, squeaked by the House 113 to 100 at the end of May. All of Missouri's congressional delegation supported it except Benton, who made a long speech against it in the House.

The Kansas-Nebraska Act reawakened the issue of slavery extension, supposedly put to rest by the Compromise of 1850, with explosive force. It disrupted and reshaped the political scene, as will be discussed later; and it led to three years of protracted violence along the Kansas-Missouri border. A later Kansas historian called this "the prelude to the War for the Union."

The Struggle For Kansas

Many Missourians assumed that they would be allowed to control Kansas for slavery while the Iowans and Free Soil element took charge of Nebraska. But by early summer, rumors reached northwest Missouri of major efforts by northern emigrant aid societies to assist settlers in moving to Kansas, supposedly with Free Soil intentions. Having won the struggle for repeal of the Missouri Compromise in Congress, most Missourians had no desire to see Kansas become free territory, with the added potential of serving as a haven for runaway slaves. They quickly determined that they would have to control the processes of popular sovereignty by whatever means they had available to them.

Numerous Missourians had begun slipping across the border to quietly preempt land even before President Pierce signed the Kansas-Nebraska Act. Many hoped to speculate, but others genuinely desired to take up a new homestead. A number of proslavery towns sprang up that summer and fall between Kansas City and the Nebraska line on the western side of the Missouri River. Most prominent among these were Leavenworth and Atchison, which was named in honor of the senator.

Atchison hurried home from Washington that summer to help organize the proslaveryites of Missouri into "self-defensive associations." He wrote his friend Jefferson Davis in September: "We will have difficulty with the Negro heroes in Kansas; they are resolved they say to keep the slaveholder out, and our people are resolved to go in. . . . We will before six months rolls around, have the Devil to pay in Kansas and this state; we are organizing, to meet their organization. We will be compelled to shoot, burn & hang, but the thing will soon be over; we intend to 'Mormanise' the Abolitionists." When a territorial election was held in November to choose a delegate to Congress, Missourians, led by Atchison, crossed into Kansas in large numbers to cast their ballots for the proslavery candidate,

Missourians crossing into Kansas to vote. *Courtesy State Historical Society of Missouri*

who was overwhelmingly elected. Atchison argued that his Senate colleagues had rejected his proposal for a ninety-day residence requirement for voting in the Kansas-Nebraska Act. Therefore, he proclaimed, "We will give them their own cup to drink," meaning that one needed to reside in the territory for only a day to vote.

Amos A. Lawrence, the treasurer of the New England Emigrant Aid Company, one of several northern groups established to encourage settlement, wrote Atchison in March 1855, asking him to use his influence to restrain his followers "from doing great injustice to actual settlers." He noted the contending forces had their different goals: "The stake is a large one, and the ground chosen. Let the fight be a fair one."

Atchison replied that he and his friends saw the Kansas struggle as one of survival. If the proslavery forces lost in Kansas, would the abolitionists be content to leave the institution alone in Missouri, he asked. He feared for the entire future of slavery in view of increasing northern agitation and saw Kansas as the battleground on which the issue had to be decided.

Atchison had spent much of the winter touring the South to encourage emigration from that area to Kansas. Realizing that Missouri could not carry the proslavery burden there alone, he argued that southerners must send their sons to help in the cause. "We must have the support of the South," he urged. "We are fighting the battles of the South. Our institutions are at stake. You far Southern men are now out of the nave of the war; but if we fail it will reach your own doors, perhaps your hearths."

The Legislative Deadlock Over the Senatorship

While Atchison sought to arouse southern support for the Kansas cause, the Missouri General Assembly was deciding the final contest between him and Benton. Old Bullion had been defeated for reelection to the House in the fall of 1854 by a strong Whig candidate who benefited from the presence of an anti-Benton Democrat on the ballot. Further embittered by this defeat, the Benton forces determined all the more to make a strong stand in the legislature for the senatorial seat. The results of legislative races in the 1854 election had been mixed, with many three-way races, so that when the General Assembly convened in December the Whigs again held the balance of power. Only a coalition by them with one or the other of the Democratic factions would make an election possible. Unlike 1850, such a coalition failed to materialize this time. The Whigs supported Alexander W. Doniphan of Clay County, the hero of the Mexican War, throughout the entire proceedings, while each wing of the Democrats remained true to its candidate. The result was a stalemate; on the forty-first and final ballot Atchison had fifty-eight votes, Doniphan fifty-six, and Benton thirty-eight, with a majority needed for election. The legislature decided to postpone action for a year, but even then could reach no solution. Missouri would have but one senator for the next two years until a new General Assembly could resolve the deadlock. Thus Atchison left the Senate, but Benton failed to replace him.

The Proslavery Forces Win in Kansas

Meanwhile the struggle for Kansas continued. When elections were held for a territorial legislature in March 1855, Missourians again crossed the border en masse to participate. Although a census taken the previous month indicated that Kansas had less than 3,000 eligible voters, more than 6,300 ballots were cast resulting in a resounding proslavery victory. Those questioning the results found themselves in difficulty. A Parkville newspaper, *The Industrial Lumi-nary*, condemned the electoral interference. For their trouble the two editors found themselves confronting a mob which hurled their press and type into the Missouri River and ordered them to leave Platte County. Others suspected of antislavery sentiments met simi-lar difficulties.

Andrew H. Reeder, the territorial governor, refused to give certifi-cates of election in six districts where he suspected the worst fraud. This angered the proslavery supporters, and Atchison began to press President Pierce for Reeder's removal. Reeder called the legislature into session at the town of Pawnee, near Fort Riley, which he and some of his associates were trying to promote as a potential capital. Reeder claimed that Pawnee had the advantage of being 140 miles from the Missouri border where the legislators could operate in a freer atmosphere. The legislators saw things differently and promptly adjourned to Shawnee Mission near Kansas City where they adopted the revised statutes of Missouri as the general law for the territory. To these they added a number of strong proslavery measures to further tighten their grip on the reins of government. They called for Reeder's dismissal; and Pierce obliged with a new governor, Wilson Shannon, who, realizing where the power lay, cooperated with the proslavery forces.

The Kansas Free State Movement

In spite of the efforts of the proslaveryites, Free Soil immigrants be-gan arriving in Kansas in considerable numbers in 1855. Finding themselves frustrated politically by the obvious proslavery leanings of the territorial and national governments, they decided to organize for the protection of their interests and to prepare for the forthcom-ing election of a territorial delegate to Congress. They met at Big Springs on September 5, four days after the arrival of Governor Shan-non, and organized the Free State party. They were led by former Governor Reeder and James H. Lane, a former Indiana congressman who had recently immigrated and who would prove a real thorn in the side of Missourians over the next decade. Their resolutions repu-diated the charges of abolitionism that had been hurled at them and denounced the proslavery legislature in scathing terms.

When the delegate election was held in October, the Free State party boycotted it on the grounds that it would not be conducted fairly and held their own eight days later. There was little evidence of

Lawrence, Kansas Territory, in ruins after the proslavery raid. *Courtesy State Historical Society of Missouri*

fraud in either contest, but significantly the Free Staters brought out 300 more voters than cast ballots in the regular contest. When Congress convened, the two rival delegates presented their credentials. The House appointed an investigating committee which visited Kansas the following spring, held hearings, turned in a majority and minority report, and resolved nothing. The Free Staters had long since held another election to approve their own constitution—one significantly that barred blacks from the territory be they slave or free—and, in January 1856, they established a rival government at Topeka with its own legislature and set of officers.

Violence Renewed

Violence erupted between the Free State and proslavery forces in December 1855 and continued intermittently through the following August. During that period Atchison led Missourians into Kansas on three occasions to assist the proslaveryites there, each time at the invitation of a territorial official. In May 1856, they participated in a raid on Lawrence, the headquarters of the Free State party. Led by a local proslavery sheriff, they destroyed two newspapers, a hotel, and several homes. This action drew considerable national criticism and led three days later to the "Pottawatomie Massacre" in which the an-

tislavery fanatic John Brown killed in cold blood five proslavery settlers unrelated to the raid. Atchison now moved to close Missouri
River traffic to any further Free Soil immigrants. Most boats were
stopped at Lexington, with Free Soil passengers being given tickets
on the next one returning to St. Louis. To counteract this, Jim Lane
led a group of 400 settlers into Kansas through Iowa by way of Nebraska. As tensions heightened, President Pierce removed Governor
Shannon, who had begun using federal troops in a limited fashion to
try to keep order. Shannon's successor, John W. Geary, finally restored peace.

The Election of 1856

Against the turbulent Kansas backdrop, Missourians and the nation
went to the polls in the fall of 1856 to choose new officials. The Kansas-Nebraska Act had forced major political realignment at both the
state and national levels. The Whig party proved incapable of holding together its shaky coalition of various interest groups. In the
South it yielded to the Democratic party, which painted itself as the
true protector of that section's interests in line with the doctrines of
John C. Calhoun. In the North the new Republican party, born in the
wake of the Kansas-Nebraska Act on a free soil-free labor platform,
had made significant gains and now stood as the Democrats' chief rival. Along the border, including Missouri, and in many cities faced
with an inundation of foreign immigrants, the Whigs gave way to the
American or Know-Nothing party. This group sought to detract from
the slavery issue by appealing to the nativist prejudices of those who
disliked the changes that the immigrants brought with them.

The situation in Kansas had kept the Missouri political cauldron
boiling for much of the past two years. The proslavery supporters
continued a constant bombardment of appeals for support of their
efforts in Kansas. They had held a three-day mass convention at Lexington in July 1855 to which twenty-four counties and the city of St.
Louis sent delegates, both Democrat and Whig. Meanwhile the anti-
Benton forces took a firmer hold on the state Democratic machinery.
Governor Sterling Price had moved increasingly into the anti-Benton
camp, but his actions had been generally limited to making emotional speeches against those who sought to make Kansas into an antislavery state and thereby threaten Missouri.

Unable to unite on the selection of a senator over the past two
years, the Democrats were in no better harmony for the election of

1856. Their state committee included members from both factions, and each group issued a separate invitation for the Democrats to meet in convention at Jefferson City on the same day, April 21, but in different locations. A few compromisers led by former Governor King tried to bring the two sides together but in vain. The anti-Benton Democrats, who now controlled the regular party machinery and thereby had their delegates seated at the national convention later that summer, nominated Trusten Polk of St. Louis as their candidate for governor. Although he had not held active office before, he had long been an active party worker in the proslavery camp.

The less numerous Benton backers nominated Old Bullion himself as their candidate, which lessened considerably any hope for coalition with other political elements. In reality, Benton's managers, Frank Blair and B. Gratz Brown, were already leaning toward the fledgling Republican party, which chose Benton's son-in-law, John C. Frémont, as its candidate for President later that summer. The platforms of the two groups were very similar, but Benton refused to have anything to do with the Republicans. For all his trials at the hands of his own party, he still could not bring himself to relinquish the Democratic label. This failure to compromise meant that the Benton Democrats controlled a mere remnant of their earlier strength.

Many former Benton Democrats found themselves more comfortable in the new American party. Indeed Blair and Brown met with James S. Rollins, the Whig candidate for governor in 1848, and other Know-Nothing leaders before any of the conventions to try to work out a coalition effort against the anti-Benton Democrats. The American party, meeting a few weeks before the Democrats, chose Robert C. Ewing, a former Benton supporter, as its candidate for governor and divided the rest of the ticket equally between Bentonites and former Whigs. They were a little dismayed when the Benton Democrats failed to endorse this ticket and put forward Old Bullion himself instead. The interim, however, had seen a St. Louis city election in which the strong German element there had swept a Benton Democrat into the mayor's office against a Know-Nothing. This caused Blair and Brown to have second thoughts, especially since they needed German votes for their own candidacies for Congress and the Missouri House, respectively. Benton might not be an ideal gubernatorial candidate, but he did not threaten them locally. And besides, they still hoped, erroneously as it turned out, to carry him into the Republican fold.

The campaign that followed was a spirited one. Missourians went to the polls in August just as difficulties in Kansas reached their highest level. They elected Trusten Polk governor with 41 percent of the vote. Ewing garnered 35 percent, while Benton ran a distant third with 24 percent. The new legislature would be solidly anti-Benton Democrat. This marked Old Bullion's final defeat—he was to die two years later—and ended the Benton Democrats as a separate group. Blair and Brown, both of whom secured election, led most of the remnant into the new Republican party during the next four years. In the national election in November, the state went solidly for James Buchanan, the Democratic candidate for President, who moved into the White House succeeding Franklin Pierce, who had become too controversial for the Democrats to offer him a second term.

The Election of 1857

The administration of Governor Trusten Polk proved to be a short one. When the legislature met in January 1857, it found itself faced with the problem of electing two United States senators. The Atchison seat still remained vacant, and Senator Geyer's term had expired. With the proslavery Democrats solidly in control, the General Assembly moved quickly to fill the vacancies. Atchison had withdrawn from any further consideration a year earlier, so the Democrats chose

George Caleb Bingham's painting *Stump Speaking* from a line and mezzotint engraving by Louis-Adolphe Gautier. *Courtesy State Historical Society of Missouri*

Congressman James S. Green of Louisiana, one of Atchison's lieutenants, as his successor for a four-year term. To replace Geyer they selected their new governor, Polk, for reasons not altogether clear.

Polk's "promotion" necessitated a new election for governor under the 1820 constitution. Lieutenant Governor Hancock Lee Jackson, who succeeded to the office temporarily, called it for August 1857, and political tensions heated up again. The National Democrats, as the party in power now called themselves, nominated Robert M. Stewart of St. Joseph, one of the proslavery leaders in the state senate, as their candidate. They confidentially predicted a repeat of their victory of a year earlier. Realizing that their only hope of success lay in unity, Blair, Brown, and Rollins forged a coalition of Know-Nothings and Benton Democrats that they called simply "the Opposition ticket." Rollins became their candidate, with the hope that his moderate views on most issues could bridge the gap between the various coalition elements. It was a closely fought contest, with many countervailing forces at work. No one doubted where Stewart stood on the issues, but Rollins vacillated, with his diverse allies pulling him in various directions. For all his difficulties, however, Rollins lost to Stewart by only 334 votes—the closest gubernatorial race in Missouri history. The results seemed to indicate a fairly close division in the state between those ardent proslaveryites who had been pushing the Kansas issue and the more moderate element that feared any potential disruption of the Union.

Slavery Loses Out in Kansas

Two months after the Missourians voted, their neighbors in Kansas went to the polls to choose a new territorial legislature, a delegate to Congress, and county officials. While the territory had been restive during the past year, violence had been held to a minimum. With federal troops keeping order, there had been no armed incursions from Missouri since August 1856. Under the urging of Robert J. Walker, President Buchanan's newly appointed governor, and their own leaders, the Free Staters participated in a regular territorial election for the first time in three years. The military guarded those polls where danger might be anticipated, and the election came off peaceably. In two cases of suspected proslavery fraud, Governor Walker decided forcefully for the Free Staters. That group carried both the legislature and the delegate's race. It appeared that a new day was dawning for Kansas.

One last chapter remained to be played in the proslavery struggle for Kansas. Earlier that summer an election had been held for a constitutional convention. With the Free Staters boycotting it, the proslavery element had won most of the delegate seats. This group met at Lecompton, the territorial capital, in October and drew up a proslavery constitution. In spite of a referendum called by the new territorial legislature in January 1858, which rejected the document overwhelmingly, President Buchanan submitted it to Congress with his endorsement in the hope that this would resolve the slavery issue once and for all. Led by Senator Douglas, who denounced the Lecompton Constitution as a fraud, Congress sent it back to the people of Kansas for another referendum which had the same result as the first. Slavery had been defeated finally in Kansas.

While the Missourians' methods in attempting to bring Kansas into the slavery fold may be criticized as harsh and shortsighted, it should be pointed out that David Rice Atchison and those who followed him believed strongly that the survival of slavery in Missouri and the rest of the South depended on what happened in Kansas. People who are emotionally involved in a cause often do things they would not condone under ordinary circumstances. This was undoubtedly true here. In the end the South did not have the necessary population ready to move to Kansas to offset the migration from the North. Most slaveholders did not care to risk valuable property in slaves in an unsettled situation. Those southerners who did come were yeoman farmers without slaves, the younger sons of planters looking for adventure, or would-be speculators. While the North sent its share of adventurers and speculators also, the bulk of its emigrants were those who came to settle the land and stay.

The struggle in Kansas left an unfortunate legacy of violence along the border. Kansas Jayhawkers made periodic raids into the counties of western Missouri in the spring of 1858 looking for revenge, plunder, and excitement. On May 19 a group of Missourians attacked some Free Staters in Linn County, Kansas, killing five and wounding five others. This became known as the Marais des Cygnes massacre and received considerable attention in the eastern press. The situation became so serious that Governor Stewart called out the militia that fall to patrol the area while his counterpart in Kansas did the same on that side of the border. The only incident after that was a raid by John Brown in December 1858, in which he led eleven slaves to freedom. But with the coming of the Civil War the Kansans swept back into western Missouri, supposedly to uphold the Union cause,

Dred Scott, Missouri slave whose freedom was denied by the Supreme Court. *Courtesy State Historical Society of Missouri*

with the result that the area was racked by guerrilla warfare throughout that long conflict. And after that the hatred died slowly among some border families.

The Dred Scott Case

Even as the Kansas struggle was playing out its final drama, the U.S. Supreme Court handed down one of its most momentous decisions in March 1857, resolving a case that had originated in Missouri some ten years earlier. The Dred Scott case provided the Court's interpretation of the issue of the extension of slavery into the territories and added further fuel to the smoldering fires of sectional agitation that were wracking Missouri and the nation.

Dred Scott had been the slave of Dr. John Emerson, an army surgeon stationed at Jefferson Barracks near St. Louis in the 1830s. When his master was transferred to the Rock Island arsenal in Illinois and later to Fort Snelling in Wisconsin Territory, Scott went with him. During their travels, Dr. Emerson purchased another slave, Harriet, who became Scott's wife. All of them returned to St. Louis in 1838 where the two slaves remained in the Emerson household until the doctor's death in 1843. Thereafter the Scotts sought to purchase their freedom from Mrs. Emerson, who turned them down. Helped by certain white friends, they then brought suit in St. Louis County circuit court seeking their freedom on the grounds that they had been taken into a free state (Illinois) and a territory (present-day Minnesota) that was free under the Missouri Compromise.

Few doubted that the Scotts would win their case as it made its way up to the Missouri Supreme Court, for that body had consistently decided similar ones in favor of the plaintiffs. But by the time the case got to the high tribunal in the early 1850s, the political kettle in Missouri was boiling, and the court's anti-Benton majority saw this as an opportunity to strike another blow for the proslavery cause. In March 1852, the state supreme court by a two to one majority (Chief Justice Hamilton R. Gamble, a Whig, dissenting) overturned eight previous cases to rule that the Scotts remained slaves because they had voluntarily returned with Dr. Emerson to Missouri. Following a precedent of the U.S. Supreme Court of the previous year involving Kentucky slaves in similar circumstances, the Missouri judges declared that the state did not have to abide by outside laws with regard to those persons fully within its jurisdiction.

Mrs. Emerson meanwhile had remarried and control of the slaves passed to her brother, John A. Sanford, who administered the estate for her daughter. Sanford lived in New York, which made it possible to take the case into the federal district court at St. Louis. Sanford asked the judge there to dismiss the case on the grounds that Scott as a black was not a citizen of Missouri and hence had no right to sue. When the judge ruled for Sanford, Scott appealed to the Supreme Court, which handed down its decision on March 7, 1857, three days after President Buchanan's inauguration. By this time the Scotts' situation, which had received little attention at the state level, had become a cause célèbre, with prominent attorneys appearing on both sides. The majority of the Court decided against the Scotts on two counts: (1) as a black, Scott could not be a citizen and hence he had

Jefferson City, 1859. *Courtesy State Historical Society of Missouri*

no right to use the federal courts; (2) under the Constitution, Congress had no right to legislate regarding slavery in the territories. Thus the Missouri Compromise had been null and void from the beginning so that Scott could not claim freedom by having lived in territory covered by that agreement. The second part of the decision confirmed what John C. Calhoun and the more extreme southerners had been saying all along. The Dred Scott decision hardened the demands of this group against the Republicans' free soil stand and undoubtedly helped lead the nation closer to civil war. As for Scott and his wife, they were now purchased by a friend and manumitted under Missouri law.

Debate Over Emancipation

The closing years of the 1850s saw the debate sharpen on the issue of slavery in Missouri. Fearful of the deteriorating situation in Kansas, early in 1857 the proslavery Democrats in the General Assembly introduced a joint resolution denouncing emancipation and warning any of its advocates to keep their hands off Missouri's slaves. It passed overwhelmingly; but during the course of the debate in the House, B. Gratz Brown took the occasion to put up a trial balloon for the Republican party which he and Frank Blair were seeking to organize in Missouri. His appeal was primarily to the white working class as he announced his belief that black slave labor was detrimental to the interests of free white labor. Brown claimed that the agitation over the slavery question in Kansas had hindered Missouri's economic growth because white immigrants bypassed the state to settle in Kansas, Nebraska, and Iowa. He pointed out that Iowa had grown sevenfold faster than Missouri had. What was his answer to this problem? Brown called for emancipation as the solution that would stimulate Missouri's economic growth. In saying this, Brown made it clear that he was not in favor of freeing the blacks for humanitarian or other purposes. Rather he wanted to emancipate the whites to realize their fullest potential as free labor within the Missouri society. To accomplish this end he urged the gradual elimination of slavery, with full compensation to owners. A year later his cousin, Congressman Frank Blair, would add to this an elaborate colonization plan to return free blacks to Africa.

Brown and Blair were careful to keep a moderate stance and certainly were not abolitionists. But their move toward the "Black Republicans," as many Missourians called the new party, drove away enough supporters to cost them their legislative and congressional seats in the 1858 election. Through their control of the St. Louis *Missouri Democrat*, Brown and Blair now became increasingly outspoken for the Republican creed of free soil-free labor. Their friendship with a rising politician in neighboring Illinois by the name of Abraham Lincoln created an alliance that would carry them to much greater heights in the wartime and postwar years.

The majority Democrats, meanwhile, led by Governor Stewart, continued to hammer out their proslavery speeches and resolutions. They scored strongly in the 1858 election to strengthen their grip on the legislature. Early in 1860 that body passed legislation declaring all free blacks unwelcome in Missouri. Those already there would have the choice of leaving or being sold into slavery. This was too strong even for the strident Stewart, and he applied a pocket veto after the close of the session.

The decade of the 1850s had seen Missouri torn by controversy that mirrored what was happening in the nation at large. The Kansas-Nebraska Act, in which Missouri congressional leaders had played a major role, had ruptured the old parties around which the state's voters had rallied for two decades and ushered in a period of agitation and confusion. Although it appeared that most Missourians favored a strong proslavery stance, the outward appearance of the legislature proved deceiving. For one thing it was not truly proportional as it is today. The rural areas tended to be overrepresented at the expense of the fast-growing urban areas of eastern Missouri. Then, too, party labels held much greater allegiance than they do today, and many Missourians found it hard to desert the Democratic party that they and their fathers had supported for so long.

But Missouri was changing as the next chapter will reveal. New immigration from the northern states and overseas was pouring into the state throughout the 1850s, and economic forces dominated by eastern capital were beginning to woo Missouri from its allegiance to the South by way of the Mississippi River. When war came, it would find the large majority of Missouri's people on the side of the Union in a struggle that would cost the state dearly. Indeed the troubles in Kansas were only a harbinger of worse times to come.

Suggestions for Reading

The political events of the late 1840s and the 1850s are well covered in Perry McCandless, *A History of Missouri, Vol. II, 1820 to 1860*, rev.

ed., Columbia, University of Missouri Press, 2000. The standard biographies of the two senatorial rivals of this period are William N. Chambers, *"Old Bullion" Benton: Senator from the New West*, Boston, Little Brown, 1956, and William E. Parrish, *David Rice Atchison of Missouri: Border Politician*, Columbia, University of Missouri Press, 1961. Regarding the early efforts to form a Republican party in Missouri, one should read William E. Parrish, *Frank Blair: Lincoln's Conservative*, Columbia, University of Missouri Press, 1998, and Norma L. Peterson, *Freedom and Franchise: The Political Career of B. Gratz Brown*, Columbia, University of Missouri Press, 1965. Christopher Phillips, *Missouri's Confederate: Claiborne Fox Jackson and the Creation of a Southern Identity in the Border West*, Columbia, University of Missouri Press, 2000, details the career of yet another important political figure. The story of an intriguing group of entrepreneurs can be found in Jeffrey S. Adler, *Yankee Merchants and the Making of the Urban West: The Rise and Fall of Antebellum St. Louis*, New York, Cambridge University Press, 1991.

The best overall study of the Kansas War is James A. Rawley, *Race and Politics: "Bleeding Kansas" and the Coming of the Civil War*, Philadelphia, Lippincott, 1969. The efforts of antislavery Kansans to persuade Missouri slaves to escape to freedom is told in Richard B. Sheridan, "From Slavery in Missouri to Freedom in Kansas: The Influx of Black Fugitives and Contrabands into Kansas, 1854–1865," *Kansas History*, Spring 1989. The Dred Scott case is well analyzed in Don E. Fehrenbacher, *The Dred Scott Case: Its Significance in American Law and Politics*, New York, Oxford University Press, 1978, reissue, 2001. The politics of the Kansas-Nebraska Act are placed in national perspective by Roy F. Nichols, *The Disruption of American Democracy*, New York, Macmillan, 1948; while Allan Nevins, *Ordeal of the Union*, 2 vols., New York, Charles Scribners Sons, 1947, does the same for the Kansas War.

An Expanding Missouri, 1830–1860

Population Explosion

The three decades prior to the Civil War witnessed a tremendous growth in population within Missouri. The 1830 federal census reported 140,455 residents settled largely in a T-shape along the state's two great rivers. Thirty years later that number had increased tenfold and stood at 1,182,012, with all of the state's present 114 counties having been established except Worth in the far northwest corner. Intermediate censuses revealed 383,702 Missourians in 1840 which nearly doubled to 682,044 by 1850. Throughout the first twenty years of this period the majority of Missouri's citizens continued to be southern in origin although an increasing stream of foreign immigrants began pouring into the state in the 1830s and 1840s.

But during the 1850s, while the percentage of native-born Missourians remained relatively stable and that of southern-born increased 44 percent, the population of northern-born residents jumped 180 percent while those of foreign birth increased by 110 percent. By 1860 northern- and foreign-born residents outnumbered southern-born residents within the state's population for the first time. Most of the rapidly growing number of northern immigrants settled in the upper tier along the Iowa border and in the rapidly developing urban area of St. Louis. Many of those who were foreign born remained in St. Louis, but they also spread along the Missouri River as far west as Cole County. Considerable pockets of foreign-born newcomers could also be found in Marion County in the northeast and in Lafayette, Buchanan, and Platte counties at the opposite end of the state. Of the southerners who continued to come, many were from the hill country of Tennessee and Kentucky who moved into the Ozark region—the last significant area of Missouri to be populated—which, while similar to the area from which they had come, possessed better soil and water resources than that to which they were accustomed. These people did not own slaves and hardly fitted the pattern of previous southern migration.

While black population grew proportionately from 25,091 in 1830 to 114,931 by 1860, it declined significantly in its ratio to the booming white population. Whereas the proportion of whites to blacks stood at $4^1/_2$ to 1 in 1830, it had been increased to 9 to 1 by 1860. All of this indicated that the face of Missouri was changing; and southerners, who had dominated the state and its politics for so long, would find the more recent immigrants challenging their power framework when the Civil War broke out.

The Coming of the Immigrants

A persistent theme in nineteenth-century American history is European immigration to this country. Coming primarily from the countries in western and northern Europe before the Civil War, the immigrants poured into the United States at an unprecedented rate. Complex reasons motivated these people to uproot themselves from a familiar environment and to seek out an unfamiliar one in America. Some came to be landowners; some to practice a political ideology; some to experiment with social and economic theories; some to follow religious beliefs without interference from the established authorities; some simply to survive. Bullied by political or religious forces, they traveled here to escape abuse and persecution; or they came to get away from adverse conditions such as epidemics, depression, plagues, and the threat of starvation. "The Fatherland is dear to me," one immigrant lamented, "but stones are not bread." Many came, as Francis Parkman noted, because of an "insane belief in a better life."

Whatever their motives it took courage and a strong will to embark for a new land. The Scandinavian immigrants in one of their folksongs ask the haunting question, "Where do the wild swans fly?" and they might have wondered too where they would go and what they would find in America. They also needed physical stamina to endure the long ocean voyage with its difficulties and dangers. "A man is of all sorts of luggage," Adam Smith observed, "the most difficult to be transported."

Because the census reports did not distinguish between native-born and foreign-born Americans until 1850, it is difficult to determine the exact number that came before then. But the federal census showed 160,541 foreign-born residents in Missouri by 1860 which constituted approximately 13.6 percent of the state's population. Of this group the Germans were the largest in number and had the greatest influence on Missouri's early development. By 1860 they made up 55 percent of the total immigrant population. A number of Germans had migrated to Missouri from other states, a good example being Henry Geyer, noted jurist and Missouri senator, who came from Maryland. Most of them, however, entered the country at New Orleans and traveled by steamboat to St. Louis, where they either stayed or fanned out to areas adjoining the Mississippi and Missouri rivers.

A significant forerunner of the thousands of Germans who came later was Göttfried Duden. A wealthy German intellectual, trained in law and medicine, he purchased 270 acres of Missouri farmland in present-day Warren County and settled there in 1824. Finding that plowing through his books was more satisfying than plowing his land, Duden returned to Germany in 1827 where he wrote thirty-six letters that he compiled into a book entitled *Bericht uber eine Reise nach den Westlichen Staater Nordamerikas (A Report of a Journey to the Western States of North America)*. Duden "mingled fact with fiction," picturing Missouri as a "new fatherland in America." Oppressed by poor economic conditions and ruled by a harsh conservative government, many Germans found the book appealing, came to Missouri believing in Duden's Report, and found that he had misrepresented some of the facts. They did not find a Garden of Eden, but rather a thinly populated state and rigorous frontier conditions. Many called him *der Lugenhund* ("lying dog") and returned to Germany. But others accepted the conditions as they were, faced up to the trials of adjusting to a new environment, and planted the seeds of numerous German communities throughout the state.

One of the early German townships was Hermann in Gasconade County, founded in 1837 on land owned by the German Settlement Society of Philadelphia. Overlooking the Missouri River 100 miles west of St. Louis, Hermann reflected the general characteristics of German communities. Selecting isolated areas of fertile hill country on or near a river, the Germans maintained tightly knit communities that reinforced their Old World customs and traditions. Independent

Hermann, Gasconade County, 1860. *Courtesy State Historical Society of Missouri*

and thrifty, they brought their businesses and crafts with them. They used their secrets to grow grapes, make wine, and brew beer. In 1848 Hermann wineries produced 10,000 gallons of wine and increased that to 100,000 gallons by 1856. Two wineries, Stone Hill (1847) and Hermannhof (1852), are still in operation today.

Martin Stephan, a Lutheran pastor in Saxony, led seven hundred of his followers to Missouri in 1838 after he had been suspended by church authorities for his religious beliefs and practices. Influenced by Duden's Report, Stephan envisioned a "new Canaan" where he and his followers could follow their religion without opposition. Settling in St. Louis and Perry County, the Stephanites never questioned their leader's ecclesiastical authority, but they did come to reject his lifestyle. In 1839 Stephan was charged with adultery, deposed from office, and exiled to Illinois. For seven years he tried to return to Missouri and regain control of the Lutheran colony but all efforts failed, and he died penniless and alone in 1846.

After Stephan's expulsion Carl Walther, another minister who had followed Stephan from Saxony, assumed leadership of the colony. A man of high ethical standards with organizational ability, Walther stood for strict adherence to the Reformation principles laid down by Martin Luther in the sixteenth century. Under their new leader the church grew and prospered. Ten years after the fall of Stephan, Walther led his people and Lutherans in Ohio and other states into the German Evangelical Lutheran Synod of Missouri. Better known as the Lutheran Church-Missouri Synod, this Protestant denomination has become one of the largest in the United States with churches, publications, seminaries, schools, and service agencies throughout the country.

A Prussian immigrant, William Keil, and five hundred of his followers founded the Society of Bethel in Shelby County in 1845. Bethel was an experiment in communal living similar to the German-American sect known as the Amana Society. The little village survived until 1883 and is now being restored by an energetic group of interested townspeople. The eccentric Keil left Bethel after the Civil War to found a similar society in Oregon but kept a strong control over the original group. On the long overland journey to Oregon he transported a watertight coffin containing a preservative solution and the body of his deceased son whom he had promised to take to Oregon.

The German immigrants added variety to Missouri life. German scholars, clergy, musicians, and authors enriched the state's cultural heritage. By the 1830s German gunsmiths in St. Louis were making the "Hawken" or "Missouri rifle," which helped to open the American West to white settlement. A pair of buckskin gloves made at Bethel received a prize at the New York World's Fair in 1858. Germans became steamboat builders, brewers, cabinetmakers, and wine makers. German sausage, scrapple, and sauerkraut now rate as favorite foods with the American public. The Germans contributed much to the urbanization of St. Louis with their industriousness. They were also excellent agriculturalists. Among their most important contributions were their pioneer efforts in scientific agricultural methods. German agriculturalists influenced the establishment of the State Board of Agriculture in 1856, with two German immigrants who had worked for scientific farming methods for twenty years serving on the first board. Germans also brought with them an intense dislike for slavery, and they would be found in the forefront of the Union cause when civil war broke out. Theirs, then, was a major contribution.

Second in number to the Germans were the Irish—some 43,000 strong by 1860, half the size of the German population. They came to America and Missouri in the 1840s when a potato famine brought extremely difficult times to their homeland. Unlike the Germans, who were often well-to-do, the Irish had few resources. Although they had been farmers at home, they lacked the money to buy land in this country and consequently settled mostly in urban areas such as St. Louis where they took a variety of jobs as day laborers. In Missouri they worked on the wharves and aboard the steamboats. With the coming of the railroads they furnished much of the labor for their construction. Outside St. Louis the heaviest concentrations of Irish would be found in Jackson and Buchanan counties. Beyond the Germans and the Irish, the number of immigrants from other countries into Missouri was relatively small.

The Early Urbanization of St. Louis

Once "an encamping ground of the solitary Indian trader" and a village of only 3,500 in 1818, St. Louis emerged within forty years as the seventh largest city in the United States with a population of 161,000 by 1860. Favorable geographic and economic conditions boosted it from a small town to a large urban center by midcentury. Its location at the confluence of the Missouri and Mississippi rivers was certainly a major factor in its growth.

Like other cities on the Ohio and the Mississippi, St. Louis grew with the river trade. Before the coming of the steamboat, St. Louis had become an important trade and commercial center largely as the result of the fur trade and the migration of settlers through it into the interior of the state. The steamboat added new dimensions to the economy by expanding the trade area into the northwest frontier and to the upper reaches of the Missouri River, by increasing the volume of trade, by employing hundreds of people, and by transporting considerable numbers of newcomers into the city. Timothy Flint, an early western traveler, estimated that "more than half of the whole number" of people moving west came by water. Steamboat building in St. Louis developed into one of the city's most important businesses.

Because the United States government regarded St. Louis as a strategic location in case of war, the city prospered from government business. Jefferson Barracks, established in 1826 ten miles south of the city, served as the center for most of the government's western operations so that troops and supplies on their way to secure American territorial expansion beyond the bend of the Missouri River passed through there. The Santa Fe Trail also bolstered the economy for decades as did the traffic and industries tied to the westward movement.

St. Louis became a manufacturing center for wagons, guns, saddles, blankets, furniture, barrels, and clothing. The lead-mining industry in Missouri, Illinois, and Wisconsin grew rapidly, and St. Louis furnished it capital, laborers, supplies, storage, and transportation. The influx of immigrants moving into the city not only increased its population but expanded its economy by introducing new trades and crafts. St. Louis produced approximately two-thirds of the state's manufactured goods in terms of monetary value—a figure that stood at $42 million by 1860.

Because of its size and location, St. Louis served as the principal financial center for the state and the western region beyond. The conservative position of the Missouri General Assembly with regard to the control of banking practices has already been discussed in Chapter 5. The Bank of Missouri, chartered in 1837, served as the state's sole legal institution for twenty years. Its restrictive currency policies alienated many in the St. Louis business community in a time of freewheeling speculation, industrial development, and commercial activity. The unsuccessful efforts to liberalize the state's banking laws in the 1840s have also been discussed in Chapter 5.

By the 1850s many rural Missourians had come to distrust the growing financial power of St. Louis, where the Bank of Missouri was located. When the bank's charter came up for renewal in 1857, the General Assembly passed a general banking law to replace the Bank of Missouri and promptly chartered eight other banks with the right to issue paper notes. By the end of 1859 the state was fairly well supplied with banking offices. Nine chartered banks with forty-one branches were in operation and issuing currency. St. Louis remained the center of banking and finance, with eight chartered banks having a combined capital of $12,500,000 as well as twelve savings banks and twenty-one private banks. "Wildcat" banking—banks operating without state authority—did not disappear, but they were generally held in check as chartered and private banks maintained sound banking practices.

The process of urbanization itself created problems for the citizens of early nineteenth-century St. Louis. City fathers wrestled with such concerns as a clean water supply, garbage disposal, unpaved streets, fire protection, lawlessness, and inadequate housing and health care facilities. Cholera epidemics occurred in 1832, 1848, and 1853 killing thousands and causing mass evacuations. One resident complained in the 1830s that the city was one of "hogs and dogs," referring to the animals that strayed at will through the city streets.

One of the city's most ambitious leaders in tackling urban problems was William Carr Lane, who served seven terms as mayor in the 1820s and 1830s. After a stint as an army surgeon during the War of 1812, Lane came to St. Louis to practice medicine. Elected mayor in 1823, he not only dealt with the annoying problems of the growing city but also insisted that a "suitable system of improvements always be kept in view." Lane believed in profiting from the experiences of other cities, planned progress, and a strict adherence to the financial resources available. During his service as mayor he pioneered public health services, encouraged free schools, and worked for paved streets, a municipal waterworks, an improved wharf, public fountains, parks and shade trees. His progressive views on urbanization, which he gladly shared with other cities, made him one of the most capable and farsighted leaders in early American urban history.

Despite the hardships, city dwellers enjoyed some advantages. Technological and scientific advances came quickly to St. Louis. Gas first illuminated the city in 1847. That same year the telegraph linked St. Louis with the East, making it possible to keep abreast with world and national developments and to disseminate the news with speed

St. Louis, 1860. *Courtesy State Historical Society of Missouri*

and accuracy. The first railroad to begin construction in Missouri started at St. Louis, and in the following decades the city became the second leading railroad center in middle America. St. Louisans enjoyed a number of good newspapers, the most prominent being the *Missouri Republican* and the *Missouri Democrat*, whose names belied their real political affiliations. The city had two German-language newspapers by the eve of the Civil War, the *Anzeiger des Westens* and the *Westliche Post*.

Although a Protestant minister once declared that "St. Louis is no more fit for a Christian than hell is for a powderhouse," the church and related activities did improve the caliber of city life. The dominant Roman Catholic element constructed a cathedral, parish churches, and performed many Christian services. Protestant churches also made inroads on the St. Louis religious scene. The Baptists built a brick church in 1821; the Episcopalians constructed a wooden one shortly thereafter. Methodists and Presbyterians started out by meeting in rooms provided by the city before establishing their own church buildings. In January 1836, the first Jewish congregation convened.

Father Francois Neil and three other priests opened the St. Louis Academy in 1819, which for a few years educated some of the sons of prominent St. Louis families. Bishop Rosati started St. Louis College in 1828, which received its charter as St. Louis University four years later to become the first university west of the Mississippi. Across the Missouri River at St. Charles, George and Mary Sibley established a girl's school, Lindenwood, to which many St. Louis families sent their daughters. Various other private schools existed from time to time, and a rudimentary system of public schools began in the 1830s. Missouri's first public high school was established in St. Louis in 1853, a year which also saw the founding of Eliot Seminary (Washington University). In 1857 the St. Louis school system opened a normal school to train teachers for its growing needs.

Few cities have had as colorful a history as St. Louis. Its French and Spanish legacy, the rawboned spirit of the fur traders and frontiersmen, and the influx of the immigrants, particularly the Germans, diversified its culture. As noted in Chapter 6, it also developed a small but significant free black community which would furnish leadership in post–Civil War efforts for better education and rights of freed slaves. In the prewar era the leadership of men like William Clark, Thomas Hart Benton, and William Carr Lane contributed to its progressive character. Its place on the Mississippi and Missouri rivers enlivened its commerce. Today it remains one of the most interesting and distinctive of American cities.

Other Missouri Towns

Other towns were developing in the interior of the state and along the Mississippi, but none rivaled St. Louis in size or importance. The 1860 census revealed eleven other communities with a population exceeding 2,500—all of them river towns except Independence, which, nevertheless, had access to a landing. The largest was St. Joseph, with 8,932 inhabitants. It was the center of a small meat-packing industry and had some local manufactories. Independence and Kansas City (which was not officially organized until 1850) supplied the western trade while Hannibal depended upon its river traffic and, after 1858, its position as one of the terminals of the Hannibal and St. Joseph Railroad. Communities along the Missouri River, notably Glasgow, developed tobacco manufacturing and a rope and bagging industry based on local hemp. Most towns simply provided the necessary services for the surrounding agricultural area with little or no impact beyond their immediate trade region.

Steamboating on the Western Waters

As already noted, the steamboat played a major role in the expansion and economic growth of Missouri. When Robert Fulton explained to Napoleon the concept of boats powered by steam, the French emperor exclaimed, "What sir, you would make a ship sail against the wind and currents by lighting a bonfire under her decks? I pray you excuse me. I have no time for such nonsense." Shortly thereafter, in August 1807, Fulton's steamboat, the *Clermont*, steamed up the Hudson River to Albany and back to New York in five days. "Such nonsense" spread rapidly to the Ohio River and its tributaries. Writing to a friend in 1812, Fulton said, "The Mississippi . . . is conquered. . . . The steamboat which I have sent to trade between New Orleans and Natchez carried 1500 barrels =150 tons . . . against the current 313 miles in 7 days, working in that time 84 hours." Steamboating increased a hundred-fold between 1820 and 1860, making it a leading industry in the West. No part of the country was more dependent upon steam transportation than middle America.

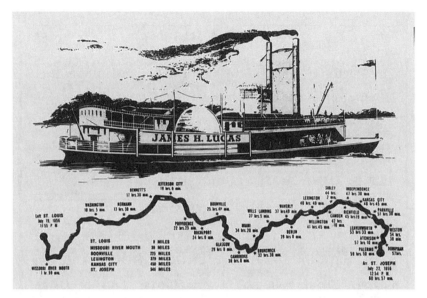

Steamboat *James H. Lucas,* 1856, with a map of its stops between St. Louis and St. Joseph.
E. B. Trail Collection, courtesy State Historical Society of Missouri

The era of Missouri steamboating opened in 1817 with the arrival of the *Zebulon M. Pike,* the first steamboat to land at St. Louis. In the following decades, the city would become an important port and the fourth-ranking steamboat construction center on the inland waterways. By the early 1830s more than 500 steamboats docked annually at St. Louis, and that number quadrupled during the following decade and then doubled again in the 1850s. By then approximately 3,000 steamboats carrying nearly one million tons of freight tied up annually at the St. Louis levee. Much of this traffic came upriver from New Orleans or from the east along the Ohio. Navigational hazards caused steamboat traffic on the upper Mississippi to develop more slowly.

In May 1819, the *Independence* became the first steamboat to ascend the Missouri River. Laden with a cargo of sugar, flour, whiskey, iron, castings, and passengers, it traveled as far as Franklin in Howard County. The following month Major Stephen H. Long started upriver, on his way to the Yellowstone country, with troops and supplies to impress the Indians and British fur traders. His flagship, the *Western Engineer,* was described by the *St. Louis Enquirer* as "a huge serpent, black and scaly . . . a monster of the deep . . . smoking with fatigue and lashing the waves with violent explosion." What a sight this steamboat and others accompanying it must have been to the

Advertisement for steamboat departures from St. Louis. *E. B. Trail Collection, courtesy State Historical Society of Missouri*

Indians and the early settlers along the banks of the Missouri! Plagued by hidden obstacles and mechanical breakdowns, only one boat got as far as Fort Osage. The abortive efforts of Long's steamboats signaled with "vomiting smoke" the continued advance of white civilization into the interior of Missouri.

Twenty years after the first steamboat passed Jefferson City, 260 landed there with such names as *J. M. White*, *L. S. Thorne*, *Island Queen*, *Calypso*, and *James Howard*. Steamboats extended their operations to Glasgow, Lexington, Westport Landing, Liberty Landing, Weston, St. Joseph, and on to Fort Benton on the upper Missouri some 2,200 miles from the port of St. Louis.

When George Sibley, the factor at Fort Osage, first learned that steamboats were to travel the Missouri River, he predicted that "while steamboats might navigate the swift current of the Missouri, they would have to be of peculiar construction and have greater power than those used elsewhere." Constructing lighter vessels with broad shallow hulls, steamboat builders also designed lighter, more powerful engines and boilers that could use the muddy water of western rivers. The paddle wheel, placed at the stern to provide a greater thrust, powered the boat through the current. Resembling a white gingerbread house on a raft, some steamboats could navigate in thirty inches of water transporting forty tons of freight and eighty passengers. On the Ohio and Mississippi rivers there were some steamboats 300 feet long that could carry as many as 300 to 400 passengers.

The average lifetime of most steamboats was five years. Although steamboat transportation was the "way to go" in the 1840s and 1850s, it was not without risks. Of all the steamboats lost between 1811 and 1851, more than 40 percent were destroyed by floating trees, ice, snags, sandbars, and similar obstructions. Spring floods caused much damage and created many hazards for steamboat traffic. The worst possible accident, a boiler explosion, could happen with such suddenness that passengers and crew had only a few seconds to escape the flames and the sinking boat. One of the worst such incidents on the Missouri River occurred on April 9, 1852, when the *Saluda* exploded near Lexington, killing more than 100 persons on board. A passenger on a Missouri River steamboat understandably wrote in his travel diary,

> We was crowded
> Now we are traveling up the river.
> Crowded in that little steamer.
> But still we felt to ask the Lord
> To protect us all on board.

Steamboating contributed greatly to the new state's economic progress. It provided jobs, encouraged commerce, and created new markets for eastern goods and western products. It stimulated such enterprises as the fur trade, lumbering, and mining and agriculture as well as those industries associated with developing and processing the products of agriculture and forestry. Steamboats spurred town development along the Missouri River. The town wharf became the scene of a lively trade in the same way that the depot would become the town's economic hub in the railroad age. When steamboats appeared on the smaller rivers—the Osage, the Gasconade, and the White—they contributed even further to the growth of the hinterland. Linking the more settled eastern side of the state with the primitive areas in the western part, steamboats carried immigrants, supplies, and the mail. The government also used them to transport troops and provisions to secure American territory beyond the bend of the Missouri River.

The steamboat era produced a body of literature and folk tales, as well as a cast of characters that have enriched America's literary and folk heritage. Mark Twain's *Life on the Mississippi* remains one of the classic accounts of that "golden age." In one of his chapters, Twain sketched the sleepy village of Hannibal transformed into a place teeming with excitement when the cry, "S-t-e-a-m-boat a-comin'!" was heard. And then, in a matter of minutes the freight had been un- loaded, passengers had gotten off and on, and the steamer had moved on. With its disappearance around the bend of the river the town returned to its summer lethargy.

The Civil War interrupted steamboat traffic. After the conflict the steamboat declined rapidly as it could not keep pace with the ex- panding railroad system that soon penetrated into every area of middle America.

Overland Transportation

Most attempts at the development of a system of roads in Missouri proved less than successful. Although the state made some efforts to en- courage construction, the bulk of the work was left to the counties; and hence the quality varied widely. Most arteries were town-to-country dirt roads that the counties maintained with occasional state support, in- cluding some federal funds from the sale of public lands. Their condi- tion was usually wretched, particularly in bad weather, so that wheeled vehicles were not common beyond an immediate locality. Some bud- ding entrepreneurs sought to develop private toll roads in the two de- cades before the Civil War, with a number of companies being chartered by the General Assembly. This was part of a national pattern as the builders considered planking and gravel as means of overcoming the problems caused by weather. Most of these failed, however, as the weather and competitive water routes proved too much. Probably the most successful was that running from the Mississippi River for forty- two miles through Ste. Genevieve, Iron Mountain, and Pilot Knob. Originally plank, it was later converted to macadam or gravel.

The acquisition and development of California and the South- west following the Mexican War created the necessity for some kind of regular transportation to service those areas. As had been the case with the development of the Santa Fe and Oregon trails, Missouri stood as the eastern terminus of such efforts. In 1855 the firm of

Russell, Majors, and Waddell opened for business in Lexington to carry freight across the Great Plains. Within three years it had 3,500 covered wagons with 40,000 oxen and 4,000 people operating across the prairies. Much of its business came from government contracts to supply western outposts, but it handled private shipments as well. It quickly became overextended, however, and fell victim to its creditors by the eve of the Civil War.

While the question of a transcontinental railroad was debated in the halls of Congress and elsewhere during the 1850s, an enterprising pair of contractors, John Butterfield and William G. Fargo, agreed to establish a stage route to the Pacific for the purpose of carrying passengers and mail. Receiving a government mall contract in 1858, the two partners established the Overland Mall Company, more frequently known as the Butterfield Overland Mail. It operated a stage route from Tipton across southwest Missouri and on to California, with stages traversing the route in twenty-four days. The trip was far from comfortable for those who road the Concord stages that were used, but it was an improvement over the covered wagon and at a fare of only $200.

The Coming of the Railroads

Many Missourians believed that railroads held the key to the state's long-range economic progress and development. A state convention in 1836 strongly endorsed the building of two railroad lines across the state—one to parallel the Missouri River and the other to run into the mining regions southwest of St. Louis. The General Assembly incorporated eighteen different railroad companies the following winter, but the Panic of 1837 quickly squelched efforts to accomplish any building.

Interest revived in the mid-1840s, and in 1847 the General Assembly granted a charter to the Hannibal and St. Joseph Railroad to build a line between those two towns. A variety of problems delayed the start of construction for another six years, and even then the work moved slowly. Finally completed in 1859 with the assistance of $3 million in state aid and extensive federal land grants, the Hannibal and St. Joseph proved a major boon to northern Missouri. Its completion created a potential threat to St. Louis' commercial interests and worked to the advantage of that city's lakeside rival, Chicago. Because of its ties with the Burlington Railroad, whose financiers had helped in its construction, the Hannibal and St. Joseph pro-

Kansas City Levee, 1858. *Courtesy State Historical Society of Missouri*

vided a cutoff for Missouri River traffic across the northern part of the state and into Chicago. This provided a more reliable all-weather route for the traders of the upper Missouri Valley than the route to St. Louis via the Missouri River, which was frequently plagued by ice in winter and shallows at other times of the year.

This is not to say that St. Louis stood idly by in the railroad game. It held a national railroad convention in 1849 that attracted 900 delegates, half of whom came from Missouri. It helped provide the impetus for the incorporation of the Pacific Railroad the following year to link St. Louis with the western border and, it was hoped, eventually with the Pacific coast. In 1851 railroad supporters managed to push through the General Assembly a state bond issue of $3.5 million which was divided between the Pacific and the Hannibal and St. Joseph. These bonds could be sold by the companies to help finance construction. The railroads would pay six percent annually to the state and eventually repay the entire amount in twenty years. In the meantime the state held a first mortgage on their lines as security.

The Pacific broke ground in 1851 and edged slowly westward. it reached Jefferson City by 1855; but by the eve of the Civil War it had extended only to Sedalia, still ninety-five miles short of its ultimate destination at Kansas City. Its developers were well intentioned, but cost overruns were high and inefficiency from lack of experience hampered management. Undoubtedly there was a certain amount of waste and corruption. The Pacific route was also the scene of Missouri's first major rail tragedy. In celebration of the completion of the line to Jefferson City, the company invited a large party of St. Louis citizens to take an overnight trip to the capital in November 1855. Pulled by a twenty-eight-ton locomotive, the eleven-car excursion train was crossing a newly constructed bridge over the Gasconade when it collapsed, plunging ten cars into the river. Thirty-one people were killed and some seventy injured. The disaster renewed public criticism over the safety of the new transportation, but it did not curtail railroad construction.

Three other railroads, of the many chartered, actually laid track during the 1850s. All received state subsidies similar to those given the Pacific and the Hannibal and St. Joseph. The North Missouri Railroad was designed to link St. Charles through the north central part of the state with the Iowa border. By 1860 it had reached Macon, where it bisected the Hannibal and St. Joseph. Further construction had to wait until the end of the war. The St. Louis and Iron Mountain Railroad stretched southwest from the river city to Pilot Knob, a distance of eighty-six miles, to serve the mining region. The Southwest

Construction along the Pacific Railroad from a painting by Frank Nuderscher. *Courtesy State Historical Society of Missouri*

Branch of the Pacific Railroad was designed to ultimately link Springfield and southwest Missouri with St. Louis. It tied in with the main
line at Pacific Junction, thirty-seven miles west of the metropolis. At
the outbreak of the Civil War it had reached Rolla, still 100 miles
short of its Springfield destination. All of these railroads experienced
difficulties similar to those of the Pacific. For all their high hopes at
the beginning of the decade, Missourians found only 810 miles of
track laid with the Hannibal and St. Joseph being the sole railroad to
have reached its destination. For all their disappointments, however,
most were still convinced that the "iron horse" carried the hopes of
the future in terms of transportation; and the postwar period was
witness to an all-out effort to complete the state's rail network, as explained in Chapter 11.

For all its difficulties in the 1850s, Missouri was a state on the
move. Although it was caught up in the throes of the antislavery
struggle that was engulfing the nation, it was also undergoing considerable internal change that would have a strong impact on the way in
which it viewed the Civil War that broke over the nation in 1861.

Suggestions for Reading

Perry McCandless, *A History of Missouri, Vol. II, 1820 to 1860*, rev. ed.,
Columbia, University of Missouri Press, 2000, is an excellent treatment of Missouri in the years leading to the Civil War. James Neal
Primm, *Economic Policy in the Development of a Western State, 1820–
1860*, Cambridge, Harvard University Press, 1954, details the role of
government in the growth of Missouri's economy. An important
work on the economic development of St. Louis during this period is
Jeffrey S. Adler, *Yankee Merchants and the Making of the Urban West:
The Rise and Fall of Antebellum St. Louis*, New York, Cambridge University Press, 1991. See also Charles Van Ravenswaay, "Years of Turmoil, Years of Growth: St. Louis in the 1850s," *The Bulletin*, July
1967. Yet another aspect is covered in Andrew Hurley, ed., *Common
Fields: An Environmental History of St. Louis*, St. Louis, Missouri Historical Society Press, 1997. Richard C. Wade, *The Urban Frontier*,
Cambridge, Harvard University Press, 1959, is a scholarly treatment
of the early development of St. Louis compared with Pittsburgh, Cincinnati, Louisville, and Lexington.

For the history of urban and town development in western Missouri, see A. Theodore Brown, *Frontier Community: Kansas City to*

1870, Columbia, University of Missouri Press, 1963; Eugene T. Wells, "The Growth of Independence, Missouri, 1827–1850," *The Bulletin*, October 1959; Sheridan A. Logan, *Old St. Jo: Gateway to the West, 1799–1932*, St. Joseph, J. S. Logan Foundation, 1979; Edward M. Shepard, "Early Springfield," *Missouri Historical Review*, October 1929; and Stuart F. Voss, "Town Growth in Central Missouri," *Missouri Historical Review*, October 1969, January and April 1970.

For the significance of German immigration on the social and economic history of Missouri, see *The German-American Experience in Missouri*, ed. Howard W. Marshall and James W. Goodrich, Princeton, Princeton University Press, 1986, and Charles Van Ravenswaay, *The Arts and Architecture of German Settlements in Missouri: A Survey of a Vanishing Culture*, Columbia, University of Missouri Press, 1977. A good short introduction is Robyn Burnett and Ken Luebbering, *German Settlement in Missouri: New Land, Old Ways*, Columbia, University of Missouri Press, 1996. An insightful article on an important promoter of German immigration is James W. Goodrich, "Gottfried Duden: A Nineteenth-Century Missouri Promoter," *Missouri Historical Review*, January 1981.

A good historical summary of steamboats on the Mississippi and Missouri rivers before the Civil War is Walter Havighurst, "Transportation on the Mississippi River System," in *The New Encyclopedia of the American West*, ed. Howard R. Lamar, New Haven, Yale University Press, 1998. For an understanding of river transportation within the larger area, one should consult Louis C. Hunter, *Steamboats on the Western Rivers*, Cambridge, Harvard University Press, 1949. For a colorful account of the experiences of a river pilot on the Mississippi River, see Mark Twain, *Life on the Mississippi*, New York, Harper, 1951. An interesting study is William E. Lass, "The Fate of Steamboats: A Case Study of the 1848 St. Louis Fleet," *Missouri Historical Review*, October 2001. The early history of railroad building and transportation in the state prior to the Civil War can be found in three *Missouri Historical Review* articles: Paul W. Gates, "The Railroads of Missouri, 1850–1870," January 1932; Robert E. Reigel, "The Missouri Pacific Railroad to 1879," October 1923; and Donald B. Oster, "The Hannibal and St. Joseph Railroad, Government and Town Founding, 1846–1861," July 1993. The state's banking system is well treated in Timothy Hubbard and Lewis E. Davids, *Banking in Mid-America: A History of Missouri's Banks*, Washington, Public Affairs Press, 1969.

NINE

The Civil War

The Election of 1860

The decade of the 1860s opened with one of the most fateful elections in American history. The Democratic party split at its national convention at Charleston in April 1860 over the issue of slavery expansion. The regular Democrats nominated Senator Stephen A. Douglas of Illinois for the presidency on a platform that called for popular sovereignty in the territories, while the bolters chose Vice-President John C. Breckinridge of Kentucky and urged acceptance of the Dred Scott decision, which clearly upheld slavery. The Republicans nominated Abraham Lincoln of Illinois on a platform that insisted the territories be free. The American party renamed itself the Constitutional Union party and nominated Senator John Bell of Tennessee on a vague platform that called for maintenance of the Constitution, the Union, and the laws.

Missourians found themselves similarly divided. Claiborne Fox Jackson had been nominated for governor by the Democrats before the Charleston convention. He had authored the Jackson Resolutions of the late 1840s which had first prompted the Missouri divisions over the question of slavery in the territories. In the new party crisis he wisely decided to stay with the regular Democrats. Although he faced a rival nominee from the bolters, he held enough strength to gain a narrow victory over Sample Orr of Greene County, the candidate of the Constitutional Unionists. The parties of Jackson and Orr seemed to represent a middle-of-the-road position on the great national issue of slavery. This appealed to most Missourians who had no desire to follow what were generally considered the more extreme positions of the Republicans and the Breckinridge Democrats.

At the national level Lincoln was chosen President as the Democratic split allowed him to combine a small popular plurality with an electoral college majority. Significantly, however, Lincoln did not carry a single southern or border state. In Missouri he polled 17,028 votes—mostly in St. Louis and the German counties along the Missouri River—and ran a poor fourth.

Missouri's Reaction to the Sectional Crisis

Led by South Carolina, the lower South began withdrawing from the Union in December 1860. Lincoln was not scheduled to take office until March 4, 1861, and Congress tried to work out a compromise in the meantime. But Republicans and Democrats could not agree, and the departing Southern states did not care. As political and economic paralysis hit the nation during the winter of 1860–61, Missourians found themselves sharing in the atmosphere of uncertainty. "The times were never so hard in St. Louis as they are now," a concerned mother reported to her son in Saline County, "money is scarce and labour is scarcer, hundreds of industrious men are out of employment and the amount of distress in this city never was so great." Anxious eyes turned toward Jefferson City as Governor Jackson prepared to assume office. All wondered what directions his new administration might take.

In his inaugural address on January 3, 1861, the new executive made his sympathies unmistakably clear. While devoted to the Union, he declared that it must ensure equality for both Northern and Southern states where slavery in the territories was concerned. The North had brought the nation to this crisis by its seeming unwillingness to accept such a principle. This being the case, Jackson emphasized: "Missouri, then, will in my opinion best consult her own interest, and the interests of the whole country, by a timely declaration of her determination to stand by her sister slaveholding States, in whose wrongs she participates, and with whose institutions and people she sympathizes." He proposed a state convention to decide Missouri's relationship with the rest of the Union and asked for authority to strengthen the state militia.

That not all of the state's citizens agreed with their governor quickly became evident. Free Soil sentiment was especially strong among the Germans of St. Louis and the lower Missouri Valley. Led by Congressman Frank Blair, whose brother would sit in Lincoln's cabinet, they organized paramilitary Home Guard units. Secessionist sympathizers countered with their own Minute Men groups under the leadership of Lieutenant Governor Thomas C. Reynolds, who openly advocated disunion.

The State Convention of March 1861

With tension mounting, the General Assembly called for a convention to meet in late February and consider what would be the best course for Missouri. It carefully provided, however, that any action taken by that group should be submitted to a vote of the people before becoming final. In the meantime the legislature found itself badly divided on whether to give the governor broad powers in reorganizing the militia.

Missourians held mass meetings in January to select candidates for the convention. These revealed that most of them preferred to take a cautious approach to secession. They were concerned with what the surrounding slave states of Arkansas, Kentucky, and Tennessee might do. None of these states seemed to be moving toward secession at the moment. What protection could a new Confederacy offer to Missouri, which stuck like a sore thumb into the heart of Northern territory? Where did the state's greatest economic interests lie—with an agrarian South or an increasingly industrialized East?

In the final balloting only pro-Union delegates were elected. These differed, however, on whether they would place any conditions on Missouri's staying put. Many strongly opposed any form of force against the Southern states that had already seceded. Meeting for eighteen days in St. Louis, the convention decided that Missouri had no cause for leaving the Union at present. It urged that a national convention be called by the state legislatures to ratify a recently proposed constitutional amendment guaranteeing slavery. Beyond that it pleaded for caution and compromise by both North and South. The convention agreed to meet again, at the call of a committee, if later events changed the situation.

The Outbreak of Civil War

The Confederate attack on Fort Sumter, South Carolina, on April 12 pushed the nation into civil war. The President called for 75,000 volunteers to put down the rebellion and gave a quota to each state. Governor Jackson curtly refused to cooperate, whereupon Frank Blair volunteered 4,000 of his Home Guard for the assignment. Lincoln accepted them, and they were provided with arms from the United States arsenal in south St. Louis. Surplus guns from that facility were sent across the river for Illinois troops.

Blair moved quickly to consolidate the Union military position in St. Louis. He had the local commander, General William S. Harney, a conservative veteran whom he feared might be pro-Southern, recalled to Washington for consultation. In Harney's absence the responsibility for the newly mustered troops fell on Captain Nathaniel Lyon, a staunch antislavery man who had only recently arrived at Jefferson Barracks from military service on the Kansas plains. Lyon had already indicated his willingness to work closely with Blair to ensure Union control of the vital St. Louis arsenal and its approaches. He now received a commission as brigadier general of volunteers and deployed his troops throughout south St. Louis to protect the arsenal against secessionist threats. Lyon also secured authorization to muster in another 10,000 volunteers.

The possibility of a secessionist move against the arsenal was not idle speculation. Governor Jackson, following the attack on Fort Sumter, had decided that the changing circumstances warranted Missouri's withdrawal from the Union. His concern then became how and when to accomplish it. Following a secret meeting in St. Louis with some of his followers, he decided on a twofold plan of action: to call the legislature into special session to secure the reorganization of the militia giving him greater control, and to order the existing militia into one-week training camps as a coverup for an attempt to seize the St. Louis arsenal and its arms.

The Camp Jackson Affair

By the time these two plans could be put into effect early in May, Lyon and Blair had made their moves in relation to the arsenal. Although this made it impossible for the governor to carry out his real intentions, the militia still went into camp across the state on Monday, May 6. In St. Louis they established Camp Jackson, which received several boxes marked "marble Tamaroa" from downriver on Tuesday. These contained arms and ammunition from the Baton Rouge, Louisiana, arsenal, which had been forwarded by Confederate President Jefferson Davis following an urgent appeal from Governor Jackson for help. Although these cases remained unopened, Lyon through his spies knew of their arrival and strongly suspected their real contents.

Almost simultaneously Lyon received word that a group of secessionists had seized the small federal arsenal at Liberty, removing its four brass guns and 1,500 stand of arms. He became more apprehensive when he toured Camp Jackson on Thursday afternoon of muster week disguised as Frank Blair's blind mother-in-law out for a carriage ride. During this outing he observed small Confederate flags flying from some of the tent poles and homemade signs at certain street intersections designating "Davis" and "Beauregard" avenues.

Convinced by all of this that the few hundred militiamen constituted a threat to his forces, Lyon consulted the local Union Committee of Safety and informed them of his intention to seize the camp Friday morning. Outnumbering the state forces better than ten to one, the federal troops met with no resistance other than written protests as they surrounded Camp Jackson on what was to have been the last day of the muster. They took the militia prisoners. As they marched their captives toward Jefferson Barracks, however, a fight broke out between the Union army and the crowd that had gathered to watch the sight. Shots rang out, and before things quieted down again twenty-eight persons lay dead. Although Lyon's official investigation placed the blame with the crowd, Missourians now felt the full impact of war.

Preparation for War

As word of the Camp Jackson affair spread across St. Louis and the state, many residents became panic-stricken. Hundreds in the city packed whatever belongings they could and fled down the Mississippi or into the country. Rumors circulated that Lyon and his troops were en route to Jefferson City. There the General Assembly, which had been leisurely considering Governor Jackson's proposals for reorganizing the militia, suddenly caught fire as word reached them on Friday evening of the Camp Jackson affair and the subsequent riot. Legislation quickly passed both houses giving the governor full power over a new State Guard, with moneys transferred from the school fund to support it. The wisdom of the Camp Jackson affair has been questioned by some. Lyon's moves had pushed the legisla-

General Nathaniel Lyon leading his troops at the Battle of Wilson's Creek. *Courtesy State Historical Society of Missouri*

ture into the very action Jackson had wanted for months. They also drove a number of "conditional Unionists" into the secession camp. In view of what they considered a federal attack upon the state, they felt they had to come to the defense of Missouri.

Governor Jackson lost no time in pushing organization of the new State Guard. He named Sterling Price, former governor and hero of the Mexican War who had chaired the recent state convention, as Guard commander. Orders went out for every able-bodied male to enroll in the defense of the state in their respective districts. Into this highly emotional atmosphere, General Harney returned from Washington to resume his command at St. Louis. He quickly restored order there and proceeded to negotiate a highly controversial truce agreement with Price. Under its terms both parties agreed to maintain order within their respective areas of operation. This angered extremists on both sides. Historians have disagreed considerably on the sincerity of the state government's motives in entering into such an agreement: was it seeking genuine neutrality or simply playing for time until it could take Missouri into the Confederacy?

Whatever the case, the agreement proved short-lived. Blocked from aggressive action now that Harney was again on the scene, Blair and Lyon successfully maneuvered Harney's removal for a second and final time. Once back in command, Lyon refused to negotiate an extension of the Harney-Price agreement. In a confrontation at the

Planters House hotel in St. Louis on June 11, he told Jackson and Price that they must yield full military control of the state to Union forces or face the consequences. When they protested, he stalked angrily out of the room, declaring: "This means war!"

The Flight of Governor Jackson

The two Missouri leaders hurried to Jefferson City where they called for 50,000 volunteers to fill the State Guard and defend the state. Then, feeling the capital indefensible, Jackson and Price retreated with a small group of followers up the Missouri River to Boonville. Lyon moved into Jefferson City with 2,000 troops on June 15. It would remain an occupied town for the rest of the war. Leaving a garrison there, Lyon followed the fleeing state forces to Boonville where he routed them on the morning of June 17. Jackson and Price now began a retreat into southwest Missouri. Here they hoped to rally the necessary volunteers to establish a base for a counteroffensive.

In the meantime Lyon secured the Missouri River and effectively cut the state in half, thereby greatly reducing the governor's chances for recruiting in north Missouri where he had considerable support. Union troops poured into the state from three sides to reinforce the successful cause. Many of these erroneously assumed that all Missourians automatically supported secession, and they proceeded to harass the civilian population. The frustration and suffering arising out of this situation brought on prolonged guerrilla warfare which would leave Missouri with a bitterness that lasted long after the conflict itself had ended.

With the action heating up on the Missouri front, President Lincoln decided to appoint a better known commander to take charge of the overall situation there and along the line of the Mississippi. His choice was General John Charles Frémont, who had gained fame as a western explorer and was the son-in-law of former Senator Thomas Hart Benton. Lyon remained in command of the forces in western Missouri and moved into Springfield simultaneously with Frémont's appointment.

The Establishment of the Provisional Government

Even as the military command in Missouri was being reorganized in July 1861, so too the political scene underwent change. Governor

Governor Hamilton R. Gamble.
Courtesy State Historical Society of Missouri

Jackson's flight from the capital had created a power vacuum in Jefferson City. The military there simply closed up the remaining state offices, and Missouri operated temporarily without an effective civilian government. Into this crisis stepped the state convention that had decided against secession the previous March. Recalled by its special committee, it met at Jefferson City on July 22 and declared that the governor and his followers had forfeited all right to rule by resisting federal forces. Those who argued that the General Assembly alone had the power to impeach and remove state officials were quickly brushed aside as the convention formally deposed the members of both the executive and legislative branches of state government. In their place it established a provisional government headed by Hamilton R. Gamble of St. Louis, former chief justice of the state supreme court and a conservative Whig attorney. Until a new legislature could be elected, the convention agreed to meet at Governor Gamble's call to take care of any necessary business. Before adjourning it repealed the recently passed militia reorganization act and reinstated the 1859 law.

The Confederates Help Governor Jackson

Claiborne Jackson had not been idle during July. Following their retreat from Boonville and a skirmish near Carthage, he and Price made camp near Cowskin Prairie in McDonald County. Less than 10,000 recruits joined them there, but Price worked hard to make these into an effective fighting force. Meanwhile the governor headed east to negotiate an agreement with the Confederacy. Taking with him former Senator David R. Atchison, a close personal friend of Jefferson Davis, Jackson arrived in Richmond on July 26, even as the convention was turning him out of office. There the two persuaded a skeptical Confederate President of the sincerity of their cause and got him to promise to pay Missouri troops cooperating with the South as soon as his congress could make the necessary funds available. Jackson in turn assured Davis that he would take the necessary steps to withdraw Missouri from the Union upon his return there.

Returning by way of Memphis, Jackson and Atchison went immediately to New Madrid. That town had just been occupied by a Confederate force under General Gideon J. Pillow that had moved into southeast Missouri to cooperate with State Guardsmen under General M. Jeff Thompson. After consulting with Thompson and several other advisers at New Madrid, the governor issued a proclamation of independence on August 5. Word came quickly that the congress in Richmond had appropriated $1 million for Missouri troops cooperating with the Confederacy.

Wilson's Creek and Lexington

The combined armies of the new "allies" had their first major engagement a few days later (August 10) at Wilson's Creek near Springfield. Price had been reinforced by Confederate troops under General Ben McCulloch and Arkansas State Guardsmen under General N. B. Pearce. They now advanced toward Springfield with an army nearly double the Union forces commanded by Lyon (14,000 to 7,000). Lyon had called for reinforcements which Frémont felt he could not spare because of the Confederate advance into southeast Missouri. He ordered Lyon to retreat; but the Union commander gave battle instead, hoping that his better trained and equipped troops could carry the day. In the fierce fighting that followed, Lyon was killed. His army fell back to Rolla. The Battle of Wilson's Creek marked a stirring comeback for Price and his State Guardsmen.

Wishing to push farther while he had the advantage, Price proposed a move into northwest Missouri in the hope of securing additional recruits and supplies. McCulloch refused to extend his lines from Arkansas that far, but Price went anyway. He scored his second consecutive triumph at Lexington during mid-September in what is known as the "Battle of the Hemp Bales." After several days of siege, Price simply wetted down a large number of bales and using them as a shield slowly advanced on the Union lines which were backed up against the Missouri River. Without reinforcement, the federal troops had to surrender. The battlefield at Lexington, dominated by Anderson House, which was used as a field hospital, is well preserved today as a state park.

Missouri Joins the Confederacy

Recruits now flocked to Price's banner. Governor Jackson, who had rejoined the state forces just prior to the battle, used the occasion to call a special session of the legislature for late October to ratify his New Madrid proclamation. With his lines too extended and Frémont organizing an army to move against him, Price retreated into southwest Missouri to await further military and political developments. What remained of the Missouri General Assembly (historians are undecided on whether a quorum actually appeared) gathered at Neosho and passed an ordinance of secession on October 28. Three days later Missouri's agents in Richmond signed an offensive-defensive alliance with the Confederacy. Missouri thereby became the "twelfth Confederate state." The Jackson government cooperated fully with Southern authorities during the remainder of the war and was represented in the congress at Richmond.

In February 1862, General Samuel R. Curtis forced Price and his State Guardsmen to leave Missouri. They joined forces with Confederates under General Earl Van Dorn in Arkansas, but Curtis pushed his army forward to defeat them at the Battle of Pea Ridge on March 7 and 8. Simultaneously General John Pope captured New Madrid so that the State Guard under M. Jeff Thompson had to evacuate southeast Missouri. After this Price and those of his command who wished to follow him formally entered Confederate military service and were transferred to duty east of the Mississippi. Claiborne Jackson continued a government-in-exile in Arkansas until his death at Little Rock in December 1862. He was succeeded by Lieutenant Governor Thomas C. Reynolds, who carried on a shadow government from his headquarters at Marshall, Texas, until war's end.

The Missouri State Militia

Even as Governor Jackson was working to take Missouri into the Confederacy, his Union counterpart, Governor Gamble, was getting his new government established. Gamble quickly found himself involved in a number of controversies with General Frémont over where their respective lines of civilian and military authority lay. A staunch conservative, Gamble was interested in cooperation with rather than domination by federal authorities. Yet with Missouri facing an empty treasury, he had to rely increasingly on financial aid from Washington, especially for the payment of a new state militia that he wanted to organize.

Disturbed by the belligerent attitude of out-of-state troops toward Missouri's rural population, Gamble hoped that the establishment of a new militia would make it possible for the state's own citizens to patrol their home front and keep order. He believed that many who would not serve outside Missouri might be willing to enlist for such a purpose. Frémont was only the first of several military commanders who saw this move as a potential threat to his authority. The Lincoln administration, desiring the fullest possible use of manpower, pushed for a compromise. The federal government would pay and arm Missouri militia if the troops could be directed by the Union commander at St. Louis. That way he could coordinate the total military effort in the state. There were constant stresses and strains on this arrangement, but it continued in effect until the last year of the war. During that time some 50,000 to 75,000 Missourians enlisted in a home front militia even though they probably would not have served the Union cause elsewhere. By so doing they freed that many regular troops for service on the major fronts.

Martial Law in Missouri

Closely related to the controversy over the militia was the question of martial law. Once established at the end of August 1861, it remained in effect throughout the war as one commander after another imposed a variety of sanctions on the state. With Missouri torn by intense guerrilla warfare, Governor Gamble and his supporters had little choice but to yield to military authority and cooperate with it wherever possible. Without martial law there would have been no way they could have kept even the small appearance of order that did exist.

Operations under martial law touched the life of every Missouri citizen. Military passes were necessary to move from one area of the state to another. Trade was licensed, and the military exercised an indirect censorship over newspapers in that they could close down any they thought to be hostile to the war effort. Military regulations governed the sale and use of firearms as well as the hours and nature of places of amusement. For example, they forbade the sale of liquor after noon on Sunday in the hope that this would ensure a sober work force the following day.

Enforcing an increasingly complex set of rules was the provost marshal system, which became the basic police power within the state. Headed by a provost marshal general, who was part of the military setup in St. Louis, the system consisted of district provosts and their deputies, who had virtually unlimited powers of arrest and confinement within their areas. Persons could be detained for indefinite periods on the least suspicion of disloyal activity. They were not subject to ordinary legal proceedings because martial law provided for the suspension of the writ of habeas corpus under which a suspect had to be informed of the charges against him or be released within a short time.

Temporary stockades were established throughout the state. From these prisoners charged with serious crimes were funneled into either Myrtle Street prison or Gratiot Street prison in St. Louis. Myrtle Street had been a "slave pen" before the war, while Gratiot Street had been a medical college whose proprietor had joined Governor Jackson in Arkansas. In these places one would find guerrillas, political prisoners, army deserters, hardened criminals, and Confederate prisoners of war crammed together in overcrowded and unsanitary facilities. Many political prisoners, after a military hearing, would either be released on heavy bond or banished into some Northern state for the duration of the war. Those who engaged in more hostile activities like sabotage or guerrilla warfare might be executed or placed indefinitely in the new federal prison across the river at Alton, Illinois.

General Sterling Price's troops behind the hemp bales, Battle of Lexington. *Courtesy State Historical Society of Missouri*

When refugees flooded into St. Louis during the winter of 1861–62 following the heavy fighting in southwest Missouri, General Henry W. Halleck, who succeeded Frémont, resorted to yet another tactic of martial law—assessment. To enforce loyalty, Halleck supported the provisional government's requirement of a test oath. Those who swore allegiance to the Union by mid-December 1861 would be assumed to be loyal. Those who refused were labeled "secesh" and subjected to fines or confiscation of property to help pay the costs of supporting the refugees. Out-state, suspected disloyalists, including some who had taken the oath, were assessed in relation to their wealth to help pay for the ravages of guerrilla warfare in their area. In the Liberty district alone, according to press reports, provost marshals required 612 persons to post bond for good behavior during 1862. These bonds ranged from $1,000 to $10,000 and totaled $840,000. At the other end of the state, the Palmyra provost reported taking in more than $1 million from "several thousand traitors" for the same period.

Undoubtedly many Missourians took the oath reluctantly. To refuse to do so could cause them untold difficulties including possible banishment. All kinds of abuses crept into the system as the provosts exercised a highly arbitrary power over suspects. Once accused, persons could have great difficulty proving their innocence before a military tribunal. Frequently they might wait weeks for even a hearing. When a military company was foraging on the countryside in search of supplies, oaths meant little where need existed. Many Missourians violated their oaths under pressure from guerrilla relatives, friends, or following a change of heart. Matters usually went even harsher for these persons if they were discovered.

Guerrilla Warfare

Martial law was most strictly applied where guerrilla warfare was worst. This in turn intensified the activities of the guerrillas. Missourians found themselves caught in a vicious cycle as both guerrillas and militia terrorized the countryside. It was frequently difficult to tell friend from foe when encountering a party on horseback, and a miscalculation could prove fatal to life or property. Old animosities from prewar days often came into play as individuals from both sides sought to repay grudges. Guerrillas in Missouri were usually of two kinds: Confederate raiders such as Colonel Joseph Porter, who came north to recruit Southern sympathizers and to harass Union outposts in the summer of 1862; and irregular "bushwhackers" such as William Clarke Quantrill, who became a legendary folk hero along the western border and spawned a tradition of lawlessness that carried over into the postwar era.

The movement by Colonel Porter and some eight other "partisan rangers" followed the collapse of Confederate hopes for regaining Missouri by regular warfare following the Battle of Pea Ridge. Believing that many Missourians would join the Confederate service if but given the chance, Governor Jackson, from his exile in Arkansas, supported the move to send the rangers north to recruit and do whatever behind-the-scenes damage they could to Union forces. Each partisan was to operate within a different area of the state. Porter played havoc through northeast Missouri (he had joined the State Guard from Lewis County a year earlier) for six months. His force varied in size but on occasion numbered several hundred.

A tragic climax to his activities came in October 1862 with what is known locally as the "Palmyra Massacre." During a raid on that town, Porter's rangers carried off a Union citizen, Andrew Allsman, who was never seen again. In retaliation the local military commander ordered that ten Confederate prisoners, chosen at random, would be shot if Allsman did not reappear within ten days. The time passed, and no word came from the unfortunate captive. So, on October 18, amid considerable protest (for most of the prisoners were local guerrillas), the sentence was carried out, each victim standing at the foot of his own coffin to face the firing squad. As for Colonel Porter, he met his end in a small skirmish in Wright County the following January.

A native of Ohio, young Bill Quantrill had been involved in a variety of legal and illegal activities along the western border before the war. During the winter of 1861–62, this natural-born leader organized an irregular guerrilla band to strike back at Union troops from Kansas who had been looting western Missouri farms and towns indiscriminately that summer and fall. Although Governor Gamble protested the actions of the Kansans, General Halleck replied that he could do little to control them. Quantrill and his followers responded by taking matters into their own hands. Supported by a sympathetic and harassed population, they made good use of the cover afforded by the vast wooded stretches along the border. It was referred to as "hiding in the bush" and hence the term bushwhacker. One could never be quite certain where these guerrillas might put in an appearance, as they kept the border in a constant state of turmoil.

Union authorities countered with increasingly strict measures, especially against the civilians who were suspected of aiding the guerrillas. The situation reached a climax in the summer of 1863 when General Tom Ewing, commanding the border district, rounded up all of the women known to have any association with the Quantrill band. He was keeping them in a makeshift prison when it suddenly collapsed from overcrowding early in August. In the rubble five of the women lay dead. Several others were seriously injured. While there is no proof, as the guerrillas claimed, that Ewing deliberately promoted the tragedy, Quantrill's men moved quickly in retaliation. On August 21 they raided the unsuspecting town of Lawrence, Kansas, gunning down 150 men and boys and leaving behind more than $2 million in property damage.

Order Number Eleven

General Ewing responded with a policy that he had been urging on his superiors throughout the summer—the mass evacuation of all those suspected of hiding or otherwise helping guerrillas within a four-county area. All persons living more than a mile's distance from a Union military outpost in Jackson, Cass, Bates, and the northern half of Vernon County were ordered to leave their homes within fifteen days. Those who could prove their loyalty might remain within the military district. Others had to move elsewhere. Ewing called in Kansas troops to enforce his orders and thereby made an already unfortunate situation even worse. The noted artist George Caleb Bingham left a vivid picture of this tragedy in his painting *Order No. 11*. Most of those uprooted had inadequate transportation for even the barest essentials in the way of furniture and clothing, and there were no guarantees regarding the safety of property left behind. Much of the border area lay in ruin within two weeks and became known for years as the "Burnt District." "It is heart sickening to see what I have seen since I have been back here," one officer told his wife. "A desolated country and men & women and children, some of them almost naked. Some on foot and some in old wagons."

George Caleb Bingham's painting *Order No. 11* from a line and mezzotint engraving by John Sartain. *Courtesy State Historical Society of Missouri*

The Emancipation Issue

Yet another problem confronted Missourians in the midst of war. This was the question of the future of slavery. In the same orders in which he proclaimed martial law on August 30, 1861, General Frémont called for the confiscation of the property, including slaves, of all those who had taken up arms against the Union. The slaves would be freed. Such a policy ran counter to the programs of both Governor Gamble and President Lincoln. The governor had made it clear in assuming office that he had no intention of interfering with slavery. Lincoln had indicated throughout 1861 that his main concern was the preservation of the Union. With Kentucky proclaiming its neutrality and Missouri seemingly swaying in the balance following the Battle of Wilson's Creek, the President had no desire to alienate the large mass of conservative slaveholders in those two states. Consequently he asked Frémont to reconsider that part of his proclamation. When the general refused, Lincoln revoked it unilaterally.

Many Missourians who opposed slavery, especially the Germans in the eastern part of the state, had welcomed General Frémont's stand. They believed that Governor Gamble had brought undue pressure on the President to reverse his military commander. When Lincoln removed Frémont for military and political incompetence early in November 1861, these Missourians ignored the real reasons and pictured the commander as a martyr to the antislavery cause.

The movement to end slavery gathered momentum that winter both in Missouri and at the national level. As the war moved back and forth across western Missouri, numerous slaves fled their owners, seeking refuge within Union lines. Frémont had encouraged fleeing slaves while he was in the field against Price; but his successor, General Halleck, ordered that all runaways be turned back from his lines. Still the newspapers were filled with notices of absentee slaves. Slowly Missourians began to question how slavery would fit into the state's postwar future. While the Germans and others opposed slavery on moral grounds, many began to see it as the cause for the conflict and all the misery it had brought. If the war did not root out slavery, the fighting would have been in vain. Still others feared that the continued use of slave labor would handicap the state in attracting new capital and immigration with which to rebuild after the war.

When Congress convened in December 1861, the drive against slavery moved forward on two fronts. President Lincoln proposed freeing the slaves in the border states while providing some kind of payment to their owners. Most of the congressmen from those areas, including Missouri, rejected this. Meanwhile, under pressure from its radical antislavery members, Congress outlawed slavery in the District of Columbia and provided for a tighter confiscation act that called for the seizure of Confederate property, including slaves, who would be freed. Climaxing all this activity, Lincoln announced his preliminary Emancipation Proclamation in September 1862, which paved the way for freeing the slaves in the Confederate South.

All of this tended to encourage those in Missouri who believed that the time had come to end slavery there. With elections for a new legislature set for the fall of 1862, they saw this as the opportunity to debate the issue. Missourians soon found themselves divided into three groups: the "Charcoals," who favored moving quickly toward emancipation and supported the enlistment of blacks in the armed forces; the "Claybanks," conservatives who had begun to realize that slavery was doomed but wished to phase it out gradually; and the "Snowflakes," who clung firmly to the belief that slavery could survive the war. This last group were a definite minority, as most voters divided fairly evenly between Charcoals and Claybanks.

The Western Sanitary Commission ministering to the wounded.
Courtesy State Historical Society of Missouri

Governor Gamble, who had joined the Claybanks during the fall campaign, urged the new General Assembly to pass a program of gradual emancipation when it convened at the end of December 1862. But the legislators argued long and hard over method and got nowhere. Efforts by Senator John B. Henderson and Congressman John W. Noell in Washington to provide compensation in the event of legislative action also failed. Consequently Governor Gamble called the old state convention into session for the fifth and final time in July 1863. Taking a personal hand in its proceedings (he was still a member), Gamble guided through an emancipation plan which provided that slavery would be abolished in Missouri on July 4, 1870, with varying degrees of apprenticeship, depending upon the age of the slave at the time he was freed. The Charcoals were led by Charles D. Drake, a St. Louis lawyer who had been converted to the antislavery cause a year earlier. They pushed in vain for more immediate action. Having failed to carry the day in the convention, they launched the Radical Union party of Missouri in September and took their cause to the people.

Many of Missouri's slaves declined to wait quietly for the "day of jubilee" to come in 1870. They fled their owners' farms in ever-increasing numbers. This proved especially true in the border counties where they were sometimes encouraged by the district military commanders, who promptly enlisted them in the Union army. Although many Missourians protested this kind of action, they became increasingly reconciled to it as time went on. Their acceptance increased noticeably when President Lincoln approved a compensation of $300 to loyal owners for each slave thus recruited. The general public also found the program easier to take when they learned that black enlistments counted against the state's draft quota. In the end Missouri officially furnished 8,344 blacks, including 665 who served as substitutes for white draftees, to the nation's armed forces.

The Western Sanitary Commision

Various groups sprang up to assist not only the runaways from Missouri but the increasingly large number of slaves who arrived in St. Louis from farther south by way of the Mississippi. Most important in coordinating relief work in the Mississippi Valley was the Western Sanitary Commission, established in September 1865, by General Frémont at the instigation of William G. Eliot, a local Unitarian minister and the founder of Washington University. The Western Sanitary Commission quickly worked to provide adequate military hospitals in St. Louis for the wounded in the wake of the Battle of Wilson's Creek. During the following winter it outfitted railroad cars and floating hospitals to move the wounded from the various battlefields to the general military hospitals in St. Louis and elsewhere. It forwarded all kinds of supplies to the battlefronts to alleviate suffering.

The commission also found itself involved with numerous other enterprises from aiding refugee whites and blacks who flooded into St. Louis from the southwest to providing soldiers' homes (similar to present-day USOs) for military on leave. It also sought to regulate conditions in Union military prisons in the area.

One of the commission's most important undertakings was its work with the freed slaves. Under the leadership of its president, James E. Yeatman, the commission sought to create fair working conditions for the former slaves on leased plantations in the Mississippi Valley. It set up schools for freed slaves and furnished a variety of relief supplies and services. In 1864 it established a Freedman's Orphans Home in St. Louis under the supervision of the Ladies Union Aid Society. This latter group had worked throughout the war as an auxiliary of the Western Sanitary Commission providing all kinds of clothing and supplies for troops and refugees.

The two groups raised funds through a variety of appeals and programs. Of these, the most auspicious was the Mississippi Valley Sanitary Fair. Held in St. Louis in May 1864, it ran for three weeks and netted $554,591 for the cause. The fairgrounds covered a square block, with many displays geared to a patriotic motif. One of the main attractions was "a wreath wrought of hair collected from the heads of a large circle of United States generals, and nearly all the members of the President's Cabinet."

The Radical Union Party

Most Missourians found the times increasingly hard. The war-torn conditions around the state discouraged both commerce and agriculture. Except for St. Louis and those few places out-state that served as military outposts, economic stagnation was the order of the day. Money for any purpose became a scarce commodity. While Missouri's banks remained open, they floated a sea of paper money that had no specie backing. The shortage of coins made postage stamps a popular monetary substitute although their sticky backs could cause users some problems in hot weather. Farming suffered as federal troops and guerrillas competed with each other for supplies, and much of the agricultural labor force became increasingly migratory. One observer reported that Kansas City was "shabby and dilapidated" in the midst of constant raiding. A cloud of uneasiness seemed to cover the entire state.

The Radical Union party, which had been organized in the fall of 1863, sought to take political advantage of this unrest. Condemning the conservative policies of Governor Gamble, it called for a speedup in the emancipation process so as to create a favorable atmosphere for the attraction of white immigrants and outside capital investment. The Radicals painted themselves as progressives who could move Missouri into the vanguard of the future. Although they narrowly lost a special judicial election in the fall of 1863, they consolidated their strength sufficiently in the legislature that winter to elect one of their leaders, B. Gratz Brown, to the United States Senate. And before the session ended they had arranged to put before the people in the fall of 1864 a referendum for a new convention to reconsider the issue of slavery.

The conservative cause was greatly injured in January 1864 when Governor Gamble became ill with pneumonia following a fall and died. Lieutenant Governor Willard P. Hall of St. Joseph succeeded him and headed the provisional government during its final year. The conservatives received a further setback that summer from the failure of their delegates to the Republican National Convention to gain seats over a rival Radical slate. The Radicals controlled the party machinery to put up their own slate of candidates for state office that fall, forcing conservatives either to accept these or go over to the revived Democratic party.

The Centralia Massacre

Guerrilla warfare increased during the summer and fall of 1864. Quantrill had been unable to hold his band together in winter quarters, and it fragmented into several groups. Foremost among these was the one led by "Bloody Billy" Anderson, so named because of his unrelenting savagery (one of his sisters had been killed and another badly hurt in the collapse of Ewing's makeshift prison the previous summer, leaving Anderson thirsting for vengeance). Anderson cut a wide path through central Missouri that summer, climaxing on September 27 with the infamous "Centralia Massacre." Arriving in the central Missouri town early that morning, Anderson and his followers proceeded to terrorize the inhabitants. Around ten o'clock in the morning the stage from Columbia rolled in, carrying among its passengers Unionist Congressman James S. Rollins; these quickly found themselves relieved of their personal belongings but escaped unharmed. Rollins passed himself off as a local farmer of Southern leanings. When the noon train arrived from St. Charles, the Anderson gang barricaded the tracks and forced its passengers into the depot. Twenty-five unarmed furloughed Union troops were on board. Anderson stood these in line, calmly ordered them to strip, and then shot them one by one. He spared only one lone sergeant brave enough to step forward when the guerrilla leader asked if there were any commissioned or noncommissioned officers among them. The gang took Sergeant Thomas Goodman with them as a hostage and later released him after they had roared out of town.

Price's Raid

Later events proved that the guerrilla activity was intended to soften Missouri up for an invasion of Confederate regulars under General

Union Military Bond issued by the State of Missouri, 1865. *Courtesy State Historical Society of Missouri*

Sterling Price that fall. Price and Governor Thomas C. Reynolds had long been urging Confederate authorities in Arkansas to authorize a return to Missouri. They pointed to the success of General Jo Shelby's raid into southwest Missouri in January 1863, when he had captured Springfield briefly and brought back a lot of supplies. They finally secured the agreement of General E. Kirby Smith, who commanded west of the Mississippi, early in August 1864. Smith hoped that such a movement might keep Union troops from General William T. Sherman, who stood at the gates of Atlanta, as well as gather badly needed recruits and supplies. Reynolds wanted the capture of Jefferson City so that his government-in-exile might be restored to its rightful capital. In preparation, Price sent orders to the guerrillas to step up their raiding north of the Missouri River to draw Union troops away from the southern part of the state, thereby making his invasion easier.

Price entered Missouri on September 19 with some 12,000 troops, two years and seven months after he had been driven out in early 1862. He came full of hope that a pro-Confederate population would rise up to greet him. He met instead a mixed reaction and in the end retreated to Arkansas with little accomplished. Disaster first struck when Price mismanaged his army against a small Union garrison at Pilot Knob. From there he moved west along the Missouri River, coming in sight of the Missouri capitol's dome but bypassing the heavily fortified Jefferson City to the south. Union forces hemmed him in near Kansas City, handed him a major defeat at the Battle of Westport on October 23, and sent him scurrying down the Kansas border into Arkansas.

The Election of 1864

Missourians went to the polls two weeks later and voted overwhelmingly for the Radical ticket and a new state convention. Fifty-two thousand fewer persons cast ballots than had done so in 1860. Many had gone into exile, either voluntarily or otherwise. Others had been disfranchised because of their unwillingness or inability to take the test oath of loyalty. Those who remained were tired of war. They looked to the future rather than the past and hoped for a new day as the conflict rapidly drew to a close. Missourians were about to enter a new era, one that would prove almost as turbulent as that through which they had just come.

Suggestions for Reading

The best overall treatment of Missouri during the Civil War is to be found in William E. Parrish, *A History of Missouri. Vol. III, 1860 to 1875*, rev. ed., Columbia, University of Missouri Press, 2001. An excellent account of the problems of guerrilla warfare and martial law is Richard S. Brownlee, *Gray Ghosts of the Confederacy*, Baton Rouge: Louisiana State University Press, 1958. For a penetrating insight into the effect of guerrilla warfare on the general populace, one should consult Michael Fellman, *Inside War: The Guerrilla Conflict in Missouri During the American Civil War*, New York, Oxford University Press, 1989, and Thomas Goodrich, *Black Flag: Guerrilla Warfare on the Western Border, 1861–1865*, Bloomington, Indiana University Press, 1995. The careers of Missouri's two most noted guerrillas are covered in Edward E. Leslie, *The Devil Knows How to Ride: The True Story of William Clarke Quantrill*, New York, Da Capo Press, 1996, and Albert Castel and Thomas Goodrich, *Bloody Bill Anderson: The Short Savage Life of a Civil War Guerrilla*, Mechanicsburg, PA, Stackpole Books, 1998. For detailed sketches of the men who rode with Quantrill, see Joseph K. Houts, Jr., *Quantrill's Thieves*, Kansas City, Truman Publishing Company, 2002. An in-depth examination of Missouri's first major battle and its participants can be found in William Garrett Piston and Richard W. Hatcher III in *Wilson's Creek: The Second Battle of the Civil War and the Men Who Fought It*, Chapel Hill, University of North Carolina Press, 2000.

An interesting contemporary insight into life in wartime St. Louis is offered by Galusha Anderson, *A Border City During the Civil*

War, Boston, Little Brown, 1908. An excellent overview of the city's struggles during the conflict is Louis S. Gerteis, *Civil War St. Louis,* Lawrence, University of Kansas Press, 2001. An intriguing fictionalized account based on real incidents in St. Louis is Winston Churchill, *The Crisis,* New York, Washington Square Press, 1962. The role of the St. Louis Germans is to be found in Steven Rowan and James Neal Primm, eds., *Germans for a Free Society: Translations from the St. Louis Radical Press, 1857–1862,* Columbia, University of Missouri Press, 1983. William E. Parrish, "The Western Sanitary Commission," *Civil War History,* March 1990, provides a comprehensive study of that agency, which was centered in St. Louis, and its work. The story of its auxiliary is told in Paula Coalier, "Beyond Sympathy: The St. Louis Ladies' Union Aid Society and the Civil War," *Gateway Heritage,* Summer 1990, while Robert Patrick Bender, "'This Noble and Philanthropic Enterprise': The Mississippi Valley Sanitary Fair of 1864 and the Practice of Civil War Philanthropy," *Missouri Historical Review,* January 2001, details that important undertaking of these agencies. Michael Fellman, "Emancipation in Missouri," *Missouri Historical Review,* October 1988, gives a good overview of that topic, while Lawrence O. Christensen, "Black Education in Civil War St. Louis," *Missouri Historical Review,* April 2001, offers insights into another aspect of it.

The key figures at the outset of the war receive biographical treatment in Christopher Phillips, *Damned Yankee: The Life of General Nathaniel Lyon,* Columbia, University of Missouri Press, 1990; William E. Parrish, *Frank Blair: Lincoln's Conservative,* Columbia, University of Missouri Press, 1998; Christopher Phillips, *Missouri's Confederate: Claiborne Fox Jackson and the Creation of a Southern Identity in the Border West,* Columbia, University of Missouri Press, 2000; George Rollie Adams, *General William S. Harney: Prince of Dragoons,* Lincoln, University of Nebraska Press, 2001; and Robert E. Miller, "Daniel Marsh Frost, C.S.A.," *Missouri Historical Review,* July 1991. General John C. Frémont's impact on Missouri's controversies is covered by William E. Parrish, "Frémont in Missouri," *Civil War Times Illustrated,* April 1978, and Robert L. Turkoly-Joczik, "Frémont and the Western Department," *Missouri Historical Review,* July 1988. Yet another important Union figure receives biographical treatment in James L. McDonough, *Schofield: Union General in the Civil War,* Tallahassee, Florida State University Press, 1972. A key member of Lincoln's cabinet from Missouri is dealt with in Marvin R. Cain, *Lincoln's Attorney*

General: Edward Bates of Missouri, Columbia, University of Missouri Press, 1965. Unfortunately, no published biography exists for Missouri's wartime Union governor, Hamilton R. Gamble.

Missouri's relationship with the Confederacy is discussed in William E. Parrish, "Missouri," in W. Buck Yearns, ed., *The Confederate Governors,* Athens, University of Georgia Press, 1985. Biographical studies of Missouri's leading Confederate generals are Robert E. Shalhope, *Sterling Price: Portrait of a Southerner,* Columbia, University of Missouri Press, 1971; Donald J. Stanton, Goodwin F. Berquist, and Paul C. Bowers, *The Civil War Reminiscences of General M. Jeff Thompson,* Dayton, Ohio, Morningside House, 1988; and Daniel O'Flaherty, *General Jo Shelby: Undefeated Rebel,* Chapel Hill, University of North Carolina Press, 1954.

Radical Rule

The Radical Union Party sat firmly in the saddle as Missouri moved into the post–Civil War era. This new political force included an amazing variety of discontented groups: Germans, who had begun arriving in Missouri in large numbers during the 1850s, with their strong antislavery bent and forward-looking social outlook; small farmers and poor whites of the Ozark and north Missouri regions, who had little interest in slavery but were disturbed by the guerrilla warfare that had torn up their areas; St. Louis merchants and would-be capitalists, who saw the state's potential for economic growth after the war as dependent upon getting rid of slavery; and a few ardent abolitionists, who sincerely wished to improve the lot of the black population. Most were newcomers to politics and eager to make the most of its opportunities for economic power.

Considerable violence still existed as the war wound down early in 1865. But the Radicals already anticipated the conflict's end and were anxious to get on with the task of reconstruction as Governor Thomas C. Fletcher took the oath of office on January 2. "Being victorious everywhere," he urged his followers, "let magnanimity now distinguish our action; and, having nothing more to ask for party, let us, forgetful of past differences, seek only to promote the general good of the people of the whole commonwealth."

Had the Radicals heeded their governor they might have had a more far-reaching political influence on the state. They had a progressive, farsighted program that laid a strong foundation for Missouri's postwar growth. But they let fear of and revenge toward their political enemies overshadow their positive programs, and this ultimately split and destroyed their party.

The main arena in which the Radicals hammered out their program was the new state convention that met on January 6, 1865. Overwhelmingly Radical, most of its delegates lacked political experience. Only three had served in the wartime convention. Two-thirds of the members were under the age of fifty. No single occupation dominated, there being about an equal number of farmers, lawyers, merchants, and doctors.

Charles D. Drake

The dominant figure in the convention was Charles D. Drake, who had played a major role in creating the Radical coalition in 1863. He

had made a detailed study of the existing state constitution to see where it needed changing and had also studied the policies of other states from which Missouri might profitably borrow. Drake quickly asserted himself within the convention. Remembering his speaking efforts on behalf of the party, the Radical delegates from rural Missouri supported him in nearly every crucial vote. Although Drake sometimes had to trim his sails to suit their temperament, his imprint on the document that the convention produced was so strong that it became known as "Drake's Constitution."

The End of Slavery

The convention passed a simple ordinance providing for immediate emancipation on January 11, with only four dissenting votes. Large-scale celebrations immediately broke out in St. Louis, Jefferson City, and other Radical centers. When Congress sent the Thirteenth

Above: Senator Charles Daniel Drake. *Courtesy State Historical Society of Missouri*

Amendment ending slavery nationwide to the states for ratification the following month, the General Assembly promptly approved it. Considerable feeling existed that the convention should deal only with emancipation and voting rights and then adjourn, leaving to the General Assembly the solution of other problems facing the state. Drake and others, however, saw this as the ideal opportunity for a complete overhaul of the state's constitution. These Radicals feared that if conservative forces later regained power they might try to undo Radical programs for the social and economic betterment of both races in Missouri unless constitutional protections were provided.

The Constitution of 1865

Drake and his coworkers produced a generally progressive constitution for the mid-nineteenth century. They established broad guidelines for the General Assembly to follow in encouraging industrial growth and corporate development, in developing Missouri's resources, and in providing a broad-based public education system for both races, with a fair method of financing. In an effort to make both state and local government more responsible to the people, they shortened the terms of the governor and other elected officials from four years to two years and gave the voters greater opportunity to influence policy through the referendum power. Numerous restrictions were placed on the General Assembly's powers to pass special-interest legislation in the hope of curbing prewar abuses. Interestingly, one of Drake's proposals, which spoke to a modern-day controversy, failed to secure the support of his rural backers. This would have reduced the House of Representatives to one hundred districts without regard to one vote per county. Representation would have been strictly proportional throughout the state, something accomplished by the courts only in the 1960s.

Who Shall Vote?

One of Drake's main concerns was that African Americans not be set free and forgotten. He tried to secure an amendment to the emancipation ordinance giving them full civil rights short of the ballot and the right to hold office. A controversial proposal, this failed at that point; but Drake fought hard and successfully to later incorporate black civil rights into the constitution. He held back on voting and office holding only because he feared that these proposals would lead to the defeat of the entire constitution when it was sent to the people for approval. Most white Missourians shared the racial prejudices of their time, which argued that blacks were unfit for such equality. Perhaps with time and education whites would accept blacks as voters and officeholders. Drake was willing to bide his time.

When the Germans demanded voting rights for aliens who had declared their intentions of becoming citizens, Drake yielded, although he had personal misgivings about this. When it came to another "alien" group, however, he drew the line. Drake went to extreme lengths in proposing that former Confederates and Confederate sympathizers not only be disfranchised but barred from public office, the jury box, the practice of law, and serving as teachers and ministers or as corporation officials and trustees. The new constitution provided for a test oath under which persons had to swear that they had never committed any one of eighty-six different acts of supposed disloyalty against the state or the Union. By this means Drake hoped to ensure absolute Radical control for an indefinite future against a conservative comeback. It would take an absolute majority of the General Assembly to repeal the test oath requirement for voting, and this could not be done until after January 1, 1871; the legislature would have to wait an additional four years to do away with the oath in the other cases.

These provisions touched off some of the strongest controversy surrounding the constitution. Many argued that Missourians who had followed Governor Claiborne Jackson in the early months of the war and then repented should not now be punished. After all, the provisional government had promised amnesty to all who took an oath by December 1861. Many of those taking advantage of that offer had been good citizens since then. Now they would be punished after the fact. Drake replied that many who had taken that oath had later violated it. His followers, many of whom had suffered at the hands of guerrillas, agreed.

Purging the Courts

Not content with ensuring "loyal" officials for the future, the convention went one step further by passing what came to be known as the "Ousting Ordinance." This began as a Radical attempt to purge the judiciary "from the Supreme Bench down" of "hostile" conservative elements. In the end it included all county courts, county recorders, and circuit attorneys. Some 800 offices were declared vacant effective May 1, 1865, and the governor was given the power to fill them by appointment until the next election.

Ratifying the Constitution

Completing its work on April 10, the convention set June 6 for a referendum election. Drake attempted to ensure a favorable result by providing that no one could participate unless he had taken the new test oath. The constitution also allowed Missouri's soldiers in the field to vote. In the end it was the military who carried the constitution by a scant margin of 1,862 out of a total of 85,478 votes cast. The civilian vote went against it by 965.

The conservatives voted solidly against the new constitution while the Radicals split over the issue. Governor Fletcher and many of the Germans believed that Drake and his followers had gone too far in their restrictions against Southern sympathizers and seriously questioned the need for a completely new document. They did not actively campaign against the constitution, however, leaving that to such conservatives as former Attorney General Edward Bates and others. Bates wrote a series of effective letters with the theme: "The Convention was revolutionary, in its origins, in its character and in its acts."

Drake and his supporters countered with the need to effectively curb disloyalty, an argument strengthened by President Lincoln's assassination in the midst of the ratification campaign. They also stressed that the constitution represented the only possible way to social and economic progress. Its acceptance would open the door for a flood of new capital and immigrants, who were merely waiting to see what course Missouri planned to take before committing themselves there or elsewhere.

Testing the Test Oath

The Radicals quickly closed ranks after the election, but controversy over the constitution continued. The Missouri courts soon became the arena for a showdown over the validity of the test oath, particularly as it affected lawyers and preachers. The constitution required the members of the various professions to take the oath by September 2. But the deadline passed with many non-Radical lawyers failing to comply. Enforcement of the oath varied as the state made no provision for its general policing. Several out-state judges refused to re-quire the oath in their courts. In St. Louis, however, nonconforming attorneys found themselves barred from court practice. Two test cases resulted that involved Samuel T. Glover and Alexander J. P. Garesche. When the Missouri Supreme Court upheld the test oath, Garesche appealed to the U.S. Supreme Court.

Meanwhile another case involving Father John A. Cummings, a young Roman Catholic priest from Louisiana, was proceeding in the same direction. Father Cummings was one of numerous members of the clergy who declined to take the test oath because it was against their conscience. Arrested for preaching illegally, he refused to make bond and became an overnight sensation as he sat in the Pike County jail. Defended by some of the country's ablest trial lawyers, who had become interested in the case through the intervention of Frank Blair, Father Cummings also appealed an adverse decision by the Missouri Supreme Court upholding the test oath to the higher level.

The U.S. Supreme Court handed down its decision in *Cummings v. Missouri* on January 14, 1867. By a five-to-four majority, it reversed the judgment of the Missouri high tribunal on the grounds that the test oath constituted both *ex post facto* legislation and a bill of attain-der. By this it meant that the test oath was designed to punish some-thing that occurred before it was passed. Such an act is forbidden by the Constitution. Simultaneously, in the case of *ex parte* Garland, the court also threw out a federal law requiring a stringent test oath for attorneys practicing before it. Consequently not only was a free pul-pit restored in Missouri, but Garesche, Glover, and other lawyers found themselves welcomed once more to the bar of the St. Louis courts after an absence of a year and a half.

Frank Blair offered yet another challenge to the test oath in the late fall of 1865 when he tried to vote in a local St. Louis election us-ing his own oath, which simply declared his allegiance to the state and nation. The election officials refused his ballot and demanded that he take the test oath, but Blair declared he could not do so be-cause he had taken up arms against the legitimate state government of Governor Claiborne Jackson in 1861. Still barred from the polls, Blair brought suit against the poll judges, asking $10,000 damages. With his strong Union record, Blair felt certain that he could win and thereby overthrow the test oath for voting. It took the case four years

The Oath of Loyalty required under the 1865
constitution. McClurg would later become
governor. *Western Historical Manuscripts
Collection, University of Missouri-Columbia,
courtesy State Historical Society of Missouri*

to make its way to the U.S. Supreme Court. Then, in a rare four-
to-four division that tribunal upheld its Missouri counterpart that
the oath could be required at the
polls. In the meantime, Blair had
moved into the front ranks of the
conservative opposition to Radical rule in Missouri.

Election of 1866

The whole controversy over the
constitution spilled over into the election of 1866; moreover President Andrew Johnson's split with congressional Radicals over reconstruction policies added strong national overtones to the state contest. Blair and others organized the Conservative party and put on a
spirited campaign. President Johnson made an appearance in St.
Louis on their behalf. The Radicals, through their control of the General Assembly, tried to curb Conservative strength by passing a strong
registration act. Largely the work of Drake, this law provided that local Radical officials would have almost unlimited power in determining the loyalty of any individual wishing to register to vote. When
they exercised these powers broadly, it heightened further existing
tensions.

Lawlessness and Vigilantes

In the midst of this political activity, Missourians faced renewed lawlessness similar to that which had plagued them during the war. Readjustment after such a conflict is never easy. Those who had remained loyal might understandably resent the return of former
neighbors who had served the Confederacy, especially in areas that

had been hard hit by guerrilla strikes. Some communities posted notices that former rebels would not be welcome regardless of how
sorry they might be. In Jackson County, Radical grand juries indicted
some former Confederates for wartime crimes even though they had
been pardoned earlier by President Johnson.

Given these circumstances, compounded by the economic difficulties of postwar readjustment, it is not surprising that many Confederate veterans returned to the bush. Reports of robbery and occasional murder began appearing in the newspapers. A group of armed
men, possibly the Jesse James gang in its first major adventure, rode
into Liberty on February 13, 1866, and held up the Clay County Savings Association. The bandits escaped with $60,000 and killed a boy
who ran into the street to give the alarm. Major Ransom, the Radical
clerk of the circuit court, was gunned down on a street in Kansas City
in July. A few weeks later Isaac Fowley, a black, was tied to a tree and
horsewhipped near Jefferson City by a gang of whites who ordered
him to leave the county within ten days if he wanted to continue living. These were only a few isolated incidents among many to be
found in the public press. A St. Louis newspaper noted in November
1865:

> Never in the memory of the most ancient citizen . . . has rascality
> stalked so boldly about our streets as at the present time. Houses are
> entered every night by burglars, and the inmates robbed, while a
> bolder class of rogues, who disdain the labor of climbing porches,
> picking locks, and experimenting with window fastenings, attack citi-
> zens on public thoroughfares and cooly relieve them of their watches,
> jewelry and money. These operations are carried on by sun light and
> gas light.

As violence continued, voluntary groups of "regulators" sprang
up in many western Missouri counties. Usually composed of Radical
partisans, they took the law into their own hands and dealt out
heavy-handed "justice." Groups such as the Honest Men's League of
Greene County frequently acted first and talked later. Governor
Fletcher found it necessary to call up the militia and even to appeal
for federal troops on occasion to help keep order. As the summer
wore on, the activities of these vigilantes seemed increasingly politically motivated.

Election Results: 1866

The Radicals retained control of the legislature by overwhelming majorities in the fall election and carried seven of the nine congressional districts. They later picked up another of these when their secretary of state, Francis Rodman, claiming the registration of too many illegal voters, threw out the ballots of Callaway County. Thereby he changed a Conservative win in the Ninth District into a Radical victory. The legislature also refused seats to both the senator and representative from Callaway, leaving it without representation for two years.

Charles D. Drake reaped a personal harvest from the Radical triumph when the legislature sent him to the United States Senate to replace an ailing B. Gratz Brown. Brown, who disliked the extremism of Missouri's more ardent Radicals, tried to make one last contribution to the cause of moderation before his retirement. He called a meeting of Radical leaders at the Planters House in St. Louis on November 20. There he argued that the recent election put them in a good position to make peace with their foes. He urged that they adopt "Universal Suffrage and Universal Amnesty," which would include extension of the voting rights to both the African Americans and the pro-Southern element and the removal of the test oath as a requirement for the practice of a profession. Brown caught Drake and the Radical extremists completely off guard. About a third of them angrily walked out. Those who remained adopted Brown's proposals by a large majority, but the highly partisan legislature refused to go along. Nevertheless, the seeds had been planted for the Liberal Republican movement that would split the Radical party four years later.

The Equal Rights League

Missouri blacks had not been idle during all this turmoil. St. Louis had developed a small but active free black community before the war. This group now took the lead in organizing the Missouri Equal Rights League in October 1865 to secure voting rights for their race. They received the support of Governor Fletcher and a number of Radical legislators. Early the following year they brought in John M. Langston, a prominent black attorney from Oberlin, Ohio, for a statewide speaking tour. This was highlighted by Langston's appear-

James Milton Turner, prominent black leader among Missouri Radicals. *Courtesy State Historical Society of Missouri*

ance before an informal joint session of the legislature where he was well received.

J. Milton Turner

Out of the league emerged the strongest of Missouri's postwar black leaders, J. Milton Turner, who served as the group's secretary. Born a slave, Turner's freedom had been purchased by his father, a well known black veterinarian in the St. Louis area. Educated at secret black schools and briefly at Oberlin College before the war, he had established a strong friendship with the family of Governor Fletcher for whom he worked. Using his natural talents and political ties to the fullest, Turner played an active role in every crusade of the black community's drive for fulfillment. He frequently met hostility, and reported staying one night in a home in southeast Missouri where he was attacked by a mob and managed "to escape for his life at midnight, barefooted in the snow."

The Problems of Freedom

Life was not easy for Missouri's blacks as they moved from slavery to freedom. While those who had been educated struggled to secure their full civil rights, the vast majority concerned themselves with the everyday problems of making a living in the midst of a prejudiced white majority. Many blacks had been uprooted from homes and familiar patterns of living they had known. They often served as ready-made targets for roving bushwhackers. Friendly whites tried to help some relocate, frequently outside the state; but the possibilities for a new start were limited by both cost and the ingrained prejudices of those among whom they would settle.

According to the 1870 census, African Americans made up only 6.9 percent of the state's population. Only Delaware among the former slavehold-ing states had a smaller number of blacks. The Missouri black population had even declined slightly; there were 3,572 free blacks and 114,931 slaves in 1860 compared with 118,071 black residents ten years later. Many left the state during the last two years of the war. Of those who remained, the vast majority settled in the counties along the state's two great rivers, with nearly one fourth of them locating in the St. Louis area because of its greater economic opportunities.

The Freedmen's Bureau, established by Congress to help African Americans adjust, and various charitable agencies sent workers into Missouri to coordinate welfare efforts and set up schools. Governor Fletcher and other Radical officials also tried to assist. A major concern of bureau agents was to supply enough clothing and rations to the destitute during the winter of 1865–66. Whenever possible, they helped arrange labor contracts for blacks with nearby farmers. They also assisted black couples with the new Missouri law requiring them to be legally married if they had not had the benefit of a wedding ceremony while they were slaves. The agents made arrangements for black schools, with instructors furnished by various missionary groups. In Springfield, for instance, the bureau sponsored two teachers who taught approximately 150 pupils. They climaxed their first year with ceremonies attended by Governor Fletcher and State Superintendent of Schools T. A. Parker. The bureau's agent at Cape Girardeau reported that about eighty had enrolled in a school taught by a black man, who worked under difficult circumstances.

Things did not always go easily. A former Springfield congressman wrote the federal military commander in June 1865 that the area contained hundreds of refugee blacks from Arkansas who were "cowered and frightened." A black church had been burned a few nights earlier and its members fired upon when they tried to put out the blaze. Black schoolchildren were stoned as they made their way to classes. Their white teachers were sometimes shunned and harassed.

It is difficult to determine how often such incidents as these occurred. Relatively few were disclosed by the press, and the reports of bureau agents tended to be far more positive than negative. By the winter of 1865–66 many blacks who had sought refuge in the towns began drifting back to the countryside. Too few economic opportunities existed in town so that the unskilled had nowhere to turn except to go back to where they had come from. Many resumed work under conditions that left them not much better off than they had been before the war. They were usually paid small monthly wages or received a share of the crop.

Some blacks managed to save sufficient funds to purchase their own land. In these instances they were generally as prosperous as any person in their immediate environment could be. Others acquired homesteads that Congress made available without racial restrictions in Missouri and four other states. The Freedmen's Bureau estimated that some four thousand black families had been able to take advantage of this opportunity in spite of the lack of teams and farm implements needed to start any large operation. By the early 1870s, the blacks in several counties had prospered sufficiently to hold their own agricultural fairs.

Those blacks who remained in town engaged in various trades or secured employment as servants. A St. Louis school survey revealed black parents in the late 1860s working primarily as laborers, laundry workers, deliverypeople, and boatmen. The 1870 census indicated that most of those out-state followed similar occupations. Few appeared to be very wealthy, although a substantial minority apparently owned homes valued from a few hundred up to two thousand dollars. Those who had prospered as free blacks in St. Louis before the war with their barbering salons, catering services, and other enterprises continued to do so.

Newspaper accounts indicate that most public meetings segregated their audiences. Blacks generally sat on one side of the hall and whites on the other. Both races apparently accepted this practice as a matter of course since it had been the custom in many churches with mixed congregations before the war. A particular problem in St. Louis concerned the use of public transportation. Blacks had to stand on the uncovered front platforms of streetcars or walk. Attempts to correct this by legislative action hit snags, and the matter finally had to be resolved in the courts. In May 1868, public transportation companies were ordered to end discrimination and allow blacks to ride inside their cars.

Although blacks had had their own churches in St. Louis and other large towns prior to 1861, most of those in rural areas went to their owner's church if they attended at all. Emancipation brought increased separation by mutual consent. In addition to churches and

Sunday schools, blacks established lodges and brotherhoods similar to those of whites.

Radical Republicans and Education

Education became a major concern for the black community. Prewar opportunities had been limited by legal restrictions. Because of a high rate of illiteracy, black leaders realized the importance of schools in helping achieve economic, political, and social advancement. St. Louis blacks had established their own board of education midway through the war to coordinate the private schools that had sprung up. By war's end they employed eight teachers for some 600 pupils. This did not include a high school of an additional fifty or sixty students in the basement of the Church of the Messiah taught by two women from New England who were paid by contributions "from friends in Massachusetts." These schools were constantly handicapped by inadequate funding and disagreements between blacks and whites over teacher qualifications. Blacks preferred teachers of their own race, regardless of qualifications, if they could be found, while whites were reluctant to give up their control. Out-state, private schools run by various charitable groups operated in Columbia, Rolla, St. Charles, St. Joseph, Sedalia, Warrensburg, and Weston during 1865–66 while blacks waited for state funding under the new constitution.

As part of their progressive program to build a better Missouri, the Radicals did a great deal to promote public education for both races. A system of free public schools fit perfectly into their image of their party as the protector of the Union and the champion of opportunity. Although legally established two decades before the war, public education had lacked widespread support in Missouri. Considering "a general diffusion of knowledge and intelligence [as] being essential to the preservation of the rights and liberties of the people," the new constitution charged the General Assembly with maintaining free public schools for all youths between the ages of five and twenty-one. Separate schools could be established for blacks if it deemed this desirable. All eligible pupils might be required to attend for a minimum of sixteen months some time before the age of eighteen.

The General Assembly acted early in 1866 to provide a thorough and detailed public school system for both races. it gave local boards

A primary school for freedmen. *Courtesy State Historical Society of Missouri*

the authority to build schools and tax their districts to cover the costs of a four-month term without having to submit the levy to the voters for approval. This greatly aided badly needed school construction while increasing school taxes dramatically. One administrator, who started teaching at this time, recalled that "frame school houses sprang up like mushrooms in the night."

Each township or city board of education had to establish and maintain one or more separate schools for black children within their respective areas if they had more than twenty black children. These black schools had to be kept open the same winter term as the white schools. Should there be less than twenty black children, the board could appropriate their share of any tax levy for their education as it saw fit. Subsequent laws improved on this situation, and considerable progress was made toward fulfilling the expectations of the lawmakers at the local level before conservative legislatures dismantled much of the machinery a decade later.

Much of the progress was due to the vigorous leadership of State Superintendent of Schools Thomas A. Parker, whose annual report for 1870 revealed an increase in the number of public schools over the past three years from 4,840 to 7,547. The number of pupils enrolled had jumped from 169,270 to 280,473 during the same period. There were 9,080 black students by 1870, also a significant increase. Still, fifty-five counties with a total count of 2,984 black children had no schools for them. In relation to potential, about 21 percent of the state's eligible black children were receiving some kind of education as compared with 59 percent of the eligible white children.

St. Louis was fortunate in having William Torrey Harris as its superintendent from 1868 to 1880. An advanced progressive who would later perform important service as U.S. commissioner of education, Harris expanded the curriculum in the St. Louis schools to include natural science and phonetic reading. He also established O'Fallon Polytechnic Institute as a center for practical education. With the help of Susan Blow, he instituted the first public kindergarten in the United States at Des Peres School in the fall of 1873. This was an innovation borrowed from some of the German private schools. Harris also worked with Parker in promoting new educational ideas around the state, particularly through teacher institutes.

Teacher's Colleges

Parker worked energetically to provide an adequate staff of teachers. He reorganized the Missouri State Teachers Association and toured the state, holding clinics and institutes. Everywhere he lobbied for the organization of state normal schools or teacher's colleges. The legislature established two such institutions at Kirksville and Warrensburg in 1870, the closing year of Parker's term of office (St. Louis had created its own teacher's college in 1857). That same year the General Assembly granted state aid for the operation of a normal department at Lincoln Institute in Jefferson City to help prepare black teachers. Lincoln had had an interesting origin in that it was established in 1866 through funds raised by Missouri's black regiments to provide for the education of their own race. After considerable struggle and additional help from the Freedmen's Bureau and various Radical contributors, Lincoln had achieved enough stability to make it a good investment for the state. In 1879 the legislature

took the final step of funding its total operation, and it became a
state school.

University of Missouri

Capping the public school system was the University of Missouri,
which found itself a storm center of controversy during the Radical
period. Located in the staunchly conservative community of Columbia, it early became a target of zealous Radicals who thought that
Boone County did not provide the right atmosphere for the education of the state's future leaders. They talked of reestablishing the
university at Jefferson City, "where the state officers can at all times
look after its interests," which implied political supervision of faculty
and curriculum. Led by Representative James S. Rollins of Columbia,
friends of the university launched a campaign that not only stopped
this move but persuaded the legislature in 1867 to make a general
appropriation to the school for the first time in its history. There followed a three-year struggle over whether the university should also
receive the federal funds provided for the establishment of an agricultural and mechanical college under the Morrill Land Grant Act of
1862 or whether these should go to a new and separate institution.
In 1870 the legislature finally gave three quarters of these funds to
the university, reserving the remainder for the establishment of a
School of Mines at Rolla, where it would be closer to the industry it
proposed to serve.

Private Education

When viewed from an overall perspective, Missouri made significant strides in the field of public education during the postwar
years. The state also had thirty-seven private colleges and forty-five
academies in 1870. The ravages of war and the trend toward public
education had led to a decline of the latter, yet they still represented
the principal means of high school training outside of St. Louis and
a few of the larger towns. Most academies existed as a part of some
private college, the great majority of which were church related.
These private schools provided the traditional classical liberal arts
curriculum that many nineteenth-century Americans considered essential for entering the various professions such as medicine, the
ministry, and the law.

Cultural and Sports Activities

Most Missourians responded eagerly to the various cultural advantages that were available to them in the postwar era. Many towns established some type of subscription library while public lectures, popularly called lyceums, and concerts were sponsored by various groups. One journal noted that Hannibal, Kansas City, Macon, St. Joseph, Sedalia, Warrensburg, and "several others of our growing young cities" had had lecture series during the winter of 1869–70. In addition, theatrical groups and circuses regularly made the rounds of Missouri towns to provide entertainment. Amateur theatricals, both in English and German, were also popular. St. Louis, of course, had a variety of entertainments available on a regular basis because of its size and easy accessibility.

Sports enthusiasts, both participants and spectators, found plenty with which to amuse themselves. Cycling and ice skating were among the most popular pastimes in their respective seasons. Trotting and pacing races were held regularly in St. Louis while in rural Missouri any long and vacant strip of road might be the scene of an impromptu horse race on a Saturday or Sunday afternoon. For those to whom this proved too tame, steamboat racing sometimes offered an alternative. These were generally limited to the Mississippi, however, as the Missouri's channel was not especially suited to this kind of competition.

The St. Louis Cock Pit still featured matches between fighting roosters every evening in the late 1860s, but this sport was on the decline as its human counterpart became the local rage. Many of the eastern states restricted boxing by legislation, so St. Louis became a popular center for what was then a rather dirty sport. Fighters used their bare knuckles and thought nothing of treating them with hot mustard or of blowing a little red pepper into their opponent's eyes to add zest to the match.

Baseball emerged as America's "national pastime" and Missourians enthusiastically accepted the new sport. In a state still marked by considerable wilderness, hunting and fishing remained favorite pastimes. Fairs of all sorts regained their popularity after having been suspended during wartime. By 1870 more than forty counties and towns were sponsoring such events. Most took place in late summer or early fall, providing an opportunity for farmers to display their recently harvested produce and merchants to show their wares.

Religious and Other Organizations

Missourians of the postwar decade were joiners, attracted to a wide
variety of organizations, old and new. Religious life flourished. The
census of 1870 revealed that the number of churches had more than
doubled over the decade to stand at 3,229. The Methodists were the
largest denomination, although divided into northern and southern
branches. Baptists and Presbyterians ranked next, with the Disciples
of Christ, the Roman Catholics, and the Lutherans following in that
order. Such interdenominational groups as the Missouri Sunday
School Association were also established to promote the exchange of
ideas and training methods, especially in the rural areas. Most
churches would hold lengthy revivals in the fall or spring to try to
reach the unchurched in their communities.

Fraternal organizations enjoyed a considerable growth as did
groups with exclusive membership based on national origins, especially among the Irish and Germans. Both Kansas City and St. Louis
had YMCA and YWCA groups. The Germans had similar organizations called Turnvereins. The Grand Army of the Republic and other
Union military associations were quite popular while the Radicals
were in control. But they went into decline when the Democrats returned to power in the 1870s. There was an active Fenian movement
in St. Louis whose purpose was to promote Irish independence.

Newspapers

By 1870 Missouri had 279 newspapers with a circulation of 522,866.
Of these, 225 were weeklies, but the 21 dailies had a circulation of
86,555. Newspapers were the window to the outside world for most
of Missouri's citizens. In them they found not only accounts of political happenings, with a heavy smattering of editorial opinion, but
also items of social gossip, advertisements of a variety of services and
goods, and stories of romance and nostalgia. The press promoted a
multitude of good causes, both political and otherwise, and to look
through its pages today gives one an interesting insight into the lives
of Missourians of a hundred years ago.

The High Tide of Radicalism, 1868

The Missouri press strongly reflected the political divisions of the
day. It was not a time for neutrality by individuals either, especially

in the light of the strong party feeling that had emerged following the war. The Radicals reached the height of their political power in Missouri in the election of 1868. They faced a revived Democratic party that year; but, with the help of the registration act, they had little difficulty in crushing it. They elected Joseph W. McClurg, a wartime militia colonel and three-term congressman, as governor and carried their entire state ticket by approximately 20,000 votes. The Radicals kept control of both houses of the legislature by wide margins. With the continued help of their secretary of state, Francis Rodman, who again threw out the votes of certain "disloyal" counties, they held on to eight of their nine seats in Congress. General Ulysses S. Grant had no difficulty in securing the state's electoral votes for President. Only one disappointment marred the results for the Radical leaders: the decisive defeat of a black suffrage amendment that had been put to the voters by the General Assembly. Although supported actively by Drake, Governor Fletcher, and every other Radical leader of consequence, prejudice among the party's rank and file overcame all moral and political arguments in its favor. The desertion of their leaders on this issue by Radical voters, combined with almost solid opposition from the Democrats, produced a negative result of 74,053 to 55,236. Many Missourians feared a large wave of black immigration if their state proved more liberal than its northern neighbors who were rejecting similar amendments. Consequently voting for Missouri's blacks had to await the ratification of the Fifteenth Amendment in 1870.

Carl Schurz

Missouri Radicals found a new leader in the election of 1868, one who carefully played upon a growing popularity to reach the U.S. Senate. Carl Schurz, long a leader among German Americans and within the national Republican party, had moved to St. Louis in April 1867 to become co-owner of the *Westliche Post,* one of the largest German-language newspapers

Senator Carl Schurz.
Courtesy State Historical Society of Missouri

in the country and a strong Radical journal. With this background he moved rapidly to the political forefront in Missouri. He delivered the keynote address at the Republican National Convention in 1868 and then reserved the final six weeks of the campaign to aid Missouri Radicals. With Senator John B. Henderson falling into disfavor because of his refusal to vote for President Andrew John-son's conviction on impeachment charges, an opening was created into which Schurz neatly inserted himself.

Some moderates thought that Schurz's election might pave the way for the enfranchisement of blacks and the "rebel element" at the same time. These hopes were quickly dashed. The majority of the Radicals in the legislature showed little desire to deal with the suffrage question in any form in 1869, with another election still nearly two years away.

Women's Suffrage

The legislators, meanwhile, faced yet another group demanding its right to vote: the women of Missouri. A delegation of ten women arrived at the capital in February 1869 to present their case. They represented the Women's Suffrage Association of Missouri, which had been organized two years earlier. Many of their leaders had worked with the Western Sanitary Commission and other wartime agencies, and they believed that their contributions deserved some consideration. Radical leaders welcomed them—Governor McClurg signed one of their petitions—and listened politely. The women met with various groups of legislators over a two-day period but with no results. One house member told a reporter that the women had "unsexed themselves by coming here with their demands." Undaunted, the suffragists continued their agitation in St. Louis and elsewhere but with as little success.

Revision of the Test Oath

Two events the following year changed the mood of the General Assembly in regard to the other disfranchised groups: the refusal of the U.S. Supreme Court to overthrow the test oath for voting in the Blair case mentioned earlier, and the final ratification of the Fifteenth Amendment, which gave blacks voting rights nationwide. The blacks of Missouri went eagerly to the polls that spring of 1870 for various local elections and, led by J. Milton Turner, began to demand full recognition from the Radicals. The legislature now submitted three amendments for the fall election: one would modify the test oath to a simple declaration of support for national and state constitutions; the second would eliminate it completely for jurors; the third would repeal the oath as a requirement for office holding and for corporate or educational activity and remove all racial barriers to political office.

Unfortunately for them, having done this the Radicals could not agree on openly endorsing the amendments at their state convention that summer. The Radical regulars, led by Senator Drake and Governor McClurg, simply wanted to let the amendments stand by themselves with the rank and file being free to accept or reject them as they would. The liberals, led by Senator Schurz and B. Gratz Brown, insisted that the party had to endorse its own proposals to show good faith. This latter group was also becoming dissatisfied with President Grant at the national level and began calling for civil service and tariff reform.

The Liberal Republican Movement

As a result of this disagreement, the Radical Union party split at its convention in the summer of 1870, with the bolters forming the Liberal Republican movement. While the regulars renominated McClurg for governor on a typical Radical platform, the Liberals endorsed Brown and strongly recommended acceptance of the amendments. The Democrats pursued what some called "the Possum Policy." They decided against nominating a statewide ticket so that they might take advantage of the Radical split, but they shrewdly ran candidates in most legislative races where they thought they had a chance of winning. Most Democrats supported Brown, who won the election by some 40,000 votes. All of the amendments passed easily. The Democrats carried the lower house of the legislature and enough seats in the Senate to control that body through a coalition with the Liberals. Most of the blacks, voting for the first time in a statewide contest, stayed with the Radicals on the assumption that its leaders, both state and national, had been their closest friends.

Missouri politics in the last half of the 1860s had been marked by a turbulence not soon forgotten. Riding the whirlwind of discontent arising out of the war years, the Radicals had swept everything before them in 1864. Fearful that Missouri might lose its rightful place in the newly emerging national order, they tried to reconstruct the state along progressive lines. Radical concern that the representatives of the conservative forces of the past might undo their handiwork at some future time led them to excessive measures for holding down the opposition. This caused hatreds that died hard. Like their counterparts farther south, the Missouri Radicals created within the opposition an esprit de corps, based on a martyr complex, that enabled the Democrats to stay in power in Missouri for the next thirty-five years.

When Drake resigned his Senate seat in December 1870 to accept a judicial appointment from President Grant, the Democrats in the legislature managed enough votes on a joint ballot of the two houses to send Frank Blair to Washington as his replacement. They also pushed through a drastic modification of the registration system with the assistance of the Liberals. Beyond that though things stalemated over the next two years.

The Return of the Democrats

In 1872 Schurz and Brown carried the Liberal movement to the national level in an effort to prevent the reelection of President Grant.

Missouri's Second State Capitol, 1842–1911. *Courtesy State Historical Society of Missouri*

Although the Democrats supported them, Grant easily won a second term. In Missouri though, it was a Democrat, Silas Woodson of St. Joseph, who won the governorship with Liberal support. The Democrats also carried both houses of the legislature. They no longer needed the Liberals, who became disillusioned and soon returned to the Republican party as the Radicals began calling themselves in 1872. During their long exile from state offices over the next three decades, Republican strength would remain concentrated in the southwestern and northern border regions and in the German-dominated counties along the Missouri River.

Governor Woodson inherited a highly restless state from his predecessor. The lawlessness of the previous decade still held Missouri in its grip as the activities of the James gang and others continued. A financial panic that hit the country in the fall of 1873 did not help matters. Many counties were becoming unhappy with their railroad debts, especially where there had been lack of construction. However, this problem will be discussed in the next chapter. Many farmers and small-town businessowners began to believe that the railroads frequently discriminated against the small shipper on freight rates, gave poor service on shipments, and ignored or delayed dealing with claims on losses.

Election of 1874

In October 1873, representatives of the various farm clubs and organizations around the state held a protest meeting in Jefferson City. Out of this grew a movement that resulted in the organization of the People's party in 1874 to try to solve their problems. It nominated William Gentry, a prominent farmer from Pettis County, as its candidate for governor and sought a balanced ticket that would appeal to a wide variety of interests. The party platform called for cheaper currency, payment of the state debt and reduction of government expenses and taxes, regulation of the railroads, improvement of the public schools, and an end to lawlessness. Now it was the Republicans' turn to "play possum." They had been thoroughly demoralized by their setbacks of the last three years, and many of them believed that a coalition with the People's party was the only hope of unseating the Democrats.

The party in power nominated Charles H. Hardin, prominent Mexico attorney and state senator, for the governorship. In an effort to hold the rural vote against "Farmer Gentry," it ran Norman J.

Colman, prominent agricultural journalist, for lieutenant governor. This proved a successful move when played with the Democratic pitch that their opponents were simply the tools of the discredited Republicans. Hardin won by 37,000 votes, and the People's party ceased to exist. Following the election the term of Senator Schurz ended, and the Democrats promptly replaced him with Francis M. Cockrell of Warrensburg, who had been a Confederate general. Cockrell would remain in the U.S. Senate for the next thirty years, and his presence there did much to keep the Missouri Democratic party united.

The Constitution of 1875

One other question had been decided in the election of 1874: should Missouri have a new constitution? The legislature had put the matter to a referendum, with only halfhearted support from Governor Woodson, who thought a constitutional convention would be too expensive an undertaking during hard times. The matter created little enthusiasm during the campaign and won approval by only 283 votes out of 261,670 cast—an indication that many Missourians had learned to live with the Drake Constitution, once its anti-southern provisions had been removed.

As might be expected, the new convention that met in May 1875 differed markedly from the last one. It contained only eight Republicans, while fifteen of its members had been in Confederate service (fifteen had been in the Union army). Most of the delegates were affluent, with a strong conservative bent. Two-thirds were lawyers, and most had had some prior political experience at either the state or local level. The convention met for three months and produced a basically conservative document that reflected the changing mood of the times. It increased the power of the governor at the expense of the legislature by giving the chief executive the right of item veto over appropriation bills while advancing from a simple majority to a two-thirds majority the necessary margin for legislative override. The new constitution limited the legislature to biennial sessions and drastically curtailed the powers of that body by including a list of thirty-two specific topics on which the legislators were forbidden to pass any local or special law. Strong curbs were placed on the exercise of fiscal power at both the state and local levels, with prohibitions on lending, debt, and taxation putting the state into a literal straitjacket, which would hamper future growth while forcing the practice of false economy.

The convention unanimously adopted the new constitution on August 2 and sent it to the voters, who approved it at the end of October in an election marked generally by its apathy. Only 105,000 persons even bothered to cast ballots. Yet this document remained the state's basic law for the next seventy years and required many amendments to meet changing times. The next thirty years witnessed the entrenchment of conservative interests in state government through the continued control of the Democratic party. Many of its leaders had strong roots in prewar politics and had served one side or the other during the war. While they could not undo completely the progress of the postwar era, they did slow it significantly. In particular, they dismantled much of the machinery for statewide educational reform that Thomas A. Parker had established, and placed more power with the local school boards. After a decade and a half of almost continuous turmoil, the basic conservatism of Missouri's people had reasserted itself.

Suggestions for Reading

The story of Missouri during Reconstruction is best covered in William E. Parrish, *A History of Missouri, Vol. III, 1860 to 1875*, rev. ed., Columbia, University of Missouri Press, 2001. One should also consult Parrish, *Missouri Under Radical Rule, 1865–1870*, Columbia, University of Missouri Press, 1965. A comparison of Missouri with other border states may be found in Richard O. Curry, ed., *Radicalism, Racism, and Party Realignment: The Border States During Reconstruction*, Baltimore, Johns Hopkins Press, 1969.

Biographical treatments of important Reconstruction political figures are found in William E. Parrish, *Frank Blair: Lincoln's Conservative*, Columbia, University of Missouri Press, 1998; Hans L. Trefousse, *Carl Schurz: A Biography*, Knoxville, University of Tennessee Press, 1982; Norma L. Peterson, *Freedom and Franchise: The Political Career of B. Gratz Brown*, Columbia, University of Missouri Press, 1965; Gary R. Kremer, *James Milton Turner and the Promise of America: The Public Life of a Post–Civil War Black Leader*, Columbia, University of Missouri Press, 1991; Henry Boernstein, *Memoirs of a Nobody: The Missouri Years of an Austrian Radical, 1849–1866*, trans. and ed. by Steven Rowan, St. Louis, Missouri Historical Society Press, 1997; and Lynn Morrow, "Joseph Washington McClurg: Entrepreneur, Politician, Citizen," *Missouri Historical Review*, January 1984. Missouri's most famous outlaw receives a thorough re-examination in T. J.

Stiles, *Jesse James: Last Rebel of the Civil War*, New York, Knopf, 2002, which places him within the political context of Reconstruction. For an earlier biography, which also analyzes the development of the myths surrounding him, see William A. Settle, Jr., *Jesse James Was His Name*, Columbia, University of Missouri Press, 1966. An excellent biography of a leading Radical educator is Kurt F. Leidecker, *Yankee Teacher: The Life of William Torrey Harris*, New York, Philosophical Library, 1946. His feminine counterpart, who began the kindergarten movement in St. Louis, is described in Joseph Menius, *Susan Blow*, St. Clair, MO, Page One Publishing, 1993.

The Radicals' impact on education is analyzed in Arthur E. Lee, "The Decline of Radicalism and Its Effect on Public Education in Missouri," *Missouri Historical Review*, October 1979, while J. Michael Hoey provides an excellent account of the struggle for recognition by parochial schools in "Missouri Education at the Crossroads: The Phalen Miscalculation and the Education Amendment of 1870," *Missouri Historical Review*, July 2001. Lawrence O. Christensen, "Race Relations in St. Louis, 1865–1916," *Missouri Historical Review*, January 1984, is a good discussion of that topic while black schools are dealt with in Henry S. Williams, "The Development of the Negro Public School System in Missouri," *Journal of Negro History*, April 1920. Martha Kohl, "From Freedom to Franchise: The Debate over African-American Enfranchisement, 1865–1870," *Gateway Heritage*, Spring 1996, offers a good analysis of that topic. The work of the American Missionary Association in Missouri is well covered in Joe M. Richardson, *Christian Reconstruction: The American Missouri Association and Southern Blacks, 1861–1890*, Athens, University of Georgia Press, 1986.

Kohl, "Enforcing the Vision of Community: The Role of the Test Oath in Missouri Reconstruction," *Civil War History*, December 1994, deals with another important issue. The following articles in the *Missouri Historical Review* may be helpful with additional information on their respective topics: Lily Ann Dickey, "The Pastimes of Missourians Before 1900," January 1943; Isidor Loeb, "Constitutions and Constitutional Conventions in Missouri," January 1922; Monia C. Morris, "Teacher Training in Missouri Before 1871," October 1948; Morris, "The History of Women's Suffrage in Missouri, 1867–1901," October 1930; and G. Hugh Wamble, "Negroes and Missouri Protestant Churches Before and After the Civil War," April 1967.

ELEVEN

A Maturing Economy, 1860–1890

Pony Express

The Pony Express marked the end of one era and the beginning of another in Missouri. Horsepower made its last and ultimate effort, but lost to the telegraph, just as the stagecoach gave way to the railroad.

Although it is not certain, the idea of a Pony Express apparently came from William Russell, a partner in the famous Missouri freight company of Russell, Majors & Waddell. Russell hoped that besides providing rapid mail service between Missouri and California the Pony Express would demonstrate the practicality of a central overland route and win a federal mail contract for his firm. The entrepreneur believed that a successful express would unseat the Butterfield Company, which held the government mail contract and traveled the longer southern route to California. Russell proposed to employ lightweight riders who would ride swift horses in relays. He predicted that these riders would get mail and messages to California in half the time that it took Butterfield's stagecoaches to get them there via the southern route.

Russell's company bought 500 horses, built 190 stations at 25-mile intervals, and hired 200 station attendants and 80 riders who weighed no more than 125 pounds. On April 3, 1860, the first rider left St. Joseph carrying mail brought from the east over the Hannibal and St. Joseph Railroad. When the mail packet reached Sacramento, California, it had traveled 1,982 miles. An average trip took ten days. A rider usually traveled seventy-five miles before passing the fifteen-pound mail packet to a colleague. Although the Pony Express delivered letters as fast as Russell had predicted and never lost a mail sack, it failed to win the United States mail contract from the Butterfield line. Financial losses and the telegraph put it out of business after eighteen months of operation.

Railroads

The Pony Express began at St. Joseph because railroad construction had not progressed beyond that point. Indeed, of the railroads started before the Civil War, only the Hannibal and St. Joseph, which connected those two cities, had been completed during the 1850s. Total railroad mileage in the state stood at 810 in 1860. The Pacific Railroad, which was planned to link St. Louis with Kansas City by following the Missouri River, stopped at Sedalia, ninety-five miles short of its destination. The St. Louis and Iron Mountain, projected to connect the metropolis with the southeast lead-mining region, reached Pilot Knob, eighty-six miles from St. Louis. The North Missouri, with hopes of extending between St. Louis and Iowa, stretched to Macon, where it connected with the Hannibal and St. Joseph. And the Southwest Branch of the Pacific stopped at Rolla, more than one hundred miles short of Springfield, its intended destination. All of these railroads had received state subsidies, and all of them had defaulted by 1860 except the Hannibal and St. Joseph. Inexperienced management had resulted in poor construction, faulty equipment, high costs, and thus financial difficulties.

Pacific Railroad

Civil war in the state added to the difficulties. Fighting disrupted construction and destroyed tracks and roadbeds. Between 1861 and 1864 only the Pacific Railroad made any progress; it laid seven miles of track beyond Sedalia and completed grading its roadbed to Warrensburg. In February 1864, the General Assembly agreed to the Pacific's request that the state relinquish its right to first payment of bonds so that the railroad could offer new first-mortgage bonds on its uncompleted portion with the earnings of the entire route pledged to pay off the new bonds. In the fall of 1864, Sterling Price made another foray into the state, destroying part of the line. The city of St. Louis then put up another $700,000 in bonds to support the completion of the road to Kansas City, which was finally accomplished on September 20, 1865. The much desired route across the state, which St. Louis interests had pushed for so ardently for two decades, had become a reality.

In reaction to the reckless railroad financing of the 1850s, the 1865 constitution prohibited the use of the state's credit to aid any corporation or association. It also forbade the state from holding stock in companies, except as collateral for loans extended before the constitution went into effect. Local governmental units could avoid these restrictions if two-thirds of their voters approved. To further protect taxpayers, the 1865 convention submitted, and voters approved, a measure that required each railroad indebted to the state to establish a sinking fund* under the control of an independent commissioner. Railroads that failed to abide by this requirement could be foreclosed and then sold at public auction.

By the spring of 1868, new financial problems plagued the Pacific Railroad. Fearing foreclosure and sale of the road, company directors lobbied the legislature to get the state's lien** released. With $200,000 in bribes to key legislators, they secured their objective as the General Assembly released the state's claim on $11 million of the company's debt for a payment of $5 million. That action indirectly defied the provision in the 1865 constitution that prohibited the legislature from releasing state liens on railroads. It also added $6 million to Missouri taxpayers' burdens. In the early 1870s, the Pacific leased its lines to the Atlantic and Pacific and, after that line experienced difficulties, it became part of the Missouri Pacific Railroad.

North Missouri Railroad

Meanwhile, the North Missouri Railroad also suffered financial reverses. Soon after the war ended, a New York banking house subscribed $6 million to cover construction costs. Work resumed in July 1866, but bond troubles arose during the winter. James B. Eads, a St. Louis engineer, headed a syndicate of hometown and eastern capitalists who subsequently took control of the road. In January 1868, the road's directors appealed to the General Assembly to release it from the state's lien on its bonded indebtedness for a nominal cash payment. In line with its procedure in the parallel case of the Pacific Railroad, the General Assembly granted the request. This meant that the North Missouri no longer had to pay loans the state had made to it although taxpayers still had the responsibility for paying off the state

*A fund accumulated to pay off a public or corporate debt.
**A lien is an agreement whereby the holder of a debt may take the property of a debtor who fails to make payment.

bonds. The legislature did require the road to reach Iowa within nine months, to finish a branch from Moberly to Missouri's western border within eighteen months, and to construct a bridge across the Missouri River at St. Charles within three years. It also required the road's directors to post a bond with the state treasurer as a sign of good faith.

Previous experience with defaulting railroads and a strong commitment to getting track laid led to the General Assembly's decision. In settling for only $200,000 against a lien of $6 million, the legislature's wisdom must be questioned, although there is no evidence of bribery in this case.

At least the North Missouri met all of its construction deadlines, including the completion of the St. Charles Bridge in May 1871. Neither success at meeting deadlines nor the General Assembly's generosity saved the railroad from insolvency, however. Reorganization and two other sales followed, and by the end of the 1870s the North Missouri had become a part of the Wabash system.

Southwest Pacific Railroad

Financial and other difficulties had so beset the Southwest Branch, which had become the Southwest Pacific, the St. Louis and Iron Mountain, the Cairo and Fulton, and the Platte Country railroads, that the state foreclosed its liens against them in 1866 and by the end of that year had sold each of them. The Southwest Pacific went to a corporation headed by John C. Frémont for $1.3 million. Governor Fletcher's name appeared among the list of stockholders. Congress granted the new company 17 million acres of land. A flurry of speculation followed, but the railroad collapsed under the burdens of labor strikes, "brittle English rails," and poor management. The Frémont group defaulted on its first payment to the state, causing Fletcher to seize the road and to place it under state control again.

In 1868 the same legislature that had been so generous with other railroads sold the reclaimed road at an attractive price to a new syndicate, which called itself the South Pacific. It did require the South Pacific to spend $500,000 within a year on construction, to have rails to Lebanon within two years, and to have trains running to Springfield within three and one-half years. For his services in the transaction Governor Fletcher collected $3,000 as a legal fee.

The General Assembly allowed the South Pacific to issue $7,250,000 in bonds and to sell the lands already granted it to finance its building program. The legislature also authorized it to construct a line extending the thirty-seven miles between the town of Pacific and St. Louis, thus providing Pacific with direct access to the latter city. The state required the company to post a $1 million bond and to deposit $1.5 million in other bonds with the state treasurer.

Work progressed well as tracks reached Springfield on May 1, 1870, and the Kansas border in October 1870. During the latter month, the Atlantic and Pacific Railroad purchased the company. Before financial difficulties forced it into receivership in 1875, it had pushed rails into Indian Territory. In 1876 the road became a part of the St. Louis and San Francisco Railroad.

St. Louis and Iron Mountain Railroad

Not long after the Frémont group purchased the Southwest Pacific, it also bought the St. Louis and Iron Mountain and the Cairo and Fulton railroads from the state for only $900,000. Governor Fletcher approved the sale in 1866. The new owners agreed to extend the Iron Mountain south from Pilot Knob so as to intersect with the Cairo and Fulton tracks within three years and to lengthen it within five years to a point in Missouri just across the Mississippi River from Columbus, Kentucky. Three days after Fletcher had approved the sale, the Frémont syndicate resold the roads to Thomas Allen of St. Louis for $1,275,000. Critics charged Fletcher and the railroad commissioners with collusion because of the low price paid for the railroads initially. After the resale those protests became louder and more widespread although no wrongdoing was proven.

While controversy continued, Thomas Allen laid track. He completed the St. Louis and Iron Mountain to Belmont, across the Mississippi from Columbus, Kentucky, in August 1869; made it to the Arkansas border three years later; and connected his road with Texas railroads in 1874. The Iron Mountain linked St. Louis with the southwest, solidifying the Missouri city's position as that region's trade center for the next two decades. In 1881 the entire line passed into the hands of the Missouri Pacific Railroad.

Missouri Valley Railroad

The state also foreclosed the Missouri Valley Railroad, which had formerly been called the Platte Country. Designed to link Kansas City with St. Joseph and the Iowa border and to eventually bring the trade of northwest Missouri to St. Louis, the Missouri Valley went through a series of reorganizations between 1866 and 1868. In the latter year, its management too came before the General Assembly and told the legislators that it could either complete the road or pay its $994,000 debt but not both. Following its newly established policy, the General Assembly decided that finishing construction took precedence over debt payment. To ensure completion, the state required the railroad to place in the treasury bonds worth $668,000 and stock certificates valued at $100,000. For every mile of track laid, the state agreed to return $12,000 to the road. When the Missouri Valley's tracks reached Iowa, the state would cancel the $100,000 in stock. The company met its December 1, 1869, deadline for completion. In May 1870, it consolidated with the St. Joseph and Council Bluffs Railroad, linking Kansas City to a point opposite Omaha, Nebraska. Later the Chicago, Burlington, and Quincy Railroad absorbed the entire line.

By the end of 1870 all of the roads had reached their projected destinations. In the five years following the Civil War, approximately 1,200 miles of track had been laid. The 1868 legislature's decision to speed construction of the various roads with little regard for repayment of loans to the state had succeeded, but at great cost to taxpay-

Eads Bridge, St. Louis. *Charles Trefts Collection, courtesy State Historical Society of Missouri*

ers. In January 1868 the railroads owed Missourians $31,735,840. They paid only $6,131,496, leaving taxpayers with $25,604,344 in bonds and interest to retire. The state treasurer made the last payment on that debt in 1903.

Public investment in constructing the state's railroads and the questionable financial practices that sometimes accompanied railroad financing in Missouri mirrored developments in the nation. The federal government granted more than 125 million acres and loaned more than $60 million to western railroads. Corruption in railroad financing involving government officials occurred on the national level, and speculators such as Jay Gould looted their own railroads.

Despite these problems, railroads transformed life in the nation and in Missouri as property values increased and population grew. Missouri farmers cultivated a larger percentage of the land and began to produce specialized crops for a national market. New towns arose, and cities developed new industries. Isolation and provincialism declined as the railroads brought metropolitan newspapers and products to rural districts and made it easy for people to travel.

Bridging the Missouri

For both Kansas City and St. Louis, bridges across their major rivers meant access to the national market. Both cities had been located next to rivers because of transportation advantages; when railroads supplanted waterways as avenues for carrying goods, rivers changed to obstacles.

Civic leaders in Kansas City sought to connect their city with the Hannibal and St. Joseph Railroad in 1860 through the construction of a bridge across the Missouri and a line to Cameron. The war interrupted their efforts, but even as the Pacific Railroad inched toward their city, Kansas Citians continued to covet the Hannibal and St. Joseph connection because of its link with Chicago and the east.

Led by Robert T. Van Horn, a sometime congressman, editor of the *Western Journal of Commerce,* and a full-time Kansas City promoter, Kansas Citians interested officials of the Burlington Railroad, which had acquired the Hannibal and St. Joseph route, in the project. The construction of the bridge and spur was completed on July 3, 1869. In the next eight months more than 4,000 trains crossed the Missouri.

James B. Eads Spans the Mississippi

Bridging the Mississippi at St. Louis proved to be a more difficult task. The approximately 30,000 Kansas Citians knew that their hopes for future greatness would never be realized without a bridge, and they worked with vigor to get it. St. Louis had already become a metropolis in 1870, doubling its population in a decade to 310,869. Some St. Louisans—for example, ferry interests—failed to see the urgency of building a bridge, and rival interests in Illinois opposed the Missouri effort. Moreover, at St. Louis engineers encountered a wide and deep river with a bottom composed of shifting soils. Building a bridge there was much more challenging than the construction of those at Hannibal and Quincy, which had already been accomplished.

James B. Eads proved to be the man for the job. He used engineering genius, dogged persistence, and political wiles in meeting the challenge. During the 1840s and 1850s, Eads had become intimate with the river by walking on its bottom in a diving bell that he invented and used in his ship salvage business. During the Civil War he designed and built iron-clad ships for the Union. After the war Eads secured approval for his projected bridge from Congress and the Missouri and Illinois legislatures. Construction began in 1867, and in 1868 St. Louis taxpayers approved a $1 million bond issue to

underwrite some of the construction costs.

With three arched spans of more than 500 feet each, the bridge rests on granite piers that reach bedrock approximately 90 feet below the river bed. Eads used steel, manufactured to his specifications, in the bridge's trusses. No other bridge had such long arches, went so far to reach bedrock, or used steel so extensively in its construction. A two-level struc-

James B. Eads, the builder of Eads Bridge.
Courtesy State Historical Society of Missouri

ture, trains traveled on the lower roadway and carriages and passengers crossed on the upper level.

Eads designed and built only one bridge. An unschooled engineer, the St. Louisan and his bridge, nevertheless, achieved great distinction. Eads became the first civil engineer elected to the Hall of Fame for Great Americans and "the first native-born American to receive the Albert Medal from the Royal Society of Arts in Great Britain." Experts called his effort an engineering masterpiece; present-day engineers continue to rank it as one of the world's great bridges.

The St. Louis engineer added to his illustrious reputation in 1879 by constructing jetties at the mouth of the Mississippi. Structures that narrowed the width, the jetties caused the river to scour its own bottom, removing sediment and deepening the channel. The jetties made it possible for large ships to dock at New Orleans and increased traffic on the Mississippi.

Continued Railroad Construction

The bridges at Kansas City and St. Louis helped tie Missouri into the emerging national railroad network. In a similar way feeder lines linked smaller Missouri towns with the major railroads between 1870 and 1890. Railroad mileage in the state more than tripled during those years to stand at 6,142 in 1890. By 1918 only the Ozark counties of Dallas, Douglas, and Ozark lacked railroads as Missouri had 8,529 miles of track.

Individual counties and lesser subdivisions provided much of the funding for railroad construction after 1870. In their enthusiasm to secure a railroad link, counties sometimes sold bonds to support projected railroads that were never built. A number of counties experienced difficulty in paying their railroad debts, and numerous court cases resulted. The last county bonds were retired in 1940.

Railroads rapidly replaced steamboats as the most important carriers of freight and passengers. Traffic on the Missouri and lesser rivers declined precipitously. On the Mississippi the number of steamboat arrivals at St. Louis varied little between 1850 and 1880, from 2,899 in the former year to 2,871 in the latter year. The amount of freight carried, however, revealed the increasing dominance of the railroad. For example, in 1866 steamboats transported 53,506 bales of cotton to St. Louis, and trains hauled only 1,921 bales. Six years later railroads had surpassed steamboats in carrying cotton by

33,132 to 26,577 bales. In 1880, with the completion of the Eads Bridge and more trackage, railroads brought 464,291 bales of cotton to St. Louis, while steamboats deposited only 32,279 bales on the levee.

The James Gang

Train robberies developed as an unexpected result of railroad expansion. The James brothers, Missouri's most famous outlaws, added that form of banditry to their stock of illegal acts. Frank and Jesse James rode with the notorious Quantrill guerrillas during the Civil War. As noted in Chapter 10, officials accused the James gang of robbing the Liberty bank in 1866. During the next eight years additional crimes ascribed to them included nine bank holdups—six in Missouri, two in Kentucky, and one in Iowa. Train robberies near Council Bluffs, Iowa, and Gads Hill, Missouri, enhanced their notoriety as did the killings that accompanied several of their holdups.

Conditions had become so bad by 1874 that Governor Silas Woodson condemned Missouri banditry. Then in 1876 the James gang tried to rob a bank in Northfield, Minnesota. Law officers killed three and captured three others; only Frank and Jesse escaped. Their whereabouts over the next few years was a matter of constant speculation. In 1880 the James gang became an issue in Missouri politics when Republicans charged that successive Democratic administrations had been lax in bringing the outlaws to justice.

Just months after Thomas T. Crittenden, the newly elected Democratic governor, took office, six gunmen robbed a Chicago, Rock Island, and Pacific train in Daviess County. The gang killed two railway employees. The *Kansas City Journal* and *St. Louis Post-Dispatch* demanded that Crittenden stop the robbing and killing. After meeting with railroad representatives, the governor announced a reward of $5,000 for the capture of Frank or Jesse James and an additional $5,000 for the conviction of either of them.

On September 7, 1881, bandits robbed the Chicago and Alton express at Blue Cut in Jackson County, the last train robbery in the state attributed to the James brothers. The state's press again attacked the Democratic administration because of its failure to act. Six months later a member of the James gang, Bob Ford, shot and killed Jesse while he dusted a picture in his home at St. Joseph where he had been living under an assumed name. Bob and his brother Charles Ford pleaded guilty to a charge of murder, but subsequently

Governor Crittenden pardoned them. Now the governor received a storm of criticism for encouraging and then condoning murder.

Frank James remained at large until October 5, 1882, when he surrendered himself to the governor. He later stood trial for the murder of a railroad employee, but the jury found him not guilty. Other trials ensued with the same result, and by the end of 1885 no further charges remained. The stealing, killing James brothers became romantic figures and passed into folk legend.

Population Growth

The period of lawlessness represented by the James gang seemed out of step in a state experiencing the population and urban growth of Missouri. As shown in the following table, Missouri's population more than doubled between 1860 and 1890. The state ranked eighth in population among the states in 1860. In 1870 it rose to fifth and retained that position until 1910. Thus Missouri's total population grew at a rate at least equal to that of the rest of the country. Augmented by immigrants from Europe that railroads and a state immigration society recruited, the state's white population grew by 137 percent. Missouri's black population increased by only 27 percent between 1860 and 1890, which placed that rate of growth far below the 60.8 percent increase recorded on the national level. Other areas proved more attractive to blacks than the former slave state.

Of Missouri's 161,234 blacks in 1900, about one-third lived in St. Louis (35,516) and Kansas City (17,567). Blacks lived in a variety of neighborhoods within each city, some in pleasant surroundings but many in deteriorating slums. While harsh discrimination against blacks existed in various areas of life, systematic segregation in housing awaited a later period. Although blacks were being disfranchised in most southern states at the turn of the century, they never lost their right to vote in Missouri.

Missouri's Population, 1860–90

YEAR	TOTAL POPULATION	WHITE	BLACK
1860	1,182,012	1,063,489	118,503
1870	1,721,295	1,603,146	118,071
1880	2,168,380	2,022,826	145,350
1890	2,679,185	2,528,458	150,184

The most dramatic population change occurred where railroad development was greatest. Between 1860 and 1870 the thirty counties in which the most railroad building took place accounted for 56 percent of the state's population increase. Kansas City and St. Louis had worked diligently to secure railroad connections, and they recorded significant population growth as a result. Kansas City went from a small town of 4,418 people in 1860 to a bustling city of 132,716 in 1890 and reached 163,752 by 1900. St. Louis's population rose from 160,773 to 451,770 between 1860 and 1890 and stood at 575,238 by 1900. Although Kansas City replaced St. Joseph as Missouri's most important western city, the latter's population jumped from 8,932 in 1860 to 52,324 in 1890.

The railroad changed Springfield from a small town of 3,442 in 1860 to a city of 21,850 in 1890. Sedalia did not exist in 1860, but it became a railroad shop and counted 4,560 people in 1870 and 15,231 by 1900. Discoveries of lead and zinc coincided with the extension of the South Pacific Railroad to create Joplin in 1871. Nine years later its population numbered 7,038, and it had increased to 26,023 by 1900.

While Missouri remained predominantly rural during this period, a trend toward greater urbanization developed. In 1880, for example, Missouri counted only fourteen cities with more than 4,000 people, and those living in towns of 2,500 or more composed 26 percent of the population. By 1890, twenty-nine Missouri cities had more than 4,000 people and urban dwellers composed 32 percent of the population, while 36 percent of the nation's population lived in urban areas. in 1910, more than 41 percent of Missouri's population lived in cities compared with less than 13 percent of Arkansas's, 30 percent of Iowa's, and more than 61 percent of Illinois's.

Kansas City

The rise of Kansas City shows, perhaps in an exaggerated fashion, the forces that transformed society during the last part of the nineteenth century. Because of aggressive, committed leadership, Kansas City succeeded in bridging the Missouri River four years before St. Joseph did so in 1873 and, as a result, outdistanced the northern city. Located next to the western plains, Kansas City benefited from railroad construction and agricultural development in that region, serving as a processing center for farm products before sending them to eastern markets via the Cameron spur and the Hannibal and St. Joseph Railroad. At the same time the Pacific Railroad connected the city with Missouri's hinterland and St. Louis. In 1887 twenty-four railroads entered Kansas City.

Farmers shipped their cattle and livestock on those trains to the Missouri city. In 1870 two Burlington railroad officials, L. V. Morse and James Joy, purchased five acres of land for a livestock yard. The next year they expanded the yard to almost fifteen acres, began construction of the livestock exchange building, and incorporated as the Kansas Stockyards Company. By 1880 farmers shipped just under a million cattle, hogs, and sheep to the Kansas City market.

When the yards opened, three local firms packed meat. In the same year Plankington and Armour, a national firm, joined them. Ten years later the Armour plant, as it was called, employed 600 workers and consumed 2 million board feet of lumber, 3,000 tons of salt, and $60,000 worth of barrels annually. Other national firms entered the competition, including the Fowler Brothers and Jacob Dold

Main Street, Kansas City, 1900. *Courtesy State Historical Society of Missouri*

in 1880 and Swift in 1887. By 1890 eight meat-packing companies had invested $1.5 million, employed a labor force of 6,200, paid wages of over $4 million per year, and consumed raw materials valued at almost $30 million per year. At the turn of the century only Chicago surpassed Kansas City as a meat-packing center.

To paraphrase a local poet, not only meat but also bread made Kansas City. In 1871 Kansas City received about 687,000 bushels of corn and 350,000 bushels of wheat. Five years later 5,769,295 bushels of corn and 1,820,297 bushels of wheat entered the city. Business leaders built elevators to store the grain and mills to grind it into flour. An increase in Missouri's farm acreage and, more significantly, the introduction of hard-kerneled winter wheat into Kansas resulted in further expansion of Kansas City's storage and milling facilities. Kansas wheat production went from 25 million bushels in 1875 to 75 million bushels in 1892. Technology to turn the hard wheat into flour developed in Minneapolis in 1871; Kansas City millers soon adopted it. In 1879 chilled iron rollers replaced mill stones, making it easier to grind grain into fine flour. By 1900 Kansas City ranked ninth in the nation as a producer of flour.

With its expanding industries and population, Kansas City experienced rapid physical growth between 1870 and 1900. One historian asserted that real estate was the city's most dramatic business.

St. Louis, 1890. *Courtesy State Historical Society of Missouri*

Developers platted ten additions during the difficult economic times between 1873 and 1876, thirteen additions in 1879, and twenty-seven in 1880. The boom collapsed in 1887 because of overexpansion and did not resume until after the Panic of 1893 subsided. Unlike some cities that underwent similar real estate expansion, Kansas City succeeded in avoiding the worst effects of urban sprawl because of concerted efforts of civic leaders such as William Rockhill Nelson.

Nelson arrived in the Missouri city from Indiana in 1880. Already thirty-nine, he established the *Kansas City Star* and *Times* and through their pages urged Kansas City residents to support the planned development of their city. Before his death in 1915, he had seen the rather scruffy, chaotic place where he had established the *Star* transformed into a city with beautiful parks, extensive boulevards, and the most up-to-date conveniences.

St. Louis

Across the state St. Louis emerged in 1870 as the third most important manufacturing city in the country. Only New York and Philadelphia ranked higher in the number and value of manufacturing establishments. During the decade between 1860 and 1870 Missouri's manufacturing work force tripled and capital investment quadrupled. St. Louis County accounted for 75 percent of that development.

Important St. Louis industries in 1870 included the production of iron, flour, beer, clothing, and furniture. The state's iron industry centered in St. Louis and produced $9 million worth of iron on an investment of $6,130,000. St. Louis County's thirty-one flour mills employed 684 people and had $3,850,000 invested in them. The city's fifty breweries employed 761 workers and had a value of $5 million. In 1873 the Anheuser Company became the first brewery to bottle beer for extensive distribution and developed a national market for its product. Clothing manufacturers numbered nearly 500 and employed 3,900 workers. Furniture produced in St. Louis adorned many rural as well as city homes. All told, the St. Louis area counted nineteen industries in 1870 that claimed a capital investment of more than $1 million each.

In the years after 1870 St. Louis added to its industrial base. New manufacturers produced chemicals, medicines, paving bricks, sewer pipes, and white lead. In 1872 the first shoe plant opened in St.

Louis. By 1899 the city had twenty-six shoe factories employing 5,500 workers. St. Louis also manufactured street cars. In 1890 more than 3,000 of its people worked in that industry. Missouri led the nation in the manufacture of tobacco products in 1890, with a majority of the plants in St. Louis. Processors made more chewing tobacco than any other product. They mixed the tobacco with honey, licorice, sugar, spices, rum or a combination of those ingredients. St. Louis chewing tobacco carried such names as "Sweet Buy and Buy," "My Wife's Hat," "Revenge," and "Wiggletail Twist."

In summary, the annual value of St. Louis's manufactured products amounted to $20 million in 1860; it exceeded $228 million in 1890. In the latter year approximately one fifth, 94,000, of the city's people worked in its industries.

Organized Labor

Increased industrialization spawned organized labor. As factories expanded, relationships between owners and managers and their employees became distant. Factory workers frequently labored for long hours for low wages under unsafe conditions. Individual workers achieved little success in bargaining for improved conditions with employers who did not know them and could easily replace them. By organizing, negotiating as a group, and using the lever of withholding their labor as a last resort, workers sought to change their positions.

To coordinate the efforts of craft unions, an umbrella organization called the Workingmen's Union of Missouri came into existence in 1864. It started a newspaper two years later that listed a number of unions, most of them in St. Louis. They included the Ships Carpenters and Calkers Union, Laborers and Helpers Protective and Benevolent Union, St. Louis and Hollow-Ware Moulders Union, the Carpenters and Joiners Association, the journeymen Harness Makers Trade Society, Lodges Number 1 and Number 4 of the Railroads Men's Protective Union, the Journeymen Tobacconists Union, and the Eight Hour League. In 1866 the league succeeded in getting an eight-hour day law passed, but it had so many loopholes that it could not be enforced.

Other workers organized in the ensuing years. During the 1880s the Knights of Labor, a national union, attracted 5,000 followers in St. Louis, and in 1887 the American Federation of Labor chartered the St. Louis Central Trades and Labor Union. At a meeting in 1891, the delegates from various craft unions organized the Missouri Federation of Labor.

Strikes against railroads in 1877, 1885, and 1886 affected Missouri. After the panic of 1873, working conditions for railroad laborers deteriorated, and during the summer of 1877 workers struck in various parts of the nation because of a 10 percent reduction in wages. In St. Louis the railroad walkout developed into a general strike when many of the city's industrial workers left their jobs. The executive committee of the Workingmen's party, a socialist organization whose membership included a large number of German trade unionists, directed the general strike. St. Louis officials became so alarmed that they organized a local militia, called the Committee of Public Safety, to "restore order." Authorities railed against the strike leaders, and workers returned to their jobs. The general strike had lasted a week and pointedly revealed the underlying discontent that existed within the St. Louis work force.

The 1885 and 1886 railroad strikes produced less spectacular results. Kansas City strikers even received favorable public support in 1885. That year Jay Gould, a railroad magnate, persuaded the Wabash Railroad's management to restore wage cuts. In 1886 a more widespread strike against all of Gould's southwestern lines halted all freight movement on the Missouri Pacific and Wabash through Kansas City. The governors of Missouri and Kansas intervened on the side of Gould, public opinion swung against the strikers, and the Knights of Labor had to yield. Many Kansas City strikers lost their jobs.

Other Cities and Industries

St. Joseph had a head start on Kansas City as an outfitter for western travelers, as a meatprocessing center, and as a city connected with eastern markets through the railroad that bore its name. Apathy and the reluctance of vested interests to move ahead rapidly kept the city from capitalizing on its early start. As noted above, it waited until 1873 to bridge the Missouri River. It did not build a stockyards until 1879, and that was obsolete before it was finished. St. Joseph built a larger stockyards in 1887, but it failed to turn a profit until the mid-1890s when Swift purchased it. In 1898 Swift built a modern meatpacking plant thereby making St. Joseph an important city in that industry.

Industries in other towns included the manufacture of boats and tobacco products in Hannibal, the production of cotton and woolen goods and the manufacture of wagons and carriages in Springfield, and the manufacture of zithers and corncob pipes in Washington. Other states made boats and the items associated with Springfield, but few indeed ever produced zithers or corncob pipes. Franz Schwartzer began making the stringed instrument that was called a zither in the Missouri town in 1866. Henry Tibbe started a corncob pipe factory there six years later. Today Missouri remains the sole producer of that item.

The mining industry ranked first among the industrial activities of out-state Missouri. The demands of the Civil War pushed the state's lead and iron ore production to its capacity. In 1869 lead-mining techniques changed dramatically when the St. Joseph Lead Company introduced a new diamond drill at its Bonne Terre mine. That innovation allowed deeper mining activities and resulted in greatly increased production.

After the railroad penetrated southwest Missouri in the early 1870s, lead mining boomed in that region. in 1870 E. R. Moffett and J. B. Sargeant discovered a rich vein of lead in the vicinity of Joplin Creek. Prospectors flocked to the digs; and when Joplin incorporated in 1873, 4,000 people lived there. Zinc production also helped make Joplin a boomtown. By 1874 zinc production had reached 23,500 tons per year providing more than $200,000 in income. By 1875 Joplin had educational facilities for its 1,620 children, twelve dry goods and clothing stores, twelve blacksmith shops, five hotels, sixteen physicians and an equal number of lawyers, two banks, and seventy-five saloons. Saturday nights roared in Joplin.

Coal mining increased in importance after the Civil War. By the late 1860s the state was producing more than a million tons annually and led all states west of the Mississippi in coal production until 1874, when Iowa surpassed it. Using strip-mining techniques, miners exploited the deposits in northeastern and west central Missouri. Railroads made it possible to ship to a national market. For example, Bates County in west central Missouri produced 19,385 tons of coal in 1880 and consumed all of it. By 1890, after the railroads came, it mined 755,989 tons, 93 percent of which went to markets outside the county. In 1900 Missouri was mining approximately 3.5 million tons of coal per year.

Other mining products included limestone for building and clay for brickmaking. In 1870 St. Louis County had thirty-two limestone quarries. Commercial mining of limestone building stone began at Carthage in 1880. The state capitol is built of Carthage stone. The number of brickmaking establishments in Missouri increased from 76 in 1860 to 277 in 1890. In that thirty years the value of their production went from $683,775 to almost $3 million.

Telephone

By 1890 telephone lines linked many Missouri towns and cities. Hannibal boasted the first exchange in the state and the second in the world, when technicians completed it in 1878. St. Louis installed an exchange the same year; Kansas City finished its telephone system in 1879. By October 1885, telephone lines spanned the state, allowing residents of St. Louis and Kansas City to talk to each other.

Agriculture

Like other aspects of economic life, agriculture underwent extraordinary growth during the period. The number of improved acres in Missouri increased from 6,246,871 in 1860 to 19,792,313 in 1890. During the same years the number of farms went from 92,792 to 238,043, while their size declined from an average of 215 acres to 129 acres. Farmers doubled their hog production and tripled their cattle production. Missouri raised 5,200,000 hogs in 1889 and 2,290,000 head of cattle in 1890. The state also increased its production of horses from 287,157 in 1867 to 950,566 in 1892, and its production of mules from 60,988 to 248,850 during the same period. As shown in the following table, the number of acres devoted to the state's chief field crops greatly increased, whereas the yields in bushels per acre either remained about the same or declined because expansion brought less fertile soil into production.

Missouri Crop Yields

	CORN		OATS		WHEAT	
		Yield		Yield		Yield
Year	Acreage	Per acre	Acreage	Per acre	Acreage	Per acre
1866	1,520,115	30.8	112,000	30.7	214,790	16.5
1871	2,299,736	38.0	488,000	28.3	957,089	13.4
1876	3,687,050	27.8	651,000	20.2	1,229,032	12.4
1881	5,650,100	16.5	959,000	23.8	2,382,700	8.6
1886	6,484,600	22.2	1,306,000	23.4	1,662,721	13.2
1891	6,796,318	29.9	1,158,000	25.3	1,892,082	13.6

New machines and scientific techniques aided farmers as they increasingly specialized their operations and produced food that trains carried to growing cities. Sulky plows that had wheels and a seat for the driver, improved corn planters and shellers, spring-tooth rakes, endgate seeders, binders, threshing machines, hay balers, and hoisting forks all made farming easier but required more capital outlay. Missouri farmers increased their investments in farm machinery from $8,711,508 in 1860 to $21,830,719 in 1890. The state university's College of Agriculture and the State Board of Agriculture, established in 1863, provided farmers with information about agricultural improvements. Norman J. Colman, a member of the State Board of Agriculture for fifty years, conducted agricultural experiments on his farm in St. Louis County and publicized the results through his lecturing and in his magazine, *Colman's Rural World*. A strong supporter of the College of Agriculture, Colman also advocated the establishment of farmers' clubs and agricultural fairs as forums for the exchange of information.

In the Ozarks, apples and grapes became important crops. Herman Jaeger of Newton County crossed Virginia and wild Ozark grapes in 1867 to create a new hardy variety. French growers later imported seventeen carloads of Jaeger's cuttings to cross with their grapes to make them more resistant to the grape louse. For his contribution France awarded Jaeger its Legion of Honor.

For Jaeger and all other Missourians, the state had become much different between 1860 and 1890. In the latter year an all-weather transportation system crisscrossed the state and tied it to a national market system. A bustling, eager Kansas City stood on its western border, and a much larger, more diversified St. Louis stood on its eastern side. People lived in places that had been prairie; crops grew where deer had roamed; and miners dug where trees had grown. Certainly, Missouri had matured.

Suggestions for Reading

Comprehensive treatments of the period 1860–1919 are to be found in William E. Parrish, *A History of Missouri, Vol. 3, 1860–1875*, rev. ed., Columbia, University of Missouri Press, 2001, and Lawrence O. Christensen and Gary R. Kremer, *A History of Missouri, Vol. IV, 1875 to 1919*, Columbia, University of Missouri Press, 1997. Volume 2 of Floyd C. Shoemaker's *Missouri and Missourians: Land of Contrasts and*

People of Achievement, Chicago, Lewis Historical Publishing Company, 1943, is encyclopedic. The chart on agricultural production was condensed from his detailed charts. On railroads between 1830 and 1860, see J. Christopher Schnell, "Chicago Versus St. Louis: A Reassessment of the Great Rivalry," *Missouri Historical Review*, April 1977; H. Roger Grant, "Courting the Great Western Railway: An Episode of Town Rivalry," *Missouri Historical Review*, July 1982; and John W. Million, *State Aid to Railways in Missouri*, Chicago, University of Chicago Press, 1896. The development of the lower Mississippi River is discussed in Florence Dorsey, *Road to the Sea: The Story of James B. Eads*, New York, Rinehart, 1947.

Kansas City has received considerable attention in recent years with the publication of A. Theodore Brown, *Frontier Community, Kansas City to 1870*, Columbia, University of Missouri Press, 1963; Charles N. Glaab, *Kansas City and the Railroads: Community Policy in the Growth of a Regional Metropolis*, Madison, State Historical Society of Wisconsin, 1962; William A. Wilson, *The City Beautiful Movement in Kansas City*, Columbia, University of Missouri Press, 1964; and A. Theodore Brown and Lyle W. Dorsett, K. C.: *A History of Kansas City, Missouri*, Boulder, CO, Pruett Publishing Co., 1978. Sherry L. Shirmer and Richard D. McKinzie, *At the River's Bend: An Illustrated History of Kansas City, Independence and Jackson County*, Woodland Hills, CA, Windsor Publications, Inc., 1982, supplements the Brown-Dorsett volume by stressing social history. George Ehrlich, *Kansas City, Missouri: An Architectural History*, Kansas City, Historic Kansas Foundation, 1979, provides an unusual insight into the city.

James Neal Primm, *Lion of the Valley, St. Louis, Missouri, 1764–1980*, 3d ed., St. Louis, Missouri Historical Society Press, 1998, provides a modern and thorough survey of the city's past. Gary Ross Mormino, *Immigrants on the Hill: Italian-Americans in St. Louis, 1882–1982*, Urbana, University of Illinois Press, 1986, William Barnaby Faherty, *The St. Louis Irish*, Columbia, University of Missouri Press, 2001, and Walter Kamphoefner, *The Westphalians: From Germany to Missouri*, Princeton, Princeton University Press, 1987, help explain the immigrant experience. An older survey of the city is Ernest Kirschten, *Catfish and Crystal: Bicentenary Edition of the St. Louis Story*, New York, Doubleday, 1960. Eric Sandweiss, ed., *St. Louis in the Century of Henry Shaw: A View Beyond the Garden Wall*, Columbia, University of Missouri Press, 2002, provides a series of essays about St. Louis. See also William Barnaby Faherty, *Henry Shaw: His Life and*

Legacies, Columbia, University of Missouri Press, 1987. J. Thomas Scharf, *History of St. Louis City and County,* 2 vols., Philadelphia, L. H. Everts & Co., 1883, remains useful, and William Hyde and Howard L. Conard, eds. *Encyclopedia of St. Louis,* 4 vols., Louisville, Southern History Co., 1899, should not be ignored. David T. Burbank, *Reign of the Rabble: The St. Louis General Strike of 1877,* New York, A. M. Kelley, 1966, discusses that episode in detail, while the baseball scene is revealed in Jon David Cash, *Before They Were Cardinals: Major League Baseball in Nineteenth Century St. Louis,* University of Missouri Press, 2002. Yet another important topic is covered in Selwyn K. Troen, *The Public and the Schools: Shaping the St. Louis System, 1838–1920,* Columbia, University of Missouri Press, 1975.

Histories of other cities include Alan R. Havig, *Columbia: From Southern Village to Midwestern City,* Woodland Hills, CA, Windsor Publishing Co., 1984; Phyllis Dark, *Springfield of the Ozarks,* Woodland Hills, CA, Windsor Publishing Co., 1981; and G. K. Renner, *Joplin from Mining Town to Urban Center,* Northridge, CA, Windsor Publications, Inc., 1985. See also Michael Cassity, *Defending a Way of Life,* Albany, State University of New York Press, 1989, for an interpretation of Sedalia's early history. An interesting study of a single farm is David Hamilton's *Deep River: A Memoir of a Missouri Farm,* Columbia, University of Missouri Press, 2001.

Among numerous articles one should note Margaret Lo Piccolo Sullivan, "St. Louis Ethnic Neighborhoods, 1850–1930: An Introduction," *The Bulletin,* January 1977, and the following in the *Missouri Historical Review:* James W. Goodrich and Donald B. Oster, eds., "'Few Men But Many Widows': The Daniel Fogle Letters, August 8–September 4, 1867," April 1986; Robert E. Smith, "Nothing Seemed Impossible: Frank N. Moore and the Mineral Cities Railway," July 1986; Janet C. Rowe, "The Lock Mill, Loose Creek, Missouri: The Center of a Self-Sufficient Community, 1848–1900," April 1981; George G. Suggs, "Child Labor in the Tiff Mines of Washington County, Missouri," July 1993; Louis Potts and George F. W. Houck, "Frontier Bridge Building: The Hannibal Bridge at Kansas City, 1867–1869," January 1995; Bonnie Stepenoff, "'The Last Tree Cut Down': The End of the Boothill Frontier, 1880–1930," October 1996; J. Michael Cronan, "Trial of the Century!: The Acquittal of Frank James," January 1997; Siegmar Muehl, "The Wild Missouri Grape and Nineteenth-Century Viticulture," July 1997; Larry G. Bowman, "Christian Von der Ahe, the St. Louis Browns, and the World's Championship Playoffs, 1885–1888," October 1997.

TWELVE

Angry Farmers
and Urban Reformers

After the Civil War farmers writhed in economic distress. In debt as participants in the agricultural expansion described in Chapter 11, they watched wheat prices fluctuate from one dollar per bushel in 1870 to forty-three cents per bushel in 1890, and corn prices range from forty-five cents per bushel in 1870 to twenty cents per bushel in 1890. Government policies that forced the value of money upward by recalling paper money and ending the coinage of silver, and banking policies that increased interest rates worsened the farmers' plight. Farmers thus struggled to pay debts with deflated dollars and declining prices for their crops.

In addition, they faced the forces of consolidation described by Lawrence Goodwyn in *The Populist Moment: A Short History of the Agrarian Revolt in America:*

> Everywhere the farmer turned he seemed to be the victim of rules that somehow always worked to the advantage of the biggest business and financial concerns that touched his world. To be efficient, the farmer had to have tools and livestock that cost him forbidding rates of interest. When he sold, he got the price offered by terminal grain elevator companies. To get his produce there, he paid high rates of freight. If he tried to sell to different grain dealers, or elevator companies, or livestock commission agents, he often encountered the practical evidence of secret agreements between agricultural middlemen and trunk line railroads. The Northern Pacific named specific grain terminals to which farmers should ship, the trunk line simply refusing to provide railroad cars for the uncooperative.

Background to Populism

Farmers protested against these conditions by forming cooperatives and seeking regulation of the railroads. They acted under the auspices of the National Grange, which was the first significant farmers' organization. Oliver H. Kelly, a former clerk in the federal Bureau of Agriculture, began the Grange in 1867; he started it in Missouri in 1870. Five years later it claimed more chapters in Missouri than in any other state. As the Grange developed, members divided over the direction that the farm movement should take. Some advocated greater political activism, while the majority advised continued concentration on social and educational uplift.

Third Parties

The People's party of 1874, which was discussed in Chapter 10, was the first effort at a third party movement arising out of farmers' discontents. Its failure to unite the farm vote illustrated a problem that would persist in Missouri throughout the late nineteenth century. Dying after only one election, the People's party found successors in the Greenback and Union Labor parties. They placed candidates on the ballot in every Missouri election between 1876 and 1888. Taking their name from United States paper notes issued during the Civil War, the Greenbackers advocated the issuance of United States notes as legal tender, a federal tax on incomes, an eight-hour day law for labor, equal pay for each sex, and the availability of public lands for actual settlers only. Greenbackers polled their largest number of votes in 1880 with 36,338 for governor, which was less than 10 percent of the total. Adhering to the same principles and including many former Greenbackers among its leaders, the Union Labor party ran candidates in 1888 and 1890. At times third parties fused with Republicans in local and state-wide elections, but with limited success.

Third parties had difficulty in Missouri for a number of reasons. First, people usually acquire party allegiance from their parents. Tradition, familiar symbols, and emotional ties all work against breaking with political inheritance. Second, by their nature new parties face difficult organizational problems, including internal ideological divisions among their members. Usually without office, a third party lacks patronage, the party glue, with which to build its structure.

Third, in Missouri some farm leaders owed the Democratic party past electoral support, and they continued active participation in that party. Fourth, Missouri Democrats took third-party issues as their own and claimed that they could achieve reform. Fifth, in Missouri examples of fusion with Republicans left a bad taste in many rural mouths. Many farmers blamed Republicans for the Civil War and the excesses of Reconstruction. They wanted nothing to do with third parties that fused with the Grand Old Party, or GOP. Sixth, in the South and in some regions of Missouri, Democratic rule meant the practical exclusion of blacks from politics; third parties meant that blacks might be the balance of power. Seventh, third parties failed to attract significant labor votes because they offered rural-oriented platforms.

Examples of Democrats taking over farmers' issues abound. For instance, in 1875 the General Assembly established a Board of Railroad Commissioners as a regulatory body. It proved ineffective because its penalties were too lenient, but its establishment quieted some farmer criticism just before the 1876 election. Democratic gubernatorial nominee John S. Phelps of Springfield and his colleagues swept the election. In 1878 the state Democratic party platform echoed its Greenback counterpart by calling for the repeal of the federal Resumption Act of 1875. That act, passed by a Republican majority in Congress, provided for placing the greenbacks issued during the Civil War on a par with gold beginning in 1879. Implementation of the Resumption Act would have contracted or deflated the currency. Another Democratic plank demanded repeal of the federal law of 1873 that had ended the coinage of silver.

Democratic Representative Richard P. Bland of Lebanon championed the free coinage of silver in the 1870s and continued to be identified with that issue until it dropped from sight in 1900. He cosponsored the Bland-Allison Act in 1878 which required the U.S. Treasury to purchase at least $2 million but not more than $4 million worth of silver per month. Republican President Rutherford Hayes vetoed the measure, but Congress passed it over his veto. The Democratic Congress also passed legislation that required the continued circulation of $346,618,016 greenbacks still being used.

In 1880 Thomas T. Crittenden of Warrensburg and his Democratic colleagues easily defeated their Greenback and Republican opponents. Governor Crittenden made no obvious overtures to agricultural demands, except for breaking up the James gang as described in

Chapter 11. Crittenden's Democratic successor, John Sappington Marmaduke of St. Louis, however, called a special session of the legislature to urge increased state supervision of railroads. Marmaduke had defeated Nicholas Ford of Andrew County, a Greenback-Republican fusion candidate, by about 10,000 votes and believed that legislative action was necessary. The General Assembly responded with a law that forbade unjust discrimination in freight charges, empowered the railroad commission to set maximum rates, and established substantial penalties for offenses. This reflected the general mood of the times for five months earlier Congress had enacted the Interstate Commerce Act as the first federal effort to regulate railroads. Governor Marmaduke died on December 28, 1887, and Lieutenant Governor Albert P. Morehouse of Maryville served out the remainder of his term.

The Alliance Movement

Meanwhile farmers in Missouri turned to the National Farmers' Alliance and Cooperative Union of America and the National Agricultural Wheel in their efforts to improve their conditions. Formed in Texas during 1884–85 and later combined with a Louisiana organi-

Founders of Missouri Farmers Alliance, painting by Sid Larson. *Midcontinent Farmers Association*

zation, the Farmers' Alliance entered Missouri in 1887. By August 1888 it had organized 615 sub or local alliances in thirty-eight southern counties. The Agricultural Wheel began in Arkansas in 1882 and entered Missouri in 1886, the same year that eight state wheels formed the national organization. In 1889 the Alliance and Wheel united, forming the Farmers' and Laborers' Union of America.

Still called the Farmers' Alliance, the new organization advocated that farmers form cooperatives, educate themselves about the issues of the day, and learn scientific farming techniques. Through the lecturer system whereby paid and unpaid individuals discussed farm problems and literature that advocated reform, farmers learned new approaches to farming and broadened their knowledge of society. Uriel S. Hall of Moberly served as state lecturer in Missouri during 1889. One contemporary Missourian called the alliance movement a national university that inspired and stimulated farmers to think. By 1889 Norman Colman, editor of *Colman's Rural World,* estimated membership in the movement at 200,000.

Election of 1888

Although political discontent surfaced in the form of the two third parties already mentioned, Democratic candidates retained all of the statewide offices in 1888. Democrat David R. Francis, a grain dealer, former president of the St. Louis Merchants' Exchange, and former mayor of St. Louis, captured the governorship from his Republican opponent, E. E. Kimball of Nevada, by 13,233 votes. Democrats also won ten of fourteen congressional races and continued their control of both houses of the General Assembly. While losing nationally in his bid for reelection, Democratic President Grover Cleveland defeated his Republican opponent, Benjamin Harrison, in Missouri by 25,691 votes.

During the next legislative session the Democratic majority tightened regulation of the railroads and provided for a state grain inspector. In addition, Governor Francis recommended and the legislature wrote the state's first antitrust law. The Missouri Supreme Court declared it unconstitutional in 1891, but a revised law passed in the same year met the court's objections. By such actions the Democrats showed an awareness of farmer discontent and moved to curb it.

Farmers Formulate a Program

In December 1889, leaders of the recently formed Farmers' and Laborers' Union of America invited representatives from various farm
and labor organizations to meet in St. Louis to discuss national consolidation. Regional antagonisms between northern and southern
farm organizations and inadequate appeals to labor made unifica-
tion impossible. The St. Louis meeting, however, led to the formula-
tion of a series of demands that served as the basis for subsequent
political platforms proposed by farmers. It also exposed the recently
proposed subtreasury plan to a large audience.

Cooperative self-help had failed in Texas, where the best organized effort had been made, because of lack of credit from banks and
an unwillingness of manufacturers to do business with the cooperatives. Consequently, C. W. Macune, a major figure in the Texas farmers' movement, proposed the subtreasury plan. It called for the federal government to make loans to farmers with their crops as collateral. The government would store the crops in its warehouses, and
farmers would receive loans of up to 80 percent of their crops' current market value. Interest on the loans would be 1 percent per an-
num. Farmers would receive certificates that stated the amount and
quality of stored goods. Certificates could be sold. Holders of certificates would have to redeem the crop in one year or the commodity
would be sold at public auction. Macune's plan would have revolu-
tionized agricultural financing by making the government the source
of credit, by guaranteeing low interest rates, by making it possible for
farmers to market crops at the most advantageous time, and by in-
jecting several billion dollars worth of negotiable certificates into the
currency every harvest time.

Beyond this, the so-called St. Louis Demands urged the federal
government to abolish national banks and their notes and to substitute federal treasury notes. The farmers wanted the federal government to coin all of the silver available and to regulate the volume of
currency according to need. Discoveries of silver mines in the West
had greatly increased the supply and reduced the value of silver; its
unlimited coinage would have inflated the currency.

Farmers also demanded that Congress prohibit speculation in agricultural and mechanical production. They asked the government to
reclaim land owned by aliens and land that had been granted to rail-

roads and other corporations and was not being used. They called for the passage of equitable tax laws and government economy. And they wanted the federal government to take control of and to operate the railroads and telephone and telegraph lines. Both that demand and the subtreasury plan drew harsh criticism because they smacked of socialism. Other proposals included a graduated income tax, direct election of the President and United States senators, and equal enforcement of the laws.

Missouri Farmers Split

When delegates of the Missouri Farmers' Alliance met in Sedalia during August 1890, they debated the merits of the subtreasury plan and of creating a third party. Those opposed to the subtreasury plan and the idea of a new political party prevailed under the leadership of Uriel S. Hall of Moberly. The convention elected Hall president of the organization, endorsed the St. Louis Demands but not the subtreasury plan, and committed alliance members to support only those candidates who signed a pledge to work for alliance principles.

Democratic candidates signed the pledges without hesitation, and the party and alliance scored an easy victory in the 1890 election. The Democratic platform included practically all of the farmers' requests because alliance members had dominated the party's convention. Democrats won all three statewide contests, all 14 congressional seats, 16 of 18 state senate seats, and 106 of 140 house seats. All of those elected to Congress had signed the pledge, as had all except 34 members of the General Assembly. Legislation passed during the 1891 session of the General Assembly met all of the alliance demands that could be accomplished at the state level, except for prohibiting allen land ownership.

More conservative members of the farmers' movement seemed content to accomplish their objectives through the Democratic party. Those who supported the subtreasury plan believed that only a third party could secure its passage. That division caused membership in the Missouri Alliance to decline and paved the way for the election of Leverett Leonard of Saline County as president of the organization in 1891. Leonard favored both the subtreasury plan and third-party politics and led the movement in that direction. Delegates to the 1891 alliance convention also removed Phil Chew's *Journal of Agricul-*

ture as the official organ of the alliance because Chew had opposed the subtreasury plan. The organization then depended upon various weekly newspapers to present the alliance message.

Election of 1892

After a series of conventions, elements of the Farmers' Alliance and Industrial Union, the Knights of Labor, and other farmer and labor groups met at St. Louis to form the People's party in February 1892. In July at Omaha, Nebraska, the party nominated James B. Weaver of Iowa for President. He had been the Greenback party nominee in 1880. The Populists, as the People's party members were called, adopted a platform based upon the St. Louis Demands, including the subtreasury plan.

Third party organizing progressed in Missouri also and resulted in the birth of the People's party of Missouri at Sedalia on June 21– 22, 1892. Delegates selected Leverett Leonard as the party's gubernatorial candidate and wrote a platform that called for the St. Louis Demands and the subtreasury plan. In addition, Missouri Populists promised free textbooks for public schools, abolition of child labor, the eight-hour day for industrial laborers, equal pay for women and men for equal work, and submission of a women's suffrage amendment to the state's voters. Because of criticism from some alliance members, Leonard resigned as president of that organization three days after the convention adjourned.

Representing a rump of the farmers' movement, the People's party had little success in taking control of the state from the Democrats. The older party played upon the movement's division by nominating Uriel S. Hall for a congressional seat. The Democrats also adopted a platform that included a plank calling for the free coinage of silver at a ratio of sixteen ounces of silver to one ounce of gold. When the Missouri Alliance met in convention at Moberly on August 23, it refused to endorse the People's party's platform or slate but expressed sympathy for its views.

Missourians cast over 540,000 votes for President in 1892, but James B. Weaver, the People's party candidate, received only 41,204 of them. Weaver failed to carry a single county, as former Democratic President Grover Cleveland defeated incumbent Republican Benjamin Harrison by a margin that almost equalled Weaver's total vote. Leonard received 4,000 fewer votes than Weaver, as Democrat William J. Stone of Nevada won the governor's race by almost 30,000 votes. Uriel S. Hall and twelve other Democrats won congressional seats while two went to Republicans. Not a single People's party candidate won. Democratic tactics, rural conservatism, and traditional adherence to the old party made the third party in Missouri ineffective.

Panic of 1893

Not long after Cleveland's inauguration, the nation began to feel the impact of the depression of 1893. Easy credit and a mushrooming population had produced a surge of industrial and business expansion during the 1880s. Sales slowed in 1893 when the distressed agricultural sector of the economy could not pick up the slack created by a reduced demand for goods in Europe. Fewer sales meant less profit, making it difficult to pay debts. A number of businesses declared bankruptcy; unemployment rose, which further reduced demand; and so it went.

Cleveland responded to the panic by engineering the repeal of the Sherman Silver Purchase Act of 1890. It had required the U.S. Treasury to purchase $4.5 million worth of silver each month and to pay for it in treasury notes. Cleveland feared that the purchase of silver would erode the value of the dollar, just what the farmers wanted.

Missouri suffered from the depression but for a relatively brief period. During 1893–94 the bottom fell out of farm prices and unemployment reached new heights, but in 1894 the state commissioner of labor statistics reported that the worst was over and that the state's economy was beginning to recover. A magazine writer in 1897 observed that St. Louis suffered "no serious results of the panic. . . ."

Election of 1894

With economic distress in the land and their President in the White House adhering to the gold standard, Missouri Democrats approached the 1894 election with apprehension. Governor Stone and Representative Richard Bland opposed Cleveland on the money question by advocating the free coinage of silver at sixteen to one. Former Governor David R. Francis stood with Cleveland and gold, although he was not doctrinaire. The two forces clashed at the state Democratic convention, but decided to compromise by calling for the coinage of both metals without specifying a ratio.

Tranquility prevailed at the Republican convention in Excelsior Springs. Leaders of the party smelled victory and wanted to do nothing to jeopardize it. They endorsed bimetallism and blamed Cleveland's opposition to high tariffs for the depression.

Political and economic conditions seemed to be tailor-made for the People's party when it met in convention at Kansas City. In an appeal to labor, its platform condemned various aspects of government intervention in labor-management conflicts. Other planks reiterated longtime demands such as government control of the railroads. As in 1892, the Missouri Alliance refused to endorse the Populist slate.

Republican anticipation proved correct. That party won the three statewide races being contested, ten of fifteen congressional seats, and a majority in the lower house of the General Assembly. Democrats retained the five other congressional posts, but because of People's party candidates in the races, longtime Democrats Richard P. Bland, William H. Hatch, and Marshall Arnold lost their seats.

Populist and Republican congressional candidates in 1894 increased their votes over 1892 totals, while Democratic candidates polled 46,638 fewer votes in 1894 than in 1892. The Populists added more than 7,000 and the Republicans increased by 3,581. Those increases accounted for fewer than one-fourth of the Democratic losses, however, and it is clear that a large number of Democratic voters just stayed home. Missouri Populists had to be discouraged by the 1894 results, particularly when they noted that the People's party on the national level had increased its total votes by 42 percent between 1892 and 1894.

Besides winning in Missouri for the first time in twenty-six years, Republicans also scored a national victory by capturing both houses of Congress. Undaunted, Cleveland adhered to the gold standard and did nothing to alleviate the crushing impact of the depression.

Election of 1896

Led by Governor Stone and "Silver Dick" Bland, Missouri silverites moved to take over the state Democratic party in preparation for the 1896 election. By April 15, 1896, when the Democratic state convention met, they had succeeded. The Democratic platform contained planks that called for the coinage of silver at sixteen to one and unanimously resolved to support Bland for the Democratic nomination for President.

Threshing wheat in Adair County around 1910. *Courtesy State Historical Society of Missouri*

On the first three ballots at the national convention, Bland received the most votes, but the sixty-one-year-old warhorse failed to generate the enthusiasm of the eloquent, aggressive William Jennings Bryan of Nebraska, who delivered a rousing speech condemning the gold standard. Delegates nominated Bryan and jubilantly declared their support for the free coinage of silver. Gold Democrats walked out and nominated a separate slate of candidates.

The national Republican convention convened in St. Louis. It nominated William McKinley of Ohio for the presidency on the first ballot. He advocated high tariffs and the gold standard. Republican silverites walked out and emulated the gold Democrats.

The national People's party convention accepted Bryan as its presidential candidate, but chose Thomas E. Watson of Georgia, a former Populist member of the House of Representatives, as its vice-presidential candidate. In so doing the Populists rejected Arthur Sewall of Maine, the Democratic vice-presidential nominee, because of his banking and railroad connections. By accepting the Democratic nominee for President as its own and free silver as the dominant, almost sole issue, the People's party lost its vigor.

In the election, Bryan carried Missouri by 363,667 votes to 304,940 votes for McKinley. Democratic gubernatorial candidate Lon V. Stephens of Cooper County defeated his Republican opponent Robert E. Lewis of Henry County by 351,062 to 307,729 votes. Orville E. Jones of Knox County, the Populist candidate, withdrew from the race a few days before the balloting, apparently recognizing his hopeless plight. In congressional races, ten straight Democrats along with two Democratic-People's party fusion candidates and three Republicans won. Bland succeeded in returning to Congress.

In Missouri the 1896 election marked the practical end of the farmers' movement as an organized social force and the People's party as an important political force. The number of votes for People's party candidates declined by almost 20,000 from 1894 to 1896. The party presented some candidates for office in 1898, but they received negligible support. The Progressives, who followed the farmer reformers, would pass much of the legislation advocated by them including direct election of United States senators, initiative and referendum, graduated income tax, and women's suffrage.

The Interim Between Populists and Progressives: Governors Stephens and Dockery

Frugality in government set the tone of Lon V. Stephens's administration. For example, when the United States entered the Spanish-American War in 1898, the federal government activated Missouri's militia consisting of five regiments of infantry and one battery of light artillery. Stephens refused to mobilize them until the federal government provided funds for their support. Delays followed, and Missouri troops remained ill clad and ill equipped, while other states' troops participated in the fighting. None of Missouri's five infantry regiments left the United States during the war, although one regiment did aid in the occupation of Cuba after the war ended. The artillery battery served briefly in Puerto Rico, but not in battle. Some of the 3,500 Missourians who volunteered in the regular service saw action in both Cuba and the Philippines. Stephens' cheapness drew harsh criticism.

Although the war lasted for less than a year, it created an increased demand for goods and services that stimulated Missouri's economy. For food alone, the federal government spent $500,000 per week in St. Louis. In addition, Europeans increased their demand for American farm products, which raised prices. And gold discoveries in Australia, South Africa, and the Klondike in Canada increased the money supply. As a result, full prosperity had returned by 1900.

During Stephens' administration, policies that the Populists had supported became law. The General Assembly prohibited children under fourteen years of age from working in dangerous or harmful places, established a six-day week for bakery and confectionery workers, and an eight-hour day for miners. Other laws limited interest rates to 2 percent per month and strengthened the state's antitrust powers.

In the 1900 election Democrats achieved another victory in Missouri. Issues arising out of the Spanish-American War received the most attention. Democrats, led by their presidential candidate William Jennings Bryan, opposed the imperialism represented by the annexation of Puerto Rico and the Philippine Islands and condemned the brutal tactics being used to subdue Philippine rebels who were fighting against American occupancy. The Republicans, led by incumbent President William McKinley, pointed to national prosperity and improved American prestige and power as reasons for voters to reelect them. Bryan carried Missouri by 351,922 to 314,092 votes, but he received almost 12,000 fewer votes than he had in 1896. McKinley garnered nearly 14,000 more votes in Missouri than he had four years earlier and of course won the national election. Vice-President Theodore Roosevelt succeeded to the presidency in 1901, when an assassin killed President McKinley. Alexander M. Dockery of Daviess County, the Democratic candidate for governor, defeated his Republican opponent, Joseph Flory of St. Louis, by more than 32,000 votes. Democrats won thirteen of fifteen congressional races and retained control of the General Assembly.

During the next four years the state administration paid off the bonded debt, provided more support for public institutions than had been appropriated during the previous twelve years, and created a Board of Labor Arbitration and Mediation; however, the public paid more attention to political events in Washington, DC, and St. Louis than those in Jefferson City. In the nation's capital Theodore Roosevelt used the presidency in new ways and set a national tone for governmental action that captured the country's attention. In St. Louis Joseph W. Folk, a young circuit attorney, received statewide and national recognition for his attacks on political corruption.

The Progressives

While Roosevelt was a Republican and Folk was a Democrat, both believed in and became advocates for a diverse political movement called Progressivism. Whereas the farmers' movement originated in the economic distress experienced in the agricultural states of the South and Midwest, the Progressive movement developed out of a continued desire by organized labor, middle-class urbanites, and

Governor Joseph W. Folk. *Courtesy State Historical Society of Missouri*

farmers to reform business and governmental practices. Corruption in city and state government brought reformers to the movement as did the effort to apply religious principles to everyday activities. Investigative journalists known as muckrakers exposed corruption, slum conditions in cities, and illegal business practices to public attention. Progressivism attempted to accommodate the new industrialism to traditional American values of private property, individual rights, and democracy. Although diverse in their backgrounds and interests, Progressives agreed that government should protect the public interest against special privilege, that government could be a major instrument of reform; and that if access to the political process was open, needed changes would be easily achieved. The movement surfaced during the 1890s in various American cities and in the states of Wisconsin, California, Oregon, and New Jersey in the early 1900s.

In Missouri the early Progressive movement was dominated by Joseph W. Folk. Born in Brownsville, Tennessee, in 1869, he clerked and kept books, read law with his father, and graduated from Vanderbilt University in 1890. Folk came to St. Louis in 1894 to practice law with an uncle. By helping to negotiate an end to a transit strike in 1900, he gained the friendship of organized labor in St. Louis. When the Democratic city committee met to discuss a slate of candidates, a member mentioned Folk's name for circuit attorney. After the city convention nominated him, Folk campaigned on the issue of better law enforcement.

Soon after his election, Folk received a visit from Edward J. Butler, the boss of St. Louis's Democratic party. Born in Ireland in 1838, Ed Butler's career contained elements of an American success story. He had immigrated to New York in 1850 where he apprenticed himself to a blacksmith. Moving to St. Louis just before the Civil War, he owned his own shop within two years. Hard work and shrewd real estate and corporate investments made him wealthy. During the 1870s, he began supporting Democratic candidates for the municipal assembly, and by the 1890s he had established himself as a political broker and dominant force in St. Louis politics. Butler gave Folk a list of individuals to whom he had promised jobs in the circuit attorney's office. The boss's power depended upon his ability to deliver services, including promised positions. Folk rejected Butler's candidates for office, saying that as circuit attorney he was neither a Democrat nor a Republican.

Next, Folk began prosecuting members of the Butler machine who had voted numerous times in the 1900 election. It made no difference to the circuit attorney that he had benefited from the election frauds; he succeeded in convicting a number of repeaters. Those actions caused a number of Democratic politicians to question his party loyalty.

In 1902 Folk answered the question by launching a full-scale investigation of political corruption in St. Louis that led directly to Boss Butler. By securing the election of his subordinates to the municipal assembly, Butler had established a group called the "combine," which would grant favors for a price. He served as liaison between businessmen seeking legislation and the combine, taking a slice of the bribe before distributing it to his cohorts.

Beginning with a case involving railway franchises in St. Louis, Folk uncovered three other specific instances of bribery that directly or indirectly implicated Butler. Evidence brought to grand juries by Folk produced four indictments of Butler for bribing a variety of city officials. The accused secured a change of venue to Columbia for his first trial. Found guilty and sentenced to three years in prison, Butler appealed the verdict to the Missouri Supreme Court, which overturned the lower court's decision. Later Butler secured an acquittal in another case tried on a change of venue in Callaway County. Thus, the boss escaped jail, but he had lost his influence. The circuit attorney received national publicity because of a *McClure's Magazine* article by Lincoln Steffens entitled "Tweed Days in St. Louis." A number of Missourians began to push the circuit attorney for the governorship.

Folk was agreeable but realized that many party leaders opposed his advancement. In addition to revealing Democratic scandals in St.

"Father Time Chasing Snakes While Consumers Look On and Dance," cartoon by L. M. Glackens, *Puck Magazine,* February 29, 1912, indicates the feeling of Progressives that reform's time had come. *Courtesy State Historical Society of Missouri*

Louis, he had provided evidence to a Cole County grand jury that caused Democratic Lieutenant Governor John A. Lee to resign in disgrace in 1903. Lee had distributed bribes to six state senators who voted to retain a law against alum being used in baking powder, which gave the Royal Baking Powder Company a monopoly in Missouri. As a result of the case, a parade of Democratic leaders appeared before the grand jury.

Election of 1904

Nevertheless, Folk delegates dominated the Democratic state convention, nominated their hero for governor, and wrote a progressive platform. It called for a statewide direct primary law, the elimination of tax privileges held by corporations, the removal of city police from politics, and the municipal ownership of utilities. Folk summarized his progressivism in what came to be called the "Missouri Idea," the elimination of corruption and special privilege from government.

Although about 40,000 fewer Missourians, many of them Democrats reacting to corruption in their party, cast ballots in 1904 than had done so in 1900, those who voted gave strong support to Progressive candidates. For the first time since 1868, the Republican candidate for President, Progressive Theodore Roosevelt, carried the state. Indeed, the Republicans, most closely identified with Progressive ideas because of Roosevelt, took all of the state offices, except for governor, and a majority of seats in the General Assembly. Because of that majority, the General Assembly selected Republican William Warner of Kansas City to replace the thirty-year veteran Francis Cockrell in the United States Senate. With Republicans also winning ten of sixteen congressional seats, Folk's success in the governor's race represented a personal victory and further demonstrated the progressive leanings of voters.

As governor, Folk worked successfully with a Republican and then a Democratic General Assembly to pass a number of Progressive measures. The legislature repealed the controversial Alum Law of 1899 that Lieutenant Governor Lee had helped pass, passed a compulsory school attendance law that required children between eight and fourteen years of age to go to school, and made it necessary for lobbyists to register. It also established maximum railroad freight rates. In an effort to open the political system, it provided for a primary election system and the initiative and referendum. The General Assembly aided education further by creating state teachers colleges at Maryville and Springfield.

The governor and his Republican attorney general, Herbert Spencer Hadley of Kansas City, cooperated to enforce laws against monopolies. Hadley prosecuted the Standard Oil Company and after three years won a decision against the oil giant in 1908. The attorney general also brought suits against the International Harvester Company and some lumber companies for violating state laws. Hadley won those cases and secured a reputation that almost equalled the governor's for progressive political action.

Election of 1908

In 1908 Hadley's popularity led to his election as the first Republican governor of Missouri since 1870. The Republican presidential candidate, William Howard Taft, also carried the state, and Republicans

Cartoon by John McCutcheon, *Chicago Tribune,* 1904, showing Missouri's departure from its longtime allegiance to the Democratic party in the election of that year. *Courtesy State Historical Society of Missouri*

won a majority of seats in the General Assembly. Elliott W. Major, a Democrat, became attorney general, and Democrats won ten of sixteen congressional races. Folk tried to unseat his fellow Democrat, William J. Stone, as United States Senator, but without success.

Hadley continued the Progressive policies of his predecessor. In an attempt to control election fraud in Kansas City and St. Louis, the legislature created bipartisan election boards for each city. Other laws established a state Food and Drug Commission, a Bureau of Vital Statistics, and a tax on oil designed to raise revenue. The General Assembly also passed laws regulating working conditions and hours for women. Hadley failed, however, to secure legislative approval of additional revenue measures, a state public service commission, and a compensation law that would have provided money to workers who were injured while working.

During the winter of 1911, the capitol building attracted a bolt of lightning and burned. Following Governor Hadley's suggestion, in

August voters approved a bond issue to finance construction of a much larger capitol. Workers broke ground in 1913, and during the next decade constructed a beautiful building out of native stone from southwest Missouri. In 1924 Missourians participated in the dedication of the completed structure.

Election of 1912

The year before the 1912 election, James Beauchamp Clark of Pike County—Champ to his contemporaries—advanced to the office of Speaker of the United States House of Representatives, becoming the first and only Missourian to hold that position. Elected to the House in 1892, defeated in 1894, and returned in 1896 and each election thereafter, Clark led the House fight to break the power of his predecessor, Speaker Joseph Cannon, over the legislative machinery. Generally progressive, Clark's record led to his name being placed in nomination for President at the Democratic national convention in 1912. He achieved a majority of the convention's votes when New York's delegation switched to him on the tenth ballot but could not muster the two-thirds then needed for nomination. On the thirteenth ballot William Jennings Bryan insinuated that Clark had made a deal with Wall Street and announced that so long as New York state voted for the Missourian he would withhold his support. That broke the Clark candidacy and on the forty-sixth ballot Woodrow Wilson, Progressive governor of New Jersey, won the nomination. Clark returned to Missouri and campaigned for Wilson, who carried the state, although the Republican candidate Taft and Progressive "Bull Moose" party candidate and former Republican President, Theodore Roosevelt, received a larger combined vote.

The Democratic gubernatorial candidate, Elliott W. Major of Lincoln County, who had been a successful attorney general under Hadley and adhered to principles similar to his two immediate predecessors, easily defeated Republican John McKinley of Uniontown. Albert D. Nortoni of St. Louis received about half as many votes as McKinley and about one-third as many as Major, while running on the Progressive party ticket. Democrats won all of the other statewide offices, controlled both houses of the General Assembly, and took fourteen of fifteen congressional seats.

As governor, Major continued to follow the legislative agenda of the Progressives. Working with a Democratic-controlled General Assembly, he succeeded in creating a Public Service Commission to

Congressman
Champ Clark of
Bowling Green, who
would later be
Speaker of the
House, and his son
Bennett, who would
later serve as U.S.
Senator from
Missouri, on the
steps of the U.S.
Capitol, 1893.
*Courtesy State
Historical Society
of Missouri*

regulate utilities, providing increased financial support for public
schools, and abolishing the contract labor system in the state's prisons. The legislature also passed the first comprehensive securities act,
providing for the supervision of corporations, and approved the Seventeenth Amendment to the U.S. Constitution, which established
the direct election of United States Senators. An earlier General Assembly had ratified the Sixteenth Amendment, which allowed for a
graduated income tax. Both amendments took effect in 1913.

Thus during the administrations of Governors Folk, Hadley, and
Major many of the reforms advocated by the farmers' movement became law. Both populism and progressivism represented responses
to industrialization and consolidation within the American eco-

nomic system. It is obvious that neither movement proved adequate, for the two forces continued apace. Nevertheless, with populism preparing the way, Progressive legislation modified some of the harsher effects of economic change. Further efforts would have to be delayed for by the end of Governor Major's term international problems had replaced economic questions in the minds of most Missourians.

Suggestions for Reading

Lawrence Goodwyn, *The Populist Movement: A Short History of the Agrarian Revolt in America,* New York, Oxford University Press, 1978, is an incisive, well-written history of that movement. For the farmers' movement in Missouri, Homer Clevenger, "The Farmers' Alliance in Missouri," *Missouri Historical Review,* October 1944, should be consulted. Other related articles in the same journal include C. Joseph Pusateri, "Rural Urban Tensions and the Bourbon Democrat: The Missouri Case," April 1975; Hazel Tutt Long, "Attorney General Herbert S. Hadley v. the Standard Oil Trust," January 1941; and William T. Miller, "Progressive Movement in Missouri," July 1928. Julian S. Rammelkamp, "St. Louis: Boosters and Boodlers," appeared in *The Bulletin,* July 1978.

Raymond A. Young, *Cultivating Cooperation: A History of the Missouri Farmers Association,* Columbia, University of Missouri Press, 1999, details the growth of that organization, while George F. Lemmer, *Norman J. Colman and Colman's Rural World,* Columbia, University of Missouri Studies, 1953, shows why one agricultural leader could not leave the Democratic party for a third party. Important biographies of Missouri governors during this period include Ruth Warner Towne, *William J. Stone and the Politics of Compromise,* Port Washington, NY, Kennikat Press, 1979; Harper Barnes, *Standing on a Volcano: The Life and Times of David Rowland Francis,* St. Louis, Missouri Historical Society Press, 2001, and Steven L. Piott, *Joseph W. Folk and the Missouri Idea,* Columbia, University of Missouri Press, 1997.

Three articles by Jeanette and Robert H. Lauer in the *Missouri Historical Review* also treat with this period: "St. Louis and the 1880 Census: The Shock of Collective Failure," January 1982; "The St. Louis Provident Association: An Elitist War on Poverty, 1860–1899," April 1983; and "Cheltenham: The Search for Bliss in Missouri," January 1987. Steven L. Piott contributed two articles to the *Missouri Histori-*

cal Review dealing with monopolies: "Missouri and Monopoly: The 1890s as an Experiment in Law Enforcement," October 1979, and "Missouri and the Beef Trust: Consumer Action and Investigation, 1902," October 1981. This same ground is covered in Piott's *The Anti-Monopoly Persuasion: Popular Resistance to the Rise of Big Business in the Midwest*, Westport, CT, Greenwood Press, 1985. Lawrence O. Christensen, "Race Relations in St. Louis, 1865–1916," *Missouri Historical Review*, January 1984, is a good survey of that topic.

The most recent book on this period is Lawrence O. Christensen and Gary R. Kremer, *A History of Missouri, Vol. IV, 1875 to 1919*, Columbia, University of Missouri Press, 1997. It counters the thesis of David Thelen, *Paths of Resistance: Tradition and Dignity in Industrializing Missouri*, New York, Oxford University Press, 1986. See also Lawrence O. Christensen, "Small Town Missouri in 1890," *The Midwest Quarterly*, Spring 1990; and in the *Missouri Historical Review*: Gregg Andrews, "Immigrant Cement Workers: The Strike of 1910," January 1995; Kenneth W. Keller, "Merchandising Nature: The J. J. Weber and Sons Nursery," April 1995; Steven L. Piott, "Joseph W. Folk and 'The Missouri Idea': The 1904 Governor's Race in Missouri," July 1996; Marian M. Ohman, "Missouri's Turn-of-the-Century Couple: 'Lon' Vest and Margaret Nelson Stephens, Parts 1 and 2," April and July 1997; and Michael J. Steiner, "Toilers of the Cities and Tillers of the Soil: The 1889 St. Louis 'Convention of the Middle Classes'," July 1999. In *Gateway Heritage*, see Howard S. Miller, "The Politics of Public Bathing in Progressive St. Louis," Fall 1989; and Geoffrey Fahy Morrison, "America's Ring Tailed Roarer: Speaker of the House Champ Clark," Spring 1990.

Missouri Develops Culturally

The Frontier Artist

Nineteenth century Missouri society, rooted as it was in the frontier experience, was not always friendly toward the artist. Thomas Hart Benton wrote in his autobiography, *An Artist in America*, that the state's rural society was lacking in "aesthetic sensibility." Born in Neosho in 1889, Benton grew up among people only a generation or two removed from the early settlers who had pioneered the region. Like their forefathers they worked hard from sunup to sundown with few hours left over for leisure-time activities. They often regarded with suspicion and hostility any able-bodied man who wasted away his precious hours in drawing pictures. Benton left Neosho at his first opportunity for places more hospitable to the artist and his work. He did not return until years later, when his father lay in the hospital dying of cancer.

Although Benton may have resented the rural, small-town opinions of the artist and his work, he, like many artists before him, thrived on the subject matter found in Missouri and on the western frontier. Whereas frontier society may have discouraged some artists, the frontier itself attracted them. Many early nineteenth century artists came to sketch and paint frontier villages, scenes of striking natural beauty, the awesome Missouri and Mississippi rivers, the various frontier types, and the Indians.

Major Stephen H. Long took two artists on his expedition of 1819–20 to "furnish sketches of landscapes . . . distinguished for their beauty and grandeur . . . miniature likenesses or portraits of distinguished Indians . . . groups of savages engaged in celebrating their festivals, or sitting in council." The artist's record made on an official expedition or on casual wanderings answered some of the questions curious Americans had about new territories and states. It also enriched the cultural life of the United States and documented much of its history.

The French artist Charles Alexandre Lesueur (1778–1846) traveled across Missouri in the early 1800s sketching and painting scenes of frontier life. Karl Bodmer (1809–93), a Swiss painter, joined the company of Maximillian Prince of Weid on his journey into the American West (1832–34). His watercolors of the Plains Indians and frontier landscapes were included in Maximillian's book on his travels in North America. A Philadelphia artist, Chester Harding (1792–1866), arrived in St. Louis in time to paint the portrait of the aging Daniel Boone. Harding was quite successful at portraiture, charging $25 for each one. Returning to Boston he painted well over a thousand portraits during his career. John Mix Stanley (1814–72) exhibited paintings of Indian life in St. Louis. Sarah Miriam Peale (1800–1885), the niece of Charles Wilson Peale, who included among her famous clients the Marquis de Lafayette, moved to St. Louis in 1847, where she resided for thirty years, painting portraits and still lifes.

George Catlin (1796–1872), a self-taught artist, devoted his life to painting the Indian tribes between the Allegheny and the Rocky mountains. Arriving in St. Louis in 1832, he traveled along the Missouri River to its upper reaches and the Yellowstone River preparing hundreds of canvases depicting Indian life. His monumental work, *Illustrations of the Manners, Customs, Conditions of the North American Indian* (1841) is not only considered a book of artistic merit but also one of scientific and historical value.

John James Audubon (1785–1851), naturalist and artist, undertook a "long journey" in 1843 up the Missouri River and beyond to collect specimens and to sketch wildlife native to the region. Audubon's "Missouri Expedition" did not reach the Rocky Mountains due to his failing health, but it did return with considerable information from which Audubon made what his editor called the "most beautiful and perfect specimens of art. I doubt whether there is anything in the world of natural history like them. I do not believe that there is any man living that can equal them." It was said that Audubon's journals often contained "blarney" but his illustrations and paintings were "truth tellers."

George Caleb Bingham (1811–79)

Missouri's most successful portraitist and genre painter in the several decades before the Civil War was George Caleb Bingham. When the Binghams moved from Augusta County, Virginia, to Franklin in 1819, George Caleb was only eight years old. Short, slender, and never robust in health, Bingham lost all his hair as a result of a severe case of the measles when he was nineteen and wore a wig for the rest of his life. As a youth, he worked at a variety of occupations including cigar roller, apprentice to a cabinetmaker, engraver, student of law and theology, and painting. Using homemade pigments, he demonstrated an artistic talent that led friends to urge him to seek a career in art. He spent three months in Philadelphia and then moved on to Washington, DC, where he worked as an engraver and part-time portraitist from 1840 to 1844. His homecoming in 1845 began the most productive period of his life.

From 1845 to the late 1850s the artist never wandered far from the Missouri River. Captivated by its romance and history, Bingham painted some of his most significant works. Representative of his Missouri River canvases were

Fur Traders Descending the Missouri (1845), *Jolly Flatboatman* (1846), *Raftsmen Playing Cards* (1847), and *The Trappers Return* (1851). Skilled in figure drawing and the use of color and lighting, Bingham created not only realistic scenes of frontier life but conveyed its mystery and loneliness. Once a person has viewed *Fur Traders Descending the Missouri*, he can never forget the image of the black bear cub that is tied to the stern of the boat mirrored in the cloudy waters of the great river.

George Caleb Bingham, self-portrait.
St. Louis Art Museum

Often using a linen tablecloth, Bingham painted the portraits of many prominent farmers, judges, lawyers, educators, politicians, merchants, and their wives who lived in the river towns of Kansas City, Arrow Rock, Boonville, Columbia, Jefferson City, and St. Louis. Today the Bingham portraits and sketches provide a colorful and accurate documentation of the style and dress of antebellum Missourians.

Influenced by the Jacksonian era before the Civil War when the democratic impulse seemed to lift the commoner to loftier positions of political equality and social status, Bingham took an increasing interest in state politics. He won a seat in the state legislature as a Whig in 1848 after being defeated by a narrow margin in 1846. He served as the state treasurer from 1862 to 1865 and as Missouri's adjutant general in 1877. Although his political endeavors may have decreased his artistic productivity in later life, his feeling for the democratic process at work in the frontier regions of Missouri showed itself in such works as *The County Election* (1852), *Canvassing for a Vote* (1852), *Stump Speaking* (1853–54), and *Verdict of the People* (1855). Each painting depicted in detail political democracy vigorously at work in Missouri small towns and hamlets.

During the 1850s the Bingham family spent some time in Dusseldorf where the artist studied the European masters. The European experience did little to enhance his craft, for his later work appears more imitative of the old and traditional than creative of new themes and techniques.

Order No. 11, recognized as one of his most famous paintings, was completed and exhibited in 1868. It depicts the execution of the 1863 order of Union General Tom Ewing forcing western Missouri residents to leave their homes because of suspected aid to Confederate guerrillas. Bingham attempted through his painting to carry out his reported threat to General Ewing that he would make him "infamous with pen and brush as far as I am able." Although Bingham was a Union man, his sense of fair play was offended by *Order No. 11* and the heavy-handed way it was enforced by Union soldiers. The painting shows a white-haired patriarch defending his home against Union officers, one of whom has his right hand on a revolver, as the flames and smoke of burning buildings fill the horizon. This painting is owned by the Cincinnati Art Museum. A later, slightly larger version completed in 1870 is a valued part of the Bingham collection at the State Historical Society in Columbia.

The remaining years of Bingham's life were lived in Kansas City, where he died in 1879. In the old Union Cemetery, a quiet, well-wooded burial ground near downtown Kansas City, a modest tombstone marks the grave of one whom many regard as Missouri's greatest nineteenth century artist.

Carl Wimar (1828–62)

With George Caleb Bingham, Carl Wimar emerged as one of the most important artists in mid-century Missouri. Born in 1828 in Sieburg, Germany, Wimar emigrated to St. Louis when he was fifteen years old. Early in life he chose a career in art and developed an interest in the Indians who slipped in and out of St. Louis on trading ventures and government business. A generous bequest enabled him to return to Dusseldorf for more training and study. While there he did a number of paintings based on sketches of his favorite subject matter, frontier scenes of Indian life. Three of his most celebrated works of this period were the *Captive Charger* (1854), *The Buffalo Hunt* (1855), and *The Attack on an Emigrant Train* (1856). When he resumed his work in St. Louis in 1856, he recognized immediately that the Indian traffic in and out of the expanding city had declined. Since his subjects no longer came to him, he journeyed up the Missouri River to the land of Crows, Yankton, Brules, Poncas, and Mandans, traveling as far northwest as Fort Benton near the Canadian border in what is now Montana to study their life and culture. He sketched, collected Indian trinkets, costumes, and weapons, and took pictures with primitive photographic equipment. During the long winter months on the upper Missouri River, he scrutinized these materials and painted from them Indian scenes and western landscapes. *Indians Approaching Fort Benton* (1859), considered by some to be his masterpiece, prophesied the end of the dominance of the Indian tribes in the western plains and mountains. Shortly before he died of tuberculosis in 1862, Wimar painted the first murals west of the Mississippi River in the rotunda of the Old Courthouse in St. Louis.

Schools and Galleries

Toward the end of the century, as Missouri became less isolated, interest in collecting and exhibiting art increased. Art groups and societies were founded in St. Louis and Kansas City and in several small towns. St. Joseph and Joplin had art leagues and galleries. A room in old Thespian Hall at Boonville was set aside to display artwork. In Sedalia the art gallery was in the public library. Hercules L. Dousman of St. Louis added a wing to his residence to house his art collection, which he opened to the public. From Dousman's modest beginning came the City Art Museum, which took over the central art building of the St. Louis World's Fair when it ended in 1904. In 1907 the citizens of St. Louis voted a tax to support the museum. William Rockhill Nelson of Kansas City, the civic-minded editor and owner of the *Kansas City Star*, led the way in establishing an art gallery in that city. The beautiful Nelson Art Gallery, located in the Country Club Plaza district, was made possible by his generosity.

A number of art schools started in the late nineteenth century in addition to the organization of departments of fine arts in various colleges and universities. In 1875 Washington University offered a free evening art class. Several years later the university took over the St. Louis School and Museum of Fine Art and made it a separate department. A group of Kansas City artists banded together and organized the Kansas City Art Association and School of Design in 1888. The Fine Arts Institute of that city came into existence in 1906. The Kansas City Art institute, which was to have on its faculty such artists as Thomas Hart Benton, was founded in 1907. Colleges that added art departments were Central Missouri Teachers College (1871), Washington University Department of Drawing and History of Art (1896), University of Missouri School of Fine Arts (1901), Southwest Missouri State Teachers College (1906), and Northwest State Teachers College (1906).

One of St. Louis's most valued art treasures is not found hanging in a gallery but rather rising ten stories above the downtown area. Designed in 1890 by Louis Henri Sullivan (1856–1924), the Wainright Building at the corner of Seventh and Chestnut was to have an influence on the development of skyscraper architecture in this country for five decades after its completion. Modern architects still regard it as a classic in style as well as in function and construction. Although by today's standards in skyscrapers, it is not very tall, the whole artistic design of this building gives the impression that it soars much higher than its ten stories. Its preservation has recently been guaranteed by its use as a state office building.

Thomas Hart Benton (1889–1975)

Missouri's most famous artist of the twentieth century had a career that spanned seventy-five years. Before attending Western Academy in Alton, Illinois, from 1906 to 1907, the young Benton drew cartoons for a local Joplin newspaper. Leaving Neosho while still in his teens, he studied art in Chicago, Paris, and New York before he became a government draftsman in Norfolk, Virginia, toward the end of World War I. During this period of his life, Benton began to crystallize his ideas about subject matter, and he turned more and more to themes of American history, folklore, the West, and rural America, which some believe reflected his early rural, small-town background. In the 1920s he continued to move in this direction until by the 1930s he had become one of the leading figures in the midwestern branch of the regional school in which artists concentrated on American scenes.

During the 1930s his reputation as a muralist grew with his work for the New School of Social Research (1930–31), the Whitney Museum of Art (1932), and the Indiana mural for the Chicago World's Fair (1933). Commissioned to paint a mural for the house lobby in the State Capitol at Jefferson City, Benton angered many Missourians who charged that he had immortalized too many shady characters in Missouri history. Included in the mural were Boss Tom Pendergast, the Kansas City political figure whose powerful machine corrupted city government; the scene of Frankie shooting her two-timing lover, Johnny, made famous by the

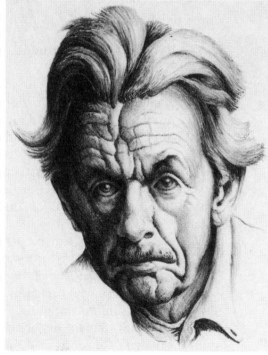

Thomas Hart Benton, self-portrait.
*Courtesy State Historical Society
of Missouri*

popular folk song; and Jesse and Frank James, Missouri folk heroes in the post–Civil War era who, after all, were bank robbers and murderers. Benton's censors claimed he had insulted the people of Missouri and had painted a lie. The controversy, however, did much to stimulate an interest in art, to encourage federal programs for artists during the Great Depression, and to solidify Benton's position as one of Missouri's outstanding artists. In the mid-1930s Benton returned to Missouri where, until 1940, he was the director of the Kansas City Art Institute.

During World War II Benton did an eight-painting series entitled *Years of Peril*, which showed the threat of the Axis powers to the western democracies. This striking series was used by the government for propaganda purposes after the intervention of the United States in the war in 1941. A longtime admirer of Benton, Harry S Truman asked him to paint a mural for the Truman Library and Museum in Independence. The mural, *The Opening of the West*, is the first thing visitors see when they enter the building. Just before he died, Benton completed a mural for the Country Music Hall of Fame in Nashville, Tennessee. Today his work marks him as an artist of achievement and significance.

Samuel Langhorne Clemens, "Mark Twain" (1835–1910)

As Missouri's population increased in the nineteenth century, so did its newspapers. They reported national and local news, included material from popular authors and journalists, and took stands on political issues, economic matters, and political candidates. A Missouri town usually took great pride in its newspaper and boasted that it had finally arrived when the first one began publication. Early newspapers provided training and experience for future editors, reporters, and authors, as the career of Missouri's best known writer clearly indicates.

Samuel Langhorne Clemens, better known as Mark Twain, began his literary career working for his brother Orion, who owned and published the *Hannibal Journal*. Born in Florida, Missouri, in 1835, Clemens had moved with his family to Hannibal, "a little white town drowsing in a summer morning," at the age of four. From 1839 to 1853 it would remain his hometown, the place from which he drew the material for some of his most popular books. Sam Clemens left Hannibal in 1853 to seek more promising positions on newspa-

Mark Twain, painted by Edouard Gelli for 1904 Louisiana Purchase Exposition.
Courtesy State Historical Society of Missouri

pers in St. Louis, New York, and Philadelphia, but he ultimately returned to Keokuk, Iowa, where the family had opened another newspaper.

At the age of twenty-one, Clemens decided to work his way down the Mississippi. He apprenticed to a river pilot, thus beginning a vocation that he once described as the "most satisfying one of my life." From 1857 to 1861 the Mississippi River was his world, a world in which he met all kinds of people, heard lots of stories and lies, learned the language of steamboating and of the river, and stored the knowledge that was to flow through the first part of *Life on the Mississippi* and his greatest novel, *Huckleberry Finn*. Many times the young Sam Clemens heard the reassuring cry of the leadman, "Mark twain," which meant that the river was two fathoms deep and safe for passage. When he became a writer, he adopted these words for his pseudonym.*

The Civil War abruptly ended Clemens's career as a river pilot. He turned briefly to soldiering until a skirmish near Hannibal made him realize that a man could get killed in such a profession. He went west to join his brother, Orion, who had become secretary to the governor of Nevada Territory. Over the next few years, Sam Clemens did some prospecting in western mines but turned back to journalism eventually at which time he began to sign his newspaper pieces "Mark Twain." In 1864 a short story, "The Celebrated Jumping Frog of Calaveras County," brought him national attention. His popularity

*In *Life on the Mississippi* Twain claimed he borrowed his pseudonym from Captain Isaiah Sellers, a river crony of steamboating days, who "used to jot down brief paragraphs of plain, practical information about the river, and sign them 'Mark Twain'. . . ."

grew as he traveled and lectured extensively. Eventually he settled in the East, with a permanent home in Hartford, Connecticut.

Mark Twain's Missouri background first surfaced in the satirical *The Gilded Age* (1873), a book written in collaboration with Charles Dudley Warner. The authors so keenly ridiculed the tawdry elegance, political corruption, and social sham of post–Civil War America that the book's title has often been used to denote that era. Multitalented Twain was not only a masterful storyteller but also an excellent satirist of the American scene.

The Adventures of Tom Sawyer (1876), based largely on Twain's nostalgic recollections of his own boyhood in Hannibal, was in part a reaction against the "goody good" children's books of his day. In Tom Sawyer the youngsters are human beings, mischievous, prankish, and immature, but with feelings, imagination, and occasionally a twinge of conscience. The book follows a number of plot lines: Tom's puppy love affair with Becky Thatcher, his befriending of the illiterate Huck Finn and the social outcast Muff Potter, his adolescent revolt against Aunt Polly, and the frightening encounter with the murderous Injun Joe when Tom and Becky are alone and lost in a cave. Each episode points to a young lad growing up and becoming a man. Tom starts out doing something childish and ends up doing something manly. In a way the book is also about the adventures of a small frontier village, Hannibal (St. Petersburg in the book), maturing on the west bank of the Mississippi River—its society, religious beliefs and practices, its folklore, its joy, and its problems. Over a hundred years have passed since its publication and yet it remains what one critic has called "the best book on a boy ever written."

The first part of *Life on the Mississippi* (1883) is a compilation of a series of articles Twain wrote for *The Atlantic* in 1874 entitled "Old Times on the Mississippi." Filled with the history of the river, its geography, and his own experiences as a steamboat pilot before the Civil War, these articles glorify and romanticize his years on the river. The book was quite popular and did much to establish Twain as an author of unusual talent as well as a humorist. Character studies abound. Twain told of the villainous Brown, a steamboat pilot, he had "killed in seventeen different ways—all of them new"; of Isaiah Sellers from whom he had taken the name Mark Twain; and of Horace Bixby, the man who taught him to be a steamboat pilot.

Bernard DeVoto, in his penetrating study, *Mark Twain At Work* (1951), believed *Life on the Mississippi* set the stage for the writing of

The Adventures of Huckleberry Finn (1884). A sequel to *Tom Sawyer*, *Huckleberry Finn* is one of the great novels in American literature. Here Twain told the exciting story of Huck and the runaway slave Jim on their raft trip down the Mississippi River. Some of the scenes and stories in the novel came from his boyhood days in Missouri. He modeled Jim after a slave on his Uncle John Quarles's farm near Hannibal where Twain spent many carefree summers as a youth. In the story Jim not only gained his freedom but his manhood as well. The attitudes, the changing times, the lifestyles of society along the shores of the river make the book a social document as well as a historical novel. Never antiquated, but fresh, insightful, and humorous, Huck increased the literary fame of his creator.

Because of Twain's ties with the state, he earned the sobriquet "son of Missouri." Those boyhood days in Hannibal, his work on the newspapers, and the days on the river, all a part of his Missouri experience, showed through his writings. When he died in 1910, the "son of Missouri" had become a man of the world.

Eugene Field, "The Children's Poet" (1850–95)

Yet another Missouri writer, who would gain fame because of his poetry for children, had his start as a newspaper reporter. No one knows for certain whether Eugene Field was born on September 2 or 3, 1850. Friends accused him of giving both dates so that anyone who failed to bring him a present on the second could give him one on the third. His father, a lawyer, moved to St. Louis from Vermont and served as the legal counsel for Dred Scott, the controversial slave who sued for his freedom before the Civil War. Field attended several colleges, including a short stint at the University of Missouri in 1870. In 1873 he married a young woman from St. Joseph and started a newspaper career there with the *Gazette*. He later joined the *Chicago Morning News* and also worked for the *St. Louis Journal*, the *Kansas City Times*, and briefly in Jefferson City covering the news of the state government. His most productive years as a columnist and author were with the Chicago newspaper in which appeared his popular column "Sharps and Flats." Sold on the Midwest as a good place for a journalist, Field turned down a number of attractive offers to join eastern metropolitan newspapers.

The popularity of the versatile and imaginative author stemmed mainly from poems written for and about children. The sentimental

Eugene Field, painting in governor's reception room at state capitol by Gari Melchers. *Massie-Missouri Commerce, courtesy State Historical Society of Missouri*

"Little Boy Blue" was about a child's death while "The Gingham Dog and the Calico Cat" and "Wynken, Blynken and Nod" were more lively and entertaining. Although Field's own assessment of his poetry was that it "was popular but rotten," most modern anthologies of American poetry usually include several of his poems for children. In ill health for most of his life, he died at an early age. His St. Louis home has been renovated and opened to the public. In addition to the Victorian furnishings and decor, an unusual collection of nineteenth century children's toys and knickknacks is displayed.

Kate O'Flaherty Chopin (1851–1904)

Thomas O'Flaherty came to St. Louis when he was eighteen and became a successful businessperson and a respected member of St. Louis society. His wife Eliza was the descendant of a French family that had settled in old Kaskaskia early in the eighteenth century. Their daughter Kate was born in 1851, a few years before O'Flaherty died in the tragic collapse of the Gasconade Bridge. Unlike her mother, who was outgoing and vivacious, Kate was shy and retiring, hiding away in the family attic and reading the works of Sir Walter Scott, Henry Fielding, and Edmund Spenser. Although she attended Sacred Heart Convent where she was introduced to French literature, theology, and elementary science, she believed that the time she spent reading in her attic retreat was the most edifying of her life. After she graduated from the convent, she blossomed into a social belle of St. Louis society. She met and fell in love with Oscar Chopin, a native of Louisiana who then worked in a St. Louis bank.

Not long after their marriage, the Chopins moved to New Orleans, and in 1879 to the family's Cane River cotton plantation near a small Creole village some twenty miles from Natchitoches. Kate Chopin found plantation life quite appealing. She grew to love the Creoles, the black servants, the everyday life of a cotton plantation, and the genteel manners of the Old South that still persisted after the Civil War. When swamp fever took the life of her husband in 1882, the young widow, unable to manage the plantation and to raise her large family alone, sold out, returned to St. Louis and, by chance, entered a new career.

Impressed by her charming letters, friends urged Chopin to write in her spare time. Reluctant at first to do so, she wrote stories for children that sold immediately. Later she wrote stories for mature audiences based on her associations and experiences as a plantation mistress in Louisiana. These stories appeared in some of the leading magazines of the day before they were collected into two books, *Bayou Folk* (1894) and *A Night in Acadia* (1897).

Kate Chopin's second novel, *The Awakening* (1899), was condemned by the critics, not because of her literary style but because of the plot, which they considered improper and immoral. The story dealt with a young wife and mother who inwardly longed to be loved as a human being instead of being merely admired as a convenient fixture in her husband's life. Outwardly the young woman conformed to society's expectations, but inwardly she dared to question if there were not more to life. Although the critics of her time were severe in their censure of Kate Chopin and her book, modern critics claim she was at least two decades ahead of her time and a forerunner of important twentieth century women authors. The present-day women's movement has created renewed interest in Kate Chopin and her works. Stunned by the events surrounding *The Awakening*, she ceased writing and before she could begin again died of a brain hemorrhage in 1904.

Harold Bell Wright (1872–1944)

A literary critic once wrote that Harold Bell Wright was the "beguiler of millions." Regardless of how critics felt about Wright, millions of Americans bought and read his books. He was one of the most popular authors in the first decades of the twentieth century, and it took railroad boxcars to haul his latest book to stores throughout the country. Wright published an average of one book every two years from 1900 to 1935, and many of them landed on the national bestseller list. Two of his books, *The Shepherd of the Hills* (1907) and *The Winning of Barbara Worth* (1911), are on the list of all-time best sellers. Many of his stories were later made into motion pictures. His autobiography, *To My Sons* (1934), covers only the early formative years of his life. In his retirement he devoted himself to his farm, Quiet Hills, near Escondido, California.

Born in Rome, New York, Wright experienced an unhappy childhood. His mother, who became the model of a number of female characters in his books, died when he was ten. Unable to raise his family without his wife, Wright's father farmed out his children to relatives and neighbors. Because he moved from one family to another, Wright's education was limited to a few years in country schools. In his late teens Wright struck out on his own, traveling through Ohio from place to place as a house painter and decorator. Converted by a Christian evangelist, who preached a doctrine of love and sacrifice as the way to salvation rather than the more traditional "hellfire and damnation," the young man decided to study for the Christian ministry. Poor health and eyesight ended his formal education after two years in a preparatory school at Hiram College in Ohio. Somewhat depressed, Wright tramped his way to the Missouri Ozarks, arriving there early in the 1890s. After preaching in hill-country churches for a short time, the Christian Church in Pittsburg, Kansas, invited him to become their pastor.

At Pittsburg, Wright wrote his first book, *That Printer of Udell's* (1903), a collection of sermons preached as a continuing story from one Sunday to the next. Although the book was not a financial success, it encouraged Wright to try again when poor health drove him back to the Ozarks. He completed his second book, *The Shepherd of the Hills,* while a pastor of a Kansas City church, and then went to Lebanon where he gathered material for a third book, *The Calling of Dan Matthews* (1909), which he finished after he left Missouri for California. *The Shepherd,* the story of a city man who found peace and happiness serving the hill people, became one of the most widely read books in American fiction. *The Calling,* a story of a young minister who found more thorns than roses in ministering to a small-town church, angered the people of Lebanon. By today's standards *The Calling* is very mild, but Wright's neighbors and church members thought he had drawn an unfair caricature of their hometown and church. Wright left Missouri in 1907, returning only on a few occasions. He spent the rest of his life in California and Arizona writing mostly westerns. He fought his greatest battle against tuberculosis, which he overcame by living in the Arizona desert. All together, Wright wrote nineteen books, but Missourians should note that only four of them have anything to do with the Missouri Ozarks.

Although he was not a great author, Wright was immensely popular in the first several decades of this century. His books entertained people in a time when there was no radio, no movies, and no television. For students of history, they provide a look at what Americans were like, what they read, what were their values and attitudes in a period before World War I. Wright's Ozark books provide a look at the natives of that region, their dialect, and their ways long before the country had been discovered by vacationers and retirees. Ironically, he once warned the Ozark folk that their country would be changed when the railroads came, bringing a great influx of people; and yet *The Shepherd* did more to publicize the hills of southwestern Missouri than any other piece of literature. Today the appellation "Shepherd of the Hills Country" is given to the area in and around Branson. Frank Luther Mott, a prominent educator at the University of Missouri, summed up the impact of Wright and his novels: "Probably America is better off for having read a lot of Harold Bell Wright. His stuff is wholesome, occasionally somewhat stimulating in ideas, and very often picturesque; and millions found it entertaining."

Reedy's Mirror

William Marion Reedy (1862–1920), the son of a St. Louis policeman, graduated from St. Louis University when he was just eighteen years old. The young Reedy turned to journalism, beginning a stint with the *Missouri Republican*. After several years of newspaper report-ing and freelance writing, Reedy joined the *St. Louis Mirror*, a weekly journal that covered a variety of intellectual and literary topics. Im-pressed by Reedy's interesting and witty articles, James Campbell, the owner, promoted him to editor in 1893. When Campbell retired a few years later, he turned the *Mirror* over to Reedy. Under Reedy's di-rection, the *Mirror* became an important part of the cultural life of middle America.

Highly intelligent and talented, Reedy never hesitated to com-ment on a range of subjects, including religion, art, social issues, eco-nomic questions, politics, and literature. Although the *Mirror* was not widely read by the working class, Reedy sided with the worker's griev-ances against management. The *Mirror* introduced and encouraged a number of young, promising authors including Edgar Lee Masters, Homer Croy, Sara Teasdale, and Fannie Hurst. Reedy did much to dispel the "cultural and literary wasteland" image that easterners had of the Midwest. He died unexpectedly at the Democratic National Convention in 1920.

Three Important Poets

In the 1880s St. Louis was the birthplace of three important poets: Sara Teasdale, Marianne Moore, and T. S. Eliot. Teasdale, (1884–1933) came from a family proud of its ancestors, who had fought in the American Revolution. Because of frail health, she was educated at home by a tutor and then in a private school. After graduation she traveled in Europe, returning to St. Louis to live with her parents. Her first poem, published in the *Mirror* in 1907, was the beginning of a literary career that established her as one of America's leading poets. From 1914 until her death, Teasdale lived in New York. Some of her well-known collections of poems are *Rivers to the Sea* (1915), *The An-swering Voice* (1917), *Flame and Shadow* (1920), and *Dark of the Moon* (1926). She died before completing her biography of Christina Rossetti, the nineteenth century poetess who most influenced her own writing.

Born and reared in Kirkwood, Marianne Moore (1887–1972) at-tended Bryn Mawr and resided most of her life in New York. Her po-ems covered a wide range of interests, from natural science to the arts and sports. As an avid baseball fan inspired by the 1968 World Series, she wrote an essay, "One Poet's Pitch for the Cardinals to win the World Series," in which she predicted Bob Gibson, the ace of the Cardinal pitching staff, would win two games. (He won two, lost one, and Detroit won the series.) Charles Guenther, a St. Louis poet and translator, once wrote, "As for her 'place,' several cities may claim Marianne Moore, [for] she was at home in many. . . . She wrote me long ago that there was 'no city more cultured than St. Louis.'"

Thoms Stearns Eliot (1888–1965) was born and educated in St. Louis. After attending Harvard, he became a British citizen. Recollections of his St. Louis boyhood influenced the opening lines of the third of his *Four Quartets* (1943), when he wrote of the Mississippi River, "I do not know much about gods; but I think that the river is a strong brown god . . . almost forgotten by the dwellers in cities. . . ." Some of his notable works were *The Wasteland* (1922), *Murder in the Cathedral* (1935), and *The Cocktail Party* (1950).

The Sound of Music

From earliest times Missouri has been a land filled with the sound of music. Singing the ditties of their native land, the early French voyageurs dispelled their loneliness as they rowed the rivers of Louisiana in search of the Indian trade. The Creole settlers along the Mississippi and Missouri rivers made music in their leisure and at their religious celebrations. When the American pioneers moved into Missouri after the Louisiana Purchase, they brought with them many of the folksongs of the frontier and contributed a few of their own. In the backcountry the Indians sang and danced in their tribal ceremonies. The Osage factor, George Sibley, recorded in his diary in 1816 how his wife Mary played her piano with a drum and fife attachment while outside their quarters the Osage warriors danced and chanted in their camp near the fort.

The liturgical music of Catholicism, the foot-stomping hymnody of Protestant rural churches, and the simple tunes of Ozark mountaineers have all become a part of Missouri's rich and varied musical heritage. The German immigrants in St. Louis encouraged the music of the European masters. In time that city could boast of the second symphony orchestra established in the United States. Practically every town had a band, an orchestra, or a chorus to sing and play at special occasions. Missouri produced some serious composers as well as popular songwriters. In the popular vein, the music of the state is most closely tied to the history of ragtime and jazz in the American musical experience.

Ragtime

The origins of American jazz can be traced to black life in Africa and to the experiences under the institution of slavery in this country. During the 1890s ragtime, one of the early forms of jazz, fused with the Negro spirituals, the spirited marches of the black fraternal orders, and the lively gospel songs to produce a "new music." Ragtime syncopated the beat, and by the turn of the century it had become immensely popular with the American people. It remained so until the mechanical piano was replaced by the phonograph record and radio performances of orchestral jazz in the 1920s and 1930s.

Born in Sedalia and St. Louis, ragtime spread to Kansas City, Chicago, New Orleans, and the musical centers back East. The main instrument of ragtime was the piano, while blues, another early form of jazz, relied primarily on the human voice. Ragtime pianists were in great demand in nightclubs, bordellos, theaters, and the sheet music departments of downtown stores. One of the first ragtime artists was Tom Turpin (1873–1922), who spent most of his life in Sedalia and St. Louis. One music scholar said that long before Americans recognized ragtime, Turpin was "swinging and playing the blues." Turpin composed ragtime tunes; but because the average pianist found them difficult to perform, few of his compositions were published. By 1896, however, several of his tunes had hit the music market, including "Harlem Rag" and "St. Louis Rag." A popular white composer, Percy Wenrich (1880–1952), born in Joplin, wrote ragtime in a slightly different style than his black counterparts. Combining the ragtime beat with English balladry, Wenrich composed such tunes as "The Smiler—A Joplin Rag" (1907), "Put on Your Old Gray Bonnet" (1909), and "When You Wore a Tulip and I Wore a Big Red Rose" (1913).

Scott Joplin (1868–1917)

Although ragtime, blues and, later, modern jazz were a performer's music, rather than a composer's, Scott Joplin tried through his

compositions to make ragtime "respectable." Joplin came to St. Louis from his birthplace of Texarkana in 1885, earning his way by playing the piano. He performed his distinctive piano technique at the World's Columbian Exposition in Chicago in 1893 before he moved to Sedalia. Organizing the Queen City Negro Band in 1896, Joplin added to the piano a clarinet, E-flat tuba, coronet, and drums. The Sedalia band was not only a novelty but an exciting one. Sedalia favored the ragtime players and their compositions. The success of Joplin's famous "Maple Leaf Rag" (1899) encouraged him to seek greater opportunities in St. Louis. There he composed "The Entertainer" (1902), the tune that started a Joplin revival nearly seventy-five years later when it was used as theme music for the highly successful motion picture, *The Sting* (1974). Neither his ragtime ballet, "The Ragtime Dance" (1902), nor his first opera, "Guest of Honor" (1903), achieved similar popularity. "Guest of Honor," first performed at the St. Louis World's Fair in 1904, is believed by some scholars to be based on the life of the famous abolitionist and black celebrity Frederick Douglass. Later in New York, Joplin composed "Treemonisha" (1911), an opera that did not receive its first complete performance until 1972, when it was performed at the Atlanta Symphony Hall. Although Joplin failed to elevate ragtime to the status of serious music and died a victim of syphilis in 1917, the Pulitzer Prize Committee awarded him exceptional posthumous recognition in 1976 for his contributions to American music.

"I Hate to See De Evenin' Sun Go Down"

"St. Louis Blues" (1914), one of the most popular songs in the history of American music, made W. C. Handy (1873–1958) famous. Handy, a blues composer and publisher, once said that his songs were "little more than notations on themes picked up in the wanderings along the river." Once, when he was stranded in St. Louis and "down on his luck," he had to sleep on the levee. Years later he said, "If you ever had to sleep on the cobbles by the river in St. Louis you'll understand" the opening lines of St. Louis Blues; "I hate to see de evenin' sun go down." When asked to explain the origin of the blues, Handy said it came from "the humor of the [slave] song, the syncopation of ragtime and the spirit of Negro folk song. . . ." Although not a native of St. Louis, Handy's song did much to make St. Louis one of the centers of blues, and later modern jazz, in the country.

The Louisiana Purchase Exposition (St. Louis World's Fair, 1904)

The cultural highlight of the early twentieth century was the St. Louis World's Fair. Construction began in 1901, with the opening planned for 1903 to commemorate the 100th anniversary of the Louisiana Purchase. Because of the immensity of the project, the opening was postponed until April 1904, but before its closing seven months later more than 19 million people passed through its gates. The fairgrounds covered most of Forest Park and the entire campus of Washington University. The total area was 1,240 acres, with buildings occupying 128 acres of floor space. The agricultural display alone took 23 acres.

Most of the buildings were temporary. The Palace of Education and Social Economy displayed educational work from kindergarten to university level as well as schools for the blind, the deaf, the mute, and agricultural, polytechnic, and commercial endeavors. Festival Hall seated 3,600 and had a dome covered with gold leaf that was larger than the one of St. Peter's Basilica in Rome. There were Palaces of Electricity, Machinery, Transportation, and Mines and Metallurgy. The Palace of Transportation contained fourteen railroad tracks that extended from one end of the building to the other for a total of fourteen miles of track. There were many national exhibits, including the French Pavilion, a reproduction of the Gran Trianon at Versailles, and entire villages of Philippine headhunters, African natives, and tribes of American Indians. Each state had a building copied after one of its famous buildings. There were restaurants, replicas of castles, waterfalls, sunken gardens, and a floral clock with hands seventy-four feet long that moved five feet every minute

Rising 264 feet above the fairgrounds was the giant Ferris wheel, which one observer said "plowed the clouds." Brought from the Chicago World's Fair and christened the "observation wheel," the wheel carried thirty-six cars, each one seating sixty people. When the fair was over, the wheel was demolished by dynamite.

The Palace of Fine Arts, which displayed some of the greatest art treasures in the world, was one of the permanent buildings. It later became the City Art Museum. The beautiful statue of Louis IX, sculptured by Charles Niehaus and recognized as one of his finest works, stands in front of the building overlooking the city of St. Louis. Confirmed in displays and exhibitions were the finest artistic and scientific achievements of mankind of the past century.

The St. Louis World's Fair was one of the most spectacular events in the history of Missouri. It not only honored the pioneers who developed the Louisiana Purchase, but it served to encourage the arts and to mark the beginning of a century dominated by technology, the machine, science, and power.

Suggestions for Reading

In recent years George Caleb Bingham and his art have generated a great deal of enthusiasm, resulting in a number of interesting and informative biographies. The most complete treatment of Bingham's life and paintings is E. Maurice Bloch, *The Paintings of George Caleb Bingham,* Columbia, University of Missouri Press, 1986, while Nancy Rash, *The Paintings and Politics of George Caleb Bingham,* New Haven, Yale University Press, 1991, discusses the interrelationship of the artist's work with his political career. The career of Carl Wimar is well covered in Rick Stewart, Joseph D. Ketner and Angela L. Miller, *Carl Wimar: Chronicler of the Missouri River Frontier,* New York, Harry N. Abrams, 1991. Henry Adams, *Thomas Hart Benton: An American Original,* New York, Knopf, 1989, is an excellent summary of the artist's life and work. For a discussion of Benton's Missouri murals, see Bob Priddy, *Only the Rivers are Peaceful: Thomas Hart Benton's Missouri Murals,* Independence, Herald Publishing House, 1989.

Mark Twain has received considerable biographical attention. An excellent recent treatment is Everett Emerson, *Mark Twain: A Literary Life,* Philadelphia, University of Pennsylvania Press, 2000. Two older books dealing with Mark Twain and his Missouri background are Dixon Wecter, *Sam Clemens of Hannibal,* Boston, Houghton Mifflin, 1952, and Minnie M. Brashear, *Mark Twain, Son of Missouri,* Chapel Hill, University of North Carolina Press, 1934. The career of Eugene Field is covered in Lewis O. Saum, *Eugene Field and His Age,* Lincoln, University of Nebraska Press, 2001. The life and works of Kate O'Flaherty Chopin are examined in Emily Toth, *Kate Chopin,* Jackson, University of Texas Press, 1990, while Lawrence V. Tagg, *Harold Bell Wright: Storyteller to America,* Tucson, Westernlore Press, 1986, tells that author's story. The career of William Marion Reedy takes center stage in Max Putzel, *The Man in the Mirror: William Marion Reedy and His Magazine,* Columbia, University of Missouri Press, 1998. William D. Drake, *Sara Teasdale: Woman and Poet,* San Francisco, Harper & Row, 1979, deals in an interesting manner with that writer and her work, while Marianne Moore receives biographical treatment in Charles Molesworth, *Marianne Moore: A Literary Life,* Lincoln, University of Nebraska Press, 1990. For T. S. Eliot, see Peter Ackroyd, *T. S. Eliot,* New York, Simon and Schuster, 1984, and Lyndall Gordon, *T. S. Eliot: An Imperfect Life,* New York, Norton, 1999. Students can find selected works by these authors by consulting their web sites or their school's card catalogs.

Rudi Blesh and Harriet Janis, *They All Played Ragtime,* New York, Oak Publications, 1966, is a good overview of this musical craze. Scott Joplin's career is the subject of two recent biographies: Edward A. Berlin, *King of Ragtime: Scott Joplin and His Era,* New York, Oxford University Press, 1994, and Susan Curtis, *Dancing to a Black Man's Tune: A Life of Scott Joplin,* Columbia, University of Missouri Press, 1994. The best recording of Joplin's compositions is Vera Brodsky Lawrence, *The Collected Works of Scott Joplin,* 1971. Yet another Missouri black performer-composer of note in this period is depicted in Jack A. Batterson, *Blind Boone: Missouri's Ragtime Pioneer,* Columbia, University of Missouri Press, 1998.

A fascinating account of the St. Louis World's Fair is Dorothy Daniels Birk, *The World Came to St. Louis,* St. Louis, Bethany Press, 1979. It should be supplemented with Martha R. Clevenger, ed., *"Indescribably Grand": Diaries and Letters from the 1904 World's Fair,* St. Louis, Missouri Historical Society Press, 1996. Two interesting articles dealing with specific aspects of the Fair are Robert A. Trennert, "A Resurrection of Native Arts and Crafts: The St. Louis World Fair, 1904," *Missouri Historical Review*, April 1993, and Michael Lerner, "'Hoping for a Splendid Summer': African American St. Louis, Ragtime, and the Louisiana Purchase Exposition," *Gateway Heritage*, Winter 1998–1999.

FOURTEEN

World War I and the 1920s

On June 28, 1914, Serbian rebels assassinated the Archduke Franz Ferdinand of Austria-Hungary. By the end of August, Europe had plunged into war, as one country after another honored its alliances. The secret treaties that European nations had hoped would provide them with security had linked them together to the extent that the isolated assassination produced war. England, France, and Russia, known as the Allies, faced Germany and Austria-Hungary, known as the Central Powers, in the struggle.

Public opinion in the United States was mixed. Most Americans wanted to stay out of the war, but few could remain neutral in mind as well as deed, as President Woodrow Wilson asked. With over 350,000 residents of German birth or parentage and more than 100,000 of Irish background, Missouri had many citizens who sympathized with the German cause. In the case of the Irish, they hated England with such passion that they leaned toward any nation opposing it. An even larger number of Missourians had cultural ties with the Allies, however, and blamed Germany for the war. Despite these feelings, few Missourians wanted the United States to enter the conflict in 1914.

Problems With Neutrality

The belligerents adopted policies that made American neutrality difficult to maintain. Britain controlled the seas and blockaded German and neutral ports in an effort to stop the flow of goods to its opponents. President Wilson contended that neutral ships carrying neutral goods had the right to go anywhere. The British and Americans disagreed about what commodities should be banned as war goods, and the British seized United States' ships. Wilson protested but England did not alter its policy, although it did pay for the goods that it confiscated.

To counteract England's dominance of the seas, the Germans used submarines to attack the blockading ships and disrupt trade. Submarine warfare, however, necessarily violated international rules of war, which required a ship attacking a cargo or passenger vessel to give adequate warning and evacuate the targeted ship's crew and passengers. Thin-walled submarines, whose chief weapon was surprise, lost their effectiveness if they followed such rules. Of course, submarines barely had sufficient space for their crews, much less room for passengers from another vessel.

Wilson demanded that Germany abide by the international rules of war and protested when 128 Americans went down with the British liner *Lusitania* on May 7, 1915. That sinking aroused American opinion against Germany; more sinkings—the *Arabic*, in August 1915, and the *Sussex*, in March 1916—added to the anger. After the *Sussex* went down, President Wilson threatened to sever diplomatic relations with Germany if it continued to employ submarine warfare. Germany pledged to abide by international law, if the United States could persuade Britain to do likewise. Wilson accepted Germany's pledge, while ignoring its qualification.

In September 1915, United States bankers loaned the Allies $500 million. Missouri's senior United States senator, William J. Stone, chairman of the Foreign Relations Committee, questioned the neutrality of making such a loan. He observed that financial investment on one side might lead to America's having too vital an interest in that side's success. Stone adhered to the principles of Washington and Jefferson in believing that the United States should stay out of European entanglements. The German-American Alliance, an organization whose members were mostly German and Irish, also voiced their objections to the loan. Such protests did little good. Before it entered the war in April 1917, the United States had provided much more support to the Allies, who received a total of $2.3 billion, than to the Central Powers, who received a total of $27 million. It must be pointed out, however, that even in peacetime the United States had a far greater proportion of its trade with the Allied nations.

Election of 1916

As the election of 1916 approached, Wilson added another issue to those of neutrality and loans when he proposed and Congress approved strengthening the country's military forces. At the national Democratic Convention in St. Louis, suffragists tried to add still another. Over 7,000 women, all dressed in white, adorned with yellow sashes and streamers, and holding yellow parasols, lined both sides of Locust Street for ten blocks in a silent demonstration for the vote. Delegates to the convention had to walk between them to get into the hall. The demonstration had little impact, however, as the Democrats made only a reference to women's suffrage in their platform.

Reunited after the Bull Moose split of 1912, the Republican party lost a closely contested election. Woodrow Wilson sought a second term, running on the slogan He Kept Us Out of War, and defeated his Republican opponent, Charles Evans Hughes of New York. The President carried Missouri with 50.6 percent of the vote. The gubernatorial race pitted Republican Henry Lamm of Sedalia against Democrat Frederick D. Gardner of St. Louis. During the campaign Republicans charged the Democrats with having been spendthrifts. Gardner responded by promising to run a "business administration," weeding out inefficiency and stopping waste. He also promised to build a state road system. In the second popular election for United States senator conducted in Missouri—Democratic Senator William J. Stone had won the first in 1914—Democratic incumbent James A. Reed of Kansas City faced Republican Walter S. Dickey of the same city. Reed beat Dickey by 24,456 votes, but Gardner defeated Lamm by only 2,263 votes. Democrats also captured every other statewide office, except for that of auditor, which Republican George Hackman of Warrenton won. Democrats took fourteen congressional seats and obtained majorities in both houses of the General Assembly.

America Enters the War

As 1917 opened, Germany faced a stalemate in the trenches of France and increasingly felt the effects of the English blockade. On January 30, it announced the resumption of unrestricted submarine warfare, although it anticipated that the announcement would bring the United States into the war. German officials hoped to win a victory before the United States could mobilize.

Parade in Boonville (Cooper County), 1917. *Courtesy State Historical Society of Missouri*

As predicted, the United States severed diplomatic relations with Germany on February 3, and German sinkings of American ships caused President Wilson to ask for a declaration of war on April 2. Congress approved Wilson's request for war, but Senator William J. Stone joined five other senators in voting against it; they were joined by fifty members of the House of Representatives, including four of Missouri's sixteen representatives. As noted above, Stone's adherence to isolation accounts for part of his unwillingness to support the war. Further, his association with the agrarian wing of the Democratic party placed him in opposition to eastern financial and industrial interests that he considered partly responsible for the war. Stone also disagreed with Wilson's interpretation of international law and believed that his country's legal position was indefensible. Missourians condemned his stand, but he died in 1918 before voters could take political vengeance against him.

War's Impact on Missouri

National and state campaigns began to persuade Americans that the naysayers were wrong and to stir patriotic passions on behalf of the war effort. The federal government created a Committee on Public Information. Headed by George Creel, a native of Waverly and former editor of the Kansas City *Independent*, the committee whipped up prowar sentiment and snuffed out dissent. Governor Frederick D. Gardner set the tone of much prowar sentiment when he told a St. Louis loyalty rally, "This is no time for slackers, copperheads, or soft pedalists. If there are any such among us, it is our duty to drive them out and brand them as traitors." In response to such sentiments, 4,000 "Four Minute Men" in Missouri agreed to give patriotic speeches to any group. In 1918 Congress passed a sedition act that made it illegal to criticize the government.

Anti-German sentiment naturally surfaced during the war. Uel Lamkin, state superintendent of schools, urged boards of education to hire only native-born teachers and requested that elementary schools provide instruction only in English. He also ruled that high schools that offered instruction in German would not be certified. City officials changed some German street names. Some individuals objected to the playing of German music. German-language newspapers probably blunted more serious anti-German sentiment by proclaiming their loyalty to the United States after Congress declared war. The St. Louis *Labor*, a socialist paper, refused to support the war, standing almost alone among the state's newspapers.

In addition to the drive to mobilize public opinion, officials worked to organize Missouri's resources. At the request of Secretary of War Newton D. Baker, Governor Gardner appointed a Missouri Council of Defense. Headed by Frederick B. Mumford, dean of the University of Missouri College of Agriculture, the state council organized 11,487 county and community councils. These groups spurred agricultural and industrial production. No doubt also stimulated by government price supports, Missouri farmers increased grain production by 87 percent and pork production by 20 percent during the first year of the war.

The demands of war also caused expansion in Missouri's manufacturing and mining industries. After early disruption of traditional markets in 1914 had brought on recession and a curtailment of activity, large loans to the Allies and reestablishment of trade produced increased output by the end of 1915. American entrance into the war made expansion more urgent. Missouri supplied lumber, munitions, lead, zinc, shoes, clothing, and other items to the war effort. Two St. Louis firms, Monsanto and Mallinckrodt chemical companies, experienced rapid growth because the war cut off American access to German chemicals.

The Missouri Council of Defense and local councils organized a food conservation program, promoted fund drives, and worked on every other aspect of mobilization. Under the sponsorship of the council, one million Missourians signed pledges to conserve food.

Missouri led all other states in the proportion of its citizens signing such pledges, and it ranked second in total signatures. Missourians contributed to greatly increased federal wartime costs by purchasing bonds in four "Liberty Bond Drives" during the fighting and a "Victory Bond Drive" after it concluded. Missourians raised more than their quota in every drive, perhaps because of community pressure to buy bonds.

The war brought Missourians into the military service. Over 750,000 of the state's men registered for the draft; 92,843 were drafted; and a total of 156,232 served in the war, half of them overseas. Missourians fought in key battles in France as members of the "Fighting 89th" Division and of the "Brave 35th" Division, Harry Truman's outfit. Black Missourians fought in France as members of the 805th, 806th, and 817th Pioneers. The Commander-in-Chief of the American Expedition Force, General John J. "Black Jack" Pershing, had been born in Laclede, Missouri, and attended Northeast Missouri State before graduating from West Point. Other prominent Missouri military figures included Major General Enoch H. Crowder of Edinburgh, Brigadier General Edgar H. Russell of Breckenridge, and Admirals Robert Edward Coontz of Hannibal and Leigh C. Palmer of St. Louis.

Missouri civilians who exerted national influence during the war included former Governor David R. Francis, who served as United States ambassador to Russia during the Bolshevik Revolution. David Franklin Houston, chancellor of Washington University, directed food production efforts as United States secretary of agriculture. His assistant secretary, Carl Vrooman of Macon County, publicized in speeches around the country both food conservation and the need for increased production. Edward R. Stettinius of St. Louis served as assistant secretary of war.

Women's Suffrage

Missouri women made sacrifices and aided the war effort at home and abroad. They contended with "wheatless" and "fuelless Mondays," "meatless Tuesdays," and "lightless nights," "porkless Thursdays," and "wartime" or daylight savings time. Women worked in factories and on farms; they served as nurses in hospitals and on battlefields; they rolled bandages and knit sweaters and socks; and they raised money for the war through various bond drives.

Their contributions to the war effort induced President Wilson to ask Congress for a women's suffrage amendment to the United States Constitution. As early as 1867, Missouri women had petitioned the legislature to grant them suffrage. Over the years various organizations including the Populists had supported women's voting. In 1914 Missouri women used initiative petitions to place the question on the ballot, but male voters rejected it. As noted above, in 1916 they demonstrated at the Democratic National Convention. Congress responded favorably to Wilson's request and submitted the Nineteenth Amendment to the states. Missouri became the eleventh state to ratify it; the required three-fourths of the states had approved it before the 1920 election. The Women's Suffrage Association, which had fought for enfranchisement, now became the Missouri League of Women Voters and affiliated with the National League of Women Voters.

Taking advantage of their new opportunities, Mellcene Thurman Smith and Sarah Lucille Turner won seats in the General Assembly in 1922, becoming the first women to serve in that body. Both Democrats, Smith represented a St. Louis County district while Turner served a Kansas City district. Smith, aged fifty, came from a business background and won a seat in a normally Republican area because of a clean government movement. Turner, only twenty-four and a recent law school graduate, secured support from political boss Joseph Shannon's faction of the Democratic party. While both ran for reelection in 1924, neither was successful.

However, a Republican woman from Carthage, Emma Knell, defeated her opponent by 800 votes in that election to continue women's representation in state government. Knell, an embalmer by profession, won again in 1926, becoming the first woman to win back-to-back contests. She defeated her Democratic opponent, Martha Taafe, by nearly 3,000 votes. Their race, for the first time in state history, pitted women against each other for seats in the legislature. Knell did not run again in 1928 but the General Assembly found itself with another woman member in the person of Ruby McReynolds, a Republican from Knox County, who served a single term. Knell returned in 1931 but then quit politics. No women served in the 1933–34 session; and only one woman held legislative office during the rest of the 1930s: Gladys Berger Stewart, a Republican lawyer from Douglas County, who served from 1935 to 1943.

Prohibition

A number of women supported another movement that reached fruition during the war years: prohibition. Ratification of the Eighteenth Amendment in 1919 completed a forty-year effort in Missouri to outlaw the manufacture, sale, or transportation of liquor. During the term of Clara Cleghorn Hoffman of Kansas City as president of the Women's Christian Temperance Union in 1887, the General Assembly passed a law providing that a majority of voters in a county or in any city of 2,500 could adopt prohibition. After 1893 the efforts of the WCTU were aided by the Anti-Saloon League, the most effective lobbying organization for prohibition. By 1917, 96 of Missouri's 114 counties and a number of towns had become dry. Referenda for statewide prohibition had been rejected in 1910, 1916, and 1918. Those votes revealed that Anglo-Saxon, Protestant, rural Missourians favored making Missouri dry, while German, Catholic, and urban Missourians opposed such action. In particular St. Louis and the counties of eastern Missouri with large German-American populations consistently voted against prohibition. When the Eighteenth Amendment came before the legislature, the rural-dominated General Assembly approved it by large majorities, 22 to 10 in the Senate and 104 to 36 in the House.

Politics: Republicans Take Control

The closeness of the 1916 election suggested the possibility of a future change in political power in Missouri. As they squared off, both major parties embraced a nucleus of rural Protestants and urban Catholic immigrants. According to the 1920 census, 53.4 percent of Missourians lived in rural areas, and 46.6 percent of them lived in towns with populations of 2,500 or more. Missouri, however, was more rural than the percentages indicated. With 70 percent of the urban population concentrated in St. Louis and Kansas City, 66 of the state's 114 counties had no towns of 2,500 and thus no urban dwellers. In the remaining 48 counties, 41 of them had rural majorities.

During the 1920s the Republican party controlled St. Louis through a coalition of immigrants from northern states, a large German-American population, and a significant black population. German-Americans and blacks had formed alliances with the Republican party during the Civil War period. Rural Republican areas included heavily German counties in the central-west portion of the state along the Missouri River east to St. Louis and then south along the Mississippi to Cape Girardeau. Reflecting their German social heritage, they always voted wet when given an opportunity to express themselves on prohibition. Old-stock dry Protestants composed the large majority of voters in the other three rural Republican strongholds: counties in northwest Missouri, including Mercer; counties in the southeast Ozarks, including Wayne; and counties in the southwest Ozarks, including Greene. Nonslaveholding northerners had either settled these areas originally or had come to dominate them.

Democrats usually controlled Kansas City because of the Pendergast machine's success in uniting rural Protestants, who were swelling its population, and Irish-American Catholics. The machine will be discussed later. In rural Missouri, Little Dixie consistently provided Democrats with large majorities. Composed of thirteen counties lying on either side of the Missouri River near the center of the state and extending northeast along the Mississippi River, the area became overwhelmingly Democratic after the Civil War. Kentuckians, Virginians, and their slaves had originally settled there. Southerners, with few slaves, had also settled the south central Ozarks from Maries County south to Oregon County. That region formed a second rural Democratic area. Similar settlement patterns and Civil War experiences produced Democratic majorities in the Osage plains counties surrounding Kansas City and ranging along the border between Missouri and Kansas.

The Republican surge began in 1918. On April 14, Senator Stone died unexpectedly. Democratic Governor Gardner, with senatorial aspirations of his own, appointed Xenophon P. Wilfley, a little-known St. Louis lawyer, to serve in the office until November, when voters would elect someone to finish the unexpired term. Wilfley immediately announced his candidacy for the Democratic nomination. In June, Joseph W. Folk threw his hat in the ring so that Democrats had a choice in the August primary. On the Republican side, Judge Selden P. Spencer of St. Louis opposed Jay Torrey, an Ozark apple grower, for that party's nomination.

Spencer won the Republican primary handily and began his election campaign with a united party behind him. He had run as a prowar candidate. In the Democratic contest, Folk defeated Wilfley by carrying out-state Missouri by large margins, while losing in both Kansas City and St. Louis. Name-calling marred the campaign, but it must be pointed out that Folk's candidacy alone promised Democratic division. Rural Democrats loved him, while urban leaders detested him as a party-wrecking do-gooder because of his activities as circuit attorney and governor.

Both the Republicans and Democrats adopted platforms that supported the war effort as the most important issue before the nation, advocated women's suffrage, endorsed prohibition while trying to avoid much discussion of it, and mentioned nothing about postwar settlements. Folk aligned himself with Wilson and his policies; Spencer assumed the role of a nonpartisan patriot determined to win the war.

Folk lost to Spencer by a vote of 302,680 to 267,397, marking the first major defeat for the Democrats since 1908. Republicans also gained three congressional seats for a total of five of sixteen. Predictably, Democratic leaders provided at best nominal support for Folk, who ran 18,000 votes behind the ticket. Spencer won by 35,730 votes in St. Louis and by 8,742 in out-state Missouri. Wilson had issued a public letter on October 25 pleading for a Democratic Congress, therefore the election represented at least in part, a repudiation of his policies as well as of Folk.

During the next two years, debate over President Wilson's peace proposals, particularly the League of Nations, divided Missouri Democrats. Senator James A. Reed implacably opposed the league; Wilson refused to compromise. Differences in political philosophy aggravated policy disagreements. Wilson believed in the parliamentary form of government, which necessitated party regularity and executive leadership. Reed adhered to the ideal of an independent lawmaker, subject to neither party, chief executive, nor those who elected him. Reed also opposed prohibition, whereas Wilson supported it. Old stock, out-state Missouri Democrats followed Wilson and homestate surrogates, Breckenridge Long and Charles M. Hay. Urban and Irish Missouri Democrats followed Reed. Sensing the national exhaustion of idealism and anticipating victory because of Democratic division, the Republicans in 1920 nominated party regular Senator Warren G. Harding of Ohio for President. He offered voters a "return to normalcy" or an alternative to the activitist domestic and international policies of Wilson. State Republicans nominated Arthur M.

Hyde of Trenton for governor. A progressive who had bolted the Republican party in 1912 to follow Theodore Roosevelt, Hyde promised voters a reduction in taxes and economy and efficiency in government.

Benefiting from high consumer prices and low farm prices and the increased taxes passed by Democrats to pay for new state programs, the Republicans simply overwhelmed their opponents. For the first time in fifty years, the GOP took all of the statewide offices. They also delivered the state to Harding, who whipped James M. Cox of Ohio, while Senator Spencer retained his seat by defeating Breckenridge Long of St. Louis. Spencer had opposed American entrance into the League of Nations and Long had supported it. Republicans swept to control of both houses of the General Assembly and won fourteen of sixteen congressional races. Even Champ Clark of Bowling Green, the longtime Speaker of the House, lost his seat. The Republican victory was so complete that Democrats won local races in only thirty counties.

In his first months in office, Governor Hyde recommended extensive reorganization of state government. Increased governmental responsibility had produced a maze of boards, agencies, bureaus, and commissions in Missouri. Hyde wanted the duties of this diverse group consolidated into a few departments, with department heads reporting directly to the governor. In 1921 the legislature enacted all but two of his recommendations. Claiming that reorganization represented a Republican scheme to eliminate Democratic officeholders, the Democratic State Committee successfully petitioned to bring these measures before the electorate. Besides the fourteen referred bills, voters were asked to decide on nineteen propositions, two initiative proposals, and three constitutional amendments. When confronted with numerous and complex issues on a ballot, voters usually say no. In addition, voter inclination to oppose change and Democratic allegations of a Republican conspiracy may have influenced the outcome. Voters rejected almost all of the proposals, destroying Hyde's reorganization efforts.

While voters rejected the governor's reforms, they approved a proposal to call a constitutional convention in 1922 and to allow the electorate to have a similar choice every twenty years thereafter. The 1922 convention began on May 15 and adjourned on November 6, 1923. Instead of writing a new constitution, it proposed twenty-one amendments to the 1875 document. The most important proposal called for the consolidation of all administrative functions into twelve departments, which echoed Hyde's consolidation request. Delegates also proposed to strengthen the governor's role in developing the state budget. On February 26, 1925, Missourians rejected all but six of the amendments with the result that no significant change occurred in state government until 1945, when a new constitution, discussed in Chapter 16, was finally approved. As in the case of the referendum on Hyde's proposals, voters were asked to deal with a number of complex propositions and they reacted negatively. Conservative rural voters provided the margin of defeat for twelve of the fifteen measures voted down.

Election of 1922

In 1922 the controversial Senator Reed sought reelection. He had made many Democratic enemies because of his opposition to the Eighteenth and Nineteenth amendments, his stand against outlawing child labor, and his strong opposition to President Wilson's foreign policy. Those enemies formed "Rid-Us-of-Reed Clubs" and put forth Breckenridge Long as a primary opponent. Reed defeated him by 6,000 votes and went on to beat Republican R. R. Brewster of Kansas City in the general election by 506,267 to 462,009.

The wily Democrat depicted himself as the farmer's friend and gained the endorsement of William Hirth's *Missouri Farmer,* organ of the Missouri Farmer's Association. Reed also persuaded a majority of St. Louisans to vote for him because of his antiprohibition stance. He thereby became the first Democrat to carry that city in eighteen years.

Democrats regained a majority in both houses of the General Assembly and also won eleven of sixteen congressional seats. Among the new representatives was Clarence Cannon of Elsberry, who won Champ Clark's old seat. Cannon would serve in the House with distinction for the next forty-one years and exercise considerable influence, especially in fiscal affairs. According to historian Franklin D. Mitchell, Reed's victory was fundamentally a personal one, but he, like other Democrats, benefited from an economic recession and Hyde's tax policies that had resulted in a reduction of both corporate and income taxes.

Pendergast Machine in Democratic Politics

In 1922 Reed carried the normally dry Kansas City 52,005 to 51,642 because of the support of the Pendergast machine. That organization began during the 1880s when Jim Pendergast started exchanging favors for votes in Kansas City's West Bottoms, a poor Irish neighborhood. Using his tavern as political headquarters, Pendergast won election to the Board of Aldermen in 1892. In 1900 his candidate, James A. Reed, won the race for mayor; and as each decade passed, Pendergast expanded his influence. When he died in 1911, Reed sat in the Senate, and the machine had expanded from the Bottoms into the North End.

The elder Pendergast had trained his brother Tom to head the organization. Tom, who came to be known as Boss Pendergast, widened the machine's influence by providing services and favors to middle-class as well as poor Kansas Citians and by making peace with longtime rival, Democratic leader Joseph Shannon. During the mid-1920s, Tom's expanded organization defeated Shannon's Ninth Ward machine in successive Democratic primaries. In 1925 Kansas City adopted a new city charter that instituted a council-manager form of government. In an effort to control a majority of the council seats, Pendergast offered Shannon one-third of the city's patronage if he would support the boss's candidates. Shannon agreed; Pendergast men won five of the nine council seats in 1926; and the boss strengthened his grip on the politics of Kansas City.

1924 Election and the Ku Klux Klan

Even before their decision to cooperate, Pendergast and Shannon had agreed that the Ku Klux Klan should be smashed. After its decline in the late 1870s, the Klan had revived during the "Red Scare" following World War I and experienced phenomenal growth in Missouri during 1923 and 1924. Americans everywhere feared that agents of Russia's Bolshevik Revolution might destroy their society. Many believed that Communist influences caused the economic recession and considerable labor unrest that occurred after the war. They applauded as government agents conducted a witch-hunt in which they used violence and deportation to rid the country of anyone suspected of "Communist" activity. The Klan seemed to attract individuals who found it difficult to cope with a changing America.

Cartoon by Jon Kennedy, 1920s. *Arkansas Democrat, courtesy State Historical Society of Missouri*

"Men, We've Got to Improve Our Image."

They distrusted and disliked the forces of urbanization, mechanization, and secularization that intruded on their lives. They were disturbed by the influx of a large number of blacks into northern cities, including St. Louis, during the war. They could not understand women who refused to return to kitchens after having worked in factories, nor could they accept women who sought more personal freedom. They resented the numerous Catholics who favored drinking alcoholic beverages and bore foreign-sounding names. In Missouri thousands sought safety within the Ku Klux Klan.* Denouncing Catholics, Jews, blacks, foreigners, and radicals, the Klan claimed to be "100 percent American" and used intimidation and violence to impose its views on society.

The Klan had sufficient strength to disrupt the Democratic National Convention in 1924. Supporters of Alfred E. Smith, who was wet, Catholic, and governor of New York, proposed a platform plank condemning the hooded organization by name. Those who favored William G. McAdoo of California and represented dry, Protestant, rural America succeeded in defeating the anti-Klan plank. Neither group could command the two-thirds majority required to nominate its candidate, however, and after 103 ballots, the convention compromised on John W. Davis of West Virginia. In the general election, he faced a unified Republican party supporting incumbent Calvin Coolidge and a Progressive party composed of midwestern farmers and laborers supporting Wisconsin Senator Robert M. LaFollette.

On the state level the Klan endorsed both gubernatorial candidates, Democrat Arthur Nelson of Cooper County and Republican

*Kenneth T. Jackson in *The Ku Klux Klan in the City, 1915–1930* (New York: Oxford University Press, 1967) estimates that 45,000 Missourians were inducted into the Klan between 1915 and 1944.

Sam A. Baker of Wayne County, a former state superintendent of schools. Neither party sought the endorsement, however, and both of them had anti-Klan planks in their platforms. During the campaign Baker issued an affidavit denying any Klan affiliation, thinking correctly that Nelson's earlier flirtations with it would prevent him from doing the same.

Election returns revealed another Republican victory. Coolidge's vote, however, was less than the combined votes for Davis and LaFollette. Baker won by only 5,872 votes, probably because his anti-Klan stand appealed to black voters who turned out for the Republicans in greater numbers than in the previous two elections. The GOP captured all of the state offices, won control of the lower house of the General Assembly, and increased their congressional posts to seven out of sixteen. The Democrats took nine of sixteen state senate seats being contested and retained control of that chamber.

After the 1924 election, the Klan's numbers and influence declined appreciably. People rejected many of its premises and withdrew from the violence that always lurked just beneath its facade of respectability. The Klan's image as defender of morality became tarnished by revelations of gross immorality and corruption within its leadership. National membership went from an estimated peak of 3 million in 1924 to 200,000 in 1928, and Missouri's membership dwindled to a few thousand.

Election of 1926

Aided by the demise of the Klan and the stench of defeat, Harry B. Hawes worked to bring unity to the Democratic party. A longtime St. Louis politician and a member of Congress since 1920, Hawes traveled over 8,000 miles around Missouri speaking to Democrats about unity in behalf of his senatorial candidacy during 1925. By the eve of the election, wets and drys, rural and urban Democrats had joined in support of the ticket. By a vote of 506,015 to 470,654, Hawes defeated his Republican opponent, George H. Williams, who had been appointed to serve in the Senate upon the death of Selden P. Spencer in 1925. The united party also reelected Charles A. Lee as state superintendent of schools, twelve of sixteen congressmen, and retained control of the state senate. Republicans continued to hold a majority in the lower house of the General Assembly.

The movement of black voters into the Democratic column was one of the significant results of this election. Democrats made a direct appeal to black voters by advocating better educational opportunities and other programs for them. Party leaders stipulated that public institutions for the race should be administered and staffed by blacks. Democrats agreed with the claim made by black politicians that past Republican victories had depended on black voters. They asked blacks whether their support of Republicans had benefited their race. Democratic appeals coincided with black discontent over the lack of patronage given them by Republican Governor Baker and helped to produce the significant black vote for the Democrats. *The Kansas City Call*, a black newspaper, estimated that 42 percent of black voters in that city cast Democratic ballots. Blacks voting Democratic represented a dramatic change in state politics, as that group had generally supported the Republican party.

Election of 1928

Even before the 1926 election, Senator Reed had announced his intention not to seek reelection in 1928. Instead, he chose to pursue the Democratic presidential nomination, but it went to Governor Alfred E. Smith of New York. The Democratic unity of 1926 was quickly shattered when Reed supported James Collet of Salisbury as his Senate successor against his longtime rival Charles M. Hay of St. Louis. Reed denounced Hay as a party bolter, an agent of the Anti-Saloon League, and a supporter of the KKK. Although Hay won the primary by 30,000 votes, he faced an uphill fight against his dry Republican opponent, Roscoe C. Patterson of Springfield. For governor the Democrats nominated the wet Francis M. Wilson of Platte County, and the Republicans chose Henry S. Caulfield of St. Louis, who opposed prohibition. That issue so muddled politics that Missourians had a choice of two drys for the Senate and two wets for the governorship.

The last election of the decade almost matched the Republican landslide of eight years earlier. The GOP candidate for President, former Commerce Secretary Herbert Hoover, overwhelmed Smith in Missouri 834,080 to 662,526. Caulfield beat Wilson by 52,510 votes, while Patterson defeated Hay by just over 60,000 votes. Even though he lost in Missouri by 171,554 votes, the New York governor's stand on prohibition did allow him to carry St. Louis, the first time that city had given a majority to a Democratic presidential candidate since 1888.

Democrats continued to woo black voters in Missouri in 1928. Showing their good faith, they nominated Joseph L. McLemore, a black lawyer, to run for Congress in the Twelfth District, a St. Louis district with a large black vote. He became the first black in any border or southern state to run for a House seat on the Democratic ticket. Although he lost the contest to his Republican opponent, and a majority of black Missourians continued to vote Republican in 1928, his candidacy aided the Democrats' campaign to win a majority of the 100,000 registered black voters in Missouri over to the Democratic side.

Road Building

While blacks became more important in state politics, Missouri's urban population grew, and the relationship between rural and urban societies changed. The spread of the radio and the increased use of automobiles eroded rural isolation. Demands for better roads naturally followed.

Organized support for improved roads began with bicyclists in the 1890s and developed momentum as the popularity of automobiles increased. In 1907 the General Assembly required that automobile owners register their cars and that drivers register themselves, designating the resulting fees of $5 per car and $2 per driver for road building. In 1913 the legislature created the office of State Highway Commissioner. But these early developments did little to take chief responsibility for building and maintaining roads out of local hands.

Consumers of Henry Ford's moderately priced Model T and federal legislation forced the state to assume greater responsibility for road building. As the number of autos in Missouri increased from 16,387 in 1911 to 151,027 in 1917, so did the demand for better roads. Congress passed the Federal Highway Act in 1916, which required states to develop highway construction and maintenance programs with the promise of federal funds on a matching basis, a federal dollar for every state dollar. The following year Governor Frederick Gardner asked the General Assembly to enact legislation making Missouri eligible for more than $2 million in available federal funds over the next four years. It complied by passing the Hawes

Good Roads Law, which created the state supervisory and engineering machinery to meet federal requirements.

As early as 1919, however, it became obvious that additional
funds were needed to "Lift Missouri Out of the Mud," to quote the
slogan of the Missouri Good Roads Federation. In 1920 that organization helped secure the passage of a state constitutional amendment that provided $60 million in needed road funds through a
bond issue. The next year the General Assembly passed the Centennial Road Law, transferring all responsibility for building and maintaining Missouri's roads to the state.

In 1924 voters approved a 50 percent increase in registration fees
and a two cents per gallon tax on gasoline to raise additional money
for roads, and four years later they voted another $75 million bond
issue. Those funds supported a building program that by 1931 had
completed nearly all of the primary roads connecting 90 percent of
the residents in places of 2,500 or above and 85 percent of the secondary road system that had been projected in 1921.

Improved roads stimulated car sales and vice versa. Increases in
the number of automobiles and the miles of hard-surfaced roads
transformed life in the state. The number of vehicles went from
151,027 in 1917 to 392,896 in 1922 to 764,375 in 1930. Road construction and the automobile industry caused economic growth, fostered the development of the tourist industry, and engendered gas
stations and roadhouses. Automobiles made livery stables and blacksmith shops obsolete, allowed rural people to shop in cities, weak-

"Lift Missouri Out of the Mud" road construction, 1922. *Courtesy State Historical Society of Missouri*

ened family and community restraint on individual conduct, and produced the killing and maiming associated with highway accidents. Attempts to reduce this last outcome led to the creation of the state highway patrol in 1931. In general the automobile tended to reduce provincialism, causing rural-urban experiences to become less dissimilar and life to become more standardized.

Charles A. Lindbergh: Hero

With an enthusiasm that rivaled their love of the automobile, Americans embraced the airplane. Following the first flight in 1903, airplane development progressed steadily until it leaped forward during World War I. By the mid-1920s aviation had become so routine that regular air-mail routes had been established.

Then in May 1927 Charles Lindbergh captured America's imagination when he flew a Wright Whirlwind from New York to Paris. A lieutenant in the Missouri Air National Guard and a pilot flying mail between St. Louis and Chicago, Lindbergh had accepted the challenge to fly nonstop across the Atlantic in the hope of winning a $25,000 prize. He secured most of the $15,000 needed to finance his effort from St. Louis backers and named his plane *The Spirit of St. Louis*. His feat was acclaimed in both Europe and America, and he became the hero of the decade.

Charles A. Lindbergh standing by his plane *Spirit of St. Louis,* 1927. *Courtesy State Historical Society of Missouri*

Education

With improved roads and increased use of automobiles, some Missourians tried to improve rural educational opportunities by consolidating schools. Because 85 percent to 93 percent of school money came from local funds, the better financed urban schools offered more diverse and advanced educational experiences than the poorer rural schools. Governor Sam A. Baker, who before becoming governor had been state superintendent of schools, attempted to address those problems by establishing a permanent school fund, but the legislature refused to do so. Instead, the state reduced its percentage of support for schools during the decade. Since 1910 Missouri had fallen well below the national average in expenditure for education per average child of school age. In 1931, during Governor Caulfield's administration, the General Assembly finally passed a school law that distributed state money so that every district could support a school program of minimum standard.

The education provided for black children failed to meet the rudimentary requirements. With a total of 51,000 school-age black children, Missouri provided only eight high schools. Over 4,000 black children in 1928 had no public schools at all. Only in Kansas City and St. Louis did black educational opportunities even begin to meet the Supreme Court dictum of equal, while state and local officials rigorously adhered to the separate part of the *Plessy* v. *Ferguson* decision. In that 1896 decision the Court had ruled that segregation was constitutional but that equal public facilities had to be provided for those segregated, thus, "separate but equal."

State-supported higher education fared little better. Enrollments outstripped facilities, which deteriorated because of limited maintenance money. The University of Missouri paid such low salaries that it became a "training institution" for schools in other states as faculty members gained experience there and soon departed for higher wages. Lincoln University consistently received too little funding to maintain essential services. Underfinancing plagued all state institutions during the period.

The Economy and Depression

The decade of the twenties brought prosperity and growth to certain segments of Missouri's economy, but stagnation and hardship to its agriculture. In 1920 over 400,000 of its 3,404,055 people were employed in farming and forestry, making them the state's largest occupation group. To put the matter simply, during and immediately after the war farmers used improved techniques and cultivated more land that produced glutted markets when Europe staged an unexpected and rapid recovery from World War I. Thus prices received for farm goods and land declined, while the quantity, variety, and prices of goods that farmers purchased increased. The farmers' plight is illustrated in the following table.

Year	Prices Received by Farmers	Prices Paid by Farmers
1918	202	176
1920	211	201
1922	132	149
1924	143	152
1926	145	155
1928	149	155
1930	126	145

Source: David March, *History of Missouri*, p. 1309. Note: Economists use the period 1909–14 as a period when prices paid to farmers and prices paid by farmers were on a par, with each being 100. Thus in 1914, Prices Received by Farmers would be 100 and Prices Paid by Farmers would be 100.

Farmers turned to Congress for aid and received the McNary-Haugen bill. It would have provided support for domestic farm prices through purchases in the marketplace by a government corporation, thus keeping agricultural prices on a par with other prices. Commodities purchased domestically would be sold on the world market, and taxpayers would make up the difference. The bill met defeat in the House of Representatives in 1924 and 1926, passed Congress in 1927 and, with alterations, in 1928 only to have President Coolidge veto both versions.

Farm leaders in Missouri advocated the formation of cooperatives as a partial answer to their problems. William Hirth promoted cooperatives in the pages of the *Missouri Farmer*, telling his readers that farmers would never get fair prices so long as middlemen processed and sold their produce. He urged them to join together so that they could buy in bulk and sell in an organized way.

Cartoon by Daniel Fitzpatrick,
St. Louis Post-Dispatch, **December 31, 1929.** *Courtesy State Historical Society of Missouri*

HISTORY OF 1929.

Chariton County farmers formed the first farm club in 1914, and in August 1917 delegates from thirty-eight counties created the Missouri Farmers' Association, a statewide cooperative. The MFA prospered during the 1920s, and by 1930 it was operating 375 exchanges and elevators where farmers bought supplies and marketed their crops, 300 shipping associations, 2 milk plants, an oil company, and a state purchasing department. The Missouri Farm Bureau competed briefly with the MFA in the cooperative movement, but its major thrust was in scientific farming. It worked with the United States Department of Agriculture and the University of Missouri's College of Agriculture to increase the number of county farm agents across the state.

Despite these efforts farm foreclosures became common, and farmers left the land. While the state's overall population remained relatively stable in the 1920s, with only a 6.6 percent increase for the decade, the number of Missourians living in rural areas declined from 53.4 percent in 1920 to 48.8 percent in 1930. This marked the first time that the majority of the state's citizens could be found in towns of 2,500 or more residents. While St. Louis County's population doubled, Kansas City grew by 23.2 percent, Springfield by 45.2 percent, and Cape Girardeau by 58 percent.

Urban dwellers prospered during the decade, with real wages of workers increasing, although not as much as labor productivity or industrial profits. Working conditions improved, and in 1926 Missouri even passed a workers' compensation law. Such living improvements as electric washers and dryers, toasters, mixers, refrigerators, irons, etc., became available to the average citizen. Many of these items, along with automobiles, were purchased through installment plans: "Consume now and pay later" became a major economic slogan for the decade.

Improved wages and more leisure time allowed the average person to attend movies and sports events. Professional athletics, particularly baseball, became popular. St. Louis sponsored two teams—the Cardinals and the Browns with superstars like Rogers Hornsby and George Sisler. The St. Louis Cardinals won National League pennants in 1926 and 1928, which brought World Series fever to the Gateway City. Motion pictures and their stars rivaled baseball as attractions, while that new gadget, radio, kept the stay-at-homes entertained and informed.

What had seemed to many as the beginning of an era of plenty ended abruptly on October 29, 1929, when the New York stock market crashed. The crash ended a speculative boom that had seen stock prices soar beyond the value of the companies the stock represented. During the 1920s, speculation in the market had hidden such weaknesses in the economy as the inability of mass purchasing to expand sufficiently to absorb the goods being produced. As noted above, incomes failed to keep pace with worker productivity and led to large consumer debts. Any interruption in regular purchasing had negative effects on sales that triggered worker layoffs, causing further interruptions in sales, and the cycle continued. Under that stress, companies with even minor financial difficulties might go bankrupt, throwing more people out of work and further reducing purchasing power and sales.

Reductions in incomes caused the demand for agricultural products to shrink and prices to fall. The already hard-pressed farmers defaulted on mortgages and other loans. Banks foreclosed, but the land could not be sold for the value of the loans. Similarly, banks had accepted stock as collateral for loans and when the loans could not be paid the banks held worthless stock. The gloom that permeated society led people to withdraw their savings from banks, and these combined factors created a crisis in the entire banking system. Many banks collapsed. Mechanisms to stop the events failed and the entire economic system screeched to a halt.

Suggestions for Reading

Lawrence O. Christensen and Gary R. Kremer, *A History of Missouri, Vol. IV, 1875 to 1919*, Columbia, University of Missouri Press, 1997, provides the most complete treatment of the state during World War I. Contemporary reaction to the war can be seen in a series of articles by Floyd C. Shoemaker in the *Missouri Historical Review* between October 1917 and July 1919. Two articles by Christopher C. Gibbs, "Missouri Farmers and World War One: Resistance to Mobilization," *The Bulletin*, October 1978, and "The Lead Belt Riot and World War One," *Missouri Historical Review*, July 1977, give important perspectives on the war. Gibbs, *The Silent Majority: Missouri's Resistance to World War I*, Columbia, University of Missouri Press, 1988, elaborates the themes covered in his articles. For another view, see Lawrence O. Christensen, "Missouri's Responses to World War I: The Missouri Council of Defense," *The Midwest Review*, 2nd series, 1990, and four articles by Christensen in the *Missouri Historical Review*: "Prelude to World War I in Missouri," October 1995; "Popular Reaction to the World War in Missouri," July 1992; and "World War I in Missouri, Parts 1 and 2," April and July 1996. Other articles in the *Missouri Historical Review* include: Chris Richardson, "With Liberty and Justice for All?: The Suppression of the German-American Culture During World War I," October 1996; Margaret Baker Graham, "Baptism by Fire: A Missourian in the Great War," July 2001; Barry Robert Wood, "'Holy Joe' Folk's Last Crusade: The 1918 Election in Missouri," April 1977; Donald Smythe, "Pershing after the Armistice, 1918–1919," October 1984; and Benjamin D. Rhodes, "Missouri to Murmansk: Chasing the Bolsheviks with Major Edward E. MacMorland, March–July 1919," January 1994.

Richard S. Kirkendall, *A History of Missouri, Vol. V, 1919 to 1953*, Columbia, University of Missouri Press, 1986, is the standard treatment of the 1920s, while Franklin D. Mitchell, *Embattled Democracy: Missouri Democratic Politics, 1919–1932*, Columbia, University of Missouri Press, 1968, is a superb treatment of the politics of the period and covers more than the title implies. Other pertinent topics to the period are covered in Roger D. Launius, *Seasons in the Sun: The Story of Big League Baseball in Missouri*, Columbia, University of Missouri Press, 2002; Gregg Andrews, *City of Dust: A Cement Company Town in the Land of Tom Sawyer*, Columbia, University of Missouri Press, 1996, and a related book, Andrews, *Insane Sisters or, the Price Paid for*

Challenging a Company Town, Columbia, University of Missouri Press, 1999; and Lynn Morrow and Linda Myers-Phinney, *Shepherd of the Hills Country: Tourism Transforms the Ozarks, 1880s–1930s,* Fayetteville, University of Arkansas Press, 1999.

Useful articles in the *Missouri Historical Review* on various topics include: John R. David, "Joseph K. Emmet as Fritz, our Cousin German: The Stage Immigrant and the American Dream," January 1979; Joe E. Smith, "Early Movies and Their Impact on Columbia," October 1979; Alan Havig, "Mass Commercial Amusements in Kansas City Before World War I," April 1981; David R. Knechtges, "A Chance Memoir of the University of Missouri, 1920–1923," January 1983; George Ehrlich and Sherry Piland, "The Architectural Career of Nelly Peters," January 1989; Charles A. Jarvis, "Clarence Cannon, the Corncob Pipe, and the Hawley-Smoot Tariff," January 1990; Tom N. McInnis, "Kansas City Free Speech Fight of 1911," April 1990; Mary K. Dains, "Women Pioneers in the Missouri Legislature," October 1990; William B. Claycomb, "Dr. Arthur Nelson for Governor: The 1924 Campaign," July 1992; Patrick J. Huber and Gary R. Kremer, "Nathaniel C. Bruce, Black Education and the 'Tuskegee of the Midwest'," October 1992; and Patrick Brophy, "Weltmer, Stanhope, and the Rest: Magnetic Healing in Nevada, Missouri," April 1997.

Among helpful pieces in *Gateway Heritage* are Dina M. Young, "Silent Search for a Voice: The St. Louis Equal Suffrage League, 1910–1920," Spring 1988; Marla Martin Hanley, "The Children's Crusade of 1922," Summer 1989; and Lisa Catherine Hefferman, "The One-Room School: Descriptions of Everyday Education in North Callaway County, Missouri, 1910–1940," Winter 1990–1991.

FIFTEEN

The Pendergast Era

The Great Depression

At the outset state government was too alarmed. Each regarded the crisis as a temporary business recession. Business and industry were urged to hold the line on wages and prices, while employees were encouraged not to press demands for salary increases or improved working conditions. Many leaders believed that if the most critical industries and institutions in the economic sector were provided limited financial assistance, the nation would soon recover its health. President Hoover believed that relief for the poverty stricken was a matter for private agencies and local government and that massive federal aid would destroy individual initiative and the free enterprise system. As a result, the President and Congress developed no bold plan to relieve the crisis. After 1930 Democrats controlled the House of Representatives while the Republican margin in the Senate was razor-thin. Hence political arguments frequently made action difficult. Soon the road to recovery became the road to economic shambles as the depression worsened.

At Hoover's request, Congress set up the Reconstruction Finance Corporation (RFC) in 1932 to lend money to banks and other firms to keep them from going bankrupt. It also established the Federal Home Loan Bank designed to help lending institutions discount mortgages in lieu of foreclosing on homeowners. Both agencies proved inadequate to the enormous task that confronted them. That summer Congress passed the Emergency Relief Act, which authorized the RFC to lend the states up to $300 million for relief purposes, and Missouri borrowed over $1 million to aid approximately 200,000 needy persons. In the meantime, Missouri's Republican Governor Henry S. Caulfield had encouraged the highway depart-

POLITICAL
BOSSISM

ITS A BUSINESS LIKE ANYTHING ELSE.
— BOSS PENDERGAST

Cartoon by Daniel Fitzpatrick, *St. Louis Post-Dispatch*, June 23, 1936. *Courtesy State Historical Society of Missouri*

ment to put more men to work on Missouri roads and instituted a modest relief program designed primarily to help farmers with the purchase of seed and feed. Despite these efforts, the nation and the state sank deeper each year into the economic morass.

From 1929 to 1933 the gross national product (GNP)—the total of all goods and products produced—dropped from $104.4 billion to $74.2 billion. Per capita GNP—the total GNP divided by population—decreased from $857 to $590. A dramatic indicator of the depression's severity can be found in unemployment figures, which rose from 3.1 percent in 1929 to one-fourth of the total labor force in 1933. Farm prices plummeted from $13 billion to $5.5 billion. Bank failures increased steadily.

Gloomy statistics showed that Missouri's economy declined similarly. In the state's largest industrial area, St. Louis, the value of manufactures dropped 56 percent while wages went down 53 percent. Whereas a family might grow enough food for their own table, the low prices received for wheat (38¢ per bushel), corn (33¢ per bushel), and cotton (6¢ per pound) put little money into their pockets. By 1932 many Missouri farmers had lost their farms and either turned to tenant farming or moved to the cities to swell the ranks of the unemployed. Bewildered by the distressing events of the past four years, Missourians searched for new leaders and new answers to their problems.

The New Deal Comes to Missouri

In a defeatist mood in 1932, the Republicans nominated Herbert Hoover for a second term. In the Missouri delegation at the Demo-

cratic National Convention Tom Pendergast, Kansas City's powerful
political boss, endorsed Missouri's "favorite son," Senator James A.
Reed, but did not discourage a small, energetic group of progressives
who backed the nomination of Governor Franklin Delano Roosevelt
of New York. On the crucial third ballot, the Missouri delegation increased its vote for Roosevelt, which indicated that the New York governor was not only holding but gaining in support. From there
Roosevelt went on to win the nomination and to promise, "I pledge
you—I pledge myself to a new deal for the American people."

Although crippled by polio when he was nearly forty, Roosevelt
conducted a spirited campaign, impressing the people with his confidence. When he came to St. Louis in October, thousands heard him
promise to ease the crisis, although he gave no specific blueprint of
how he proposed to do it. But in 1932 promises were enough. Missouri voters handed him the largest plurality of any presidential candidate to that date. In the state election the Democratic Judge Guy B.
Park of Platte City beat the Republican Edward H. Winter of Jefferson
City for the governorship. All Democratic candidates for Congress
were elected, and Democrats regained control of both houses of the
state legislature. The Missouri voters made it quite clear that they
wanted Democrats, instead of Republicans, to head their nation and
state for the next four years.

Following the election, the lame-duck Hoover and Congress sat
helplessly by as the nation continued its downward slide. Park, who
assumed the governorship in January 1933 before Roosevelt took office on March 4, acted on the state budget but delayed other matters
until the new President and Congress began their terms. Everyone
waited eagerly to see what kind of a "new deal" Roosevelt planned to
offer.

The Bank Holiday

The New Deal was not a well-planned, well-organized program but
rather a series of reforms and experiments developed on almost a
day-to-day basis to get the American economy moving again. Often
described by critics as a man mounting a horse and riding off in six
directions, the New Deal evolved from two basic ideas: first, when
the nation is confronted with a depression, federal and state governments have a responsibility to intervene and to use their powers and
resources to relieve the crisis; second, relief programs in the form of

government jobs or direct handouts should be created to help the people most in need. In dealing with the nation's crisis, New Dealers believed that it was better to act immediately than to plan indefinitely. When a drowning man cries, "Help!" the people safe on shore do not call a summit meeting to decide what to do. Rather they respond at once to save him. Two days after his inauguration, President Roosevelt made his first move to save a desperate nation. He declared a "Bank Holiday," closing the doors of banks and lending institutions throughout the nation. Three days later Congress enacted legislation which provided that banks could reopen for business when federal examiners found them solvent. From 1929 to 1933 more than 300 banks and trust companies had failed in Missouri, wiping out depositors' bank accounts and savings and eroding public confidence in such institutions. The Bank Holiday gave bank officials time to take the necessary steps toward placing their institutions on sound financial footing. By mid-March most of Missouri's banks and other financial institutions had reopened for business. Later that year Congress passed a bill that created the Federal Deposit insurance Corporation, a government agency that insured deposits up to $2,500. Now recognized as an important step toward economic recovery, the Bank Holiday panicked many Missourians at the time as they found only a few pieces of change in their pockets to operate households and businesses until the banks reopened.

The Efforts of Governor Park

Elected in the Democratic resurgence of 1932, Governor Guy B. Park made it clear that the economic and social conditions in Missouri demanded cooperation with New Deal programs. He requested that state funds be raised to match those of the federal government for relief purposes. The state legislature responded by passing an "occupation tax" (a tax of 0.5 percent on the gross receipts of persons engaged in the sale of goods and services). When this tax failed to procure sufficient funds, the legislature repealed it in 1934 and replaced it with a one percent sales tax.

Park also urged state leaders to take advantage of the Public Works Administration (PWA) through which funds were made available for the repair of public buildings. The PWA would make an initial grant, and then the state would borrow the rest at a low-interest rate spread over a fifteen-year period. State bonds were sold to pay off

Cartoon by S. J. Ray, *Kansas City Star,* March 10, 1933. *Courtesy State Historical Society of Missouri*

the federal loan. Approximately $16 million was spent between 1934 and 1939. This program saved old buildings, constructed new ones, provided employment, and encouraged the local economy.

The Plight of the Farmers

Although no class escaped the effects of the Great Depression, farmers and urban workers suffered the most. Heat and drought added to the farm problem in the 1930s. The summer of 1936 broke all records with nearly forty days of temperatures above 100° (38° Celsius). A plague of grasshoppers took what few crops survived the heat. Many New Deal measures passed by Congress were designed to relieve farm distress. The Agricultural Adjustment Act sought to raise farm prices by government control of farm production. The Farm Credit Administration made loans available at low-interest rates and with small payments. The Resettlement Administration relocated farmers and provided temporary loans for feed, seed, and livestock, while the Farm Security Administration assisted low-income families with loans and technical knowledge. These last two organizations assisted some 113,000 farm families between 1935 and 1939, although admittedly the sharecroppers and tenant farmers did not fare as well. While New Deal farm programs did relieve some of the agricultural distress, the farmers continued to have a rough time as long as the depression lasted.

One of the beneficial acts to Missouri farmers was the establishment of the Rural Electrification Authority (REA). When it began in 1935, only about 10 percent of rural families in Missouri and the nation had electricity. Funds were appropriated for electric cooperatives and privately owned electric companies to bring electricity to rural areas. By 1939 over 33,000 farms were being served by REA. The electrification of rural areas modernized farm life, extended the farmer's day and made life more convenient and easier. Many hardworking Missouri farmwives breathed prayers of gratitude for electricity, a convenience which their city cousins had had for years.

The Unemployed

Industrial employment in Missouri dropped from 370,787 in 1930 to 141,196 in 1933. Although statistics can tell us how many people were out of work during the depression, they cannot measure the personal hardships, the mental anguish, the emotional strain, and family tensions that the unemployed experienced. Putting people to work was not only crucial to economic recovery but also to the recovery of the people's confidence in themselves and in a better America. St. Louis and Kansas City were not the only areas affected by the high rate of unemployment. Small towns and rural hamlets across the state felt the impact as well. In April 1933, Congress established the Civilian Conservation Corps (CCC) under the supervision of the War Department. For $30 a month young men enlisted in the CCC to work on roads, dams, conservation, and reforestation projects. The state legislature cooperated with the federal government by passing a bill authorizing the government to purchase land in Missouri up to 25,000 acres for post offices, government offices, hospitals, sanatoriums, fish hatcheries, game or bird preserves, and reforestation. It is estimated that between 1934 and 1942 the CCC planted trees on 10,000 acres and removed cull and low-value trees on 115,000 acres of national forests in the state.

One month after the passage of the CCC legislation, Congress established the Federal Emergency Relief Administration that was designed to pump relief funds directly into state and local governments. Added to state funds, these were used to hire the unemployed to rebuild and to renovate some of the state's charitable and penal institutions.

One of the most strongly criticized and yet one of the most suc-

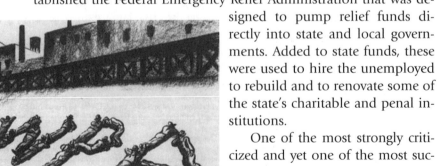

"WPA," cartoon by Daniel Fitzpatrick, *St. Louis Post-Dispatch,* February 26, 1936. *Courtesy State Historical Society of Missouri*

cessful programs established by Congress during the New Deal era was the Works Progress Administration (WPA). Angrily condemned by the New Deal haters as a giveaway to "shovel leaners" and "ditchdiggers," the WPA put people to work at paving roads, laying sewer lines and building dams, parks, playgrounds, and swimming pools. About one-fifth of the total funds appropriated went for community service projects that employed jobless teachers, artists, musicians, actors, and writers. One example of a WPA project was the compilation of a state history, *Missouri: A Guide to the "Show Me" State*, for the Highway Department by WPA authors and researchers. An extension of the WPA, the National Youth Administration (NYA), provided part-time employment for young people that kept them off the streets and made it possible for many to remain in high school and college. In all fairness, the WPA and the NYA did not permanently solve the unemployment problem, but they benefited many Missouri communities, pumped some money back into the economy through the wages they paid, and restored in many people a sense of pride that comes from doing a worthwhile job.

Black urban workers in St. Louis and Kansas City and black sharecroppers in the cotton-growing area of the Bootheel were especially hard hit in the 1930s. Not only did they have to endure the harsh economic conditions of the day, they also had to struggle against a racial discrimination that made them "the last to be hired and the first to be fired." Although black militancy had existed earlier, the 1930s saw it increase as more and more blacks strove for economic opportunity. In St. Louis, for example, blacks organized a boycott against a chain store that had a "lily white" hiring policy. A black preacher, Owen H. Whitfield, organized black sharecroppers in the Bootheel to call attention to their sad conditions. When their landlords evicted them in the winter of 1939, they camped along the roadside, prompting one newspaper cartoonist to call them "Missouri Refugees." The

"Missouri Refugees," Cartoon by Daniel Fitzpatrick, *St. Louis Post-Dispatch,* **January 13, 1933.** *Courtesy State Historical Society of Missouri*

state provided some emergency relief; but more important, their dramatic nonviolent act, which continued for nearly ten days, caught the attention of the federal government and unleashed a number of plans and projects for the area. The Resettlement Administration relocated many of them, while the Farm Security Administration made loans and grants, built communities with low-cost housing, and encouraged cooperatives.

Social Security

One of the lasting contributions of the New Deal was the Social Security Act of 1935. A very complex law, the act provided for both a pension and an unemployment compensation system. Only about half the states had such plans at the time. The Missouri General Assembly had passed a pension bill earlier that same year that provided $30 monthly for those over the age of seventy who could not earn a living. Married couples would receive $45. The funds for this program fell far short of what was needed, and only about two-thirds of those entitled to them received anything prior to 1937. During Governor Lloyd C. Stark's administration in the late 1930s, the two programs were merged, and Missouri also took steps to establish aid to dependent children and child welfare assistance as well as a retirement plan for public school teachers.

The Repeal of Prohibition

The depressed economic conditions throughout the nation added impetus to those forces opposed to the Eighteenth Amendment, which had outlawed the manufacture, sale, and use of intoxicating beverages. As mentioned in Chapter 14, prohibition had been a continuing issue in both national and state politics during the 1920s. For all of the high hopes of its original sponsors, this reform had created impossible enforcement problems and led to a vast underworld network to supply liquor to those who refused to give it up. This spawned other crime in its wake. Both Kansas City and St. Louis had their bootlegging gangs that left a trail of violence.

When Congress proposed the Twenty-first Amendment to repeal the Eighteenth, Missourians voted overwhelmingly for a state convention to approve the measure. Enough states ratified the amendment that it became effective by the end of the year. In the aftermath of repeal, the General Assembly levied taxes on the sale of liquor and

WHAT THE MISSOURI LEGISLATURE DID ABOUT RELIEF

set up a Liquor Control Board to authorize licenses for its distribution. Repeal revived the breweries in St. Louis and Kansas City, contributing greatly to their depression-plagued economy.

The Pendergast Machine in State Politics

By the 1930s Tom Pendergast, Kansas City's political boss, was at the height of his power. Studies of machine politics in American urban history have shown that the power of the boss was sustained in part by what he and his cronies did for the people that government did not do. Like other city bosses, Pendergast fed the poor at Christmas, provided coal for the widow down the street, found a job for a man out of work, and gave a helping hand to a person down on his luck, but always in exchange for their votes and support. Boss Tom's lieutenants, such as City Manager Henry F. McElroy and certain members of the city council, carried out his orders while the machine openly violated election laws, intimidated honest voters, and delivered large blocks of votes to handpicked candidates. Members of the Kansas City Police Department took bribes and looked in the other direction as crime, vice, and the rackets thrived in Missouri's second largest metropolitan area. Pendergast's enterprises feasted off lucrative city contracts.

While conducting his business from an unassuming office building at 1908 Main Street, Boss Tom and his family lived a lordly life in Kansas City's fashionable Country Club district. From the notorious north side, the machine's political tentacles reached octopus-like across the state and, so his enemies said, right into the state capitol at Jefferson City, which they dubbed "Uncle Tom's Cabin." In the early days of the New Deal, Pendergast partially controlled federal relief funds and property. Matthew Murray, for example, the WPA adminis-

trator for Missouri, was handpicked by Pendergast. This not only enhanced his political power in Kansas City, but also attracted to a degree the support of the urban middle class.

In the early 1930s, the Pendergast machine had a lot to say about
who ran for public office and who was elected. Although Boss Tom
didn't always win, ambitious Democratic politicians sought his aid
and support. When Francis Wilson, the Democratic gubernatorial
candidate in 1932, died unexpectedly before the election, the Democratic State Committee, with Pendergast's sanction, selected Judge
Guy B. Park of Platte City to replace him. A veto by Governor
Caulfield of the Democratic legislature's effort to reapportion congressional seats forced all of Missouri's congressman to run "at large"
on a statewide basis that year. Most of them beat a path to "Uncle
Tom's" office to gain his strategic support. In the election the Democrats won big, and the Kansas City vote added greatly to the margin
of victory. Pendergast's only setback came when his candidate for the
Senate, Charles M. Howell, was defeated by Bennett Clark, son of
former House Speaker Champ Clark. The younger Clark won the
nomination with the support of the American Legion and the St.
Louis voters to show an embarrassed Pendergast that despite its political power his machine was not invincible.

Senator Harry S Truman

Again in 1934 the machine showed its power when Pendergast withdrew his support from the longtime and efficient State Superintendent of Schools Charles A. Lee in the Democratic primary and gave it
to Lloyd W. King. Lee's defeat was a kind of political punishment for
what the machine called ingratitude. It was in the primary contest for
the Democratic nomination for United States senator, however, that
Pendergast's influence significantly helped open one of the most remarkable chapters in recent American political history.

The three men seeking the Democratic nomination for United
States senator from Missouri in 1934 were Congressman Jacob
Milligan of Richmond, Congressman John Cochran of St. Louis, and
Judge Harry S Truman of Independence. Senator Clark supported
Milligan while Cochran's strength came largely from St. Louis city
and county. Although backed by Pendergast, Judge Truman was not
his first choice. He simply emerged as the "available man" after others refused to run. In a lively campaign, the three politicians criss-
crossed the state, slung some mud, and drummed up support wher-

ever they could find it. As expected, the Kansas City/Jackson County vote rolled in giving Judge Truman a large majority, but what was unexpected was his surprising showing in rural areas and small towns. This wasn't to be the last time Truman would shock the political pros. To assume that the Pendergast machine was solely responsible for his nomination and subsequent election to the Senate is to ignore important factors about Truman and his skill as a campaigner. Well known throughout the state by county judges, Truman also appealed to farmers and small-town inhabitants. A political race seemed to trigger in this man a combative spirit that transformed him into an indefatigable, tell-it-like-it-is campaigner who could capture the attention of the voters. He had no difficulty in defeating the Republican incumbent, Senator Roscoe C. Patterson.

The new senator had been associated with the Pendergast machine since the early 1920s. A veteran of World War I, he had seen service in France with the Thirty-fifth Division. After the war a short-lived men's clothing business in downtown Kansas City proved unsuccessful. Then Pendergast, whose nephew Jim had served with Truman in France, picked him to run for Jackson County judge in the Eastern District. Truman won in 1922, lost reelection two years later, but in 1926 was chosen presiding judge of the Jackson County Court with Pendergast's help. He held that position until his election to the Senate, building an impressive and clean record as an administrator.

Truman was a solid if not spectacular senator. He served on the Interstate Commerce Committee, kept in touch with voters back home, supported President Roosevelt, and never wavered in his loyalty to the Democratic party. In 1940 he was reelected and during World War II chaired the important Committee to Investigate National Defense Programs. The Truman Committee saved the government about $1 billion and increased defense production during World War II. Its work stamped Truman as a persistent, patriotic politician and earned him national attention. Truman never disavowed his link with the infamous Pendergast machine, but he was never implicated in its scandalous activities.

Reform Continues Under Governor Stark

In the national election of 1936 President Roosevelt crushed his Republican challenger, Governor Alfred M. Landon of Kansas, in a lopsided victory that saw forty-six of forty-eight states go Democratic. In Missouri, Roosevelt received 60.8 percent of the popular vote to

Landon's 38.1 percent. In the governor's race Lloyd C. Stark, the well-known president of Stark Nursery near Louisiana, won over Jesse W. Barrett of St. Louis, while Democrats retained control of the state legislature. Although the Pendergast machine reluctantly supported Stark, the Democratic candidate stoutly declared his independence of the Kansas City political boss.

The advances in the area of social security during Governor Stark's administration have already been noted. Toward the end of his term in office, progress in health-care facilities was made with the building of Ellis Fischel State Cancer Hospital at Columbia. Today it is one of the leading cancer hospitals in the nation, not only in the treatment of cancer victims but also in cancer research. A state hospital at Rolla opened in 1940 for the treatment of the dreaded eye disease trachoma.

At the 1936 election Missourians ratified an amendment to the state constitution that created a bipartisan commission to oversee the wildlife resources of the state. Although the Missouri Fish and Game Commission met with opposition in the beginning, its work has done much to protect and to conserve Missouri's wildlife resources. Conservationists in the 1930s laid the groundwork for future actions to save the land, to encourage soil conservation, to protect forest resources, to set aside wilderness areas, to clean up polluted streams, and to protect fresh water in the state. In view of the present-day concern about natural resources and conservation practices, the efforts of conservationists in the 1930s increases in historical significance.

The Fall of Tom Pendergast

During the Stark administration cracks began to appear in the Pendergast machine. With the 1936 election approaching, the *Kansas City Star* declared that an honest election in Jackson County was impossible. Aroused by machine bullies and thugs who bribed election officials, threatened honest voters, sent degenerates from one polling booth to another, and even cast votes for fictitious people and dead ones, angry Kansas City citizens laid a long list of grievances before Judges Albert L. Reeves and Merrill E. Otis of the United States District Court following the election. The judges summoned a grand jury to investigate the charges of election fraud. Moved along by the dogged determination of District Attorney Maurice M. Milligan, the grand jury brought in 278 indictments, resulting eventually in 78 jail and penitentiary sentences and fines totaling $60,000.

The big fish, Tom Pendergast, escaped the grand jury's net, but Governor Stark further damaged the machine's prestige by withdrawing patronage and appointing men and women to state jobs independently of the boss's preferences. When Stark refused to appoint machine men to the Kansas City election board, he delivered another blow to the boss's control of Kansas City. A scandal emerged, involving State Superintendent of Insurance Robert Emmett O'Malley, a Pendergast figure, and Pendergast himself was exposed. Governor Stark fired O'Malley, who was later sent to prison. A federal investigation of Pendergast's involvement reached its climax in 1939 when the boss pleaded guilty to income tax evasion. A fine of $10,000 and a sentence of fifteen months in the federal penitentiary at Leavenworth, Kansas, ended Pendergast's rule of Kansas City. The Democratic machine in Kansas City/Jackson County remained a force to be reckoned with in local politics, but it no longer held Missouri's western metropolis in a political stranglehold.

"Man Shall Not Live By Bread Alone . . ."

Never was the biblical truth that "man shall not live by bread alone" truer than it was during the Great Depression. Admittedly economic and political matters held center stage for the people of Missouri, but life in the thirties was not without its style, social concerns, and cultural achievements. The severe economic conditions placed a great strain on family life, resulting in divorces, desertion, and runaway children. Nevertheless, most families rallied and met the challenge of the Great Depression together.

PEOPLE STILL ATTENDED CHURCH

Urban church membership increased during the thirties in Protestant, Catholic, and Jewish congregations; while rural churches found it increasingly difficult to keep their doors opened. New religious sects and denominations appeared on the church scene in Missouri. The Assemblies of God, with headquarters in Springfield, grew rapidly as their strong emphasis on personal salvation and the pentecostal experience attracted many converts. The Church of Christ, a group that splintered from the Christian Church (Disciples of Christ) at the turn of the century, began to establish congregations throughout Missouri as did the Reorganized Church of Jesus Christ Latter Day Saints, with its headquarters at Independence. The Unity School of Christianity, which later built an impressive plant in Lee's Summit, began to gain a nationwide following. Attendance at church activities mushroomed as people sought the solace and strength that comes from public worship and prayer meetings and enjoyed the social activities provided by various church organizations.

Some ministers preached the need for personal commitment and the promise of a better life in heaven while others became more concerned about religion's answer to the social and economic ills that beset American society. Among the latter was the Protestant clergyman and theologian Reinhold Niebuhr. Born in Wright City on June 21, 1892, Niebuhr attended Eden Theological Seminary in St. Louis, and completed two graduate degrees at Yale University. Ordained to the ministry of the Evangelical Synod of North America, Niebuhr's first charge was a church located in the industrial area of Detroit. In short time, his defense of working people and thoughtful comments on applied Christianity caught the attention of religious leaders around the country. Joining the faculty of Union Theological Seminary in New York in 1928, he taught, wrote books, and influenced several generations of Protestant pastors, Catholic priests, and Jewish rabbis. Two of his most profound works were written during the Great Depression, *Moral Man and Immoral Society* (1932) and *An Interpretation of Christian Ethics* (1935).

PEOPLE STILL SENT THEIR CHILDREN TO SCHOOL

As a result of the declining birth rate during the 1920s and 1930s, there was a decrease in public school enrollment not only in Missouri but throughout the nation. However, a higher percentage of the school-age population attended school. Missouri, like other states, had strengthened its school attendance laws and stiffened their enforcement. Public schools adjusted to the depression by cutting expenses, firing teachers, and eliminating impractical courses from the curriculum. The story is told that one superintendent of schools stored supplies in his vault, dispensing them only when his teachers could show sound reasons for their use.

During the low point of the depression, 1932–33, college and university enrollments dropped. From then until the beginning of World War II the rate of increase in the college population climbed steadily. Students who made it to college remained there because so few jobs were available beyond the ivied walls. The rah-rah atmosphere of the 1920s did not disappear from the campuses, but generally students seemed more serious minded, bent on finding out what had happened to America and seeking solutions to the current problems.

PEOPLE STILL LISTENED TO THE RADIO

When WEW at St. Louis University began broadcasting in 1921, it was the second such station in the United States. Radio became a leading industry and a major form of entertainment in a short period of time. For people living through the Great Depression, the radio had two advantages: first, it was cheap to operate and, second, one could stay at home to listen to it. The radio, after it warmed up, could transform a living room into a theater, a concert hall, a dance pavilion, or a vaudeville stage. President Roosevelt used the radio for nationwide broadcasts called "fireside chats" to bolster confidence and to seek the support of the people for New Deal programs. Radio personalities reached star status comparable with those of the Broadway stage and motion pictures. One of the most popular was Mary Margaret McBride, who had been born in Paris, Missouri. After attending William Woods College and the School of Journalism at the University of Missouri, she launched a career in broadcasting, developing a program that was especially appealing to women. Her autobiography, *How Dear to My Heart* (1940), contained many memories of her early days in Missouri.

PEOPLE STILL WENT TO THE MOVIES

Motion pictures were the most popular form of entertainment during the 1930s. Grandiose theaters were constructed in the downtown areas of St. Louis and Kansas City while every neighborhood and small town had its "motion picture show." The most popular movies were westerns, adventure stories, lavish musicals, and lighthearted romantic comedies. Clearly an escapist form of entertainment, the movies seldom dealt with controversial or realistic themes and invariably had a happy ending.

A number of Missourians went to Hollywood, the capital of the motion picture industry in the 1920s and 1930s, and became actors, script writers, technicians, extras, directors, and producers. The most famous was Walt Disney. Born in Chicago, Disney lived for a short time in Marceline, attended the old Benton School in Kansas City, and began his art and movie career there by producing advertising films. Leaving the Midwest for Hollywood, Disney made his first successful animated cartoon in 1928. Creating a simple cartoon character, Mickey Mouse, who has entertained millions for nearly eighty years, Disney made a vast fortune and expanded his endeavors into many different avenues of the show business industry. In 1937, he elevated the cartoon to a serious art form with the full-length motion picture *Snow White and the Seven Dwarfs.* He later branched out into amusement parks, building Disneyland in California and Disney World in Florida.

PEOPLE STILL CONSIDERED BASEBALL
"AMERICA'S FAVORITE PASTIME"

In the early thirties the St. Louis Cardinals had one of the most colorful and exciting teams in professional athletics. Winning the World Series in 1930, 1931, and 1934, they did their share of entertaining Missouri baseball fans. Composed of a cast of zany characters and superb athletes, they earned the nickname, "The Gas House Gang." Their pitching ace, Jerome "Dizzy" Dean, won thirty games in 1934, and then went on to the World Series where he and his brother Paul won four games between them.

Since black athletes had not crossed the racial barrier into the white-dominated big leagues, they had their own league in which they competed. In Kansas City the Monarchs played great baseball for black and white fans alike. Although they did not receive the publicity that their white counterparts in St. Louis did, they may well have had the greatest pitcher in the history of the sport. Satchel Paige threw a baseball like a bullet or as soft "as a butterfly." By the time blacks were admitted to the big leagues after World War II, Paige was past his prime, but Bill Veeck, the enterprising owner of the St. Louis Browns, brought him up to pitch in relief. Even then he could baffle the batters for a few innings with an assortment of pitches that modern ballplayers call "junk." Both Paige and Dizzy Dean now have places in Baseball's Hall of Fame.

Miniature golf became a popular pastime, as did croquet, midget auto racing, and basketball. One of the most enjoyed sports was softball, which could be played on a sand lot, in a park, or even a city street. The popularity of softball was enhanced when some of the parks and playgrounds were lighted for evening activities. The University of Missouri produced a number of outstanding teams in football and basketball before World War II erupted. One of the university's greatest teams, quarterbacked by Missouri's first All-American, Paul Christman, rose to national prominence in the early 1940s.

PEOPLE STILL WROTE BOOKS AND OTHERS READ THEM

Among the many Missouri authors of the 1930s was Fannie Hurst, who spent her childhood in St. Louis. Educated at Washington University, she became a popular novelist with such books as *Back Street* (1931) and *Imitation of Life* (1933).

Iowa-born MacKinlay Kantor drew from his years as a Missouri resident to write the story of a foxhound that had a yelp like a bugle sound in the haunting novel, *The Voice of Bugle Ann* (1935).

Henry Bellaman, a Fulton native, wrote *King's Row* (1940), a novel based on his memories of his hometown at the turn of the century. The book angered many Fultonians at the time, but entertained thousands when it was made into a major motion picture starring Ronald Reagan.

Laura Ingalls Wilder wrote a series of children's books based on her early experiences on the frontier. These stories inspired the popular television program "Little House on the Prairie." Moving to the Mansfield area in the Ozarks in 1894, the author lived there until her death in 1957.

Thomas Hart Benton, discussed earlier, wrote an autobiography, *An Artist in America* (rev. ed. 1983), that gives an absorbing account of his travels during the Great Depression years.

The End of the New Deal

When World War II started in 1939, creating demand for American goods and agricultural products, the New Deal era came to an end. In Missouri, New Deal programs and policies had assisted farmers and urban workers, although they did not solve all their problems. Politically, the New Deal put together a coalition of farmers and workers within the Democratic party that made it a major voice for liberal causes and values in the state and nation for nearly four decades.

Missourians benefited from a number of lasting New Deal reforms: the REA, Social Security, unemployment compensation, and the Federal Deposit Insurance Corporation to mention only a few.

Concrete evidence of the New Deal can be seen literally in many courthouses, schools, and other public buildings constructed during the 1930s by those desperate for a chance to work, who were paid with federal/state funds. Few communities in Missouri were not improved by WPA projects or by the work of the young workers in CCC.

The New Deal did much to make government more sensitive to the needs of those who were distressed, downtrodden, and dispossessed. Many social reforms that came later had their roots in the attitude that there are times when people may need a little help before they can help themselves. Although the New Deal did not completely defeat the Great Depression, Missouri was better off in 1939 than it had been in 1933.

Election of 1940

In the presidential contest of 1940, Missourians again showed their appreciation for Roosevelt although the question of a third term noticeably reduced his plurality. Senator Truman waged a strong campaign in the Democratic primary for renomination against the popular Governor Stark and District Attorney Maurice Milligan, who had successfully prosecuted the Pendergast machine. Stark and Milligan divided the reform vote sufficiently to allow Truman to overcome his association with the discredited Pendergast machine. Voters in Kansas City, in the wake of the Pendergast scandals, established a nonpartisan government that would last till 1959. Truman won an exciting primary by 8,000 votes and then went on to beat his Republican opponent, Manvel Davis, by a considerable margin.

The Democrats retained control of both houses of the General Assembly, but after eight years of Democratic governors, Republican

Governor Forrest Donnel. *Courtesy State Historical Society of Missouri*

Forrest C. Donnell of St. Louis won a slim victory over Lawrence McDaniel for the governor's chair. The Democrats charged that numerous irregularities had given the governor's race to the Republican, while the Republicans counter charged that Democrats were out to steal the election. On February 19, 1941, the Missouri Supreme Court ruled that Donnell was the governor, and a week later his inauguration took place. But the Democrats would not give up. They set up a legislative committee to review the election results. A recount was held, and somewhat embarrassingly for the Democrats, Donnell increased his vote total. The disgruntled Democrats accepted defeat as the Republican Donnell moved into the governor's mansion.

World War II

Governor Donnell's administration was dominated by World War II, which had broken out in September 1939. When the war began, the United States took essentially the same position that it had taken when world war commenced in 1914, that of neutrality. Despite its good intentions to stay out, the United States was drawn inevitably into the war. On December 7, 1941, Japan attacked Pearl Harbor, the American naval base in Hawaii. In the aerial combat above Pearl Harbor, an American aviator, Lieutenant George Whitman, became the first Missourian to die in the war. Describing the Japanese attack as a "day of infamy," President Roosevelt the next day asked Congress for a declaration of war against Japan. The President requested a declaration of war on Germany on December 11, 1941, after that nation had declared war on the United States.

In addition to the thousands of young men and women from Missouri who served in the ranks of the armed services, a number of native sons rose to positions of high command. One of the most successful commanders was General Omar Bradley, who grew up in Randolph County. He served with distinction in North Africa and then commanded the Twelfth Army in Germany. Bradley worked closely with General Dwight D. Eisenhower in the invasion of France and Germany in 1944 and 1945. Three Missourians who attained the rank of admiral during the war were Admiral Thomas S. Combs, who commanded the USS *Yorktown*; Admiral Charles A. Lockwood; and Admiral Freeland A. Daubin, all of whom came from Lamar in Barton County. On the home front Senator Truman carried on his work as chairman of the Committee to Investigate National Defense Programs. Donald M. Nelson of Hannibal headed the War Production Board, which spurred the production of goods necessary for the war effort. Thomas Hart Benton painted scenes portraying the brutality of the Nazi war machine that were used effectively for propaganda purposes by the United States government.

Defense contracts to Missouri industries amounted to $4.2 billion. Missourians manufactured arms and ammunition, firebrick, and medical supplies, and mined minerals essential for the war effort. Missouri farmers raised more produce, while in the cities and small towns people turned vacant lots and backyards into "victory" gardens. The use of rationing coupons for sugar, meat, gas, rubber, and other scarce items became for Missouri shoppers a part of the everyday routine. Camps for training army and air force personnel were established at Jefferson Barracks near St. Louis, Fort Leonard Wood in Pulaski County, and Camp Crowder at Neosho. A number of colleges and universities housed the V-12 program designed to train young men to be commissioned officers. Seldom a day passed when Missourians were not engaged in a drive to collect paper, scrap metal, lard, or to sell war bonds.

Unlike World War I, Missourians were united behind the new war effort. The harassment of German Americans that occurred during World War I was not repeated; however, Japanese Americans on the west coast were placed in detention camps during the war for fear of their disloyalty and the possibility of their aiding the enemy. At the same time, Japanese-American soldiers served in the U.S. armed forces. When Japan signed the final terms of surrender on board the battleship USS *Missouri* in Tokyo Bay on September 2, 1945, all Missourians rejoiced and looked forward to a postwar world with high hopes for a better life.

Suggestions for Reading

Richard S. Kirkendall, *A History of Missouri, Vol. 5, 1919–1953*, Columbia, University of Missouri Press, 1986, gives an interesting account of the Great Depression in Missouri. Not only does *Missouri: A Guide to the Show-Me State*, Lawrence, University of Kansas Press, 1986, contain much state history to 1940, but it is an example of one of the WPA projects that provided jobs for unemployed school teachers, writers, and researchers. The following articles deal with a variety of aspects of the Great Depression: Rowena May Pope, "The Hungry Years," *Missouri Historical Review*, January 1984; J. Christopher

Schnell, Richard J. Collings and David W. Dillard, "The Political Impact of the Depression on Missouri, 1919–1940," *Missouri Historical Review,* January 1991; Edgar D. McKinney, "Sharing Hardship: The Missouri Ozarks During the Great Depression," *Gateway Heritage,* Fall 1992; and Amber R. Clifford, "To the Disinherited Belongs the Future," *Missouri Historical Review,* October 1993. These two journals, together with *The Bulletin* contain numerous other articles on education, religion, literature, sports, and culture during the 1930s.

The best study of the Pendergast machine is Lawrence H. Larsen and Nancy J. Hulston, *Pendergast!,* Columbia, University of Missouri Press, 1997. Robert Ferrell, *Truman and Pendergast,* Columbia, University of Missouri Press, 1999, covers their relationship. See also Ferrell, ed., *The Kansas City Investigation: Pendergast's Downfall, 1938–1939,* Columbia, University of Missouri Press, 1999. Three articles in the *Missouri Historical Review* provide significant material on the relationship between the social structure of Kansas City and the Pendergast machine: Donald B. Oster, "Reformers, Factionalists and Kansas City's 1925 City Manager Charter," April 1978; Patrick McLear, "'Gentlemen, Reach for All': Toppling the Pendergast Machine," October 2000; and McLear, "Pendergast vs. Stark: Politics, Patronage, and the 1938 Supreme Court Democratic Primary," April 2002. Sherry Lamb Schirmer, *A City Divided: The Racial Landscape of Kansas City, 1900–1960,* Columbia, University of Missouri Press, 2002, gives further information on the politics of that city, while Virginia Laas, ed., *Bridging Two Eras: The Autobiography of Emily Newell Blair, 1877–1951,* Columbia, University of Missouri Press, 1999, shows how a woman activist influenced politics during the period. Three excellent biographies of President Harry Truman are David McCullough, *Truman,* New York, Simon & Schuster, 1992, and Alonzo L. Hamby, *Man of the People: A Life of Harry S Truman,* New York, Oxford University Press, 1995, and Robert H. Ferrell, *Harry S Truman: A Life,* Columbia, University of Missouri Press, 1994. Also helpful is Richard S. Kirkendall, ed., *The Harry S. Truman Encyclopedia,* Boston, G. K. Hall & Co., 1989. For Truman's own account of his rise in American politics, see *Harry S. Truman, Memoirs, Vol. 1,* New York, Doubleday, 1955.

SIXTEEN

The 1945 Constitution and Postwar Politics

The Constitutional Convention of 1943–44

By the early 1940s Missourians of diverse opinions agreed that the state's constitution was outdated. The constitution of 1875 had been amended over fifty times, and government under it had become unwieldy. Led by St. Louis members of the National Municipal League, a movement to secure a constitutional convention received support from farm organizations, labor unions, the Missouri State Teachers Association, and the League of Women Voters. It also had the general support of both Republican and Democratic leaders. Proponents of governmental change sought to make the executive branch more effective by strengthening the governor's powers. They wanted tax collections centralized in one department, greater compensation for legislators so as to attract better candidates, and revision of suffrage and election laws.

An amendment to the 1875 constitution required that after 1922 the question of whether to hold a constitutional convention be submitted to the electorate at least every twenty years. In the general election of 1942, by a 100,000-vote majority, voters approved calling a convention, although almost one-third of those casting ballots expressed no opinion on the proposition.

The constitution of 1875 provided a cumbersome method for the selection of convention delegates. Each senatorial district would be entitled to two, one Republican and one Democrat, while fifteen would be chosen from the state at large on a nonpartisan basis. Presumably the delegates from the senatorial districts were to be chosen by local mass meetings. In most cases, however, selection was left to party leaders.

Candidates for the at-large positions qualified by a petition process and were listed without party affiliation. Thirty-four were declared eligible for the fifteen positions, whereupon the two major parties entered the supposedly nonpartisan process by agreeing on a slate of preferred candidates. The slate was given preferential placement on the ballot by Secretary of State Dwight Brown to the dismay of other political groups.

The League of Women Voters also had drawn up a slate of candidates. Although eight names appeared on both slates, the league challenged the Brown arrangement but lost in the Missouri Supreme Court. The state political committees blitzed the state with over one million sample ballots showing their preferences and elected all of their at-large candidates in the April 1943 voting. Notwithstanding the generally partisan manner of their selection, most of the delegates were able persons who performed effectively. And the new constitution they drafted retained this method for the future.

Eighty-three delegates assembled in Jefferson City on September 21, 1943. Almost all of them were politically experienced. Forty were lawyers, and the remainder came from a variety of occupations. Only two delegates were women, and no blacks were delegates. They elected Robert Blake of Webster Groves as their president and established twenty committees to deal with various aspects of revision.

The Executive Branch

When the convention completed its deliberations on September 28, 1944, it presented a document to the voters that called for significant reorganization of state government. For example, those favoring change succeeded in placing the frequently overlapping duties of the nearly ninety agencies, departments, boards, bureaus, and commissions, which had administered the state, into five executive departments with provision for as many as five more. Departments of Revenue, Education, Highways, Conservation, and Agriculture were named in the constitution. The legislature in 1946 added Departments of Public Health and Welfare, Business and Administration, Corrections, and Labor and Industrial Relations. The constitution gave the governor better control over administration by making him responsible for assigning all agencies, boards, etc., to the appropriate executive department.

The new document also increased the governor's power to administer the state's finances by empowering him to appoint the director of revenue and the director of the budget and to dismiss them when he pleased. He retained the item veto on all budgetary items except funds appropriated for schools or money designated to pay the principal and interest on the public debt. The item veto allows the executive to veto specific provisions in a proposed budget while accepting all other parts of it.

Reformers failed in their attempts to create a state executive branch that resembled its counterpart in the federal government. They had sought to give the governor power to appoint the secretary of state, attorney general, and treasurer, keeping only the lieutenant governor and auditor as elected officials. Such a change would have consolidated too much executive power in the governor's office for the conservatives. The reformers did succeed in specifying that the auditor, secretary of state, and state treasurer could perform only duties that were germane to their offices.

While desiring to increase the governor's appointive power in the higher echelons of government, those seeking change wanted to eliminate the spoils system or patronage appointments in the various departments. After debate and maneuver, the convention decided to base employment in eleemosynary and penal institutions on competitive examination. The 1946 legislature created the State Merit System with control over the Departments of Public Health and Welfare, Corrections, and certain personnel divisions. Despite continuing promises to eliminate patronage, only about 40 percent of state government jobs came under the classified service.

The General Assembly

Efforts to reform the General Assembly were not as successful. While some suggested a unicameral or one-house legislature as more efficient and economical than the bicameral system, the convention did not discuss it seriously. It continued the system of allowing each county one seat in the lower house and thereby perpetuated rural domination of the legislature. As late as 1964, the 233,354 people living in the forty-two least populous rural counties had as many representatives as the 2,076,290 individuals residing in St. Louis, St. Louis County, and Jackson County.

Change came quickly thereafter when a federal court in Kansas City ordered the Seventy-third General Assembly of Missouri to create a system of reapportionment that complied with the dictum of one man, one vote. That order came as a result of the United States Supreme Court's ruling that malapportionment in state legislatures violated the equal protection clause of the Fourteenth Amendment (*Baker* v. *Carr*, 1962). In 1966 Missouri voters ratified a constitutional amendment providing for a reapportionment commission composed of one Democrat and one Republican from each congressional district appointed by the governor to divide the state into 163 compact districts as equal in population as possible. A similar system had already been established by the constitution for determining the thirty-four senatorial districts after each decennial census.

The Courts

The judicial branch of state government underwent limited but significant change. The constitution retained the nonpartisan court plan that the state's voters had approved in 1942. This provides for a nonpartisan judicial commission to create a list of three qualified individuals for each vacancy on the "supreme court, court of appeals or in the office of circuit or associate judge within the City of St. Louis and Jackson County." The governor must appoint one of the individuals on the list to fill the position. After an appointee has served a minimum of twelve months in office, that appointee's name is presented to voters at the next general election without party designation, and they decide whether to retain the person for a twelve-year term.

The constitution expanded the supreme court's power by making it responsible for establishing rules of practice and procedure for lower courts. It can transfer judicial personnel from courts with light case loads to those with heavy work schedules. It is also responsible for trying the impeachments of all state officers except a governor or a member of its court. In addition, the constitution broadened the high court's power to review decisions made by courts of appeals. At the local level the constitution abolished the office of justice of the peace, eliminated the fee system of paying judges' salaries, and created the magistrate court system. All judges in the judicial branch had to be licensed attorneys. In 1976 magistrate judges were replaced by associate circuit judges with expanded powers.

In summary, the 1945 constitution made no fundamental changes in the structure of state government. The principle of separation of powers among legislative, executive, and judicial branches, with each unit checking the other two, was retained. It eliminated obsolete provisions, extended women's rights to include jury service, stated that freedom of speech and press included other means of communication, guaranteed the right of employees not working for a governmental agency to organize and bargain collectively, and retained segregated schools.

Ratification

Only four of the delegates refused to sign the completed document that was submitted to the voters for approval on February 27, 1945. Sixty of the proconstitution delegates organized themselves into a public relations committee and circulated a half million copies of the new constitution with a detailed explanation appealing for support. Newspapers across the state endorsed it, as did Governor-elect Phil M. Donnelly. Opposition to the constitution proved weak, ineffective, and centered in rural Missouri. Apparently rural voters feared that the new document would enhance the political, economic, and social power of the state's urban population. In a light vote, Missouri's citizens approved it by 312,032 to 185,658, with margins of better than three to one in the metropolitan areas.

Reorganization Since 1945

Major efforts have been made to further update and improve state government about every ten years since the adoption of the new constitution. Recognizing added responsibilities and a continuing inefficiency of state government in spite of constitutional changes, Governor Phil M. Donnelly in 1953 asked the General Assembly to create a commission to study governmental operations. It responded by authorizing a State Reorganization Commission composed of four senators, four representatives, and four members appointed by the governor. The "Little Hoover Commission," as it was called (after the federal reorganization commission headed by former President Herbert Hoover), reported in January 1955 with 112 recommendations.

The thrust of the recommendations was to streamline the administration of state government by placing responsibility for certain functions in appropriate departments and by providing for better coordination and planning of state operations. A large proportion of the suggestions were passed through the legislature, and some were incorporated into state government through executive order. One change alone netted the state $18 million within the first ten years after it was made: the treasurer began to place idle funds in interest-bearing accounts. Another recommendation, adopted during Governor James T. Blair's administration, placed the Division of Budget and Comptroller under the governor's direct supervision. A third recommendation, which the General Assembly approved during Governor John Dalton's term, was the creation of a Commission on Higher Education. It sought to define state educational needs and to eliminate program duplication in state-supported universities and colleges.

In 1963 the General Assembly provided for another State Reorganization Commission. Its organization duplicated its predecessor's, except that the governor and chief officers of the senate and house of representatives were added as ex officio members. On January 12, 1965, Governor Warren E. Hearnes and the General Assembly received the commission's report, which made 115 recommendations. Forty of them repeated suggestions that the Little Hoover Commission had made, which indicated that the two study groups had similar thrusts and that some of the earlier problems had not been solved.

To streamline and make government more efficient, the commission recommended and the General Assembly created an administrative services section in the Division of Budget and Comptroller for the purpose of overseeing data processing, records management, and other services for all state agencies. Similarly, to give better direction to the executive branch, the second commission repeated a recommendation made by the first to allow governors to succeed themselves. Governor Blair had favored such a provision, and Governor Hearnes strongly endorsed the change. The General Assembly approved a constitutional amendment to allow a maximum of two terms for governor; the voters ratified the amendment in 1965. Three years later Hearnes became the first to benefit from the change when he sought and won reelection. Although other recommendations were incorporated into governmental operations in succeeding years, much still needed to be done.

Christopher S. Bond succeeded Governor Hearnes in 1972 and oversaw many of those changes. Under the Omnibus State Reorganization Act of 1974, thirteen departments and an Office of Administration became responsible for administering state government. Five of the departments were new; one old department was divided into

two separate ones; one had been created in 1972 through constitutional amendment; and the remainder had existed before the reorganization.

An act of the legislature had already created the Office of Administration, which began functioning on January 15, 1973. It was designed to coordinate the efforts of the other departments and illustrates the desire to streamline governmental operations. The Divisions of Accounting, Budget, Design and Construction, Electronic
Data Processing, Personnel, Purchasing, and State Planning and
Analysis come under its umbrella.

The names and duties of the new departments reflected the scope
of responsibilities assumed by the state. For example, under the Department of Social Services were the Divisions of Family Services,
Health, Corrections, Youth Services, Probation and Parole, Veterans
Affairs, and Special Services. In the Division of Special Services, there
were Offices of Aging, Comprehensive Health Planning, Manpower
Planning, and Economic Opportunity. This largest of departments
suggests the many aspects of life for which the state had assumed
some responsibility.

In a related area—mental health—officials elevated the problems
of the mentally ill, mentally challenged, and developmentally dis-
abled from division to department status. In so doing, the state reflected its increased commitment to improving conditions for those
suffering from those afflictions.

Reorganization divided the old Department of Education into
two departments: Elementary and Secondary Education, and Higher
Education. Over the latter presides a coordinating board, which grew
out of the Commission on Higher Education recommended by the
Little Hoover Commission. It was given greater powers for planning
and coordinating all of Missouri's higher education establishment,
planning and overseeing all federal programs for postsecondary education, and keeping the governor and General Assembly informed
about the status of higher education in the state. Both the need for
dividing education into two departments and the creation of a coordinating board reflected how large and complex Missouri's educational establishment had become.

Similarly, the new Department of Natural Resources consolidated
the work of fourteen separate agencies. Under divisions of Environmental Quality, Parks and Recreation, Planning and Policy Development, Research and Technical Information, and Administrative Services, the department oversees the use of the state's resources. The
creation of a Division of Environmental Quality reflected citizen

concern with maintaining and improving the quality of the state's air, water, and land resources.

Other departments included Consumer Affairs, Regulation and Licensing; Labor and Industrial Relations; Public Safety; Revenue; Agriculture; Conservation; Highways; and Transportation. It would appear that creating a Department of Highways and a Department of Transportation represented duplication of effort, whereas the thrust of reorganization was to eliminate overlapping and inefficiency. Yet the commitment to the automobile and the elaborate system of roads and highways needed to support it is demonstrated by continuing department status for highways. Other means of transportation—aviation, railroads, mass transit, and waterways—achieved the status of only divisions within the Department of Transportation. In 1980 those two departments were combined as a result of a referendum passed in 1979. Gas shortages since 1974 suggested to voters the increased importance of alternate forms of transportation.

Although partisanship certainly has influenced the reshaping of state government since ratification of the 1945 constitution, the process of trying to make state government responsive to citizen needs has progressed under both parties. The most recent reorganization of state government occurred under a Republican governor and Democratic-controlled legislature. Voters, of course, have played an important role in changing government through initiative petitions by ratifying forty-eight constitutional amendments and by deciding who should administer the state.

Some of the expansion of state government has come from the necessity to comply with federal regulations so that the state could qualify for federal funds. Over the years the federal government has held out the attraction of money to secure changes in states and cities. In activities as different as highway construction and education, the carrot of federal funds has stimulated developments in the states. Of course, the threat of withholding federal funds has also been used to cause changes in state and local government.

Election of 1944

During the 1940s the electorate spoke with an unclear voice, but with a Republican accent. Both parties could find some comfort in the results of the 1944 election. The state senate fell to the Republicans, and Forrest C. Donnell won a seat in the United States Senate, albeit by less than 2,000 votes. The Democrats gained fourteen seats in the state house of representatives, not enough for a majority; cap-

Cartoon by S. J. Ray, *Kansas City Star,* April 15, 1945. Kansas City Star, *courtesy State Historical Society of Missouri*

tured the governorship with Phil M. Don-nelly's victory over Jean Paul Brad-shaw of Lebanon; and won every other statewide race. They also took two congressional seats from the Republicans, giving them six of thirteen.

An important factor in the 1944 election was Harry S Truman's position as the vice-presidential candidate on the Democratic ticket. Truman had won election to the United States Senate in 1934, after having served as a judge of the Jackson County Court. In 1940 he barely won the Democratic primary but won an easy victory over Manvel Davis of Kansas City in the general election. During the next four years Truman made a national reputation for himself as chairman of the Committee to Investigate National Defense Programs. In 1944 President Roosevelt wanted to dump his vice-president, Henry A. Wallace, and at the suggestion of advisers selected Truman to run with him. The ticket of Roosevelt and Truman carried Missouri; it was the fourth straight time that the Democratic president had carried the state. Worn out after three terms of fighting depression and war, Roosevelt suffered a stoke and died on April 12, 1945, which catapulted Truman into the White House, the first Missourian to hold the office of president. To replace Truman in the Senate, Governor Donnelly appointed fellow Democrat Frank P. Briggs of Macon.

Election of 1946

The presence of President Truman in the White House did little to aid Missouri's Democrats in the 1946 election. It was a Republican year nationally as the party swept into control of both houses of Congress on a tide of postwar unrest. Missouri's voters followed the national trend. Indeed, 1946 must be considered a high tide of Missouri Republicanism. The state's voters selected Republican James P.

Kem of Kansas City over incumbent Frank Briggs to occupy Truman's old Senate seat. It was the first time that two Republicans had represented Missouri in that body since Radical Reconstruction. The party won nine congressional seats, an increase of two, and added nineteen seats to its majority in the lower house of the General Assembly. The nineteen-to-fifteen Republican margin in the senate remained the same.

One factor in the Missouri Republican success was the defection of black voters from the Democratic party. Blacks left Democratic ranks because of dissatisfaction with the distribution of Democratic patronage and New Deal jobs during the preceding years. They also became disturbed by the absence of progress in ending racial discrimination under the Democrats and by the slurs hurled at their race by Democratic politicians such as Theodore Bilbo of Mississippi. Thus, Republican Aloys Kaufmann won the mayoral contest in St. Louis during 1946 and carried predominantly black wards with as much as 65 percent of the vote. With the help of black voters, Kaufmann's party also controlled the city's Board of Aldermen.

Election of 1948

Harry Truman and the state's Democrats lured black voters back to the fold in 1948 and halted the Republican surge. Blacks returned to the party because of Truman's civil rights record and social welfare program. The President had issued executive orders banning discrimination in federal employment and in the military services and made it clear that he would enforce them. He led the Democratic ticket in seeking reelection. During the campaign Truman ripped the Republican-controlled Eightieth Congress for failing to pass legislation that would benefit farmers and other groups. According to Thomas Soapes, a student of the period, the Missouri Farmers Association publicized Truman's charges and Congressman Clarence Cannon's statement that the Republicans "had kicked the farmer in the 'slats.'" Missouri farmers obviously responded, for what had been a rural Republican majority in previous elections became a Democratic one.

While Truman whistle-stopped across the country haranguing the Republicans in his inimitable style, his Republican opponent, Thomas Dewey of New York, ran a lackluster campaign. The polls showed that Dewey had a substantial lead, and he had no desire to upset the electorate. State Republicans followed suit.

During the campaign the Democratic gubernatorial candidate, Forrest Smith of Richmond, was linked in newspaper stories with Charles Benaggio, a Kansas City politician and former Pendergast associate. In 1946 Benaggio had been accused of vote fraud, but the ballots in question disappeared from the county courthouse before he could be prosecuted. Newspapers alleged that in 1948 Benaggio had secured between $100,000 and $200,000 from a Chicago-based syndicate that he was associated with and donated it to Smith's campaign. For the contribution Smith was supposed to reduce restrictions on the Kansas City and St. Louis police forces so that gambling in the state could flourish. The allegations were never proved. After his election Smith kept a tight reign on gambling. In April 1950, Benaggio and a lieutenant were murdered; the crime was never solved.

The voters disregarded charges of corruption and elected Smith, a former state auditor, over Murray E. Thompson by 223,028 votes. They responded with equal enthusiasm to the rest of the Democratic ticket. The Democrats swept every statewide office, won control of both houses of the legislature, and defeated their opponents in twelve of the thirteen congressional elections. Truman carried the state by 150,000 votes.

Democratic Dominance, 1948–68

Democrats controlled both houses of the General Assembly from 1948 until 2000, when Republicans won a majority in the Senate.

In 1950, for example, Thomas Hennings, Jr., of St. Louis defeated Republican incumbent Donnell for his United States Senate seat during what was nationally a Republican year. indeed, no Republican won statewide office again until 1968, when John Danforth of St. Louis County defeated incumbent Norman H. Anderson from the same county for the post of attorney general. Democrats controlled the

Senator John C. Danforth.
Courtesy Congressional Office

lower house of the General Assembly until 2002 and occupied a large majority of the state's declining number of congressional seats. Reapportionment in the United States House of Representatives reduced Missouri's congresspersons to eleven after 1950, to ten after 1960, and to nine after 1980. Both of Missouri's seats in the United States Senate were occupied by Democrats until John Danforth captured one in 1976. At the presidential level, General Dwight D. Eisenhower carried Missouri for the Republicans in 1952, and Richard Nixon took the state in 1968 and 1972.

The extent of Democratic supremacy between 1952 and 1968 is detailed in the following election returns for President, governor, and United States senator.

1952

PRESIDENT

Dwight D. Eisenhower (R)	959,429
Adlai E. Stevenson (D)	929,830
Difference	29,599

UNITED STATES SENATOR

Stuart Symington (D)	1,008,521
James P. Kem (R)	858,170
Difference	150,351

GOVERNOR

Phil M. Donnelly (D)	983,169
Howard Elliott (R)	886,270
Difference	96,899

1956

PRESIDENT

Adlai E. Stevenson (D)	918,273
Dwight D. Eisenhower (R)	914,289
Difference	3,984

UNITED STATES SENATOR

Thomas C. Hennings, Jr. (D)	1,015,936
Herbert Douglas (R)	785,048
Difference	230,888

GOVERNOR

James T. Blair (D)	941,528
Lon Hocker (R)	866,810
Difference	74,718

1960

PRESIDENT

John F. Kennedy (D)	972,201
Richard M. Nixon (R)	962,221
Difference	9,980

UNITED STATES SENATOR

Edward V. Long (D)	999,656
Lon Hocker (R)	880,576
Difference	119,080

GOVERNOR

John M. Dalton (D)	1,095,200
Edward G. Farmer (R)	792,131
Difference	303,069

1964

PRESIDENT

Lyndon B. Johnson (D)	1,164,344
Barry Goldwater (R)	653,535
Difference	510,809

UNITED STATES SENATOR

Stuart Symington (D)	1,186,666
Jean Paul Bradshaw (R)	596,377
Difference	590,289

GOVERNOR

Warren E. Hearnes (D)	1,110,651
Ethan A. H. Shepley (R)	678,919
Difference	431,732

1968

PRESIDENT

Richard M. Nixon (R)	811,932
Hubert H. Humphrey (D)	791,444
Difference	10,488

UNITED STATES SENATOR

Thomas F. Eagleton (D)	887,414
Thomas B. Curtis (R)	850,544
Difference	36,870

GOVERNOR

Warren E. Hearnes (D)	1,072,805
Lawrence K. Roos (R)	691,797
Difference	381,008

Senator Stuart Symington. *Courtesy State Historical Society of Missouri*

Stuart Symington

Except for President Truman, Stuart Symington influenced national politics more than any other Missourian after World War II. He entered government service in 1945, after having risen to the presidency of Emerson Electric in St. Louis. President Truman appointed him the first secretary of the air force in 1947, and he served the federal government in several other capacities until 1952, when he won a seat in the United States Senate.

While in the Senate, Symington held key positions on the important Foreign Relations and Armed Services committees. As a respected expert on military affairs and member of those committees, he exercised great influence on the country's foreign policy and military posture during the crucial years of the cold war. In 1960 his name was placed in nomination for President at the Democratic National Convention, but he failed to become his party's candidate. After serving in the Senate for twenty-four years, he retired in 1976.

Civil Rights Movement

During Symington's years in the Senate, a fundamental change occurred in the nation's race relations. Missouri, because of its mixed racial history, was less dramatically affected than Deep South states but nevertheless was forced to make important adjustments. The most important change involved efforts to end segregation in both the public and parochial schools.

As noted above, the 1945 constitution continued the practice of separating the races in the public schools. In 1947 the Roman Catholic church under the leadership of Archbishop Joseph E. Ritter committed itself to desegregate its schools in the city of St. Louis, reflecting a movement within Catholicism that had begun in the late

1930s. The church anticipated the United States Supreme Court's de-segregation ruling by seven years. In *Brown et al. v. The Topeka Board of Education* (1954), the court ruled that separate schools for black and white children were inherently unequal and thus unconstitutional.

St. Louis desegregated its public high schools almost immedi-ately after the Brown decision and created a plan to institute com-plete desegregation within two years. Kansas City and other cities re-sponded almost as quickly. In southeast Missouri, however, where ra-tios between blacks and whites were more equal and Deep South tra-ditions prevailed, segregation was still being practiced a decade after the *Brown* decision.

Moreover, in many instances, particularly in large cities where over 80 percent of Missouri's blacks lived, residential patterns meant that schools might be desegregated by law but segregated in fact. To attack that problem, federal authorities and local officials resorted to busing and other devices. To date most black students in the state continue to attend predominantly black schools, but that circum-stance is the result of economic and social factors, not the law.

Since World War I Missouri residents have been informed about the lack of economic and educational opportunity afforded blacks by a vigorous black press led by the *St. Louis Argus* and the Kansas City *Call.* Black newspapers often quoted black politicians and other lead-ers who were willing to speak out on racial issues. After 1870 Mis-souri blacks never lost their right to vote, and they have used their ballots to reward those who defended their interests and to punish those who attacked them. Residential segregation in both Kansas City and St. Louis also meant that certain districts would contain black majorities, and that those votes could be used to elect blacks to the state legislature, a practice begun in the 1920s and maintained intermittently over the years.

In the first post–World War II election, black voters in St. Louis sent two black Republicans and a black Democrat, and black voters in Kansas City sent a black Democrat to represent them in the state house of representatives. Except for the election of Theodore D. McNeal of St. Louis as the first black to ever serve in the state senate in 1960, black representation in the General Assembly made little progress during the next sixteen years. In 1962, St. Louis districts had four black Democrats representing them, and one Kansas City dis-trict also had a black Democratic representative. One-man, one-vote reapportionment during the middle 1960s caused greater urban rep-resentation in the General Assembly and increased the number of predominantly black districts. Thus by 1978 St. Louis had two black senators, Franklin Payne and J. B. (Jet) Banks, and nine black representatives, and Kansas City had four black representatives in the General Assembly. All of the black legislators were Democrats, as the vast majority of black Missourians cast their votes for that party after 1948.

African-American Leaders

Among those who have provided important leadership both in and out of the legislature since World War II are Theodore McNeal and William Clay. McNeal worked as a labor organizer during the 1930s, becoming an American Federation of Labor official. As noted above, he became the first black to serve in the state senate. After two terms he chose not to run for reelection in 1968. Governor Hearnes appointed him to the University of Missouri Board of Curators in 1970. Twenty years earlier he would have been denied admittance to the university because of his race. In 1973 Governor Christopher S. Bond appointed him president of the St. Louis Board of Police Commissioners, the first black to head the board.

Similarly, in 1968, William Clay became the first African American to represent Missouri in the United States Congress. A St. Louis native who graduated from St. Louis University, Clay began his political career as a member of the Board of Aldermen, serving between 1961 and 1964. He became Democratic committeeman in the Twenty-sixth Ward in 1964 and used that position as his political base in winning a seat in the U.S. House of Representatives. He won election to Congress from the First District, which includes a part of St. Louis and St. Louis County and is the

Congressman William Clay, the first African American from Missouri elected to U.S. House of Representatives. *Courtesy William Clay*

only congressional district in Missouri with a population more than 50 percent black. In Congress, Representative Clay has been a spokesman for black, urban, and liberal causes. He led in organizing the Congressional Black Caucus, a group of African-American representatives who seek to advance black causes through unity. Voters returned Clay to Congress in each subsequent election, until he retired in 2000. His son, William Lacy Clay, Jr., won his old seat in the 2000 election.

Civil Rights Legislation

Black political protest and participation in state government prompted the creation of the Missouri Commission on Human Rights in 1957, a formal expression of the state's obligations in protecting civil rights. The General Assembly in 1961 made those obligations more specific by passing the Fair Employment Practices Act. The act prohibited discrimination in employment because of race, color, sex, creed, or ancestry. Pressure from the federal government and black citizens contributed to the passage of a Public Accommodations Act in 1965. The act prohibited Missouri businesses that offered goods and services to the general public from practicing discrimination. The Seventy-sixth General Assembly in 1972 passed a Fair Housing Law prohibiting discrimination in buying, selling, or renting housing.

Civil Unrest in Kansas City

Despite better political representation and provisions outlawing discrimination, blacks still faced continuing problems of poverty and unequal opportunities in Missouri. The deep frustrations that these conditions produced in blacks became forcefully obvious in Kansas City in 1968. The assassination of Martin Luther King, Jr., and subsequent failure of officials to close schools on the day of his funeral ignited a powder keg of frustration in Kansas City's black youth. On April 9, police fired tear gas into a group of one thousand African Americans, mostly youths, who had marched to city hall to protest the decision to keep schools open. The police action sparked three days of violence as young blacks set fires and looted stores on Kansas City's east side. Police, state troopers, and three thousand National Guards finally quelled the disturbance. When the major disorder ended on April 12, property loss through fires and looting totaled in the millions; 360 were in jail; 79 were injured; and 6 blacks were dead.

The Women's Movement

Women shared with blacks increased political representation after World War II. In 1946 four women were elected to serve in the state House of Representatives; by 1962 that number had declined to three. Active political organization during the 1960s resulted in women winning eight seats in 1970 and thirteen in 1976. Also in 1972 Mary L. Gant of Kansas City became the first woman to win election to the state senate. She was joined in 1976 by Harriet Woods of St. Louis County. Only three of the women in the General Assembly in 1976 were Republicans; all of them came from the state's two largest metropolitan areas.

Until 1990, the only woman to have represented Missouri in the United States Congress was Leonor K. Sullivan of St. Louis. After attending Washington University, she married Congressman John B. Sullivan. Between 1941 and 1951, she served as his campaign manager and administrative assistant. After his death in 1951, Mrs. Sullivan won his seat in the House of Representatives, which she held until her retirement in 1976. In 1990, Joan Kelly Horn defeated incumbent Jack Buechner from St. Louis County for his seat in the House of Representatives.

Election of 1968

It is difficult to know how much effect the women's movement, anti-Vietnam protest, and the rioting in Kansas City and in other cities across America had on the election of 1968. One thing is clear: George Wallace of Alabama, a candidate for President on the American ticket who used the term *law and order* as code words for smashing demonstrators and denying blacks any more progress, drew 206,126 votes out of the 1,806,502 cast in Missouri's balloting for President. He took sufficient votes away from Democratic candidate Hubert Humphrey in traditionally Democratic areas to allow Richard Nixon, the Republican candidate, to carry Missouri.

The 1968 election also produced the first Republican victory in a contest for statewide office since 1946. John Danforth, a youthful, handsome lawyer from a wealthy St. Louis family, won the race for attorney general. He polled 891,498 votes to his opponent's 819,365. Governor Hearnes was reelected by over a million votes, however, and other Democrats fared equally well. Democratic Lieutenant Governor Thomas F. Eagleton defeated Congressman Thomas B. Curtis for a seat in the United States Senate, although the race was close.

The beginnings of a Republican resurgence were clearly evident two years later when Danforth lost a fairly close election for United States senator to the distinguished Democratic incumbent Stuart Symington, but another young, wealthy, Republican lawyer won statewide office. Christopher S. Bond of Mexico defeated incumbent Haskell Holman by 200,000 votes in the race for auditor. Bond won by more votes than any other Republican who had ever contested for statewide office. Missourians seemed to be tiring of a "politics as usual" attitude that had come increasingly to dominate Democratic thinking. Like voters nationally, they proved willing to split their ballots and vote less on a straight-party basis.

Election of 1972

With two Republicans in statewide office and two-term Governor Warren E. Hearnes required by the constitution to retire, Republican chances seemed bright in 1972. In an era of resurgent conservatism, those chances were enhanced when the national Democratic ticket nominated liberal George McGovern of South Dakota as its candidate for the presidency, and the state Democratic party chose lackluster, fifty-four-year-old Edward L. Dowd of St. Louis as its gubernatorial nominee. Republican opportunities received further aid during the summer when McGovern chose and then dropped Senator Thomas Eagleton as his running mate. McGovern's action came after Eagleton disclosed that he had suffered medical difficulties, depression, and fatigue during various times in his career. For the first time eighteen-year-olds were allowed to vote in the presidential election, and the Republicans nominated a youthful slate of candidates led by State Auditor Christopher Bond.

The results of the election suggested to the *St. Louis Post-Dispatch* that the Republicans had capitalized on the youth movement. Bond won by 185,000 votes. He became the state's youngest governor at thirty-three and its first Republican chief executive since 1944. Attorney General Danforth defeated James E. Spain of Salem by more than 440,000 votes, while Republican William C. Phelps of Kansas City

Christopher Bond. *Courtesy State Historical Society of Missouri*

eked out a victory over Jack J. Schramm of St. Louis for lieutenant governor. The entire Republican slate was aided by President Richard M. Nixon's strong victory over George McGovern. Nevertheless, Democrats James C. Kirkpatrick of Windsor and James I. Spainhower of Marshall won election as secretary of state and state treasurer, respectively. Republican successes at the state level were not translated into majorities in the General Assembly or in the congressional delegation.

In campaigns for United States senator and state auditor in 1974, the Democrats won fairly easy victories. Thomas Eagleton retained his Senate seat over Thomas B. Curtis by a vote of 735,433 to 480,900, while George Lehr of Kansas City won the auditor's post over John Ashcroft of Springfield, who had been appointed to fill out Bond's term after he became governor, by a vote of 635,855 to 562,564.

Election of 1976

As the 1976 election approached, it appeared that neither party would dominate but that the Republicans had an excellent chance to retain the governorship and be competitive in the contest for United States senator. After Stuart Symington announced his retirement, three prominent Democrats vied for their party's nomination to replace him: Congressman Jerry Litton of Chillicothe, former Governor Warren Hearnes of Charleston, and Congressman James Symington of St. Louis County, the departing senator's son. The Republicans united behind Attorney General Danforth as their challenger.

Both the primary and general elections held surprises. In the hotly contested Democratic senatorial primary, Jerry Litton won the nomination only to be killed with his wife and children in a plane crash on election night. Warren Hearnes, second in the balloting, then became his party's candidate. To oppose Bond in the governor's race, Democrats chose "Walking" Joe Teasdale, a former prosecuting attorney of Jackson County who earned his nickname by walking across the state in his unsuccessful bid for the 1972 nomination for governor. Danforth defeated Hearnes handily, but underdog Teasdale scored a stunning upset, defeating Bond by 12,500 votes.

According to political analysts, Teasdale gave voters a fresh face, youth, and good looks. A reputation as a reformer and an instinct for the political jugular vein added to Teasdale's assets. During the campaign the Kansas Citian hammered at high utility bills and taxes, while Bond discussed reorganization and prenatal care. Teasdale accused Bond of being too friendly with corporations and greedy utilities, and the incumbent made inadequate responses.

A Republican strategist noted that Bond made a mistake when he agreed to debate the lesser known challenger on television. He criticized Bond and his organization for failing to campaign harder, particularly in Teasdale's home territory of Kansas City. He also noted that Bond lost support when he backed Gerald Ford's renomination for the presidency because a significant element of his party endorsed Ronald

Reagan. Last, he asserted that Teasdale's sophisticated television blitz during the last ten days of the campaign tipped the balance in his favor. No doubt a combination of these factors caused Bond to lose and Teasdale to win.

In other races incumbent Republican Lieutenant Governor William Phelps won a narrow victory over Richard Rabbitt, and Republican John D. Ashcroft beat James G. Baker for attorney general. Democratic presidential candidate Jimmy Carter carried the state over Gerald R. Ford, and Kirkpatrick

Governor Joseph P. Teasdale. *Courtesy State Historical Society of Missouri*

and Spainhower retained their posts as secretary of state and treasurer, respectively. The Democrats continued to control both houses of the General Assembly by large majorities. The Republicans added Jerry Litton's congressional seat in northwest Missouri to the one they held in southwest Missouri, but still trailed the Democrats eight to two.

The 1976 election returns unquestionably proved that Missouri politics had become competitive again. Between 1948 and 1968, the important election in Missouri occurred in August, when Democrats decided through their primary who would hold state office. Since 1968, a revitalized Republican party has made the November election the decisive one.

Regardless of the political fortunes of Missouri's strong two-party system, it is clear that Missourians have come to expect a great deal of state government, including comprehensive, public educational facilities. The constitution of 1945 provided the structure for more responsible and responsive government, and successive reorganizations of the executive branch made it possible to administer the expanded system. Finally, African Americans and women have increased their importance in the state's politics by winning more offices and raising their voices on behalf of their constituencies.

Suggestions for Reading

Every student should consult the Constitution itself, which is available from the secretary of state's office. The Official Manual of Missouri, published biennially by the secretary of state, is crammed with information about state officials, elections, and historical data. The proceedings of the constitutional convention are contained in the *Journal of the Constitutional Convention of Missouri, 1943–1944.*

Richard S. Kirkendall, *A History of Missouri, Vol. V, 1919 to 1953,* Columbia, University of Missouri Press, 1986, deals with this period in detail. Articles in the *Missouri Historical Review* which shed light on a variety of topics are: Henry J. Schmandt, "The Personnel of the 1943–1944 Missouri Constitutional Convention," April 1951; Donald Mrozek, "Organizing Small Business During World War II: The Experience of the Kansas City Region," January 1977; Thomas T. Soapes, "The Fragility of the Roosevelt Coalition: The Case of Missouri," October 1977; Donald J. Kemper, "Catholic Integration in St. Louis, 1935–1947," October 1978; Robert H. Ferrell, "A Visit to the

White House, 1947: The Diary of Vic H. Householder," April 1984; George Cook Morgan, "India Edwards: Distaff Politician in the Truman Era," April 1984; Stanley B. Botner, "Missouri's Governors: A Composite Portrayal," July 1985; Patricia L. Adams, "Fighting for Democracy in St. Louis: Civil Rights during World War II," October 1985; Brenda S. Heaster, "Who's on Second: The 1944 Democratic Vice Presidential Nomination," January 1986; Sharon Pedersen, "Married Women and the Right to Teach in St. Louis, 1941–1948," January 1987; Richard S. Kirkendall, "Truman and Missouri," January 1987; Arvarh E. Strickland, "The Plight of the People in the Sharecroppers' Demonstration in Southeast Missouri," July 1987; Thomas Soapes, "Barak Mattingly and the Failure of the Missouri Republicans," January 1993; Mary K. Dains, "Forty Years in the House: A Composite Portrait of Missouri Women Legislators," January 1993; Roy D. Blunt and Gary R. Kremer, "The 1954 Prison Riot and the Image of the Highway Patrol," April 1993; Thomas D. Wilson, "Chester A. Franklin and Harry S Truman," October 1993; Thomas Eagleton and Diane L. Duffin, "Bob Hannegan and Harry Truman's Vice Presidential Nomination," April 1996; Debra K. Pitts, "Stuart Symington and Harry S Truman: A Mutual Friendship," July 1996; Joel P. Rhodes, "It Finally Happened Here: The 1968 Riot in Kansas City, Missouri," April 1997; and Will Sarvis, "Black Electoral Power in the Missouri Bootheel, 1920s–1960s," January 2001. A pertinent article in *Gateway Heritage* is Amy M. Pfeiffenberger, "Democracy at Home: The Struggle to Desegregate Washington University in the Postwar Era," Winter 1989–1990.

A book that suggests a lot about rural Missouri in the period is Gwen Hamilton Thogmartin and Ardis Hamilton Anderson, *The Gazette Girls of Grundy County: Horse Trading, Hot Lead, and High Heels*, Columbia, University of Missouri Press, 1994. A delightful biography of baseball hero Stan Musial is James N. Giglio, *Musial: From Stash to Stan the Man*, Columbia, University of Missouri Press, 2001.

The *Kansas City Star* and the *St. Louis Post-Dispatch* ably cover Missouri's politics. Black newspapers such as the *St. Louis Argus*, the *St. Louis Sentinel*, the *Kansas City Call*, and other daily, county, and weekly newspapers can be profitably consulted for special and local information

There are a number of books about President Truman, including his *Memoirs*, 2 vols. New York, Doubleday, 1955–1956. Cabell Phillips, *The Truman Presidency*, New York, Macmillan, 1966, is a comprehensive treatment. Alonzo L. Hamby, *Beyond the New Deal: Harry S Truman and American Liberalism*, New York, Columbia University Press, 1973, focuses on Truman and the liberal movement but includes significant material on other matters as well. During the 1990s, three important biographies of Harry S Truman were published: David McCullough, *Truman*, New York, Simon and Schuster, 1992; Alonzo L. Hamby, *Man of the People: The Life of Harry S Truman*, New York, Oxford University Press, 1995; and Robert H. Ferrell, *Harry S Truman: A Life*, Columbia, University of Missouri Press, 1996. See also Ferrell, *Choosing Truman: The Democratic Convention of 1944*, Columbia, University of Missouri Press, 1994.

SEVENTEEN

An Urbanizing Missouri: Postwar Economic Development

T he trend discernible in 1930 of fewer Missourians engaged in agriculture and more employed in manufacturing and service industries accelerated during and after World War II. As a result of these economic changes, urban areas experienced impressive population growth, while rural areas suffered corresponding loss.

Population Shifts, 1940–90

Each decennial census between 1940 and 1990 recorded population growth for Missouri, but at the end of the period the state held a smaller percentage of the nation's population than it had at the outset. While the state's population grew from 3,784,664 to 5,117,073 during those fifty years, Missouri fell behind the national growth rate. In 1940, the state claimed 2.9 percent of the country's population; by 1970 it held only 2.3 percent of the nation's people. Between 1980 and 1990, Missouri's population grew by 4.1 percent, while the nation's population grew by 10.2 percent.

The United States Census Bureau defines an urban area as a community that has a population of at least 2,500. In 1940 just over half of Missouri's population, 51.8 percent, met that classification. By 1950 the urban segment of the state's people had increased to 61.5 percent, or by almost 10 percent. This segment increased by an additional 4.9 percent during the next ten years and stood at 66.6 percent. The 1970 census recorded for Missouri an urban population of 70.2 percent. Thus, 420,170 fewer people lived in rural Missouri in 1970 than did in 1940. Since 1970, 79 percent of the state's population growth has occurred in the ten counties around Kansas City and

St. Louis. About an equal rate of growth took place in the five counties near the Lake of the Ozarks and Table Rock Lake. Only Boone,
Greene, Christian, Newton, Jasper, and Cole counties, of the remainder, experienced significant growth. The remaining ninety counties
in the state increased by a total of only 1,000 people. Agricultural
counties north of the Missouri River experienced the greatest loss of
population.

Missouri's farm population had peaked in 1900, when 2 million
people lived on 284,886 farms. By 1945 the number of farms had
decreased by 14.7 percent, while the average farm size had increased
by 16 percent. During the period 1945 through 1960, this pace accelerated as the number of farms declined by 30.6 percent and the average farm size increased by 35.8 percent. The average farm size grew
from 125 acres to 197 acres during that sixty-year period. In 1975
Missouri counted 175,000 farms, with an average of 235 acres per
farm. Between 1975 and 1990 these trends continued, as surviving
farmers increased their acreage and ever more Missouri farmers left
the land during the difficult 1980s.

The Urbanization of Missouri

YEAR	PERCENT URBAN	PERCENT URBAN
1940	51.8	48.2
1950	61.5	38.5
1960	66.6	33.4
1970	70.2	29.8

Changes in Agriculture

While each census reported fewer people tilling the soil, it also
showed increased agricultural production. Mechanization and advances in plant development, livestock raising, and fertilizers help to
explain how a dwindling population has been able to produce more
goods. The use of more and improved tractors, combines, and other
labor-saving machines allowed fewer farmers to work more acres. For
example, between 1930 and 1950 the number of tractors in Missouri
increased by just under 100,000. Increasing the scale of operation
while diminishing labor costs reduced the cost of production per agricultural unit, and small farmers could not compete. Both they and

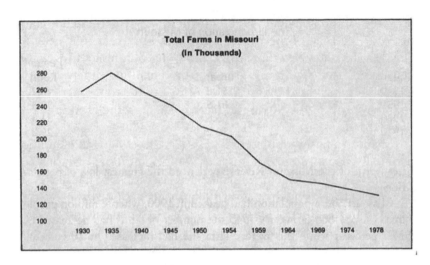

Source: Missouri Department of Agriculture

agricultural laborers were squeezed off the land because of technological change. One Bootheel county, Pemiscot, lost 32 percent of its
population after cotton-picking machines came into widespread use
during the 1960s.

The University of Missouri College of Agriculture has been instrumental in many of Missouri's farming advances. Besides educating
teachers and supervising the county extension program, which in
turn provides a variety of information to farmers and their families,
the university has led in agricultural research. Its first experiment station was established in 1888 in Columbia. Now there are agricultural
experiment centers in various locations in the state that work on particular problems in the individual area.

Agricultural Production: Crops

Corn yields per acre between 1939 and 1977 illustrate the advances
in production. In 1939 each acre of corn yielded an average of thirty
bushels. By 1964 that figure had increased to sixty-one bushels. In
1977 the average yield per acre of corn reached seventy-six bushels.

Traditionally Missouri farmers planted more acres and harvested
more bushels of corn than any other crop. By 1968, however, corn
had been replaced by soybeans as farmers harvested 3 million acres
of corn as opposed to 3.7 million acres of soybeans. In less than forty
years, soybean production in Missouri went from 1 million to 144

million bushels as soybeans became an important ingredient in the manufacture of lubricants, margarine, salad oils, shortening, soap, paints, plastics, and varnishes. The 1 million bushel harvest was recorded in 1939. Ten years later farmers produced 17 million bushels, while in 1959 they harvested 47 million bushels. The peak yield of 144 million bushels came in 1977. By 1982 soybeans and corn accounted for 69 percent of the state's total market value of crop sales.

Both corn and soybeans are produced in most areas of the state with the exception of the Ozark highlands, where rugged terrain and rocky soil make it difficult to engage in crop farming. Those regions of highest productivity for all crops are the rich valleys of the Missouri and Mississippi rivers. Counties in the Missouri River valley in the west central and northwest portions of the state and in the Mississippi Delta of southeast Missouri provide twelve of the thirteen top agricultural counties in the state, the exception being Nodaway in the northwest section of the state. Indeed, the three Bootheel counties of Stoddard, New Madrid, and Pemiscot lead all others in the production of soybeans.

Increased soybean production in the Bootheel has challenged but failed to supersede king cotton there. Cotton ranked as the state's fourth most important cash crop behind soybeans, corn, and hay, even though it is grown in quantity in only seven southeastern counties. Two of these counties, Butler and Stoddard, also produce considerable rice.

The growth of rice and cotton points up Missouri's agricultural diversity. Except for citrus fruit, the state's land and climate make it possible to cultivate nearly every other crop grown in the United States. Missouri produced quantities of apples, peaches, grapes, melons, vegetables, strawberries, seeds of various sorts, tobacco, and walnuts. Since 1947, tobacco has declined in importance, in part because of the rigid controls

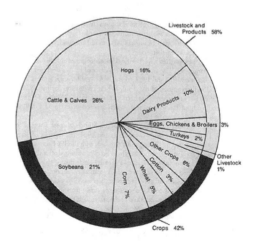

Missouri Cash Farm Receipts by Commodities, 1977. *Source: U.S. Department of Agriculture*

applied to it. In 1969 Platte County grew about two-thirds of the state's crop, although twenty-eight counties harvested some tobacco. The walnut-processing industry is centered in the Ozarks region, and Missouri leads the nation in the production of black walnuts. In the Ozarks, strawberries, grapes, and vegetables are other significant crops. Truck farmers near St. Louis, Kansas City, and Springfield also raise fruits and vegetables for those metropolitan markets.

Two other crops that have been traditionally grown in Missouri have had differing fates. The number of acres devoted to oats declined by 90 percent between 1930 and 1969. In the latter year Missouri farmers grew only 6.3 million bushels of the grain. Wheat production declined during the 1960s, but since then it has been increasing. In 1977 Missouri farmers grew 60.5 million bushels of wheat, which almost doubled the 33.1 million bushels they had grown in 1969.

A grain sorghum harvest of 61.3 million bushels also set a record in 1977. During the decade between 1954 and 1964, the number of acres devoted to that crop had been greatly reduced, with the 1964 acreage only half that of the 1959 planting. Sorghum acreage stabilized after that, but the introduction of hybrid varieties increased yields by one-third. Yields vary greatly from year to year because of weather conditions. The 1977 crop, for instance, was 50 percent greater than the 1976 yield.

The yield from Missouri's forests is more stable than sorghum production. Forests cover about one-third of the state, with the heaviest concentration in the Ozarks region. Most of the state's timberland is privately owned, but about 8 percent of it is in the Clark and Mark Twain national forests. Besides using the forest lands for recreation, firewood, and building materials, Missourians manufacture everything from oak flooring and walnut furniture to the covered wagons built in Silver Dollar City.

The growing of hay also occupies a prominent position in Missouri's agriculture. Hay is raised on more than 3 million acres, which places it with soybeans and corn as one of the state's most important crops. Those three crops occupy three-fourths of Missouri's 12 million arable acres. In 1969 the state's farmers grew 5.6 million tons of hay.

Missouri also grew more tall fescue seed than any other state and ranked second in the production of orchard grass, lespedeza, and timothy seeds in 1968.

Agricultural Production: Livestock

Most of the hay and much of the corn grown in Missouri are fed to livestock. In 1977, for example, the sale of corn contributed only 7 percent of the state's cash farm receipts, and the sale of hay was insignificant as a source of income. Soybeans, not a livestock feed, produced 21 percent of the cash farm receipts. Thus, most of the production of more than 6 million arable acres was used to feed livestock. In 1977 the sale of livestock and related products provided 58 percent of farm income.

Livestock production generally increased in Missouri between 1940 and 1970. In 1959, for example, cattle sales provided more farm income than any other source, and hog sales ranked second. Nine years later the sale of livestock and its products contributed 68 percent of agricultural income, with cattle and calves composing 31 percent and hogs making up 21 percent of the total. Between 1968 and 1977 soybean sales increased from 16 percent to 21 percent of the total cash receipts; cattle and calves declined to 26 percent; and hogs declined to 16 percent of the total farm sales. Naturally, livestock production is most important in those central and western portions of the state where quantities of corn and hay are raised. In recent years pork production has become more specialized and the grain-growing areas of northwestern and west central Missouri are raising hogs for slaughter, while in the southern Ozarks quality feeder pigs are being produced.

The state's dairy and poultry industries are also centered in the Ozarks. Like other agricultural activities, milk production has become specialized during the last thirty years. Although the number of milk cows has declined, milk production has increased. Besides milk, Missouri's dairy industry produced important quantities of cheese and butter. In 1968 the state ranked third in cheese production and eighth in butter manufacture among the states. Income from dairy products has provided 10 percent of Missouri's farm cash receipts over the last twenty years, with that from poultry products—eggs, chickens, broilers, and turkeys—composing about 6 percent of farm sales during the same period.

The least significant contributors to livestock production in Missouri are the sheep and lamb producers. That phase of the livestock industry has been in decline for a number of years. Between 1959 and 1964, sheep and lamb production declined by 46 percent. In

Ralls County farm, 1974. *University of Missouri Agricultural Extension*

1970 there were only 51,000 sheep in Missouri, and only 7 of every one 100 farms raised them. Between 1976 and 1977 production dropped by another 2 percent.

Overall Missouri ranks ninth among the states in farm cash receipts. That ranking has remained constant since 1959. In individual categories in 1975, the state ranked fourth in raising cattle, calves, hogs, and soybeans; sixth in producing hay; eighth in growing corn, and tenth in producing milk. And although less than 90,000 of Missouri's people worked on farms in 1977, about one out of five in the state's work force labored in some activity related to agriculture.

Mining

Missouri's agricultural diversity is almost matched by the variety of its mineral holdings. Missourians mine lead, zinc, shale, stone, coal, fireclay, copper, iron ore, lime, sand and gravel, barite, and silver. In 1947 Missouri ranked twenty-first in mineral production; it declined to twenty-seventh in 1961, but it rose back to twenty-first among the fifty states in 1977. That resurgence in rank should not be interpreted as suggesting great growth for the mining industry. The Mining Inspection Section of the Missouri State Department of Labor expressed pessimism about the future of lead, zinc, iron, and fireclay production in the state because of federal health and safety laws, and all of those commodities declined in amounts produced between 1976 and 1977.

Missouri's relatively high ranking in mineral production has traditionally depended upon its production of lead. Missouri has outproduced every other state, and in 1977 it supplied 82 percent of the nation's production. Lead sales composed almost 35 percent of Missouri's mineral sales in that year.

The discovery of a rich vein of lead near Viburnum in 1955 by the St. Joseph Lead Company, and the subsequent opening of mining operations in the 1960s allowed Missouri to recoup its national ranking after a decline in the 1950s. These deposits extend south from the northwest corner of Iron County for a distance of about thirty miles. Production of lead from the Viburnum deposit has replaced that of worn-out mines in the old lead area, which was located about fifty miles to the northeast of the newer find. In the older area only the mine at Flat River still operated in 1970. Mines at Fredericktown and Desloge closed in 1958; one at Bonne Terre ceased operations in 1961; another at Leadwood stopped in 1962. Mines in eastern Washington County and at Doe Run had quit operations much earlier.

To illustrate the significance of the Viburnum discovery, twenty-two companies entered the area to prospect, resulting in an expenditure of $60 million in new mine development in 1965. Furthermore, the AMAX-Homestake Company built the first smelter constructed in this country in forty years to smelt the ore, and the Frisco Railroad built the longest stretch of track constructed in recent years, 32.3 miles, to transport it. In 1977 St. Joe Minerals Corporation, Cominco American, Incorporated, AMAX Lead Company of Missouri, and the Ozark Lead Company mined 697,417 tons of lead. St. Joe Minerals produced about half of the total, with AMAX contributing over 170,000 tons.

Another of the state's minerals, coal, has become more significant as the nation has sought to find a substitute for oil. About one-third of Missouri is underlain with deposits of bituminous coal. Counties with coal extend northeastward from Jasper County in the southwestern part of the state to Clark County in the northeastern part of the state. Missouri mines produced just over 3.5 million tons of coal in 1965; that figure increased to just over 4.4 million tons in 1970; and by 1977 it reached 6.6 million tons. About two-thirds of Missouri's coal is used to generate electricity.

Compared with other economic activities, mining uses a small percentage of the state's workers. Less than 8,500 people found employment in the mines during 1977. Nevertheless, mining is important to particular areas of the state, and fashioning mineral products into useful commodities provides employment to a larger number of people. Missouri's silica sand production, for example, is the basis for glass manufacturing in Crystal City. The fireclay mined in north and east central Missouri is the raw material for the manufacture of bricks in a number of refractories in Fulton, Mexico, and Vandalia. And a portion of the limestone mined in Missouri is turned into cement in factories located in St. Louis and Kansas City.

The Urban Population

As noted above, in 1970 more than 70 percent of the state's citizens lived in areas with populations of 2,500 or more, a total of 3,279,144. Between 1940 and 1970, St. Louis' metropolitan area* experienced impressive growth, although after 1950 St. Louis city began a decline in population that shows few signs of diminishing. Population statistics reveal the pattern: St. Louis city recorded an increase of 50,000 in population during the 1940s, going from 816,048 to 856,796, only to take a nose dive of some 106,000 the following decade. By 1990 the continued decline left St. Louis city with a population of fewer than 400,000. St. Louis County's growth over the same period illustrates the increasing suburbanization of the urban population. In 1940 the county showed a population of 274,230. By 1950 it had jumped to 406,349; ten years later the county held 703,532 people; in 1970 it reached 951,353, and in 1990 it stood at 993,529. Because St. Louis city's boundaries had been fixed in 1876 and the city separated from the county, the city could increase its size only if county residents agreed. In 1959 a referendum voted on a proposal to consolidate the city and county was voted down. Ringed by incorporated towns and cities, with old and deteriorating houses, St. Louis city could not expand, and those of its people who could flee to the better housing and open spaces in the county did so.

The pattern of population growth in Kansas City has been much different from that of St. Louis. Between 1940 and 1970, Kansas
*A city and its surrounding territory.

City's population grew from 399,178 to 507,330. The greatest growth occurred between 1940 and 1950, with about 57,000 people being added, but increases of just under 20,000 and over 30,000 were recorded in the next two census years. Unlike St. Louis, Kansas City expanded its boundaries during each decade between 1930 and 1970, and thus brought areas on the fringe of development into the city. By 1990, however, Kansas City's population had experienced decline. Only 435,146 people lived there. For the first time since 1900, Missouri's largest city was below 500,000.

Both Kansas City and St. Louis have experienced growth in the percentage of their nonwhite populations. About 99.8 percent of Missouri's nonwhite population is black. In the state as a whole, the number of African Americans has increased at a faster rate than the number of whites. Between 1940 and 1960, Missouri's white population increased by 11 percent, its nonwhite population increased by 62 percent. Blacks also joined the farm-to-city movement. In 1940, 21.9 percent of Missouri's blacks lived in rural areas, but in 1960 only 9.4 percent remained there. Only 4.7 percent of African Americans lived in rural areas of Missouri in 1970. Between 1940 and 1960, the percentage of St. Louis' population that was black increased from 13.4 percent to 30.1 percent. In 1970, blacks composed 41 percent of St. Louis' people, and by 1980 that figure had reached 45.6 percent. Similarly, African Americans increased their share of Kansas City's population from 10.5 percent in 1940 to 18 percent in 1960 to 29.7 percent in 1970. Kansas City's black population declined to 27.4 percent by 1980, however.

Manufacturing Developments

In both cities the African-American population was concentrated in deteriorating central districts, whereas industries and jobs accompanied the white exodus to the suburbs. Many whites no doubt fled from central districts simply to escape blacks. Opportunities for more open space, new housing, and other factors also motivated people, white and black, to leave central city areas. Both the nature of new industries and the need for older industries to expand and modernize caused manufacturing establishments to locate in suburbs.

New industries—electronics, chemicals, aircraft, aerospace, defense, and research and development—either began or greatly expanded during and after World War II. These companies did not need to be near raw materials, for the materials that went into the products were much less important than a work force that had advanced technological, scientific, management, and information skills. Able to build wherever they pleased and desirous of attracting well-educated employees, the bulk of the new industries chose suburban sites. Employees found homes nearby that provided space, fresh air, and perhaps scenic views and even lakes. The post–World War II ideal of living in the "country" and having access to the leisure activities and employment opportunities of the city seemed to be realized by suburban Americans.

Government road building in each decade since 1950 has aided greatly the dispersion of people and industry. In Missouri the federal government constructed seven interstate highways, and five of them facilitated automobile transportation into, out of, and around Kansas City and St. Louis. Interstate 70 aids commuting to both cities and links them. Both Interstates 55 and 44 also influence living and traffic patterns in St. Louis. Kansas City's commuters travel on Interstates 29 and 35. Other four-lane highways move traffic around and through both cities.

McDonnell-Douglas plant, St. Louis. *McDonnell-Douglas, courtesy Missouri State Historical Society*

The McDonnell Aircraft Corporation exemplifies the growth of new industries in Missouri since World War II. Founded in 1939 by James S. McDonnell, Jr., with two employees, it received government contracts to build airplanes during the war. Other contracts from the navy and air force followed after World War II, and by 1962 McDonnell Aircraft had become the largest private employer in the state. The company won the design competition for a space capsule and built all of the Mercury and Gemini capsules that were flown. During the 1990s the Boeing Corporation absorbed what had become the McDonnell-Douglas Aircraft Corporation.

Michigan-based automobile manufacturers also employ thousands of Missourians in making a less glamorous form of transportation. Assembly plants in Kansas City and St. Louis produce Chrysler, Ford, and General Motors products in such quantities that Missouri ranks second in automobile production behind Michigan. The number of Missourians employed in producing motor vehicles increased from 10,464 in 1940 to 35,926 in 1970.

Since 1940 manufacturing has become increasingly important as an economic activity in Missouri. Although fewer people worked in factories than in agriculture in 1940, manufacturing led all other sources of employment in both 1950 and 1960. In 1970 service activities barely surpassed manufacturing as an employer, and that trend continued during the 1980s as the service sector grew faster than any other.

Diversity has marked Missouri's manufacturing. About three-fourths of all manufacturing done in the United States is represented in Missouri's activities. The state's abundant and various natural resources and agricultural production make it a logical place to change raw materials into finished products. A stable work force, over 30 percent of which was unionized in 1972, has provided proficient labor. Missouri's central location and excellent transportation system, including the 9-foot channel of the Mississippi and seven and $7^1/_2$-foot channel of the Missouri rivers, have long given the state important trade advantages.

St. Louis, for example, not only produces space capsules, planes, and automobiles, but also manufactures beer, drugs, clothing, shoes, chemicals, cement, food products, electrical equipment, books, and a number of other items. The famous Anheuser-Busch brewery leads all of its national competitors in the production of beer.

Home plant of Anheuser-Busch Brewing Co., St. Louis. *Anheuser-Busch, Inc., courtesy Missouri State Historical Society*

Kansas City manufactures some of the same items as St. Louis, and it is the second most important grain-milling center in the country, an important meat-packer, farm machinery producer, lumber processor, steelmaker, and even oil refiner. Kansas City is also the home of the nation's leading greeting card company, Hallmark Cards, Incorporated.

Significant out-state manufacturing cities include Springfield, St. Joseph, and Joplin. Springfield, Missouri's third largest city in 1990, contributes dairy products, other food processing, animal feeds, electronic items, paper products, trailers, trucks, and typewriters to the state's manufacturing total. St. Joseph is an important meat-processing center and produces electrical equipment, pharmaceuticals, and paper products. In Joplin the Eagle Picher Company draws upon lead and zinc resources to manufacture lead oxide and other products. Tobacco products, explosives, and mining machinery are also manufactured in Joplin.

Since World War II other Missouri towns and small cities have sought to attract industries in their efforts to stem the exodus of

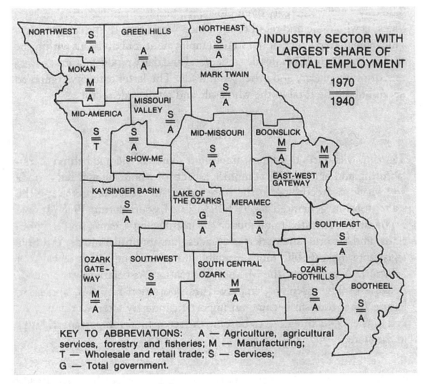

INDUSTRY SECTOR WITH
LARGEST SHARE OF
TOTAL EMPLOYMENT

1970
1940

KEY TO ABBREVIATIONS: A — Agriculture, agricultural services, forestry and fisheries; M — Manufacturing; T — Wholesale and retail trade; S — Services; G — Total government.

Missouri Regional Planning Commissions

people from rural to urban areas. And between 1940 and 1990 manufacturing replaced agriculture as the most significant source of employment for people in the south central Ozarks and in the part of east central Missouri called the Boonslick region.

Services

As noted above, between 1960 and 1990 the service sector replaced manufacturing as Missouri's most important source of employment. The service category includes those occupations in which individuals perform work for others, and the product of that work is the service that is performed. Over 100,000 more workers performed services in 1970 than in 1960, and that trend increased momentum during the 1980s. Employees in that category composed 20.2 percent of the work force in the former and 24.8 percent in the latter year. During the decade of the 1960s the greatest growth occurred in the professional services area. It showed an increase from 11.5 percent to 16.9 percent of the total work force. Other subdivisions, lodging places and other personal services, business and repair services, entertainment and recreation services, and private household, either declined or increased slightly.

Wholesale and Retail Trade

The other major category of employment, besides manufacturing and services, is wholesale and retail trade. Since World War II this category provided about 20 percent of the state's employment. Subdivisions within the trade sector include wholesale trade, food and dairy products stores, eating and drinking places, and other retail trade. The latter category composed about half of the total in the wholesale and retail trade sector.

Tourism

Tourism, Missouri's third most important source of income behind manufacturing and agriculture, combines aspects of wholesale and retail trade and services. According to the state agency in charge of promoting the state, tourism generated $2.55 billion in Missouri during 1978. People have visited the state's numerous caves, fast-flowing streams, urban attractions, and historic landmarks for decades, but not until 1946 did the state legislature make public funds available for advertising the attractions of Missouri. A year later, the Missouri Recreation Association was created. Because of advertisement, improved transportation facilities, and more leisure time, tourism became an important industry after World War II, and in the 1990s threatens to become the second most important industry in the state.

Lake of the Ozarks

What happened at the Lake of the Ozarks illustrates the development of other areas. Created during the 1930s when the Union Electric Company dammed the Osage River, the Lake of the Ozarks provided good fishing, beauty and little else until after World War II. Since 1950 the lake has become filled with powerboats, and a good portion of the 1,400 miles of shoreline has become a haven for individual cottages or large resort hotels. A multitude of businesses, which provide services for the hundreds of thousands who come to the lake every year, have grown up in the vicinity.

Southwest Ozarks

In southwest Missouri the Corps of Engineers built Bull Shoals Dam and Table Rock Dam in the 1950s. The lakes that were formed have made the southwest Ozarks region one of the largest artificially made recreation areas in the nation. Bull Shoals had over 5 million visitors in 1978, and Table Rock, Norfork, and Taneycomo lakes drew additional visitors. Development in this area has matched that which occurred around the Lake of the Ozarks earlier.

For those who do not enjoy fishing or water sports, the southwest Ozarks offers the Shepherd of the Hills Farm and Theater, Silver Dollar City, with its nineteenth century costumed craftspeople, and the Ozarks Country Jubilee. During the 1980s Branson became the country music center of the state. Tourists in the area may also visit Fantastic Caverns, Talking Rocks Cave, and Crystal Cave.

Central Ozarks

Other caves and fast flowing streams attract many people to the central Ozarks. Missouri has about 3,900 known caves, more than any other state, and at least 24 of them are commercially operated. Meramec Caverns at Stanton, Onondaga at Leasburg, and Fisher's Cave at Sullivan are in the east central Ozarks, while Bridal Cave, Fantasy World Caverns, Jacob's Cave, Indian Burial Cave, and Ozark Caverns are near the Lake of the Ozarks. Central Ozark streams have become so popular that on summer weekends one might find the beautiful Jack's Fork, Eleven Points, Meramec, or Current clogged with canoes. A trip on one of these streams without a crowd, however, is a delightful way to view the natural splendor of the Ozarks and to experience the exhilaration of negotiating rapids in a canoe.

State Parks

Many tourists float these streams and stay in one of the state parks in the Ozarks. Missouri has thirty-nine state parks, twenty-two historic sites, and one archaeological site distributed over the state. The Mis-

Lake of the Ozarks. *Charles Trefts Collection, courtesy Missouri State Historical Society*

souri State Park Board, established in 1917, began the park system and supervised its expansion after World War II. Among the most popular parks are Bennett Spring, Roaring River, Lake of the Ozarks, Alley Spring, Big Spring, Round Spring, Montauk, and Maramec Spring.

The Department of Conservation stocks a number of streams that flow through these parks with trout from its hatcheries and complements the work of the State Park Board in making Missouri attractive to citizens and out-of-state tourists alike. Created by the General Assembly in 1936, the department has labored to preserve wildlife habitat and to balance the demands of people and nature. In 1976, Missouri voters indicated their appreciation for the work of the department by approving a one-eighth cent sales tax designated for conservation purposes. In 1978 the department received $24 million from the tax and purchased more than 37,000 acres of land to be used for conservation purposes. The department's goal is to add 300,000 acres to the state's holdings.

Tourism in Kansas City and St. Louis

For those interested in visiting cities, St. Louis and Kansas City have attractions that appeal to all ages and are attended by hundreds of thousands every year. Kansas City has professional baseball (the Royals) and football (the Chiefs) teams. St. Louis, having lost its Cardinals football team to Phoenix in 1988, welcomed in the Rams in 1995. St. Louis also hosts highly popular pro baseball (the Cardinals) and hockey (the Blues) teams. Both cities also boast large entertainment complexes: Six Flags over Mid-America near St. Louis and Worlds of Fun just north of Kansas City.

Historic sites, new and old architecture, riverboats, good restaurants, museums, orchestras, theaters, libraries, zoos, and other cultural and entertainment activities make Missouri's two urban centers pleasurable and interesting places to visit. St. Louis is credited with having over sixty tourist attractions ranging from the famous Gateway Arch to the Anheuser-Busch Brewery. Kansas City's points of interest range from Fort Osage, the re-creation of the first outpost in the Louisiana Purchase, to the lovely Crown Center and country club area. Both cities have recently constructed convention centers to further boost their economies.

Out-State Missouri

In recent years, such smaller cities as Hannibal and St. Joseph have become more active in seeking tourist dollars. Hannibal, for example, has recently constructed the Clemens Amphitheater where the continuously running drama *Mark Twain and His Times* is performed. Until 1935 Hannibal had done nothing to commemorate and exploit the fact that Samuel Clemens had spent his youth there. The author of *The Adventures of Tom Sawyer* and *Huckleberry Finn* has now become a cottage industry.

Visitors to the St. Joseph area may visit the Patee House Museum, which preserves the memories of the Pony Express, the house where Jesse James died, a doll museum, the Stetson Hat headquarters, and a nineteenth-century restoration project called Robidoux Row. Other communities are similarly developing local tourist attractions on a smaller scale.

Missouri's Economic Future

Evidence of growth in the recent past would suggest that future economic development may be most dramatic in certain out-state cities and rural areas. Between 1950 and 1990 some of Missouri's most impressive growth occurred in cities with populations of less than

100,000. Two cities that had state colleges created in them in the late sixties did not share that growth. St. Joseph lost population during that span, and Joplin's population increased by less than 1 percent. In contrast, Columbia's population jumped by 60.5 percent between 1960 and 1970, while Maryville, Kirksville, Warrensburg, Cape Girardeau, and Springfield all had increases of more than 20 percent during the same decade. Jefferson City, the home of state government and Lincoln University, grew by 14.8 percent, and Rolla, the home of the University of Missouri-Rolla, recorded an increase of 21.9 percent during the 1960s. Similar growth patterns marked the 1980s.

The growth of educational institutions no doubt aided this development, but probably more important was the fact that these were relatively small cities with clean air, open space, reasonable land values, little congestion, and records of citizen safety. Population growth in the Ozarks between 1970 and 1990 seems to support the contention that the factors listed above will be important in Missouri's future development. During that time Christian, Stone, Camden, and Morgan counties recorded increases in their populations. McDonald, Ripley, Webster, Hickory, and Benton counties joined them. And Cedar, Ozark, Polk, and Texas counties tallied similar increases. Taney County's population increased by more than 35 percent during those twenty years.

The attractions of the Ozarks simply suggest the rich diversity that the state contains. Blessed with the great Mississippi and Missouri rivers, fertile prairies, rich bottomlands, timbered hills, a wealth of minerals, a central location, and a moderate climate, Missouri also has bustling medium-sized cities and two major metropolitan areas that contribute a vast diversity of manufactured commodities. A vigorous population has used imagination and skill in developing the state's mixed economy. In the future, Missourians will likely continue to produce manufactured goods that range from space capsules to beer and agricultural commodities that range from soybeans and cotton to tobacco. Moreover, people from other states and countries will continue to join native Missourians in enjoying the state's beautiful lakes, rushing streams, tree-covered hills, numerous caves, and urban attractions.

Suggestions for Reading

The best sources of information about economic trends are government publications. Decennial census reports published by the United States Department of Commerce are essential. Reports by state agencies such as the Division of Budget and Planning, Office of Administration, Department of Natural Resources, Division of Tourism, Division of Industrial Development, and Department of Agriculture are also important. Another good source of information about the state is the *Official Manual of Missouri*, which is published biennially by the secretary of state. A good compilation of material about the state is contained in Milton D. Rafferty, Russell L. Gerlach, and Dennis J. Hrebec, *Atlas of Missouri*, Springfield, Aux-Arc Research Associates, 1970. An indispensable guide to the beauty of Missouri is Thomas R. Beveridge, *Geological Curiosities and Wonders of Missouri*, Rolla, Missouri State Geological Survey, 1978.

The best history of the state during the second quarter of the twentieth century is Richard S. Kirkendall, *A History of Missouri, Vol. V, 1919 to 1953*, Columbia, University of Missouri Press, 1986. Articles of interest in the *Missouri Historical Review* include: G. K. Renner, "Strawberry Culture in Southwest Missouri," October 1969; Milton D. Rafferty, "Missouri's Black Walnut Kernel Industry," April 1975; Clarence R. Keathley and Donna M. Ham, "4-H Club Work in Missouri," January 1977; Duane Meyer, "The Ozarks in Missouri History," January 1979; Robert G. Schultz, "The Monroe Drug Company, 1876–1976: A Century of Chemical Enterprise," October 1981; Paula McNeill Quirk, "The 'Missouri Meerschaum' Pipe," October 1983; John R. Hensley, "In the Shadow of Table Rock: The Army Corps of Engineers, Civil Engineering and Local Communities," April 1986; and Stephen N. Limbaugh, "The Origin and Development of the Ozark National Scenic Riverways Project," January 1997. Among articles of interest in *The Bulletin* is Glen E. Holt, "The Future of St. Louis: Another Look Ahead," July 1978.

Modern Missouri: Educational and Cultural Development

I n significant ways educational developments since World War II illustrate changes in the broader society. Enlarged by the postwar baby boom, a growing population required an enormously expanded system of schools. An increasingly complex and technical world demanded schools that could provide children with better educations than their parents had received. An expanded middle class, holding high aspirations for its children, placed great faith in education as a vehicle for economic and social advancement. Under governmental programs such as the GI Bill (discussed later), higher education became increasingly available, and people came to accept the idea that even college educations should be supported at public expense, a concept made concrete by the community college movement. New groups, particularly women and blacks, entered colleges and universities in larger numbers than previously as the first step in gaining admittance to the economic, political, and social arenas of power dominated by white males. Thus the schools became a microcosm of society, mirroring its strengths and weaknesses.

School Consolidation

In 1947 the General Assembly passed the District Reorganization Law, which provided for the elimination of one-room, country schools and promoted the consolidation of small high schools into larger ones. This act required each county board of education to create a plan for district reorganization and to place its design before county voters for approval. The state further encouraged consolidation by allocating matching funds to be used for expanding school buildings in enlarged districts. Between 1948 and 1964, those efforts reduced the number of school districts from 8,422 to 1,028. Consolidation no doubt made it more economical to educate students. It certainly provided students with better school facilities and better trained teachers.

Further consolidation occurred when in 1969 the General Assembly passed legislation that required districts not operating schools to combine with a district that did. The state board of education would consolidate those districts failing to comply with the law within one year.

School reorganization increased the distance that students were forced to travel and compelled an increasing number of them to be bused. Between 1944–45 and 1974–75 enrollment in Missouri's public schools increased from 620,844 to 1,053,879, while the number of students transported to school rose from 103,939 to 629,000. This represented an increase from 16.7 percent of Missouri's public school population riding buses to 59.8 percent over that thirty-year period. In 1974–75 Missouri students traveled 81 million miles back and forth to school.

Busing for purposes of integration had little impact on those figures. Indeed, because maintaining segregated schools frequently required African-American students to be bused to neighboring towns, integration may have reduced the number of the miles traveled by schoolchildren because of race. For example, after integration in the 1950s, black high school students in Glasgow no longer had to travel the sixty miles per day to attend a segregated school in Dalton and those in Fulton were spared the fifty-mile round trip to Jefferson City. Integration is discussed in Chapter 14.

For most students the advantages of attending reorganized schools more than compensated them for the time they spent in traveling. Consolidation made possible broadened curricula, teachers with more and specialized training, better audiovisual facilities, better stocked and administered libraries, improved gymnasiums, and more congenial surroundings.

Consolidation, however, failed to solve all educational problems. Increased school populations and a larger percentage of children attending high schools forced public educators to teach children who ranged from the bright to the dull, from the well-adjusted and highly motivated to the incorrigible and noncaring. Moreover, society increasingly asked schools not only to educate children but to provide many of the functions traditionally performed by families. To meet these demands, school officials changed curricula to make their offerings more attractive, tried ability grouping of students, increased extracurricular activities, and expanded vocational training. By the mid-1980s many both in and out of the education profession were decrying educational frills, chastising the schools for graduating functional illiterates, and urging that the schools return to the basics: reading, writing, and arithmetic. Those criticisms have led to experimentation with competency testing, but that has added to the debate rather than resolving the question of what ought to be taught in the schools.

Financing Schools

Inadequate financing has consistently impeded Missouri's educational progress. The General Assembly provided some relief in 1955 when it submitted a proposal, which voters approved, to place in the school fund the revenue from a two cents per package tax on cigarettes. Voters also approved a constitutional amendment, submitted by the same legislature, that created the School Foundation Program. It allocated state funds to school systems on the basis of an elaborate formula that included average daily attendance, the number of teachers and their educational level, assessed valuation, and the amount of revenue raised from local taxes.

While these measures have provided increased aid on a more structured basis, the traditional reluctance of its citizens to tax themselves has caused Missouri to lag behind other states in providing money for education. In 1954–55 school districts spent $349.74 for each pupil in average daily attendance; by 1974–75 that figure had risen to $1,082. Yet in the latter year, Missouri still spent $200 less per pupil than the national average. Of states in the Midwest (Arkansas, Illinois, Iowa, Kansas, Kentucky, Nebraska, Oklahoma, and Tennessee), Missouri ranked last in percentage of revenue spent on education in 1975. In 1978–79 Missouri ranked forty-first among all the states in spending for primary and secondary education. During the 1980s Missouri fell further behind the other midwestern states in every category of support for education.

About 15 percent of Missouri's young people attend private schools, a percentage that has experienced a slight increase in recent years. Students in Catholic elementary and secondary schools compose over 90 percent of these; children in Lutheran schools make up the second largest group; and students in other religious and private schools make up the rest.

Higher Education

Like colleges and universities in other states, Missouri's institutions of higher education have experienced spectacular growth since World War II. The Servicemen's Readjustment Act, commonly known as the GI Bill of Rights, played a significant role in that growth. Among other things, it provided federal government support for those veterans who wanted to attend colleges. Almost 3 million former members of the armed services attended colleges and universities as a result of the GI Bill. Although it is difficult to gauge the social, economic, and cultural impact of all those veterans attending college, all students of the period agree that the GI Bill caused the middle class to expand greatly; abetted the technological revolution by creating a large pool of well-trained people; and provided a large audience for all forms of cultural activity.

New Building for Education

For a decade Missouri's colleges and universities coped with the influx of veterans and other students by using old barracks as dormitories, classrooms, and offices and by constructing new buildings out of current budgets. Those stopgap measures could not provide the necessary facilities, and it became obvious that increased funds were needed.

The need for new buildings on public campuses coincided with a riot and fire at the state penitentiary in Jefferson City and a major fire at the state hospital in Fulton. These led voters to approve, by a three-to-one majority, a $75 million bond issue for the construction of new and the rehabilitation of old state buildings. Within a month after passage of the bond issue, in January 1956, the General Assembly had provided $36,453,040 for construction on state college and university campuses.

Enrollments in Colleges

Campus expansion resulting from that money barely kept pace with increased enrollments. The larger number of eighteen- to twenty-four-year-olds and the tendency for larger percentages of the population to attend college caused campuses to maintain building programs during the 1960s and to continue the use of temporary buildings, a campus code word for remodeled barracks. Enrollment in public institutions of higher education increased from 16,539 in 1952 to 31,920 in 1960. It more than doubled during the next five years, reaching 71,137 by 1965; and it doubled again during the next decade, reaching 154,270 in 1975. Since 1975, the rate of growth has leveled off, but schools such as Southwest Missouri State have experienced remarkable growth. In 1990, Southwest Missouri enrolled more than 20,000 students and ranked second to the Columbia campus of the University of Missouri in enrollment.

Private colleges and universities also increased their enrollments during that time, but at a lower rate. In the mid-1950s public schools surpassed private ones in numbers of students for the first time. For example, in 1952 private schools enrolled 54 percent of all college students in Missouri. By 1960 that percentage had declined to 43.5; five years later it was 33.1; and in 1975 it was 25.9. Since 1975 enrollments in both public and private institutions have leveled off.

Women helped to swell the ranks of college students between 1945 and 1960. After the latter date the number of women going to college increased even more as many of them began to question their status in society and sought to change it. In the fall of 1979 the *Chronicle of Higher Education* reported that nationally more women than men were attending colleges and universities.

Expansion of the State System

Lower tuition rates, more room because of expansion, and the creation of new institutions all help to explain why public colleges and universities attracted ever larger percentages of the state's college students. The public demanded more educational facilities, and the state could expand with greater ease than could the private sector.

Responding to Governor John Dalton's request, in 1961 the General Assembly approved the formation of junior college districts under the supervision of the state board of education. Designed to make two years of higher education available to virtually everyone at minimal cost, junior colleges emphasize vocational education while also offering more traditional courses for those who eventually desire to earn bachelor degrees. They offer a wide range of programs leading to certification or associate degrees. Within four years such

Elmer Ellis Library, University of Missouri, Columbia. *Courtesy State Historical Society of Missouri*

districts had been created in both major metropolitan areas and in Jefferson County, Newton-McDonald counties, Jasper County, Buchanan County, and St. Francois County. Older junior colleges in those areas were incorporated into the new districts, while the established institutions in Moberly and Trenton continued as they were. Between 1965 and 1968 additional junior or community colleges were established in Neosho (Crowder College), Union (East Central Junior College), Sedalia (State Fair Community College), and Poplar Bluff (Three Rivers Community College). With the establishment of the community college system, higher education had been democratized. By 1977 Missouri's community colleges enrolled 49,434 students.

In 1963 the General Assembly created the University of Missouri System with campuses in Kansas City, St. Louis, Rolla, and Columbia. The last two campuses had been connected administratively since the nineteenth century; the Kansas City campus had been a private institution; while the St. Louis campus was completely new. With an enrollment of over 50,000 students, the university ranks among the fifteen largest in the country.

Two years later the General Assembly authorized the expansion of junior colleges in Joplin and St. Joseph into four-year institutions. Missouri Southern State College at Joplin began its new operation in 1967, and Missouri Western State College at St. Joseph took on its new

status in 1969. During the mid-1970s both schools severed earlier connections with junior college districts to become fully state supported.

Lincoln University in Jefferson City and Harris-Stowe State College in St. Louis also receive state support. Both had their origins in
the nineteenth century. Lincoln was the state's university for African-
American students but became fully integrated during the 1950s,
evolving into a regional institution that serves a larger percentage of
white than black students. Its choral and drama departments present
programs in various parts of the state that are known for their excellence. Lincoln also has an impressive collection of materials on African-American history in its library. Harris-Stowe is an amalgamation
of two colleges that originally trained teachers and had long been
supported by the St. Louis School District.

In addition the state supports five regional universities. Begun as
state teacher's colleges during the late nineteenth and early twentieth
centuries, these schools experienced phenomenal growth during the
1960s and evolved into multipurpose institutions. The General Assembly recognized their new status in 1972 by changing their names
from state colleges to state universities. Northeast Missouri in Kirksville, Northwest Missouri in Maryville, Central Missouri in Warrensburg, Southeast Missouri in Cape Girardeau, and Southwest Missouri
in Springfield make important contributions to their areas of the
state, including specialized museums, collections of books and manuscripts, and scholarly experts. During the 1990s the General Assembly renamed Northeast Missouri State University as Truman State
University and gave it designation at the state's arts and sciences university.

University of Missouri

The University of Missouri has long contributed to the state's culture.
Currently public FM radio stations on each of the four campuses provide classical music, opera, drama, intellectual discussion, and other
cultural programming to residents in every section of the state. As
part of its journalism school, the Columbia campus also operates
KOMU, a television station. The St. Louis campus has specialized
in urban studies and has developed a significant collection of urban
oral history. The Kansas City campus library houses the Robert
McClure Snyder, Jr., collection of middle western research materials.
The Rolla campus emphasizes engineering education, and its library

has an excellent collection of engineering journals. It also has a small but representative geological museum.

The Columbia campus's Elmer Ellis Library contains more than 2 million volumes, an impressive collection of rare books, and a collection of foreign and national newspapers. It is one of the finest libraries in the Midwest and shares its resources with the other campuses of the system. Besides the usual good music, drama, and art departments associated with a major university, the Columbia campus also houses in Jesse Hall, the administration building, an interesting collection of 102 paintings entitled "Missouri, Heart of the Nation." Commissioned by the Scruggs-Vandervoort-Barney department stores of St. Louis in 1946, the collection contains the paintings of fourteen nationally known artists who have depicted the state's great variety. Scruggs-Vandervoort-Barney subsequently gave the collection to the university. The Columbia-based University of Missouri Press publishes a wide variety of significant works.

With its four-campus university, five state universities, two state colleges, Lincoln University, Harris-Stowe State College, and a fifteen-campus junior college network, Missouri operates an extensive system of higher education. Like the public schools, it has seldom received adequate financing. In 1976–77 Missouri ranked forty-seventh in assessing taxes and forty-third in appropriating funds for higher education among the fifty states. Fourteen years later Missouri's support for higher education showed no improvement. The wealth of the state is considered in that ranking. Since 1975 the State Coordinating Board for Higher Education has assumed increased authority in recommending the amount of funds that various state institutions should receive and in planning for the future of higher education in the state. It attempts to weed out waste and duplication and to provide expert advice to the state legislature.

Private Schools

Twenty-five four-year and five two-year private schools provide additional educational opportunities. Many private institutions are in medium- and small-sized towns such as Culver-Stockton in Canton, Central Methodist in Fayette, Westminster and William Woods in Fulton, Missouri Valley in Marshall, William Jewel in Liberty, and Southwest Baptist in Bolivar. To use historian David March's phrase, they are "cultural oases" for their communities and regions because of their libraries; departments of music, drama and art; museums; and talented faculties. They also sponsor exhibits of artists, appearances of lecturers and musical groups, and performances by actors from around the state and across the country.

Missouri's two private universities, St. Louis University and Washington University, have cultural strengths that transcend their city and region. Washington University has a well-known school of fine arts and a representative collection of art that can be seen in the Steinberg galleries. Besides housing an art collection in its administration building, St. Louis University has the Pius XII Memorial Library, with its microfilm collection containing three-fourths of the manuscripts of Rome's Vatican Library, certainly a national cultural resource.

Historical Collections and Libraries

The State Historical Society of Missouri, located in the east wing of the Ellis Library on the University of Missouri-Columbia campus, houses collections of manuscripts, records, newspapers, genealogical material, photographs, and art. Founded by the Missouri Press Association in 1898, it is a center for research into the past of both the state and Midwest region. The society's newspaper collection contains 6,750 bound volumes and 20.5 million pages of microfilm, making it one of the most comprehensive state collections in the country. Its historical art collection includes a number of Bingham paintings and Thomas Hart Benton's famous World War II series, *Year of Peril*. Missouri and national politics are delightfully displayed in the original cartoons of Daniel R. Fitzpatrick, S. J. Ray, Bill Mauldin, and Don Hesse. Those individual collections are supplemented by the Peter Mayo Editorial Cartoon Collection, which contains over 3,000 cartoons created by 150 cartoonists. The society also has a collection of contemporary art that contains the works of more than fifty Missouri-related artists. It has fostered the establishment and growth of many local historical societies and has published over 100 volumes of Missouri history. Its journal, *The Missouri Historical Review*, has published important writings on Missouri since 1906.

Missouri researchers also have available to them the Western Historical Manuscripts Collection with offices on all four of the University of Missouri campuses. Established in 1943, it has collected a variety of research materials, including papers of politicians, writers, and academicians. It is particularly strong in materials on twentieth century Missouri politics and business enterprise.

Two other important repositories are in St. Louis. The Missouri Historical Society is a private organization founded in 1866. Since 1913 it has been housed in the Jefferson Memorial in Forest Park, a structure built with funds left over from the 1904 World's Fair. Its collections, activities, and programs focus on the Louisiana Purchase territory, Missouri, and St. Louis. Manuscripts of early St. Louisans make its holdings particularly significant for the study of the trans-Mississippi west. The society's museum displays include fine paintings, colonial Creole furniture, costumes, steamboat lore, Charles A. Lindbergh memorabilia, and the history of aviation in St. Louis. Its *Gateway Heritage,* formerly *The Bulletin,* publishes important articles on Missouri's history. The Mercantile Library also has materials important for research. Founded as a private lending library in 1845, its collection must be consulted by those interested in western and Missouri history.

The Harry S Truman Library in Independence is a major cultural resource that attracts researchers and visitors from across the nation. Completed in 1957, it houses the papers of former President Truman

The St. Louis Truman Library, Independence, etching by M. Breton. *Courtesy State Historical Society of Missouri*

and many of his associates and microfilm copies of papers relating to the presidency from other repositories. It also has a collection of books about the presidential office, museum rooms displaying aspects of a president's job, historic documents, and gifts presented to Truman while he was in office.

Researchers and general readers in the cities of St. Louis and Kansas City have access to large municipal libraries. The St. Louis Public Library offers all the facilities of an excellent library with current materials, specialized collections, and historical materials. The same can be said of the Kansas City Public Library. It also has the Missouri Valley Room, with its collections relating to the city, Missouri, and the West. In recent years numerous other community libraries and historical societies have begun collections of regional materials that are useful for an understanding of their areas.

Research in these repositories has produced many books and articles, numerous examples of which have been listed in this book's Suggestions for Reading. Without the manuscripts and other materials contained in these historical collections and libraries, it would have been impossible to produce these studies that have enriched those who have read them by adding depth of understanding, knowledge, and pleasure to their lives.

Historic Preservation

In addition to the collection of the written records of Missouri's past in various archives and libraries around the state, there has been a strong movement to preserve Missouri's significant archaeological sites and historic buildings. The work of the archaeologists got underway in the 1930s, with the efforts of concerned faculty and students at the University of Missouri working with interested private citizens. Professors Jesse Wrench and J. Brewton Berry launched a statewide archaeological survey in 1933 that later received federal funding. The Missouri Archaeological Society was organized the following year and began publishing *The Missouri Archaeologist.* Through its efforts much of the state's prehistoric heritage has been preserved, making possible our knowledge of ancient people in Missouri as described in Chapter 1.

Although various state and local groups and agencies had made efforts at preserving historic sites and buildings in Missouri before World War II, their work had been done largely in isolation. In 1953 the General Assembly reorganized the Missouri Park Board. Thereafter it made a concerted effort to blend historic preservation with recreational concerns. The board already operated state parks around historic sites at the "Old Fort" (Van Meter State Park) and Arrow Rock in Saline County and Fort Zumwalt in St. Charles County. Over the next five years it assumed control over the birthplaces of President Truman at Lamar and Mark Twain at Florida as well as General John J. Pershing's early home at Laclede. During the 1960s it expanded its program to include the acquisition of Watkins Mill in Clay County, an excellent example of a nineteenth-century milling operation, and the Lexington battlefield site. It also superintended the restoration of the First Missouri State Capitol at St. Charles, which became the focal point for Missouri's sesquicentennial celebration in 1970.

Simultaneously, the State Historical Society began a highway-marking program in the early 1950s detailing the history of towns, counties, and important sites. It also undertook to survey the state's major historic sites, county by county, publishing its results in *The Missouri Historic Sites Catalogue* in 1963.

In 1966 Congress passed the National Historic Preservation Act authorizing financial assistance to those states actively engaged in statewide programs to record and preserve their prehistoric and historic past. The law also provided for systematic listing of sites in an expanded National Register of Historic Places through state advisory councils. Missouri established the director of the State Park Board as the liaison person to the federal program and provided the director with advisory councils of experts on historic and archaeological sites. Through the efforts of these councils, the State Park Board, the State Historical Society, the Missouri Archaeological Society, and interested local groups and individuals, a great deal of interest has been stimulated in the preservation movement. In 1978 Missouri became the first state in the nation to fund a project aimed at preserving historic and cultural sites associated with African Americans. The Department of Natural Resources later refunded the project for an additional year. Missouri currently has more than 350 sites listed on the National Register, with the number increasing regularly as state and local organizations work together to preserve their heritage.

Kansas City's Cultural Resources

The William Nelson Gallery of Art and Mary Atkins Museum of Fine Arts in Kansas City contain examples of the artistic remains of a number of cultures. It was opened in 1933 with bequests from two

Nelson Art Gallery, Kansas City. *Courtesy State Historical Society of Missouri*

midwesterners: newspaper publisher William Rockhill Nelson and philanthropist Mary Atkins. Commonly known as the Nelson Gallery, it houses works by European master artists, including over 600 engravings produced as early as the fifteenth century; a collection of decorative arts, including displays of European furniture, ceramics, silver, and sculpture; replicas of early American rooms; comprehensive collections of Chinese, Japanese, Egyptian, and Indian art; the art of southwestern Indian tribes; and American paintings, including some works by George Caleb Bingham. In 1975 it shared with the National Gallery of Art in Washington, DC, the honor of being the only two museums to show the fantastic pieces of art contained in the Exhibition of Archaeological Finds of the People's Republic of China.

Other museums in that area include the Kansas City Museum of History and Science, with its collection of Indian objects, a replica of an igloo, frontier materials, and exhibits of a general store, log cabin, and Indian village. The Liberty Memorial Museum commemorates World War I and has a collection of flags, uniforms, and posters. Interesting first editions of scientific and mathematical manuscripts are displayed in the beautiful Linda Hall Library. It is one of the best scientific libraries in the country.

Kansas City's musical offerings range from the repertoire of the Kansas City Philharmonic Orchestra to that of the Starlight Theater. The former, organized in 1933, performs classical music in the Music Hall of the Municipal Auditorium, where the Kansas City Lyric Opera also appears. The Starlight Theater in Swope Park presents a program suitable to an outdoor theater with a mixed clientele. During a typical season there might be on successive weeks a ballet, an appearance by a popular singer, and a presentation of a musical comedy.

St. Louis's Cultural Resources

The largest open-air theater in the nation is in St. Louis. Founded in 1919, the Municipal Opera in Forest Park grew out of the St. Louis *Pageant and Masque*, a dramatization of St. Louis' history, which was presented in 1914. The success of that effort along with others during the next three years led to the creation of the Municipal Theater Association. It has programs similar to those offered by the Starlight Theater in Kansas City.

Devotees of what some call "serious" music and dance have a variety of opportunities to attend performances in St. Louis. The St. Louis Symphony Orchestra has a wide repertoire of classical music, which it performs around the city and county during the summer and in beautiful, refurbished Powell Hall during the winter. It is the second oldest orchestra in the country, taking its present form in 1897. In 1979 it launched a campaign to raise an endowment of $14 million; by midwinter it had commitments for half of it, indicating the importance that many St. Louisans place on a flourishing orchestra. The symphony is ranked as one of the best in the country. St. Louisans may also attend performances by the Dance Concert Society, Opera Theatre, Civic Ballet, and Metropolitan Ballet Company.

Opportunities to attend dramatic productions are plentiful in St. Louis. The American Theatre provides a stage for touring companies that bring to the city theatrical fare similar to that available in New York. The Loretto Hilton Theatre at Webster College is a repertory company that presents new plays as well as more standard ones. The Lindenwood Colleges sponsor theater through their Summerstage, and the City Players add to dramatic offerings.

Museums abound in St. Louis. The city's Art Museum on Art Hill in Forest Park is housed in one of the few surviving buildings from the 1904 World's Fair, an architectural exhibit in itself. Inside the building visitors may see decorative arts of the ancient Far and Near East; the work of modern American and European artists; sculpture, ranging from Classic, Gothic, and Renaissance to modern pieces; a representative collection of African art; and the complete file

St. Louis Art Museum. *St. Louis Art Museum*

of George Caleb Bingham's pencil sketches, along with some of his oils. The museum changed its name in 1971 from the City Art Museum to the St. Louis Art Museum when county taxpayers joined city taxpayers, who had been supporting the institution since 1907, in providing the museum support.

Specialized museums in the area include the Museum of Science and Natural History, the Space Science Museum and McDonnell Planetarium, the St. Louis Medical Museum, the National Museum of Transport, and the Museum of Westward Expansion. The last is housed in the famous Gateway Arch, which is part of the Jefferson National Expansion Memorial. Completed on the Mississippi riverfront in 1976, it is the largest museum in the National Park system, with 42,000 square feet of exhibit space. Its 600 exhibits and 1,600 graphic displays, murals, and slides present a visual history of the West during the nineteenth century. A visitor to the museum can easily walk to the Old Cathedral, completed in 1834 and once the mother church for Roman Catholics in the western part of the country. Just west of the cathedral stands the Old Courthouse. Begun in 1839, it was not completed until 1862. Its dome was decorated by the mural painters Carl Wimar and Leon Pomarede. In 1940, after the new Civic Courts Building was constructed, the people of St. Louis gave the Old Courthouse to the federal government; it is now a museum that depicts the history of the Jefferson National Expansion Memorial.

Out-State Missouri's Cultural Resources

While St. Louis and Kansas City have the greatest quantity of cultural resources, other cities and towns in the state offer their citizens numerous cultural experiences. St. Joseph and Springfield have art museums, and Joplin has the Spiva Art Center. Fulton has the Winston Churchill Memorial and Library on the Westminster College campus, which commemorates the British leader's "iron curtain" address delivered there in 1946. Springfield also has a budding symphony orchestra, the Museum of the Ozarks and, like a number of other towns, an active civic theater. Many smaller towns such as Rolla and Jefferson City have civic music associations that sponsor appearances by concert artists, orchestras, and dance groups. Sedalia annually hosts a ragtime festival that attracts thousands from across the country.

Every community of any size has a public library, and those that do not may borrow books from bookmobiles sponsored by the Missouri State Library in Jefferson City. The General Assembly created the State Library in 1946 and charged it to "furnish direct library service to Missouri citizens not having local libraries. . . ." Communities with libraries but with limited book collections may borrow volumes from the state library, which is the center of Missouri's interlibrary loan network.

Jefferson City also has the Missouri State Museum in the Capitol Building. Created in 1921, the museum contains an assortment of items including mounted birds and animals, antique musical instruments, Indian artifacts, a scale model of the battleship *Missouri*, a stagecoach, and the murals of Thomas Hart Benton. Located between the capitol and the governor's mansion is the Jefferson Landing Historic Site—a restoration of three of the community's oldest buildings. One of these—Lohman's Landing—houses a small museum emphasizing the growth of Jefferson City and the development of state government. This project was a major effort of Missouri's celebration of America's Bicentennial and was dedicated by Governor and Mrs. Christopher Bond on July 4, 1976.

Ethnic Cultural Events

In various places around the state, ethnic groups have established festivals to celebrate their heritage. For years Hermann residents have commemorated their German heritage by holding a Manifest. In Bethel they label their celebration German Heritage Days. St. Louisans honor their German background with the Strassenfest, held downtown, and the Badenfest, held on North Broadway. St. Louis Italians began honoring their heritage in 1965 by having Hill Day. That first year more than 80,000 people attended. Each time the event is held, it raises about $200,000, which is spent on improving the Hill area. Kansas City annually holds a Black Arts Festival to celebrate its black heritage. In Springfield southwest Missouri Indians honor their past by staging an annual event. Clearly, the recognition of ethnic contributions to Missouri has greatly increased during recent years.

Missouri State Council on the Arts; Missouri Committee for the Humanities

Concern about the state of the arts and humanities in American society led the Congress in 1965 to create the National Endowment for the Arts and the National Endowment for the Humanities. It is the goal of these endowments to use federal appropriations to stimulate, foster, and disseminate interest in the arts and humanities throughout the country.

In Missouri the state arms of these endowments have taken different forms. In 1965 the General Assembly created the Missouri State Council on the Arts "to stimulate and encourage the growth of arts throughout the state." The second oldest state arts agency in the country, it provides funds, usually on a dollar-for-dollar match basis with local sponsors, for dance, film, music, opera, theater, and visual arts. It also sponsors exhibitions, artists' residencies in schools and communities, and gives technical assistance to arts organizations.

The Missouri State Committee for the Humanities is a voluntary organization without state affiliation. It receives its funds from the Office of State Programs in the National Endowment for the Humanities. To receive support for a project, institutions, organizations, or individuals must make application to the committee. Applications are judged on how well a project will stimulate thought, generate discussion, and disseminate information about the humanities. Past programs supported by the committee have included debates on community issues involving experts in the humanities and local representatives; lectures by prominent academicians; conferences at which philosophical, historical, and literary topics are discussed; and public radio and television programming containing humanistic content.

Bicentennial

The United States reached the 200th birthday of its nationhood in 1976, and Missourians joined with Americans everywhere in enthusiastically celebrating the Bicentennial. Over 500 Missouri communities and colleges participated in the Bicentennial communities program, which required them to have at least one major project for civic improvement. Many of the projects were educational and cultural in nature, ranging from the massive BHAM festival of performing arts in St. Louis, to the efforts of Kansas Citians to promote a better understanding of the ethnic diversity and heritage of their community, to the creation of new museums in smaller towns like Trenton and Warrensburg. Numerous local histories were written and rewritten. Parks and community centers were created or restored. Everywhere civic pride was in evidence. While it evoked nostalgia for the past, the Bicentennial also seemed to create a determination among Missourians to renew their dedication to the building of a stronger future within their communities and across their state.

Changing Cultural Patterns

If the future emulates the recent past, life in Missouri will become less and less distinctive. Television will certainly play a significant role in that development. Indeed, since KSD-TV in St. Louis began operation in 1947 as the first completely equipped station in the country, television not only has provided the viewing public with opportunities to appreciate the best that civilization has created, but also has been a part of the technological revolution that has transformed American life. As historian Daniel Boorstin has written, "Television opened another world. It did not simply multiply the sources of news and entertainment it actually multiplied experiences. . . . Now on TV you can share the suspense of the event itself."

Television has combined with radio, newspapers, and modern transportation facilities to homogenize American life. Regional patterns continue to persist, but certainly revealing evidence of erosion is the fact that one can travel from the East Coast to the West Coast, from Maine to Florida, from Minnesota to Texas, eating every meal at a McDonald's restaurant, staying every night in a Holiday Inn, and seeing the same television program whether in Missouri or Maine.

Technological change, school consolidation, and the creation of state institutions such as the state library have almost eliminated debilitating isolation and have made opportunities for intellectual growth available to all Missouri citizens. Moreover, the state's rich cultural resources, including museums, libraries, historical societies, and musical and theatrical organizations, have become more accessible than ever before.

The legacy of Missouri includes the excitement of exploration, the danger of the fur trade, the tragedy of the Civil War, the exploitation and innovation of industrialization, and the realization of greater equality for its diverse people. Blessed with great rivers, a wealth of minerals, fertile soil, and beautiful scenery, Missourians have developed a rich and diverse cultural heritage that coming generations will certainly build upon in creating an even more exciting and interesting future.

Suggestions for Reading

Two articles by Ronald W. Johnson describe Missouri's historic preservation efforts "Historic Preservation in Missouri: Origins and Development Through the Second World War, " *The Bulletin,* July 1976, and "Historical Preservation in Missouri: A Recent View," *The Midwest Quarterly,* October 1976. See also Susan Flader, *Exploring Missouri's Legacy: State Parks and Historic Sites,* Columbia, University of Missouri Press, 1992. Alan R. Havig, *A Centennial History of the State Historical Society of Missouri, 1898–1998,* Columbia, University of Missouri Press, 1998, is a first-rate history of that institution. Kristie C. Wolferman, *The Nelson Atkins Museum of Art: Culture Comes to Kansas City,* Columbia, University of Missouri Press, 1993, details the history of that fine museum. Eleanor Martineau Coyle, *Saint Louis: Portrait of a City,* St. Louis, Folkstone Press, 1966, has photographs of the significant institutions there with a commentary about their history.

For information on education, the annual *Report of the Public Schools of the State of Missouri, Department of Elementary and Secondary Education,* provides details about the public schools as does *Missouri Social and Economic Indicators,* State of Missouri: Office of Administration Division of Budget and Planning. *School and Community,* published by the Missouri State Teachers Association, contains valuable material on the state's schools, and the *Chronicle of Higher Education* is a national periodical devoted to developments in colleges and universities. Missouri's efforts to assist the deaf are described in Richard D. Reed, *MSD: The Story of the Missouri School for the Deaf,* Fulton, the author, 2000.

Three recent studies providing the history of the University of Missouri are James C. and Vera Olson, *The University of Missouri: An Illustrated History*, Columbia, University of Missouri Press, 1988; Lawrence O. Christensen and Jack B. Ridley, *UM-Rolla: A History of UMR/MSM*, Columbia, University of Missouri Printing Service, 1983; and Blanche M. Touhill, *The Emerging University: The University of Missouri-St. Louis, 1963–1984*, Columbia, University of Missouri Printing Service, 1985. In addition, the *Missouri Historical Review* devoted its entire October 1989 issue to articles about the University of Missouri-Columbia authored by Lawrence O. Christensen, Ian A. Horwood, Pamela Ann Miner, James C. Olson, and William Taft. William E. Parrish, *Westminster College: An Informal History, 1851–1999*, Fulton, Westminster College, 2000; Virgil and Dolores Albertini, *Towers in the Northwest: A History of Northwest Missouri State University, 1956–1980*, Maryville, Northwest Missouri State University, 1980; and Paulina A. Batterson, *Columbia College: 150 Years of Courage, Commitment and Change*, Columbia, University of Missouri Press, 2000 are other valuable studies.

The state's major newspapers, the *Kansas City Star* and the *St. Louis Post-Dispatch*, publish reviews of books by Missouri writers and information about cultural institutions and activities in their cities and the state. The March 25, 1979, issue of the *Post-Dispatch* was the one-hundredth Anniversary Edition and had particularly valuable historical material. *Missouri: A Bicentennial Report* describes the many activities of the Missouri American Revolution Bicentennial Commission during that celebration. A novel volume that is a gold mine of material on Missouri women is Mary K. Dains, ed., *Show-Me Women*, 2 vols., Kirksville, The Thomas Jefferson University Press, 1989, 1993.

Articles about Missouri's culture and its cultural resources include the following in the *Missouri Historical Review*: David D. March, "Sobriquets of Missouri and Missourians," April 1978; Laura Perittare, "The Cartoon Collection of the State Historical Society," April 1979; Bartlett C. Jones, "History of Morrison Observatory, 1875–1979," January 1981; Sharon A. Brown, "Creating the Dream: Jefferson National Expansion Memorial, 1933–1935," April 1982; Lewis E. Atherton, "The Western Historical Manuscript Collection of the University of Missouri, 1943–1983," October 1983; Bonnie Wright, Robert Durant Smith, and Holden D. Smith, "And It Was

Red: Missouri's New Supreme Court Building, 1907," July 1984; Walter Ehrlich, "Birth Pangs of a Teachers Union: The St. Louis Story," Parts 1 and 2, October 1984, January 1985; Bob Priddy, "The Taos Connection: New Mexican Art in Missouri's Capitol," January 1985; Lawrence O. Christensen, "Pains of Birth and Adolescence: The University of Missouri and Its Rolla Campus, 1871–1915," April 1985; Jack B. Ridley, "Stepchil' of the University: The Separationist Controversy at the Missouri School of Mines, 1937–1949," July 1985; Lawrence J. Nelson, "The Demise of O'Reilly Hospital and the Beginning of Evangel College, 1946–1955," July 1987; James C. Olson, "MU Becomes a System," October 1993; Marian M. Ohman, "The Scruggs-Vandervoort-Barney Art Collection," January 1999; and Sean Brennan, "The Little School on the Hill: The Founding of Rockhurst College," October 2002.

NINETEEN

Missouri During the 1980s

Overview of Politics in the 1980s

Missouri's politics during the 1980s reflected national trends, just as it had in the past. At the executive level each election provided evidence of greater Republican strength. By 1990 only one Democrat served in a statewide office, and Republican John D. Ashcroft had been governor for six years. Even the office of secretary of state, so long held by Democrat James C. Kirkpatrick of Windsor, had become the possession of Republican Roy Blunt of Greene County. In 1990 Republicans John C. Danforth and Christopher S. Bond represented Missouri in the U.S. Senate, while Republicans at one point during the decade held four of Missouri's nine seats in the U.S. House of Representatives. The pattern of two strong political parties vying against each other continued, but by the end of the 1980s Republican strength seemed to be almost unchallengeable at the statewide level.

Meanwhile in the General Assembly the Democratic Party continued to exercise control. In the 34-member Missouri senate, Democrats always held a majority of at least 21 to 13 during the 1980s. In the 163-member house of representatives, while the Democrats often lost seats, the party never fell below a majority of 104 to 59. Predictably the division between the Republican-controlled executive branch and the Democratic-controlled legislature sometimes led to a government with little ability to address pressing state problems. The Hancock Amendment placed a further obstacle in the road to change.

Named after Springfield business executive Melton D. Hancock, the amendment became law through the initiative process in 1980. Passing by a vote of 1,002,935 to 807,187 on November 4, it essentially required a vote of the people to increase state or local taxes or to increase fees. No longer could traditional governmental authorities by themselves raise new revenue to address the problems of the state. Passage of the Hancock Amendment reflected a trend seen in several other states, suggesting voter distrust of elected officials and frustration at paying taxes for governmental services. Neither it nor the division in state government between Republicans and Democrats made it easy to address Missouri's societal problems; but, apparently, Missourians lacked either the unity or the incentive to deal with deteriorating roads and bridges or the problems that plagued cities, schools, and prisons as they voted for a limited government.

Elections in the 1980s

The election of James F. Antonio of Jefferson City as state auditor in 1978 gave a preview of the political trend toward Republican control of the executive branch during the 1980s. The Republicans won two statewide offices in 1980, with former Governor Christopher Bond defeating the incumbent Governor Joseph Teasdale and John Ashcroft winning a second term as attorney general. For the presidency, Republican Ronald Reagan beat Democrat Jimmy Carter by more than 100,000 votes in Missouri. Still Democrats retained three state offices as Mel Carnahan of Rolla became state treasurer, James C. Kirkpatrick returned as secretary of state for a fifth term, and Kenneth J. Rothman of St. Louis won the office of lieutenant governor. Senator Thomas F. Eagleton retained his seat by defeating St. Louis County Supervisor Gene McNary. In the U.S. House of Representatives, Republicans gained two seats as R. Wendell Bailey of Willow Springs and N. William Emerson of Jefferson County joined E. Thomas Coleman and Gene Taylor as Republican members of Congress. Bailey took the seat long occupied by Richard Ichord, a Democrat who retired, while Emerson defeated incumbent Bill D. Burlison.

John Danforth won reelection to the U.S. Senate in 1982 by fewer than 30,000 votes as his opponent, State Senator Harriett Woods of St. Louis County, became the first woman to seriously contest for a statewide office in Missouri. In the state auditor's race Republican James Antonio defeated James R. Butler by almost 200,000 votes to gain a second term. Because Missouri's population failed to keep pace with national growth, the state lost a seat in the U.S. House of Representatives in 1982. Wendell Bailey became the victim of the needed redistricting, reducing the Republicans' House delegation to three. In addition the Missouri congressional delegation lost long-time and influential Democrat Richard Bolling to retirement although it acquired another African American representative when Democrat Alan D. Wheat won election to Bolling's Kansas City seat.

State Auditor Antonio resigned his office in July 1984, and Governor Bond appointed Margaret B. Kelly, the Cole County auditor, as his replacement. Kelly thus became the first woman in Missouri's history to hold statewide office, though not for long. Later that same year Harriett Woods defeated Mel Hancock, the Republican nominee, for lieutenant governor. Woods thus became the first woman in Missouri's history to win election to a statewide office.

Woods's victory proved to be one of the few Democratic successes in 1984. Ronald Reagan again carried the state for president against Walter F. Mondale by more than 400,000 votes. John Ashcroft defeated Kenneth Rothman for governor by a margin of almost 300,000 votes. Roy Blunt won the office of secretary of state by a vote of 1,108,579 to Gary D. Sharpe's 940,236. Former Congressional Representative Wendell Bailey defeated Thomas Villa for state treasurer by fewer than 30,000 votes, while William L. Webster of Newton County completed the near Republican sweep by beating Richard

P. Beard 1,131,715 to 901,394 for attorney general. No change occurred in the state's delegation to the U.S. House of Representatives as all incumbents won reelection, keeping the division of six Democrats and three Republicans. Democrats also maintained large majorities in both houses of the General Assembly.

Republican victories in statewide elections continued in 1986. Former Governor Christopher Bond defeated Lieutenant Governor Harriett Woods for the U.S. Senate seat being vacated by retiring Thomas Eagleton

Margaret B. Kelly, the Cole County auditor

by a vote of 777,612 to 699,624, and State Auditor Margaret Kelly won a full term over Travis Morrison by 741,697 to 706,299 votes. Missouri's delegation to the U.S. House of Representatives changed as Democrat Robert Young, a member of Congress since 1976, lost his St. Louis County seat to Republican John W. Buechner, giving the Democrats a majority of only five to four. Democrats continued their 21 to 13 margin in the Missouri senate and increased their majority in the Missouri house.

For Democrats, the 1988 election results proved little more heartening than those of 1984. They did increase their margin in the state senate by one, and Mel Carnahan continued the 1980s phenomenon of Democrats holding the office of lieutenant governor, beating Republican R. B. Grisham by almost 100,000 votes. Democrats lost ground in the house, however, although they still held a safe majority of 104 to 59. They lost every other race for statewide office. Governor Ashcroft turned back the challenge of Betty C. Hearnes, wife of the former governor and the first woman to run for that office, by more than 600,000 votes. State Treasurer Wendell Bailey, Attorney General William Webster, and Secretary of State Roy Blunt were also reelected by comfortable margins. Senator John Danforth won his third term by almost 800,000 votes over relatively unknown Democrat Jeremiah Nixon. No change occurred in the Democrat/Republican ratio in Missouri's U.S. House delegation, but Republican Mel Hancock won the retiring Gene Taylor's seat from southwest Missouri. The presidential race provided more interest, but ended with the same result, as Republican George Bush defeated Democrat Michael Dukakis in Missouri by 1,084,953 to 1,001,619 votes.

Women and African Americans in Politics

In addition to Margaret Kelly and Harriett Woods, other Missouri women took a more active role in state politics during the 1980s. In 1986, for example, two women served in the state senate while twenty-eight held seats in the Missouri house. Those figures changed little during the next two elections; and while they do not represent the ratio of women to men in society, they do reveal the impact of the Women's Movement on state politics. In 1990 Democrat Joan Kelly Horn defeated John Buechner for his seat from St. Louis County in the U.S. House of Representatives, thus becoming the second woman to represent the state in that body.

Of the twenty-eight women in the Missouri house in 1986, three were African American. In addition nine black males served in the house, and three black men sat in the state senate. Indeed, Senator J. B. "Jet" Banks of St. Louis held the post of majority floor leader in that body. John F. Bass, also a Democrat from St. Louis, won a special election during 1981 and became the second African American to serve in the senate during the decade. In 1983 in another special election, Phillip B. Curls, Sr., a Democrat from Kansas City, joined them. No doubt the trends of an increasing number of women and blacks in elective office will continue as the political process becomes more reflective of the society.

Education in the 1980s

Without substantial increases in revenue and revision of the formula that distributed funds to elementary and secondary education, change during the 1980s took the form of trying to do more with less. Efforts to measure the competency of students through examination appeared as a major policy of Governor John Ashcroft. In concentrating on assessment, the governor implied that teachers did their jobs less than adequately. Another issue raised by Ashcroft concerned the length of the school year. Those, like the governor, who put emphasis on "time on task" argued that if students spent more time in the classroom, they would learn more.

At least one Missouri school district received commendation in November 1989 for such a pioneer achievement, an achievement that could serve as a model for others. The Associated Press reported that the Francis Howell School District, just west of St. Louis, had the longest running year-round program in the nation, having initiated the concept in its elementary schools in 1969 in an effort to solve overcrowding. Instead of the typical three month summer vacation, students in Francis Howell have four shorter vacations scattered throughout the year. Although officials had not found the arrangement feasible beyond the elementary level because of the problems presented by extracurricular activities such as sports, the Francis Howell model did seem to offer an alternative to be considered.

Of course, those advocating this educational reform wanted to accomplish it without increased funding. The problem of distribution of state funds became more serious as the 1980s moved forward because the old formula continued to benefit those local school districts with a sound tax base and failed to address the needs of districts experiencing population or tax-base erosion. Legislative initiative to solve funding problems always encountered the Hancock Amendment and voter reluctance to raise taxes.

The failure to deal with the continuing problems of educational funding meant deficit spending in many districts; poor teacher salaries and the inability to attract the best students to the profession of teaching; and the prospect of a bleak future for public education. Quality of instruction, given the level of support, remained surprisingly high during the decade as Missouri students ranked much above the state's rank in teacher salaries and other measurements of funding. But quality of instruction will last only as long as well-qualified teachers are in the classroom. The ability to replace good teachers with ones of similar quality became ever more problematic as salary averages, conditions in the schools, and morale deteriorated during the 1980s.

Higher education experienced similar problems. During the 1980s Missouri ranked in the low forties among the fifty states in support of higher education. As a result, students in the University of Missouri system saw their fees increase by more than one-third during the decade. Other institutions had to follow the same course; and, while prominent individuals talked about the importance of access to higher education, they did little to stem the flow of funds out of the pockets of students, which resulted in making it difficult for youngsters from families with modest incomes to attend the state's public institutions. Tuition at private schools also kept pace and surpassed the increased costs at public schools. Ironically, inadequate funding continued to hamper the achievement of what everyone believed to be the future of Missouri—a better educated citizenry, which would allow the state and the nation to compete in a world market.

By the end of the decade business leaders in St. Louis and Kansas City, educational leaders from across the state, and some political leaders had concluded that new funding for education must be found. These concerns produced considerable debate during the 1991 legislative session, with proposals being introduced to help alleviate the educational problems at both levels. Whether these could pass the various hurdles necessary to become effective remained to be seen.

The St. Louis and Kansas City Desegregation Cases

Missourians were confronted by several controversies in the 1980s that embroiled them or their representatives in serious litigation that carried all the way to the United States Supreme Court. Both St. Louis and Kansas City entered the decade enmeshed in desegregation cases seeking to bring about a better racial balance in their public schools. The two cities, like many other urban areas in the 1960s and 1970s, found themselves steadily losing white population to the suburbs surrounding them. As a result, their inner city schools became heavily African American. The NAACP Legal Defense and Educational Fund, together with local citizens and the city school boards, brought suit to correct the situation.

St. Louis had undergone court-ordered busing and mandatory school assignments within the city district in the early 1970s; but as the district's minority enrollment approached 80 percent a decade later, a move was made to bring county school districts into a new desegregation plan. In the summer of 1983, Judge William L. Hungate approved a plan that he called "one of the most creative social experiments of our time." It involved a voluntary exchange between pupils in the city schools and those of twenty-three suburban districts. Under this plan, the St. Louis city school board would improve a magnet school system to lure whites from the county, and county schools would be required to bring their African-American enrollment within 15 to 25 percent of their student population within five years. The costs were to be absorbed primarily by the state and city governments at a cost of between $30 million and $100 million. The state appealed on the ground that this was an unfair financial burden; but the Supreme Court disagreed in October 1984, and the plan went forward. Within five years some 12,000 students were attending schools outside their districts on a voluntary basis with no busing.

The vast majority were African American, with only 625 suburban students attending the magnet schools in the city. While the plan was found to have numerous problems, most St. Louisans considered it generally successful, and many still saw it as an important model for other cities across the nation.

At the other end of the state, Kansas City schools underwent a similar metamorphosis although initially on a somewhat more restricted geographic scale. In April 1984 Judge Randall G. Clark dropped eleven predominantly white suburban school districts as defendants in another desegregation suit, thereby confining the suit, initiated in 1977, to the 68 percent black Kansas City district. Two years later, in November 1986, Judge Clark ordered a plan for specialized academic programs in all of Kansas City's seventeen high schools and half of its fifty elementary schools in the hope of drawing whites from the suburbs to take advantage of these. As in the St. Louis case, the estimated costs of several hundred million dollars over the next six years were divided between the state and the local district. The following fall, after Kansas Citians had rejected proposed tax increases in four elections during the preceding fourteen months, Judge Clark went one step further by ordering sharp increases in property and income taxes to pay for the sweeping improvements needed to implement the program. This touched off a fury of protest about the constitutionality of such an order, and again the state appealed to the Supreme Court. Ruling in April 1990, that body upheld Judge Clark's authority while indicating that rather than acting independently he should have ordered local officials to raise the tax. That same month a federal appellate court, following the pattern established in St. Louis, agreed that black inner city students could voluntarily transfer to predominantly white suburban schools at state expense. The whole procedure in St. Louis and Kansas City proved to be an expensive proposition for Missouri taxpayers, but by the end of the decade both plans seemed to be moving forward successfully.

Other Educational Controversies

Two other cases involving the authority of local school officials came to the Supreme Court's attention during the decade. In May 1983, the principal of Hazelwood East High School deleted two stories about teen pregnancy and divorce from the student newspaper because he believed the stories did not adequately disguise the identities of persons involved. The journalism students who produced the paper as part of an elective course sued on the grounds that this interfered with freedom of the press. Four years later the case reached the Supreme Court. In January 1988 the Court ruled for the principal while giving administrators broad latitude to suppress controversial stories.

That summer a group of students and their parents filed suit against the school board of Purdy in southwest Missouri because it refused to allow student dances at the high school. The plaintiffs claimed that the ban was based on religious values and thus violated the concept of separation of church and state. Judge Clark, who initially heard the case, agreed. During appeal to the next judicial level, the appellate court issued a temporary restraining order, and the student council held the school's first dance that December, which about half of the students attended. The following spring, however, the appellate court upheld the school board's right to control policy. An appeal for Supreme Court review was rejected in April 1990 without comment. And thus, once again, local school authority was upheld.

The Question of the Right to Life

Missourians found themselves at the center of national controversy in two additional cases that reached the Supreme Court at the close of the decade. The first was a test of a Missouri statute declaring that "life begins at conception" and placing a number of restrictions on medical personnel performing abortions. Reproductive Health Services of St. Louis brought suit to enjoin its enforcement and carried the day in federal district court and in the U.S. Court of Appeals, Eighth Circuit. When Attorney General William Webster appealed to the Supreme Court, the case became a cause célèbre for both prolife and prochoice groups struggling over the demise or maintenance of the Court's historic *Roe* v. *Wade* decision. In July 1989 the Court upheld the Missouri statute, thus opening the door for states to place a variety of restrictions on abortion procedures.

The second case involved the question of terminating life at the other end. In January 1983 Nancy Cruzan, age twenty-five, was thrown from a car in a crash on a lonely road in southwest Missouri and severely injured, becoming comatose. Four years later she remained unconscious in the state rehabilitation hospital at Mount Vernon, kept alive by artificial nutrition through a tube introduced directly into her stomach. Her parents, advised by doctors that there was virtually no chance of her recovery, filed suit in Jasper County Probate Court in November 1987 to have the tube removed. The probate court gave the permission sought, but medical authorities appealed to the Missouri Supreme Court, which denied the petition by a four-to-three vote. The Cruzans then appealed to the U.S. Supreme Court, which in June 1990 agreed that a patient in such condition had the right to die if the patient had previously given an indication of such a desire. It thus validated the "living will" concept that had been enacted by a number of states, including Missouri. The Court found no evidence, however, that Nancy Cruzan had given any such indication before her accident and therefore denied the parents' petition. Subsequently the family was able to provide new evidence from three witnesses indicating Nancy's prior unwillingness to be kept alive under such circumstances. The local court now gave permission to remove the nutrition tube, much to the dismay of many prolife activists who maintained a lonely and sometimes violent vigil at the Mount Vernon hospital as Nancy Cruzan's life slowly ebbed away.

The Green Issues

The problems of the environment, its deterioration, and the search for solutions that will save "this fragile earth, our island home," have become worldwide concerns. The "green issues," as they have been called, range over many complex matters, such as acid rain, air and water pollution, soil contamination, global warming, zero population control, solid and toxic waste disposal, the recycling of waste materials, the conservation of natural resources, and the protection of endangered species. Few segments of American society have been untouched by the green issues and the growing public demand to protect the environment. This was evidenced by millions of people across the country celebrating Earth Day on April 22, 1990.

Although the environmental movement has made substantial progress in our nation and state, leaders point to a sense of urgency, as time is running out in many areas of concern. Peter Raven, director of the Missouri Botanical Gardens in St. Louis who is recognized as a leading authority in the study of threatened species, has warned that if greater efforts are not made "a fifth of all species of plants and animals alive today will be lost forever before they are even identified by scientists." In a race against time the Missouri Department of Natural Resources has made saving the endangered great horned owl from extinction a top priority.

The Great Horned Owl. *Photo, S. and D. Maslowski*

Difficulties in Environmental Issues

In Missouri controversy surrounds the environmental movement. This was seen in the 1990 state election when Missouri voters soundly rejected Proposition A: The Natural Streams Act. Drafted by the General Assembly in an attempt to protect Missouri's free-flowing streams, many of them in the Ozark region south of the Missouri River, Proposition A would have restricted what adjoining landowners and users of the streams could and could not do. In the weeks before the election opposition mounted as even environmentalists clashed among themselves over whether Proposition A infringed too greatly upon the rights of private property. Whether a more acceptable proposal can be found to help protect the state's streams and rivers in the public interest remains to be seen.

In addition to the political controversies raised by the green issues, environmentalists and the general public must face the perplexing problems that arise when the attempt to solve one crisis creates another. A dramatic example of this can be found in the disaster at Times Beach where dioxin-contaminated soil ruined this small community west of St. Louis. The Environmental Protection Agency plans to haul 100,000 tons of contaminated soil from sites all over the area, burn it in an incinerator located at Times Beach, and then spread the burned soil across the land for permanent storage. Although well-intentioned, the plan creates a dilemma for environmentalists. Rain could wash the burned soil into the Meramec River below Times Beach, thus increasing siltation in the river that would threaten the pink mucket, a freshwater mussel, as well as do serious damage to the river's delicate ecosystems. At this time study continues as the EPA and others seek ways to save both Times Beach and the pink mucket in the Meramec River.

Gains in the Environmental Movement

Despite setbacks and robust disagreements over policies, techniques for the management of natural resources, and priorities, the progress of the green issues in Missouri can cautiously be described as taking two steps forward and one step backward. In 1984 Missouri voters approved a 0.1 percent parks and soils sales tax, renewed in 1988, which mandated the Department of Natural Resources to further develop and expand the state park system. As a result of the increased revenue, the department has upgraded and improved the facilities of a number of parks and historic sites. Furthermore, plans now pending before the General Assembly call for adding to the acreage of Hawn State Park; Johnson Shut-Ins State Park, which would include Taum Sauk, the highest mountain in Missouri; and Crowder State Park. The purchase of Big Sugar Creek in the very southwestern tip of the state is also being considered. Missouri now has seventy-five state parks and historic sites encompassing 117,177 acres. In 1989 it was estimated that 14.7 million people visited these areas, pumping approximately $54 million into the state's economy.

One of the most ambitious projects planned by the Department of Natural Resources is the development of the Missouri River State Trail. In the 1890s the Missouri-Kansas-Texas Railroad, known as the Katy, constructed a 100-mile long railroad line, beginning near St. Charles and going west through scenic hills, farmland, woods, and bluffs along the Missouri River to Sedalia. A hundred years later the Katy abandoned the line. Since the federal government had passed the National Trails System Act, which provided that "railroad corridors" no longer needed could be used on an "interim basis" for recreational trails, state officials and public-spirited citizens proposed that the Katy line be converted to such a trail.

The Missouri River State Trail Advisory Committee was established to advise the department on the development and management of the trail. Fearing that a recreational trail open to the public would lead to trespassing and abuses of private property, landowners along the right-of-way opposed the plan. Edward D. Jones, a St. Louis business executive who made his home in rural Callaway County, not only contributed substantial resources to the trail's development but also helped to ease the disagreements between landowners and trail supporters. The trail, which is to be developed by sections, has been opened between Rocheport and McBaine (9.4 miles) for nature lovers, hikers, and bicyclists to enjoy for years to come.

On January 22, 1990, Governor John Ashcroft proclaimed the "Year of the Caves" to call attention to Missouri's 5,000 caves that have been discovered and recorded. Caves are storehouses of natural history where geologists can study the rock formations and mineral deposits beneath the earth's crust. Archaeologists have dug in caves, such as Graham Cave in Warren County, to discover more about the origin and development of primitive peoples in Missouri, who once inhabited the caves and surrounding areas. Some caves have been developed to draw tourists and hobbyists. The cave at Hannibal, which Mark Twain made famous in *The Adventures of Tom Sawyer,* is one of the state's most popular tourist attractions.

The Missouri Cultural Resource Inventory

The Missouri Cultural Resource Inventory is a body of information about Missouri's architectural, archaeological, and historic resources gathered since 1968. The Department of Natural Resources has announced that it is now available for preservationists, historians, and students of Missouri history to use. It will be especially useful for those who need documentation for nominations of archaeological and historic sites to the National Register of Historic Places.

The Missouri Historic Preservation Revolving Fund

Historic preservation projects have increased sharply in recent years. In 1979 the General Assembly established the Missouri Historic Preservation Revolving Fund, which allows the Department of Natural

Missouri Caverns. One example of Missouri's huge number of caves used extensively for study and recreation. *Courtesy Missouri Historical Society.*

Resources to acquire and preserve significant historic resources that are threatened with destruction. The fund does not restore properties but rather enables the department to market historic properties to preservationists under "restrictive covenants." The property owners can then proceed to make changes under approved guidelines. Some of the properties now being restored as a result of this fund are the Joplin Union Depot; the Missouri Theater in Columbia; the Maclay Home in Tipton, a Civil War era girls' boarding school; and the Bequette-Ribault house in Ste. Genevieve that dates back to the French colonial period and is one of four known *poteaux en terre* (post in ground) structures left in North America. White Have, the Missouri home of Ulysses S. Grant near St. Louis, has been restored and is soon to be turned over to the National Park Service.

"Breakthrough," November 9, 1990

On March 5, 1946, President Harry S Truman and Missouri Governor Phil M. Donnelly accompanied Winston Churchill, Great Britain's heroic wartime prime minister, to the campus of Westminster

College in Fulton where Churchill delivered the historic lecture "The Sinews of Peace." In one of the most prophetic statements of the post–World War II era, Churchill warned that "from Stettin in the Baltic to Trieste in the Adriatic an iron curtain has descended across the Continent" dividing the democratic nations of Western Europe and the United States from the Soviet bloc of nations in Eastern and Central Europe. The term *iron curtain* came to symbolize the division between democracy and totalitarianism, between human rights and the power of the state to suppress those rights, between the free market and communism. Churchill's words declared the existence of a cold war between the West and the East that was to dominate international relations for more than four decades. In August 1961 the iron curtain became symbolized by the Berlin Wall, a concrete barrier entwined in barbed wire, manned by soldiers and guard dogs, separating West and East Germany.

Back in Missouri at about the same time, a bold scheme was taking shape to honor the memory of Winston Churchill and to commemorate his famous address. The plan proposed to transport from London to Fulton the ruins of the Anglican Church of St. Mary the Virgin Aldermanbury and to restore it on the Westminster campus as the Winston Churchill Memorial and Library. Stone by stone the ancient church, which dated to the twelfth century, was destroyed by fire in 1661 and rebuilt by the great English architect Sir Christopher Wren, rose to memorialize a historic man and event in world history. It was dedicated in the spring of 1969.

Two decades later, in 1989, the Communist regimes behind the iron curtain began to crumble as people grown weary of Communist tyranny pressed for democratic reforms. The climactic event came in the summer of 1990, when the Berlin Wall was torn down and the reunification of West and East Germany moved toward fulfillment. Many see in those events the end of the cold war and the beginning of a new era of freedom and democracy for those nations once behind the iron curtain.

On November 9, 1990, a crisp autumn day in mid-Missouri, a large crowd gathered near the Churchill Memorial in Fulton for the dedication of *Breakthrough*, a sculpture by Edwina Sandys, one of Winston Churchill's ten grandchildren. The sculpture is a section of the Berlin Wall, eleven feet high and thirty-two feet long, with two figures, one representing a man and the other a woman, carved out of the concrete to represent the escape from bondage. Former President Ronald Reagan in the main address alluded again and again to the symbolism of *Breakthrough*—the liberation of people under Communist control and a major advance in the struggle for human freedom.

Breakthrough now stands on a campus hillside in a small Missouri town as a reminder that a remarkable epoch has ended and a new era has begun. As we begin the twenty-first century, perhaps it will serve to inspire us to continue to work for breakthroughs in human rights, in the search for world peace, in the advancement of education, in the fight to save the planet, in solutions to the problems of intolerance and racial hatred, and in the struggle to deal wisely and humanely with all of the social and moral problems that beset us.

Breakthrough and
Churchill Memorial.
Bruce Hackmann

Suggestions for Reading

The best sources for studying the recent past are the newspapers, the most complete collection of which is in the State Historical Society of Missouri. There you can also find excellent vertical files for Governors Christopher Bond and John Ashcroft as well as Senators Thomas Eagleton and John Danforth.

TWENTY

Missouri Since the 1990s

Introduction

T he 1990s saw one of the longest stretches of overall prosperity in American and Missouri history. An exuberance, a sense of confidence and optimism, seemed to permeate the society. Technology, primarily the computer and its applications, made young millionaires, and the rise of the stock market promised young and old prosperous retirements. Some even predicted an end to the normal patterns of the economic cycle, declaring that Americans now lived in a world driven by the new economy of lasting growth and prosperity. The federal and state governments even found surpluses in their budgets, and politicians delighted in passing tax cuts, something that most people, of course, applauded. The fall of the Soviet Union added to this sense of euphoria. The United States stood as the lone superpower in the world. With the Japanese economy in recession, it seemed that no other nation could challenge the ongoing strength of the American system. Then, as the twenty-first century dawned, the bubble burst.

The decline of the stock market beginning in the spring of 2000 and layoffs in a variety of industries revealed that the traditional business cycle had not gone away. The steepest declines occurred in technology stocks. Then on September 11, 2001, terrorists commandeered four U.S. commercial passenger jets. Two of the airplanes slammed into the twin towers of the World Trade Center, and another hit the Pentagon in Washington DC. In the fourth plane, passengers attacked the terrorists, disrupting their plans; the plane crashed in Somerset County, Pennsylvania, killing all aboard. Not since the Japanese attack on Pearl Harbor in 1941 had a serious strike been made on U.S. soil. For the first time since the Soviet Union's nuclear threat had disappeared, Americans felt vulnerable. To many

Americans, the future seemed more uncertain than even the period of the Cold War.

Population Growth

During the emotionally charged 1990s, Missouri's population grew by 9.3 percent, reaching 5,595,211 people. The nation's population grew by 13.1 percent, so Missouri's rank among the fifty states fell one place from sixteenth to seventeenth. African Americans made up 11.2 percent of the total in Missouri's population, while their national percentage reached 12.3. Kansas City remained Missouri's largest city with a population of 441,545. St. Louis's population declined to 348,189 during the 1990s, having stood at 351,565 at the beginning of the decade. More than two-thirds (67.8 percent) of all Missourians lived in the metropolitan areas of these two cities and metropolitan areas gained 75.8 percent of Missouri's population growth. When the five Illinois counties in St. Louis's metropolitan area were included, the 2000 census recorded a total population of 2,569,029 for the St. Louis area. When the four Kansas counties in Kansas City's metropolitan area were included, the Kansas City area counted a total population of 1,755,899 in 2000.

Among other Missouri cities, Columbia experienced an 18.3 percent increase in the decade for a total of 84,531. Its metropolitan area population rose to 135,454 for a 20.5 percent increase from the 1990 figure. Springfield grew by 7.3 percent to 151,580, while its metropolitan area total grew 23.2 percent, rising to 325,721. The city of Joplin grew by 10.2 percent and its metropolitan area reached 157,322 for a growth of 16.6 percent. St. Joseph grew a modest 2.9 percent to 73,990, and its metropolitan area's population reached 102,490 for a 4.9 percent increase. Both Cape Girardeau and Jefferson City grew in population; Cape Girardeau counted 35,345 and grew by 2.4 percent in the decade; while Jefferson City saw an increase of 10.4 percent to 39, 636 people. Missouri's African-American population rose from 548,208 to 629,391, with just over half of them living in St. Louis and Kansas City. African Americans composed 51.4 percent of St. Louis city's population, and 31.2 percent of Kansas City's. Missouri's Hispanic population increased to 118,592 in 2000. The Kansas City area attracted more than 40 percent of the state's Hispanics, while the St. Louis area held less than 20 percent. Employment opportunities in large-scale meat processing operations produced a significant increase in the Hispanic populations of Sullivan County, where Premier Farms established a huge hog-growing operation in the 1990s. Chicken processing in McDonald County also attracted a number of Hispanic laborers. Domestic labor opportunities in Branson's motels and entertainment centers attracted others to Taney County. The Hispanic school population in Sullivan County, for example, went from 6 in 1996 to 133 in 2000. McDonald County's Hispanic school population grew from 44 in 1994 to 431 in 2000. With 84.7 percent of Missouri's population listed as white in the 2000 census, other ethnic groups added small numbers to the total. Only 61,595 identified themselves as Asian, the fourth largest ethnic group.

More rural counties experienced growth during the 1990s than during the previous decade, and only 17 rural counties lost population, whereas 52 counties overall declined in population during the 1980s. Southwest Missouri counties experienced the greatest growth. Christian County grew by 66.3 percent; Taney County by 55.3 percent, and Stone County by 50.2 percent in the 1990s. The tourist mecca of Branson, with its surrounding lakes, accounts for much of this growth. At the other end of the spectrum, Worth and Atchison Counties in Northwest Missouri lost population. Atchison led all areas with a 13.8 percent decrease. The number of farms decreased across the state. In 1987, Missouri had 106,105 farms. In 1997 only 98,860 remained, as farmers like other businesspeople sought to consolidate their holdings.

Economic Growth in the 1990s

Missourians shared in the exuberance of the 1990s, and individuals in all economic categories experienced a gain in wealth. Between 1989 and 1998, using constant dollars, the poverty rate fell from 12.7 percent of the population to 10.8 percent. The national percentage of those in poverty stood at 13 percent in 1998. Hourly wages rose by 5.5 percent during the decade for the lowest 20 percent of wage earners in Missouri, and for the middle 20 percent, wages rose 3.1 percent. The unemployment rate declined from 5.5 percent in 1989 to 3.4 percent in 1999. The national unemployment rate stood at 4.2 percent in the latter year. The median family income for a family of four in Missouri rose from $50,080 in 1989 to $54,190 in 1998. In 1997 the Center on Budget and Policy Priorities calculated incomes for families with children in Missouri and divided the population into five groups of equal size. The richest 20 percent had average incomes 2.5 percent higher than the middle 20 percent and 9 times higher than the lowest 20 percent. That gap translated into the richest group seeing its average annual income increase from $88,970 in 1987 to $100,840 in 1997. The middle 20 percent had income increases from $39,960 to $40,370, and lowest 20 percent saw a meager climb, from $8,930 to $11,090. Over two decades, from 1977 to 1997, the lowest group actually lost ground, going from $12,680 to $11,090. The richest gained income during the same period, going from $85,040 to $100,840. Clearly, the rich got richer during the last twenty years and the poor, although gaining ground from the 1980s to the late 1990s, failed to even get back to their level of income in the late 1970s. In 1999, 24 percent of full time jobs in Missouri paid wages totaling less than the annual income needed to lift a family of four above the poverty line of $17,028. The number of Missourians in poverty decreased in the 1990s and fell below the national average, but left many dependent on food stamps, charity kitchens, and other supports to make ends meet.

An important change in welfare law affected Missourians. On August 22, 1996, President William Jefferson Clinton signed the Personal Responsibility and Work Opportunity Reconciliation Act. It substituted for the old welfare arrangement a system whereby the federal government provides block grants to the states to support the needy for a limited amount of time. States created their own programs and determined eligibility and benefit levels for recipients. Requirements included a provision that every able bodied recipient of aid must be in the work force by the end of two years. No one could receive aid during his lifetime for longer than a total of five years. The law prescribed that by 2002 at least 50 percent of recipients had to be in the work force, and 90 percent of those in two-parent families had to be working. In 1995, 192,948 children lived in 89,429 families receiving Aid to Dependent Children. Almost half of them lived in Kansas City and St. Louis and their surrounding counties, while an additional 8,000 children lived in five additional urban counties. More than 34,000 AFDC families lived in rural Missouri, including some 70,000 children. The full impact of the new welfare system has yet to be seen, but the fact that 24 percent of jobs in 1999 paid so little that a family of four remained below the poverty level suggests an ongoing and serious problem of poverty in both urban and rural Missouri.

A letter to the *Missouri Conservationist* magazine suggests the magnitude of the problem. In September of 2002, Peggy Kirkpatrick, the executive director of the Central Missouri Food Bank, wrote:

> In the 10 years I have been with Missouri Food Bank, I have never witnessed so many people in need. Food pantries are reporting record numbers of people needing help.
>
> I thank you for your donation of 1,742 pounds of goose meat. The food provides hope, it provides dignity and it conveys love for one to another. You are a priceless friend to this ministry to the poor.

The gap between rich and poor that grew in the 1990s could be readily seen by driving around practically any sizable city. Acres of housing developments filled with what one critic called "starter castles" surrounded the cities. Bigger seemed to always be better in the private housing market during the 1990s. Single family dwellings with thousands of feet of floor space occupied crowded manicured lots. Parked in many such driveways were Sport-Utility Vehicles, apparently the preferred mode of private transportation of the 1990s. The prevalence of these huge vehicles flew in the face of any concern about conserving energy. Rivaled only by pick-up trucks, many of which matched them in size, the SUVs became the status symbol of the affluent.

On the other end of the spectrum, Missouri towns and cities became filled with short-term loan stores, called by such names as "Check Casher," where those living from paycheck to paycheck—and sometimes not quite making it to the next pay period—could get short-term loans at high interest rates. *The Economist Magazine* noted that such "predatory lenders" preyed on low-income people, the old, minority families, single mothers, and others who could hardly afford to use such services. Called "sub-prime" lending because those with bad or nonexistent credit records used it, this form of credit "grew from $20 billion to $150 billion" in the United States between 1993 and 1998. And between 1990 and 1998, "despite a strong economy and falling [interest] rates, the rate of home foreclosures rose fourfold." Finally, the magazine noted that African-American neighborhoods had five times as many "sub-prime" lenders as did white neighborhoods. Clearly, the much-celebrated prosperity of the 1990s failed to penetrate all segments of the population.

Kevin Phillips in *A Political History of the American Rich* called the numbers stark. He wrote, "The top 1% pocketed 42% of the stock market gains between 1989 and 1997, while the top 10% of the population took 86%." Phillips feared for the nation's democracy: "The imbalance of wealth and democracy in the United States is unsustainable," he wrote. He argued that during the last the twenty years, under both political parties the society had been ruthlessly pillaged by the few at the expense of the many. While the Missouri figures are not that stark, the gap between the wealthy and the poor widened during the 1990s.

Nevertheless in 2002 Missouri children bested the national average in ten categories measuring "well-being," and received the highest rating since the Annie E. Casey Foundation began the survey thirteen years ago. Missouri ranked twenty-sixth among the fifty states. The Foundation counted 146,000 or 11 percent of Missouri children under eighteen years of age living in poor or nearly poor families with at least one parent working full time. Nationally, the Foundation found 15 percent of children in that category. Similarly, school attendance in Missouri improved during the 1990s. The rate of teens sixteen to nineteen years of age not attending school or working full time fell from 11 percent in 1990 to 6 percent in 1999. The national average in that category went from 8 percent in 1990 to 10 percent in 1999.

Like the rest of the nation, Missouri increased its technological industries. By 2000, eleven Missouri companies employed more than 1,000 people in information technology. The majority of them engaged in telephone communications, including Sprint in Kansas City and Southwestern Bell in St. Louis. Information technology employed 63,820 persons directly and created a total of 185,008 ancillary jobs. A. G. Edwards Data Processing in St. Louis employed between 2,500 and 4,999 people, as did St. Louis's Maritz Performance Improvement Company. Kansas City's Cerner Corporation employed more than 1,500 people in producing business-oriented computer software. In Monett in southwest Missouri, Jack Henry and Associates, a software firm, employed more than 1,500 people in twelve states and in 1999 had sales of $184.5 million. That town of 6,529 had fourteen information technology firms. Brewer Science in Rolla makes anti-reflective coatings and applies them to microelectronic and optelectronic chips. With branches in Europe and Asia, the company employees 230 people. The new technology allowed people to work in small places and to market their products anywhere.

Missouri continued to be the home of more traditional industries as well during the 1990s. St. Louis's Anheuser-Busch became even more dominant as the number one producer of beer. Whether in Missouri, or anyplace in the world, one could readily find a Budweiser. General Motors, Ford, and Daimler-Chrysler assembled automobiles in Missouri's two main cities, although General Motors threatened to close one of its facilities in suburban St. Louis.

Eight Fortune 500 Companies made the St. Louis area their headquarters in 2000, but by 2002 the number had been reduced by three, as consolidation occurred in many industries. Ralston Purina, a pet foods and food-processing company, sold out to Nestle, a Swiss firm, for $10.3 billion. American Airlines purchased Trans World Airlines in 2001, causing the St. Louis Rams to seek a new sponsor for the domed stadium in the city. (It became the Edward Jones Dome, named after a stock brokerage firm.) Monsanto, a chemical company that employed 70,000 people worldwide, merged with Pharmacia and Upjohn. In 1995, McDonnell-Douglas, at one time the largest private employer in Missouri, sold out to rival airplane manufacturer Boeing. The May Department Stores, Emerson Electric, Anheuser-Busch, Graybar Electric, and Charter Communications remained in the Fortune 500 and continued to maintain their headquarters in the St. Louis area.

In Kansas City, the Harley Davidson company produced motorcycles, and the Butler Manufacturing Company engineered and built steel and wooden buildings for an international market. During the 1990s, Butler closed its facility in Europe because of reduced sales, but expanded into China and continued its operations in Latin America. Ewing Kauffman, the founder of Marion Laboratories and owner of the Kansas City Royals baseball team, died in 1993. By then Marion had become a billion-dollar company; with Kauffman's death, it went to foreign buyers. Hallmark, the greeting-card company founded by Joyce Hall, experienced growth during the 1990s and remained locally owned. Three Fortune 500 companies had their headquarters in Kansas City in 2001, but Farmland Industries, the nation's largest cooperative, declared bankruptcy in 2002. Utilicorp United and Interstate Bakeries remained in the select Fortune 500. Utilicorp, which changed its name to Aquila, ranked second in the nation in selling electricity to wholesale customers and third in selling natural gas. The fall of Houston-based Enron in 2002 had a significant impact on its stock market price. Interstate Bakeries made Dolly Madison and Hostess products. Payless Cashways, a large lumber and hardware firm, and former Fortune 500 Company, declared bankruptcy in 2001.

St. Louis, Kansas City, and Springfield expanded their already significant medical centers during the 1990s. While, as one analyst noted, "The greatest stabilizing force in Missouri's economy, all sources agree, is the state's predominant middle-class which includes 1,008,426 residents receiving . . . Social Security," the aging of the Missouri population created an ever greater demand for health care and hospital treatment. Cox and St. Johns Hospitals met that need in the southwest Missouri region. In St. Louis, Barnes-Jewish, noted as one of the best hospitals in the world, and a host of other hospitals supplied medical care. Kansas City residents had ready access to the University of Kansas Medical Center, among others. And Columbia provided the Boone County Regional Hospital, the University of Missouri Medical Center, and the Truman Veterans Hospital for mid-Missouri residents. Indeed, all of Missouri's larger cities increased the quality and size of their hospitals during the decade.

At the end of the 1990s, Missouri remained a major industrial state, but as in other parts of the country, Missouri's manufacturing declined as its service sector increased. The transition to a new service economy emphasized health care, education, and technology. For example, in St. Louis, the manufacturing sector declined from having 35 percent of the area's employment and 11 percent of its firms in 1970 to 16 percent of employment and 9 percent of firms in 1997. Service employment went from 16 percent of employees and 31 percent of firms in 1970 to 44 percent of employment and 40 percent of establishments in 1997.

Missouri's agricultural economy also reflected national trends. As noted above, the number of farms declined, but their average size increased during the decade. Productive farms, those producing $100,000 and more in sales, grew in number from 9,800 to 10,200. Their size went from an average acreage of 1,071 to 1,098 between 1994 and 1999. Farms with sales of $10,000 to $99,999 dropped from 40,500 to 36,700 and their average acreage increased from 304 to 316. Recreational farms producing sales of between $1,000 and $9,999 rose in number from 60,700 to 63,100 and declined in average size from 120 acres to 116 acres. The sale of livestock and related products in 1999 produced 58 percent of Missouri farmer's income. Crops brought in 42 percent, with soybeans leading other crops in sales. Poultry production increased during the 1990s, and southeast Missouri farmers continued to derive income from cotton and rice production. Melon production added to their incomes as well. Missouri ranked second in the nation in the production of hay, sixth in the production of rice, eighth in the production of watermelons, tenth in bushels of corn grown, eleventh in cotton production, and sixteenth in milk production and in the production of red meat. Turkey production in Missouri contributed 8 percent of the nation's total, and Missouri produced 6 percent of the nation's soybeans. Without question, agriculture remained important in the state's economy.

Politics

In 1992, incumbent Governor John Ashcroft reached the end of his second and final term in office. Two statewide office holders, Secretary of State Roy Blunt and Attorney General William Webster vied for the Republican nomination for governor. After a hard-fought primary campaign, Webster defeated his opponent from southwest Missouri. The son of Richard Webster, a powerful state Senator from Carthage who had recently died, William Webster had been accused of illegal actions by Attorney General Roy Blunt, which cast a pall over his campaign for governor.

The Democrats nominated Lieutenant Governor Mel Carnahan as their candidate. The son of A. S. J. Carnahan, who had been a long-time United States Representative from the Ozarks and the first Ambassador to Sierre Leone, Mel adopted Rolla as his home after growing up in Washington DC. He graduated from George Washington University with a degree in business administration in 1954, married his wife, Jean, who also graduated from George Washington, and entered the United States Air Force. After his tour of duty, Carnahan entered the University of Missouri Law School, earning a degree and passing the bar in 1959. At twenty-six he won election as a municipal judge in Rolla, and in 1962 he won election to the General Assembly. In his second term, Carnahan became majority floor leader, an elected position. In 1966 he ran for a state senate seat and suffered his first defeat. He returned to Rolla and practiced law until 1980, when he won the race for Treasurer of the state of Missouri. In

1984, he ran for Governor, but lost in the primary to Kenneth Rothman. Then in 1988, he won election as Lieutenant Governor by almost 100,000 votes. Thus, a proven vote getter and experienced campaigner, Carnahan defeated Webster easily, gaining 59 percent of the vote with 1,375,425 votes, the most of any candidate. After the election a grand jury indicted Webster, and a jury convicted him of malfeasance in office, sending him to jail.

In 1992, Democrats carried all of the state offices contested; however, Republican United States Senator Christopher S. Bond won a second term. Roger B. Wilson became Lieutenant Governor; Jeremiah W. (Jay) Nixon succeeded Webster as Attorney General; Judy Moriar-ity won the Secretary of State office; and Robert Holden became state Treasurer. Margaret Kelly remained Auditor and the only Republican statewide officeholder except for Bond. Missourians elect their Auditor in the off-year elections. Six Democrats and three Republicans represented Missouri in the House of Representatives as James S. Talent won in suburban St. Louis for the Republicans, and Pat Danner represented northwest Missouri for the Democrats. William Emerson and Mel Hancock won their races over Democratic opponents and represented southeast and southwest Missouri, respectively. Democrats William L. Clay, Harold Volkmer, Allen Wheat, Ike Skelton, and Richard Gephardt, all long-time officeholders, retained their seats. Democrats continued to hold a majority in both houses of the General Assembly. No doubt all of the Democratic candidates were helped when Democratic nominee Bill Clinton defeated George Herbert Walker Bush, the presidential incumbent. Clinton carried Missouri.

In 1994, Margaret Kelly won the Auditor's race; Allen Wheat, the second African American to serve in the House of Representatives from Missouri, lost his race for the United States Senate against John Ashcroft, as the for-mer governor joined his fellow Republican in Washington. Democrat Karen McCarthy won Wheat's House seat, so the division in the congressional delegation remained the same, as all of the incumbents won reelection.

In 1996 William J. Clinton faced Kansan Robert Dole in the presidential contest, and Mel Carnahan faced Margaret Kelly in the race for governor. Carnahan defeated former St. Louis mayor Vincent Scheomehl in the primary to gain the nomination. Once again, Democrats defeated their opponents for president and governor, with bellwether Missouri voting in a majority for Clinton. Democratic incumbents won reelection to statewide offices, except for Judy Moriarity. Her administration of the Secretary of State's office lasted

Representative Jo Ann Emerson.
Courtesy Jo Ann Emerson

only until 1994, when she resigned in the wake of widespread controversy over her conduct of the office. Governor Carnahan appointed Cape Girardeau lawyer Rebbecca McDowell to replace her. McDowell easily won reelection in 1996. The United States congressional delegation changed as Kenny Hulshof, a Republican, defeated Harold Volkmer. Other changes included Republican Roy Blunt's election to replace retiring Mel Hancock, and Jo Ann Emerson replacing her husband in office. Representative William Emerson became ill and died and his widow won the right to replace him. Thus, Republicans picked up one seat, making the party division five Democrats to four Republicans. For the first time in Missouri history, women held three congressional seats. Both houses of the General Assembly remained in control of the Democrats.

As the new session of the state legislature organized, Democrats missed a familiar face and their leader since 1981. In 1995, Bob F. Griffin had been forced to resign as Speaker of the House of Representatives. Indicted, tried, and found guilty of influence peddling, this formerly powerful state leader was sent to prison. Griffin had served as Speaker longer than any person in the history of the state.

The two statewide races conducted in 1998 indicated how evenly divided the two parties had become. In the United States Senate race, Christopher Bond defeated his Democratic opponent, Jeremiah (Jay) Nixon, 830,625 to 690,208. And in the race for auditor, Democrat Claire C. McCaskill defeated Republican Charles Pierce, 780,178 to 719,653. Missouri's congressional delegation did not change, as all incumbents won reelection, leaving the division 5 Democrats and 4 Republicans. The division in the state senate grew even narrower, with Democrats controlling 18 seats and Republicans holding 16 seats. The Democratic majority in the House stood at 86 Democrats, 76 Republicans, and 1 Independent.

Some of those who won reelection in 1998 looked forward to only one more campaign for office. In 1992, through initiative petition, advocates of limiting the terms of legislators to a maximum of 8 years in the same office succeeded in getting their proposition on the ballot. The measure passed with 75 percent of those voting saying yes. In 1994, the eight-year limit would begin. As Kenneth Winn noted in his essay on political change in the *1999–2000 Official Manual of Missouri*, Roy Blunt thought this was "a bad idea whose time has come." Thomas Eagleton, a former United States senator said that it put forth the "weird notion that in government inexperience will always out perform experience." He called it "a phony political panacea for our complex social ills." Winn also quoted Greg Upchurch, a leader of the term limits movement, who said, "We are taking one more step toward the vision of government that truly serves the people rather than serving those in power." Only the future will tell what groups term limits serve.

Another change in Missouri politics came with campaign finance legislation. In 1994, Governor Carnahan advocated finance reform; Democratic state senator Wayne Goode and Representative May Scheve, also a Democrat, sponsored legislation in their respective chambers. Their measure limited individual contributions to $1,000. An initiative petition reduced the figure and voters approved it with 74 percent in favor. After some court action, a limit of $300 per personal contribution in the primary election, and $300 in the general election became the rule for the Missouri House. The limit for Missouri Senate races became $575 for each race, and for statewide office the figure became $1,175 for each race. Federal regulations applied to United States House and Senate seats. Contributions to political parties and contributions by political PACs had no such limitations, and the money that campaigns consume continues to rise.

As the 2000 election loomed ahead, Missourians anticipated participating in the first presidential primary conducted in the state and a strongly contested United States Senate race between Governor Mel Carnahan, who had reached the mandatory two-term limit in that office, and Senator John Ashcroft, who sought a second term. The two candidates had a record of disagreeing on many matters, dating back as far as the late 1980s, when Carnahan had served as Lieutenant Governor and Ashcroft held the governor's office. A mudslinging, highly partisan campaign ensued. Polls measured the race as neck and neck on October 15, when the candidates debated in Kansas

City. According to the newspapers, Carnahan won that debate and pulled slightly ahead. The next day Carnahan campaigned in St. Louis, with a planned evening event in New Madrid. During his various campaigns for office, Carnahan, an avid flyer, had used a private plane, most often piloted by his son Roger, known by all as Randy. That evening they planned to fly from Cahokia airport in Illinois to New Madrid. With his top aide, Chris Siefert, Carnahan boarded a six-passenger, twin engine Cessna at 7:15. Randy, an experienced pilot manned the controls. Rain and fog limited visibility to only three-fourths of a mile. After a smooth take off, weather conditions worsened, and Randy reported to the St. Louis control tower that he was having difficulty with his gyroscope. Seventeen minutes later, the control tower lost contact with the plane. Only seconds thereafter, the Cessna crashed into hilly terrain in Jefferson County, just south of St. Louis. All aboard died instantly. A part of the landing gear was the largest piece found in the wreckage. A shocked state and nation mourned the death of the Governor, his son Randy, and Chris Siefert. President Clinton, Vice President Albert Gore, cabinet officers, governors from a number of states, ambassadors from foreign countries, and just plain Missourians attended the funeral. School children from across the state sent a variety of memorials to Mrs. Jean Carnahan. Lines of distraught citizens visited the Governor's mansion to pay their respects. In time, thousands of individuals from around the world sent their condolences to the Carnahan family.

The terrible accident occurred too late for another Democrat to appear on the ballot. Nevertheless, Governor Roger B. Wilson, who had earlier announced that he was leaving politics, had the power to appoint someone to fill the office if by chance Missouri voters elected the dead Carnahan over the incumbent Ashcroft. Soon, rumors circulated that Wil-

Jean and Mel Carnahan when Governor and First Lady of Missouri. *Courtesy Missouri State Archives*

son would appoint Jean Carnahan to the post should a majority of voters select her late husband. When the ballots were in, 1,191,812 Missourians had voted for Carnahan and 1,142, 852 for Ashcroft. For the first time in Missouri history, the electorate chose a dead person over an incumbent. As promised, Governor Wilson chose Jean Carnahan to serve in the United States senate until the 2002 election. For the first time in Missouri history, a woman represented the state in the United States Senate. Later, Republican president George W. Bush chose John Ashcroft as United States Attorney General.

Missourians once again voted for the winning presidential candidate as George W. Bush carried the state by some 70,000 votes over his Democratic rival Albert Gore. Splitting their tickets, Missourians elected Democrat Robert Holden over James Talent by just over 20,000 votes in the race for governor. The post of Lieutenant Governor went to the Democrat, Joe Maxwell, but the office of Secretary of State went to Republican Matt Blunt, son of Representative Roy Blunt. Nancy Farmer, a St. Louis Democrat, defeated Todd Graves for state Treasurer by a margin of 129,000 votes, and Jay Nixon defeated Sam Jones, his Republican opponent, by a count of 1,378,296 to 855,814, the largest difference in any statewide race. In congressional races, Bill Clay retired and his son William Lacy Clay won his seat. Republican Todd Akin won Jim Talent's old seat, and Republican Sam Graves replaced retiring Democrat Pat Danner in the northwest Missouri district. Other incumbents won reelection, but the total became 5 Republicans to 4 Democrats. The Democrats also lost the state senate as Republicans numbered 18 to the Democrats 16. In the state House, Democrats remained a majority by capturing 88 to the Republicans 75 seats. Divided government, with Democrats holding the governor's office and the house of representatives and Republicans a majority in the senate, made action difficult during the next two years. Everyone looked with anticipation to the 2002 elections, when more that 100 of the state's 197 legislators would reach the limit of their terms.

The Great Flood of 1993

Within months of his inauguration as governor, Mel Carnahan and Missourians faced the ravages of the most severe flood in the state's history. In the late spring of 1993, heavy rains produced high water in the upper Midwest. Officials began holding the water behind the

Bridge washout near Glasgow during the Great Flood of 1993. *Missouri Department of Transportation*

dams that regulated the flow of the Missouri and Mississippi Rivers. The rains continued and water inundated upper-Mississippi towns such as Prairie de Chien, Wisconsin, and Davenport, Iowa. High water pressure broke levees, and more flooding occurred. Near Hannibal, Missouri, a vandal blew up a levee that prevented water from entering thousands of acres of land. A flood wall saved downtown Hannibal, but the rest of the valley flooded. In the west, the Missouri River and thirteen smaller rivers flooded a vast amount of ground, inundating Interstate 29 below Omaha, Nebraska. One heavy rain followed on the heels of the last downpour producing more flooding.

Kansas City escaped with less damage than it suffered in the 1977 flood, but the flood walls that protected that city created higher water eastward. Levees burst, forcing the closing of Interstate 70 at Columbia, flooding downtown Jefferson City, and isolating Hermann as water covered highway 19. St. Louis remained protected behind its flood barriers even though the Missouri River cut a new path where it joined the Mississippi, just north of the city. Thousands of sand bags piled high by volunteers and flood prevention barriers saved Ste. Genevieve from the rushing water. Cape Girardeau's recently built flood walls kept the flood at bay there, but the 400 residents of Pattonburg left their town to the water, eventually relocating the town on higher ground. Washed-out roads and railroad tracks marked the damage in many locales, including highway 240 west of the river town of Glasgow. According to one estimate, the flood severely damaged 12,000 private dwellings and as many as 1,500 businesses.

Governor Carnahan called out some 3,200 members of the National Guard to fight the flood. Volunteers across the state, like those defending Ste. Genevieve, helped reduce the impact of the flooding, which lasted from June into August. The Governor later called the flood the "most difficult part of his public life." The event claimed the lives of at least twenty-five people. Of course, the flooding financially injured a great many people, but especially those involved in agriculture and tourism. The costs of the massive clean-up efforts added to the millions of dollars lost directly because of the Great Flood of 1993.

Naturally, the failure to control Missouri's great rivers evidenced by the flood intensified debate about whether flood walls and efforts to make the rivers little more than canals for boat traffic had been in the best interests of society. Critics of the Corps of Engineers locks and dams and levees said the Corps had ruined the rivers and made them even more dangerous. Some said that obstacles to the free flow of the rivers should be dismantled and individuals who built on the floodplains should not be insured by the government. The debate caused one ninety-five-year-old man, who had spent his working life building levees for the Corps of Engineers, to wonder if all of his effort had been in vain and that, indeed, if it would have been better to leave the rivers crooked and meandering rather than making them straight and deep enough for barge traffic.

Education and the Carnahan Legacy

Even before the Great Flood, Governor Carnahan and the legislature had faced a crisis in education. On January 15, 1993, Judge Byron Kinder ruled that the state's formula for allocating funds to the public schools violated the constitution and that too little money went to the schools. Judge Kinder ordered an increase in school funding, bypassing the Hancock Amendment, and informed officials they had until August to address the problem. After a long spring of debate, the legislature passed Senate Bill 380. Governor Carnahan worked closely with the Democratic leadership in the House, Speaker Bob Griffin, and the Senate, President Pro Tem Jim Matthewson, and key Democratic legislators, Senator Harold Caskey, Representative Annette Morgan, and Representative Richard Franklin to craft the Outstanding Schools Act. It became law in late May. The bill raised $315 million in new taxes and another almost $50 million through reallocation for elementary and secondary schools. The Commissioner of Education, Robert E. Bartman, called the legislation "truly a watershed event for Missouri's public schools." Besides providing significantly greater funding for the schools, the act rewrote the formula for funding so as to create greater equity between rich and poor districts, although in the year 2000 funding per pupil in McDonald County in southwest Missouri stood at $4,000, while the Clayton school district spent $11,000 per pupil. The act provided for all-day kindergartens, allowed districts to hire more teachers to reduce class sizes, expanded opportunities for summer school, rewrote accreditation standards for the schools, and established new measures to gauge the progress of students through testing. The act also made provision for a revolving building fund so the state could aid districts with their building needs. Unfortunately, the state placed little money in the fund. On another front, increased funding placed computers in many classrooms and made it possible for schools to buy other new equipment. According to the *St. Louis Post-Dispatch*, education funding increased by 70 percent between 1993 and 2000.

Other major improvements in education included the Parents As Teachers Program, more provision for early childhood education that the legislature funded with revenue from gaming boats, a grant program to increase reading skills, and school safety acts that provided a zero-tolerance program towards violence and drugs.

In another area of education, court-ordered desegregation ceased in St. Louis near the end of the decade. But in 2000, only about 12,000 out of more than 200,000 students attended schools outside their home districts. In 1996 the Kansas City school board and the state created a plan to phase out state funding for desegregation by 1999. Judge Russell Clark approved the plan, but he retired in 1999, and Judge Dean Whipple took over his seat. After a series of legal manuevers, a court ruled that until the gap between white and black children narrowed, the court should retain official jurisdiction in this matter. While in some areas African-American students scored higher on tests in 2001, the test-score gap between white and black third graders remained 17 points, down from 23 points two years earlier. In eighth-grade mathematics the gap narrowed from 20.4 to 19 in two years, but in tenth-grade mathematics the gap widened from 19.3 to 30 points. Judge Whipple, whose court now oversaw the program, received no encouragement from Christine Rossel, a Boston University expert, when she testified that "No school district in the United States has ever closed the achievement gap, ever." Meanwhile, administrative turmoil in the school system made education difficult in Kansas City. During the thirty years of desegregation, Kansas City employed twenty different school superintendents. In 2000, the state withdrew accreditation from the system and threatened to take over the district. Enrollment slumped to half its 1954 level, when the United States Supreme Court rendered the *Brown* decision outlawing segregation. In the fall of 2000, only 30,000 students enrolled. Desegregation efforts in Kansas City had cost $2.1 billion, but at least the Kansas City school district no longer had disgraceful, antiquated school buildings.

During the 1990s, the legislature and the governor funneled some $700 million into capital improvements for higher education. With Carnahan's support, the legislature also provided $45 million for University of Missouri enhancement efforts during the 1990s. Not surprisingly, Carnahan became known as the education governor—school children and their teachers sent hundreds of memorials to the Carnahan family when he died so tragically.

In addition, Carnahan directed the creation of the first comprehensive economic development plan for the state, sponsored tougher crime prevention legislation, tried but failed to secure more comprehensive health coverage for Missourians, conducted the first thorough review of government operations in twenty years, worked closely with Freeman Bosley, Jr., the first African-American mayor of St. Louis, on a wide variety of projects to improve that city, and led the fight to eliminate the general sales tax on food. His actions on appointments indicated his strong support of equal rights for minorities. Between January 1993, when he took office, until May of 2000, he appointed 3,367 people, 13 percent of whom were members of minority groups. He appointed Ronnie L. White, the first African American to serve on the state Supreme Court, and Ollie W. Gates of Kansas City, the first African American to serve on the Highway and Transportation Commission. He also appointed an African-American majority to the St. Louis Police Board. In addition, Carnahan signed legislation outlawing profiling of minority drivers, and he supported adequate pay for state employees. In 1992, state employees ranked 48th among the 50 states in compensation. In 2000 they ranked 30th. During the 1990s, Missouri's average teachers' salary increased by 22 percent. A women's rights advocate, who unflinchingly supported family planning, the governor earned the strong support of the state's most prominent women's groups.

After passage of the Outstanding Schools Act, those who opposed taxation for apparently any reason tried to persuade voters to enact what came to be called Hancock II. It would have forced state government to cut local and state services by from $1 billion to $5 billion annually. Carnahan led the fight to defeat the proposal, which lost by 500,000 votes. Later he proposed and secured passage of legislation that required a vote of the people to increase taxes by more than $50 million. In 1999, Carnahan led the fight to defeat the gun lobby's effort to make carrying concealed weapons legal. He also supported funding for Missourians with disabilities to live independently, and he started a program for children's health that made it possible to cover 67,000 more children under Medicaid. Longtime state senator John Scheinder of St. Louis called Carnahan the most effective governor in dealing with the legislature since Warren Hearnes. Another pundit wrote that his "compassion for the disadvantaged and dedication to the notion of a life of public service had no modern equal in state politics."

Addressing these issues required increased personnel. Historian Kenneth Winn pointed out that the state bureaucracy increased by 17.8 percent during the 1990s. This trend marked the entire twentieth century. In 1900, Missouri's state government employed 750 civil servants to serve 3.1 million people. By 1998, the bureaucracy numbered 89,000 individuals serving a population of 5.4 million people. Certainly the state's responsibilities have increased to match this increase in personnel. For example, Attorney General Jay Nixon created an Environmental Protection Division within his office and recently achieved the first criminal conviction in the country of an Internet gambling Web site operator. State responsibilities now include taking care of the environment and supervising the Internet.

The old responsibility of housing criminals increased during the 1990s, and Missouri built two new prisons to hold them. The state built the Eastern Reception and Diagnostic Correctional Center at Bonne Terre, but never funded its operation. The South Central Correctional Center in Licking went into operation in the late 1990s. In 2000, Missouri housed 28,000 adult felons in twenty-one correctional facilities and two community release centers. The state also supervised 11,500 people on parole, and another 48,000 on probation. The increased prison population came in part from a law passed in 1994 that increased sentences for violent and repeat felons. A 1995 law emphasized teaching inmates to read and required that by 2001 all prisoners were to have earned high school equivalences to be eligible for parole. Many prisoners served time for drug convictions, and the drug methamphetamine became a serious problem in rural Missouri during the decade.

Despite the added responsibilities and increased number of employees in state government, historian Kenneth Winn asserted that Missouri's state government was recognized "as one of the best and most efficiently run . . . in the nation." Part of that efficiency came from stricter regulation of lobbyists. Careful monitoring of spending, specific limits on the value of gifts to officials and their families, and extending lobbying regulations to the executive and judicial branches made supervision easier and the ability to link lobbyist money to political action possible.

Gambling

Some of the funding for schools came from the state's share of gambling revenue. Voters approved so-called river boat gambling in 1994. But the boats could not cruise up and down the Missouri and Mississippi Rivers, because of Corps of Engineer regulations. Thus, gambling interests built structures on moats or backwaters close to the rivers. A state sponsored lottery also became an aspect of Missouri life. Supporters of legalized gambling made vague promises about funding education through taxes from the industry. But by 2000, revenue from gambling provided less than 10 percent of formula funds for elementary and secondary education. Higher education received a portion of lottery receipts, but the total figure from gambling going to the state amounted to only $160 to $180 million. By law, gamblers on the boats may not lose more than $500 per visit. Though the law is an effort to stem addiction to gambling, it is a controversial one that gambling advocates would like to see change. Not

Entertainers at the Country Jubilee, Branson. *Courtesy Missouri State Archives*

surprisingly, legalized gambling spawned a number of organizations to combat gambling addiction. With the opening of a boat on the Boonville river front in 2002, Missouri had twelve casinos along the Missouri and Mississippi Rivers.

Entertainment

Entertainment opportunities increased during the decade. By 2001, Branson had more than fifty theaters and all of the infrastructure to accommodate the 5 to 6 million annual visitors. Condominiums, restaurants, a new discount mall, and plenty of motel rooms added to the pleasure of retirees and visitors who came to see the shows. On the way to Branson visitors could see the new wildlife museum next to the famous Bass Pro store in Springfield. Kansas City boasted the new Science City in the renovated Union Station. Money for the renovation came from voter approval in 1996 of a bistate cultural tax. Planners wisely used some of the money to completely refurbish the Great Hall, so that it looked just as Harry Truman saw it when he traveled from Washington, DC, to Kansas City during his presidency. Missouri is quite fortunate to have in good condition both of the beautiful railroad stations that served St. Louis and Kansas City during the hey day of railroad travel.

St. Louis Cardinals playing in Busch Stadium. *Courtesy Missouri State Archives*

Professional football left St. Louis in 1989, when the Cardinals moved to Arizona. Interests in St. Louis, the state legislature, and private parties built a new stadium in downtown St. Louis to attract another franchise. The dome and other incentives attracted the Los Angeles Rams to make the move. They came in 1992 and seldom won until Kurt Warner quit stocking shelves in an Iowa grocery store and began throwing touchdown passes. In 1999, the Rams won the Super Bowl, vied for a chance to play in it again in 2000, and lost the Super Bowl to the New England Patriots in 2001. Kansas City fans continued to fill Arrowhead Stadium to see their beloved Chiefs. The Chiefs rewarded them by making the playoffs almost every year, although another Super Bowl appearance escaped them.

Professional baseball continued to attract millions to Kansas City and St. Louis. The Cardinals drew more than 3 million fans annually for most of the decade. Tony LaRussa became the manager in 1996, and he took the Cardinals to the post-season his first year. In 1998, Mark McGwire attracted fans to watch his assault on Roger Maris's home run record. He hit 70 home runs, while the Cardinals finished in third place. Sammy Sosa of the Chicago Cubs rivalled McGwire, hitting 66 round trippers. In 2001, Bobby Bonds of San Francisco hit 73 homers for a new record, but the McGwire-Sosa rivalry in 1998 would become a legend for Missouri baseball fans. In 2000, the Cardinals won the Central Division again, but they lost to the New York

Mets. They won their division again in 2001, but lost to Arizona, who went on to win the World Series. Sadly, the great Cardinal broadcaster of more than forty years, Mr. Jack Buck, died in 2002. Few men's deaths caused a greater outpouring of emotion. Buck had touched generations of Missourians and others who heard his broadcasts of baseball and football games and experienced his generous spirit during the more than forty years he called Missouri home. Meanwhile, the Kansas City Royals had little success in the 1990s. The St. Louis Blues hockey team entertained loyal fans and played competitively in their league.

Missouri flirted with but acquired no National Basketball Association teams. The University of Missouri, Columbia, St. Louis University, and the Southwest Missouri State University Bears, both men and women, and other regional university teams provided basketball excitement. The University of Missouri replaced its long-time coach, Norm Stewart, with the youthful Quinn Snyder. Southwest Missouri's Lady Bears captured the fans in their community, and coach Cheryl Burnett took her team to the final four of the national NCCA tournament on two occasions.

One of Missouri's great institutions ran into economic problems during the decade. The St. Louis Symphony Orchestra verged on bankruptcy by 2000. The generous matching gift of $40 million from the Taylor family of St. Louis, who own the Enterprise Leasing Car company, brought hope. Missourians responded to the threat by making the first year's required match and the superb musicians who make up the orchestra made compromises in their salary scale to keep the orchestra going, but more funds will have to be raised in the future to keep this world-class orchestra solvent.

Financial Problems in the New Century

The prosperity of the 1990s produced revenue that triggered the Hancock Amendment tax lid. The state refunded millions of dollars to taxpayers. The legislature and Governor Carnahan also responded to revenue surpluses by cutting individual income taxes, the sales tax on food, and taxes on corporations. In addition, the legislature provided many tax exemptions to businesses. These actions caused state Senator Wayne Goode and Representative Richard Franklin to warn their fellow members that such actions might produce dire results. In December 1999, Franklin, chair of the House Budget Committee, and Goode, Chair of the Senate Appropriations Committee, sent a letter to fellow legislators. They warned that recently enacted tax reductions and tax credits had reduced the expected increase in revenue from 5.1 percent to 2 percent. The letter also pointed out that for 2001 "'mandatory' as opposed to 'discretionary' expenditures. . . . (i.e., Medicaid/state medical, employee benefits and salary adjustment, 100% funding of the school formula and legislation adopted during the 1999 session, etc.)," increased costs by $150 million higher than the 'mandatory' expenditures for the current year. Thus, the budget chairs estimated at least a $100 million funding shortfall in the required programs. The legislators attributed the problems to refunds through the Hancock Amendment of "approximately $875 million over the last four years. During that same period of time, we have decreased taxes by an additional $770 million. We are now in the position of not having adequate revenue to provide the minimal services needed and expected by our citizens."

Monies awarded the state by tobacco companies as settlements in lawsuits offered one possible source of aid to the state's financial dilemma. Attorney General Jay Nixon had worked with other states's attorneys general to secure a large settlement from tobacco companies for knowingly and falsely advertising their products and thus hurting millions of Americans. Missouri's share of the settlement amounted to some $6 billion. Franklin and Goode warned against counting on those funds because on "an annual basis, the tobacco settlement represents less than one and a half percent of the state's budget." Finally, they noted that "Missouri remains in the bottom 20% of the states in state and local revenue as a percentage of personal income." In other words, Missouri retained its status as a low-tax state.

Unfortunately, the dire predictions of the two budget chairs proved accurate during 2001 and 2002. With a constitutional requirement that state revenue match expenditures, Governor Bob Holden had to cut programs as revenue declined. With only about 10 percent of the budget in the discretionary category, Holden cut deeply in certain state services. For example, the University of Missouri's budget received a more than $50 million cut in 2002. Other public universities experienced the same level of cuts, as did other state agencies such as the State Historical Society of Missouri. Of course, that meant that student fees increased. And this tuition increase came on top of a trend to place ever more of the burden of the cost of a college education on the student. In 1988, for example, the state paid 64 percent of a University of Missouri student's education.

By 1998, the state's share had been reduced to 54 percent. In terms of proportion of family income, from 1974 to 1990 it took about 4 percent of the median family's income to send an undergraduate student to a campus of the University of Missouri. In 2002, it took 8 percent of that same family's income. Other public universities experienced similar financial difficulties. At a time when education seemed ever more important in helping individuals realize their full potential and in creating a work force that would attract new industry to the state, it made little sense to make it more difficult for Missouri students to afford college.

Similarly, the Department of Transportation received too little funding to maintain Missouri's roads and bridges. Recognizing the problems, in 1992 the Highway Commission adopted a fifteen-year plan that included an increase in the gasoline tax. Before the decade ended, the Commission abandoned the plan as being more ambitious than the funds could support, but retained the increased tax on gasoline. Meanwhile, the state's roads continued their decline. One study ranked Missouri's roads and bridges "third-worst in the nation. . . ." In 2002, officials decided to try to raise funds to improve the roads through an initiative petition, Proposition B. It called for a $483 million increase in gasoline and sales taxes. In August 2002, voters defeated Proposition B by a 3 to 1 vote. Critics blamed distrust of the Highway Commission for the defeat, which prompted the *St. Louis Post-Dispatch* to evaluate the effectiveness of the Department of Transportation. The Department maintains 32,407 miles of roads, the 7th most miles in the country, and Missouri ranks 32nd in per capita road spending. The Department of Transportation spends about $1 billion annually and uses only 3 percent of its budget for administrative costs, ranking it 5th lowest among the states. The Department had about the same number of employees in 1992, (6,196) as it had in 2002, (6,179), while other Missouri state agencies grew by 22 percent. In 1977, the state spent 17 percent of its budget on roads; in 2002 that figure reached only 7.5 percent. One can only draw the conclusion that Missourians should be proud of the Department's efficiency.

Missouri has always been a "low tax" state. In 2002, it ranked "between 36th and 46th among the 50 states in tax bite per person, depending on how you crunch the numbers," observed the *St. Louis Post-Dispatch* in an August 11, 2002, editorial. Missouri's spending on transportation, education, and welfare placed it in the bottom half of the states. And yet, Missourians were more prosperous than most citizens. Unemployment was below the national average, and median income was a bit higher. In education, Missouri ranked only 35th per pupil in spending on elementary and secondary education, but in high school graduation rates it was among the highest in the nation. Student scores on the ACT and other achievement tests ranked Missouri at or above the national average.

The state's taxation system favored the rich. Two-thirds of state revenue came from personal income taxes, but "the rate top[ped] out at 6 percent for all income over $9,000 per year." So the state tax on the million-dollar earner was little different than on the middle-class worker. Although the sales tax on food ended, sales taxes on other items increased during the 1990s. Sales taxes hit the poor and lower class more than the rich. Those with little spent all of their income and paid sales taxes on all of it, except on what they spent for food. The rich saved more and found ways to avoid such taxes.

The editorial ended with this thought, "Eventually, Missouri will have to decide between striving for excellence or settling for mediocrity." Future generations will make the decision of which to do.

Suggestions for Reading

Newspapers are among the best sources for the recent past, and the State Historical Society of Missouri has the most complete collection of Missouri newspapers in the world. For excellent coverage of Governor Mel Carnahan see the Vertical File on him in the State Historical Society of Missouri. The 2000 United States Census for Missouri is available on the Internet under Missouri 2000 Census. The state posts a number of Web sites that contain much information on the recent past. A copy of the letter from Representative Dick Franklin and Senator Wayne Goode to their colleagues in the legislature, dated December 10, 1999, is in the possession of the authors. Professor Lawrence H. Larsen graciously shared his draft manuscript of the forthcoming volume 6 of *A History of Missouri* with the authors, and all those interested in the last fifty years of Missouri history should consult his book when it is published. Kenneth H. Winn's "It All Adds Up: Reform and the Erosion of Representative Government in Missouri, 1900–2000," *Official Manual of Missouri, 1999–2000,* is a fine piece of work that helped shape this chapter.

Appendix

Governors of Louisiana and Missouri Territories (1805–20)

Wilkinson, James, July 4, 1805–August 16, 1806
Browne, Joseph, Acting Governor, August 16, 1806–April 7, 1807
Bates, Frederick, Acting Governor, April 7, 1807–March 8, 1808
Lewis, Meriwether, March 8, 1808–October 11, 1809
Bates, Frederick, Acting Governor, October 11, 1809–September 17, 1810
Howard, Benjamin, September 17, 1810–June 16, 1813
Clark, William, June 16, 1813–September 13, 1820

State Governors of Missouri

McNair, Alexander, St. Louis (Democrat-Republican), September 18, 1820–November 15, 1824
Bates, Frederick, St. Louis (Democrat-Republican), November 15, 1824–August 4, 1825; died in office
Williams, Abraham J., Columbia (Democrat-Republican), August 4, 1825–January 20, 1826
Miller, John, Franklin (Democrat-Republican), January 20, 1826–November 19, 1832
Dunklin, Daniel, Potosi (Democrat), November 19, 1832–September 30, 1836; resigned to accept appointment as surveyor general of Missouri, Illinois, and Arkansas
Boggs, Lilburn W., Independence (Democrat), September 30, 1836–November 16, 1840
Reynolds, Thomas, Fayette (Democrat), November 16, 1840–February 9, 1844; died in office
Marmaduke, Miles Meredith, Arrow Rock (Democrat), February 9, 1844–November 20, 1844
Edwards, John Cummins, Jefferson City (Democrat), November 20, 1844–November 20, 1848
King, Austin Augustus, Richmond (Democrat), November 20, 1848–January 3, 1853
Price, Sterling, Keytesville (Democrat), January 3, 1853–January 5, 1857

Polk, Trusten, St. Louis (Democrat), January 5, 1857–February 27, 1857; resigned to accept election to United States Senate

Jackson, Hancock Lee, Randolph County (Democrat), February 27, 1857–October 22, 1857

Stewart, Robert Marcellus, St. Joseph (Democrat), October 22, 1857–January 3, 1861

Jackson, Claiborne Fox, Fayette (Democrat), January 3, 1861–June 31, 1861; removed from office by state convention

Gamble, Hamilton Rowan, St. Louis (Unionist), June 31, 1861–January 31, 1864; elected provisional governor by state convention; died in office

Hall, Willard Preble, St. Joseph (Unionist), January 31, 1864–January 2, 1865; provisional governor

Fletcher, Thomas Clement, DeSoto (Radical), January 2, 1865–January 12, 1869

McClurg, Joseph Washington, Linn Creek (Radical), January 12, 1869–January 4, 1871

Brown, Benjamin Gratz, St. Louis (Liberal Republican), January 4, 1871–January 3, 1873

Woodson, Silas, St. Joseph (Democrat), January 3, 1873–January 12, 1875

Hardin, Charles Henry, Mexico (Democrat), January 12, 1875–January 8, 1877

Phelps, John Smith, Springfield (Democrat), January 8, 1877–January 10, 1881

Crittenden, Thomas Theodore, Warrensburg (Democrat), January 10, 1881–January 12, 1885

Marmaduke, John Sappington, St. Louis (Democrat), January 12, 1885–December 28, 1887; died in office

Morehouse, Albert Pickett, Maryville (Democrat), December 28, 1887–January 14, 1889

Francis, David Rowland, St. Louis (Democrat), January 14, 1889–January 9, 1893

Stone, William Joel, Nevada (Democrat), January 9, 1893–January 11, 1897

Stephens, Lawrence (Lon) Vest, Jefferson City (Democrat), January 11, 1897–January 14, 1901

Dockery, Alexander Monroe, Gallatin (Democrat), January 14, 1901–January 9, 1905

Folk, Joseph Wingate, St. Louis (Democrat), January 9, 1905–January 11, 1909

Hadley, Herbert Spencer, Kansas City (Republican), January 11, 1909–January 13, 1913

Major, Elliot Woolfolk, Bowling Green (Democrat), January 13, 1913–January 8, 1917

Gardner, Frederick Dozier, St. Louis (Democrat), January 8, 1917–January 10, 1921

Hyde, Arthur Mastick, Trenton (Republican), January 10, 1921–January 12, 1925

Baker, Samuel Aaron, Jefferson City (Republican), January 12, 1925–January 14, 1929

Caulfield, Henry Stewart, St. Louis (Republican), January 14, 1929–January 9, 1933

Park, Guy Brasfield, Platte City (Democrat), January 9, 1933–January 11, 1937

Stark, Lloyd Crow, Louisiana (Democrat), January 11, 1937–February 26, 1941; served until election dispute over successor resolved

Donnell, Forrest C., Webster Groves (Republican), February 26, 1941–January 8, 1945

Donnelly, Phillip Matthew, Lebanon (Democrat), January 8, 1945–January 10, 1949

Smith, Forrest, Richmond (Democrat), January 10, 1949–January 12, 1953

Donnelly, Phillip Matthew, Lebanon (Democrat), January 12, 1953–January 14, 1957

Blair, James Thomas, Jr., Jefferson City (Democrat), January 14, 1957–January 9, 1961

Dalton, John Montgomery, Kennett (Democrat), January 9, 1961–January 11, 1965

Hearnes, Warren Eastman, Charleston (Democrat), January 11, 1965–January 8, 1973

Bond, Christopher Samuel, Mexico (Republican), January 8, 1973–January 10, 1977

Teasdale, Joseph Patrick, Kansas City (Democrat), January 10, 1977–January 12, 1981

Bond, Christopher Samuel, Mexico (Republican), January 12, 1981–January 14, 1985

Ashcroft, John David, Springfield (Republican), January 14, 1985–January 12, 1993

Carnahan, Melvin Eugene, Rolla (Democrat), January 12, 1993–October 16, 2000

Wilson, Roger Byron, Columbia (Democrat), October 17, 2000–January 8, 2001

Holden, Robert Lee, Eminence (Democrat), January 8, 2001–

United States Senators from Missouri

Barton, David, St. Louis (Democrat-Republican), August 10, 1821–March 3, 1831

Buckner, Alexander, Jackson (Democrat), March 4, 1831–June 6, 1833; died in office

Linn, Lewis Fields, Ste. Genevieve (Democrat), October 25, 1833–October 3, 1843; appointed to interim term by governor and then elected; died in office

Atchison, David Rice, Platte City (Democrat), October 14, 1843–March 3, 1855; appointed to interim term by governor and then elected

Green, James Stephen, Canton (Democrat), January 12, 1857–March 3, 1861; seat vacant for two years by failure of legislature to elect

Johnson, Waldo Porter, Osceola (Democrat), March 17, 1861–January 10, 1862; removed from office by U.S. Senate for having gone over to the Confederacy

Wilson, Robert, St. Joseph (Unionist), January 17, 1862–November 13, 1863; appointed to interim term by governor

Brown, Benjamin Gratz, St. Louis (Radical), November 13, 1863–March 3, 1867

Drake, Charles Daniel, St. Louis (Radical), March 4, 1867–December 19, 1870; resigned to accept appointment to U.S. Court of Claims

Jewett, Daniel Tarbox, St. Louis (Radical), December 19, 1870–January 20, 1871; appointed to interim term by governor

Blair, Francis Preston, Jr., St. Louis (Democrat), January 20, 1871–March 3, 1873

Bogy, Lewis Vital, St. Louis (Democrat), March 4, 1873–September 20, 1877; died in office

Armstrong, David Hartley, St. Louis (Democrat), September 29, 1877–January 26, 1879; appointed to interim term by governor

Shields, James, Carrollton (Democrat), January 27, 1879–March 3, 1879

Vest, George Graham, Kansas City (Democrat), March 4, 1879–March 3, 1903

Stone, William Joel, Jefferson City (Democrat), March 4, 1903–April 14, 1918; died in office

Wilfley, Xenophon Pierce, St. Louis (Democrat), April 30, 1918–November 5, 1918; appointed to interim term by governor

Spencer, Seldon Palmer, St. Louis (Republican), November 6, 1918–May 16, 1925; died in office

Williams, George Howard, St. Louis (Republican), May 25, 1925–December 5, 1926; appointed to interim term by governor

Hawes, Harry Bartow, St. Louis (Democrat), December 6, 1926–February 3, 1933

Clark, Joel Bennett (Champ), St. Louis (Democrat), February 3, 1933–January 3, 1945

Donnell, Forrest C., Webster Groves (Republican), January 3, 1945–January 3, 1951

Hennings, Thomas Carey, Jr., St. Louis (Democrat), January 3, 1951–September 13, 1960; died in office

Long, Edward Vaughn, Bowling Green (Democrat), September 23, 1960–December 27, 1968; appointed to interim term by governor and then elected; resigned to allow successor additional seniority in Senate

Eagleton, Thomas Francis, St. Louis (Democrat), December 28, 1968–January 3, 1987

Bond, Christopher Samuel, Kansas City (Republican), January 3, 1987–

Benton, Thomas Hart, St. Louis (Democrat), August 10, 1821–March 3, 1851

Geyer, Henry Sheffie, St. Louis (Whig), March 4, 1851–March 3, 1857

Polk, Trusten, St. Louis (Democrat), March 4, 1857–January 10, 1862; removed from office by U.S. Senate for having gone over to the Confederacy

Henderson, John Brooks, Louisiana (Unionist), January 17, 1862–March 3, 1869; appointed to interim term by governor and then elected

Schurz, Carl, St. Louis (Republican), March 4, 1869–March 3, 1875

Cockrell, Francis Marion, Warrensburg (Democrat), March 4, 1875–March 3, 1905

Warner, William, Kansas City (Republican), March 18, 1905–March 3, 1911

Reed, James Alexander, Kansas City (Democrat), March 4, 1911–March 3, 1929

Patterson, Roscoe Conkling, Kansas City (Republican), March 4, 1929–January 3, 1935

Truman, Harry S, Independence (Democrat), January 3, 1935–January 17, 1945; resigned to become vice-president of the United States

Briggs, Frank Parks, Macon (Democrat), January 18, 1945–January 3, 1947; appointed to interim term by governor

Kem, James Preston, Kansas City (Republican), January 3, 1947–January 3, 1953

Symington, William Stuart, Creve Coeur (Democrat), January 3, 1953–December 27, 1976; resigned to allow successor additional seniority in Senate

Danforth, John Claggett, Flat (Republican), December 27, 1976–January 3, 1995

Ashcroft, John David, Springfield (Republican), January 3, 1995–January 3, 2001

Carnahan, Jean Anne, Rolla (Democrat), January 3, 2001–November 26, 2002

Talent, James Michael, Chesterfield (Republican), November 26, 2002–

Index

tutional amendments of, 85–86;
divisions in, 84–86, 140, 143–45;
emancipation debate in, 150, 189;
Jackson Resolutions and, 132–34;
Prohibition passed by, 297; public
education and, 97, 209–10; railroads
and, 167, 168, 225–29, 247–48, 249,
261; reapportionment issues and,
103–4, 338–39, 350–51; reorganization of, 338–39; sectional crisis and,
173–74, 179; senators chosen by, 59–
60, 94, 140, 145–46; slave laws
passed by, 110–12; state bank chartered by, 96–97; term limits for, 428;
Thirteenth Amendment approved by,
199; toll road companies chartered
by, 166; women in, 296–97, 353,
404–5
Gentry, Col. Richard, 102
Gentry, William, 219–20
geography: of American West, 64; of
Missouri, 1, 4–6; of Platte Purchase,
95. *See also* caverns; rivers
Gephardt, Richard, 426
German-American Alliance, 291
German Evangelical Lutheran Synod of
Missouri, 157
German immigrants: elections and, 144;
festivals celebrating, 395; as influ-
ence, 155–57; music of, 283; newspa-
pers for, 161, 215–16; organizations
of, 214; political parties and, 173–74,
297–98; voting rights for, 200; WWI
and, 290, 294
German Settlement Society of Philadel-
phia, 155
Geyer, Henry S., 135, 145, 155
Geyer Act (1839), 97
GI Bill of Rights, 380, 383
Gibson, Bob, 283
Giddings, Salmon, 49
Glackens, L. M., 260
Glasgow, 126, 162, 164, 381, 431, 432
glass manufacturing, 368
Glover, Samuel T., 202
Goode, Wayne, 428, 439–40
Goodman, Sgt. Thomas, 192

Goodwyn, Lawrence, 245
Gore, Albert, 429, 430
Gould, Jay, 229, 239
governors: list of, 443–45
Graham Cave, 7–8, 413
Grand River, 3, 11, 12
Grange, 246
Grant, Gen. Ulysses S., 215, 217, 218–
19, 414
Graves, Sam, 430
Graves, Todd, 430
Great Britain: land claims of, 78; revolu-
tion against, 31–35; territories of, 2;
U.S. treaties with, 81
Great Depression: everyday life during,
327–31; farmers' plight in, 319–20;
overview of, 312, 315–16; unemploy-
ment in, 316, 320–22. *See also* New
Deal
Great Frontier concept, 18
Green, George F., 42
Green, James S., 146
Greenback party, 246, 247, 252
green issues, 410–13
Gregg, Josiah, 75–76
Gregory, Uriah, 102
Griffin, Bob F., 427, 433
Grisham, R. B., 404
Gros Ventre Indians, 67
Guenther, Charles, 283
Guthrie, Abelard, 136

Hackman, George, 292
Hadley, Herbert Spencer, 261–62
Hall, Joyce, 423
Hall, Uriel S., 249, 251, 252, 253
Hall, Willard P., 136, 192
Halleck, Gen. Henry W., 184, 185, 188
Hallmark Cards, Inc., 372, 423
Hamilton, Henry ("Hair-buyer"), 32
Hancock, Melton D., 401–2, 403, 404,
426
Hancock Amendment, 401–2, 406, 432
Hancock II (proposed), 435
Handy, W. C., 286
Hannibal: bridge at, 230; cave at, 413;
churches in, 125; 1993 flood and,

Missouri: The Heart of the Nation, Third Edition
Developmental Editor: Andrew J. Davidson
Editor/Production Editor: Lucy Herz
Indexer: Margie Towery
Cartographer for Endpaper Maps: Jane Domier
Cover Design: DePinto Graphic Design
Printer: Versa Press